THE 43RD, 1741.

HISTORICAL RECORDS

OF THE

FORTY-THIRD REGIMENT,

MONMOUTHSHIRE LIGHT INFANTRY,

WITH

A ROLL OF THE OFFICERS AND THEIR SERVICES FROM THE PERIOD
OF EMBODIMENT TO THE CLOSE OF 1867.

BY

SIR RICHARD GEORGE AUGUSTUS LEVINGE. BART.

"La gloire de l'armée Britannique lui vient, avant tout, de son excellente discipline et de la bravoure calme et franche de la nation."—GEN. FOY.

The Naval & Military Press Ltd

Published by

The Naval & Military Press Ltd
Unit 10 Ridgewood Industrial Park,
Uckfield, East Sussex,
TN22 5QE England

Tel: +44 (0) 1825 749494
Fax: +44 (0) 1825 765701

www.naval-military-press.com
www.military-genealogy.com
www.militarymaproom.com

In reprinting in facsimile from the original, any imperfections are inevitably reproduced and the quality may fall short of modern type and cartographic standards.

HAVING passed many early happy years in H.M. 43rd Light Infantry, it was a matter of surprise to me as well as to others, that of so gallant and distinguished a Regiment no memoir existed. I have endeavoured, however inadequately, to supply the deficiency.

It has been with me a labour of love to compile the following records of "old corps" from sources, both published and private—too varied and manifold to enumerate—in all points, I believe, authentic. They claim no literary merit, but the "plain, unvarnished tale" will, I trust, be received and read with interest by all who have served or may serve in the Regiment.

R^{D.} LEVINGE.

KNOCKDRIN CASTLE,
    November 1st, 1867.

Page 45, line 20, *for* Trevor Hall *read* Hull.
,, 134, ,, 1, ,, Mason ,, Nason.
,, *ib.* ,, 2, ,, Hall ,, Hull.
,, 319, *for* JOHNSTONE, JOHN, appointed **Major** on formation of Regiment, *read* JOHNSON, JOHN.
,, 337, SINGLETON, WILLIAM, *for* "Out 1843-4" *read* "Out 1743-4."

HISTORICAL RECORDS

OF THE

43RD LIGHT INFANTRY.

1739.

THE claim of the Spanish Government to the right of search, and the aggressions committed by that Power on the commerce of Great Britain, in the West Indies, by 'Guarda-Costas' and other ships acting by authority of the King of Spain, contrary to existing treaties, led to a Convention between the two Crowns, which was concluded on the 14th of January, 1739. It stipulated that compensation should be made by Spain, in reparation of hostilities committed on British subjects in the American seas. The Court of Madrid violated the Convention, and consequently, on the 23rd of October, war was proclaimed.

1740.

While the war was being carried on between Great Britain and Spain, on the 20th of October, Charles VI., Emperor of Germany, died; and the succession of his daughter, the Archduchess Maria Theresa, being disputed by the Electors of Bavaria and Saxony, a Continental war resulted. England and France, in the first instance, acting as auxiliaries, finally became principals in this contest, subsequently known as the "War of the Austrian Succession." Louis XV., King of France, supported the Elector of Bavaria, while King George II., adhering to the Pragmatic Sanction, to which nearly all the potentates of Europe had been parties, espoused the claims of the Archduchess.

1741.

Augmentations were accordingly made in the British army and navy. Ten regiments of marines were raised and embarked under Admirals Vernon and Sir Chaloner Ogle. To these were added seven regiments for the regular line, numbered from the 54th to the 60th, the first being the subject of the present Memoir.

In the Commission Book of that period, in the War Office, appears the following entry:—

"Thomas Fowke, Esq. (Lieutenant-Colonel Thomas Fowke had for many years commanded the 7th Dragoons) to be Colonel of a regiment of foot, to be raised forthwith for our service, and likewise to be Captain of a company in our said regiment.

"GEORGE R.
"HARRINGTON.

"St. James's, 3rd January, 1840-1."

On the 17th of the same month he received the following orders for raising the regiment:—

"War Office, 17th of January, 1741.

"SIR,—His Majesty having thought fit to order a regiment of foot to be forthwith raised under your command, which is to consist of ten companies, of three sergeants, two corporals, two drummers, and seventy effective private men in each company, besides commissioned officers; and to grant a warrant for allowing two pounds for each private man as levy-money, and to authorise the Commissary-General of the Musters to make out muster-rolls *complete*, for two musters, from the 25th of December last, the commencement of your establishment, the better to enable your officers to raise good and able men; I am therefore commanded by Mr. Secretary-at-War to acquaint you with this, and that his Majesty expects you will take care to have your regiment *complete* at the expiration of the two said musters.

"I am further to acquaint you that the proper orders will be sent for issuing the necessary arms, as usual, out of his Majesty's stores of ordnance; as also to the Paymaster-General of the Forces to pay you fourteen hundred pounds, being two pounds per man, as levy-money for seven hundred effective private men, and likewise to issue to you two months' subsistence for the whole regiment, from the 25th day of December last, inclusive.

"I am, &c.,

(Signed)   "RD. ARNOLD."

In Hooker's 'Weekly Miscellany' of the 27th December, 1740, it states that "a great number of brave old subaltern officers are arrived from Ireland and the islands of Guernsey and Jersey, &c., in expectation of being provided for in the regiments which are ordered to be raised with all expedition. Some of the most experienced men are to be drafted out of each company in the three regiments of Foot Guards to serve as sergeants and corporals in the said regiments."

The following officers were appointed to commissions:—

Lieut.-Colonel, Charles Crosbie.
Major, Robert Johnson.

Captains.

Edward Northall.	William Singleton.
William Pritchard.	Demetrius James.
John Sterling.	James Haliburton.
John Farie.	

Captain-Lieutenant, Sir William Boothby.

Lieutenants.

Richard Temple.	Antony Mallet.
James FitzPatrick.	Robert Elliot.
Hans Fowler.	William Sansom.
Charles Maitland.	John Lloyd.
John Carter.	Witherington Morris.

Ensigns.

John Charles Hay.	John Moore.
Hans Hamilton.	Daniel Melville.
James Preston.	Patrick Campbell.
Thomas Elliot.	John Symmes.

Chaplain, John Bourne.
Surgeon, Thomas Phillips.
Adjutant, Patrick Campbell.
Quarter-Master, Thomas Thelkeld.

At that time the colonel, lieutenant-colonel, and major were gazetted as captains of companies, and the captain's lieutenant commanded the colonel's company. Captain-lieutenants were abolished in 1803.

1741.

The business of recruiting progressed rapidly, and by the 24th of March the regiment was formed and occupied Ampthill, Hockliffe, Leighton Buzzard, and Woburn. On the 12th of August, Colonel Fowke was removed to the 2nd Foot, and on the same day William Graham was appointed to succeed him.

1742.

In April, the head-quarters being at Winchester, Colonel Graham received the following official communication :—

> "It is His Majesty's pleasure that you cause the regiment of foot under your command to march as soon as transports shall be ready to receive them, from their present quarters, in such divisions as you shall think proper, to Portsmouth, there to embark for the Island of Minorca, &c., &c.—Given at the War Office the 28th day of April, 1742.—By His Majesty's command.
>
> "WALTER YOUNGE.
>
> " *To* WM. GRAHAM, ESQ., *Colonel of H. M.* 54*th Regiment of Foot, or officer commanding the said regiment, at Winchester.*"

1742-47.

During the whole war of the Austrian succession, the 54th was employed in the protection of the island of Minorca. It consisted of ten companies of seventy men each.

On the 7th of February, 1746, Colonel James Kennedy succeeded William Graham as full colonel.

1748.

In this year the regiment numbered 815 men, including officers. On the treaty of Aix-la-Chapelle of the 7th of October, and consequent conclusion of the war, several corps were disbanded, and the numerical title of the regiment was changed from that of 54th to 43rd, by which it has ever since been distinguished.

No special records exist of the battalion while quartered in Minorca, but from private correspondence it is conjectured their time passed agreeably. The necessaries of life were abundant and cheap, ladies fair and frank, sport good and plentiful. Oyster-fishing was a general amusement of the day, and breaking up huge masses of rock to dislodge a small species of fish called *datyls*, reached by divers, who armed with hammers, fastened to the right arm, plunged into the deep, was another favourite pastime.

These were esteemed a great delicacy and must have for centuries been embedded in the crevices. It is conjectured that they were originally worked into the natural orifices of the rock by the force of the water, which had ever since supplied the necessary sustenance. They were found in clusters, each encrusted in two shells somewhat in size and shape resembling a finger slightly bent.

1749.

In July Colonel Kennedy's regiment was relieved from Minorca, and being placed on the Irish establishment, landed on the 5th of October at Cork, under command of Major Sir William Boothby, Bart. The roll of officers then present and absent, exists in the record tower of Dublin Castle. During the latter part of the year they occupied quarters at Rosscastle, Youghall, Dingle, and Castle Island.

1750.

Moved to Galway. Official army lists were not published for four years subsequent, but Faulkner's 'Irish Journal' furnishes a very detailed and quaint state of regiments on the Irish establishment, as the following attests :—

    Colonel James Kennedy.
    Captain-Lieutenant James Fitzpatrick.
1. Ensign William Dunbar.

    Lieutenant-Colonel Charles Crosbie.
8. Lieutenant James Talbot.
8. Ensign Michael Cuffe.

    Major Matthew Watkins.
7. Lieutenant Arch. Campbell.
7. Ensign John Dowdall.

1. Captain John Stirling.
2. Lieutenant John Carter.
7. Ensign H. Clements.

2. Captain John Farie.
5. Lieutenant Roger Spendlove.
5. Ensign Henry Hewitt.

3. Captain D. James.
6. Lieutenant Hans Hamilton.
3. Ensign Granville Graham.

4. Captain John Brown.
3. Lieutenant Arthur Mallet.
4. Ensign William Percival.

5. Captain R. Temple.
1. Lieutenant Charles Maitland.
2. Ensign Graham Johnson.

6. Captain Robert Elliott.
9. Lieutenant Thomas Crosbie.
10. Lieutenant David Maitland.

7. Captain Peter Pigou.
7. Lieutenant Witherington Morris.
2. Ensign John Knox.

    Chaplain John Bourne.
    Adjutant William Dunbar.
    Surgeon George Aug. Cunningham.
    Mate Water Henderson.

1751.

On the 6th of April "the body of Major Mathew Watkins, of Colonel Kennedy's regiment, was put on board a vessel for Park Gate, for interment in Warwickshire; the pall, supported by the six senior officers, and all the officers attending. On this occasion, the regiment made a very good appearance, and performed the funeral exercise and firings with great exactness and regularity."

1752-57.

From Galway they were detached to Beleek, Carrick, Foxford, Lanesborough, Jamestown, and Banaghar.

During 1752 the whole regiment was at Limerick. Colonel Kennedy arrived from England and took the command. In 1754 they moved to Dublin, and in the following year back to Galway.

During this time the sergeants and corporals of the several regiments in Ireland were drilled in an improved exercise and firings; and one man from each company was ordered to Dublin to learn the gun exercise, as every corps was to have one or two field-pieces attached.

Eight years were spent in Ireland, during which time no events of importance, either public or regimental, occurred.

The 43rd being destined to cross the Atlantic, a *resumé* of the state of North American affairs will not be here out of place.

In the year 1757 England was supposed to possess Nova Scotia, or Acadia, though such tenure was merely nominal. True, she had a settlement at Halifax, a garrison at Annapolis Royal; one at Fort Cumberland, and three insignificant stockaded intrenchments, Forts Sackville, Lunenburg, and Fort Edward, all in the southern peninsula; but the troops and inhabitants of these several places could only be regarded in the light of prisoners, the French having possession both of the north and north-east, together with the entire interior, considerably above three-quarters of the whole, besides the islands, of which Cape Breton and St. John were the principal.

The condition of our provinces west and south of Acadia was alarming, the enemy having drawn a line from Cape Canso to Cape Breton, across the bay of Fundy, to the river Penobscot, and by the frontier of Albany, to New York and Pennsylvania, including also the greater part of Virginia, by the Allegany mountains, along the Carolinas and Georgia, to the Gulf of Mexico. This immense extent of territory was secured by a chain of forts, thereby crippling England in her most valuable settlements, as well as in her fur-trading with our Indian allies on the Lakes Champlain, Erie, and Ontario.

By frequent sorties from their numerous posts, reinforced at will, they struck terror amidst the unfortunate inhabitants, whom they scalped and otherwise barbarously mutilated, sparing neither sex nor age.

Early in the year, strong reinforcements of troops and vast quantities of martial stores had been sent out. An attack long meditated, against Crown Point, was abandoned for a projected expedition against Louisbourg, the great stronghold of the French in the island of Cape Breton. Lord Loudoun, in command of the land forces, left New York with 6000 men, and others from Great Britain were ordered to join. The following orders were issued to the 43rd :—

"Dublin, February 2nd, 1757.

"SIR,—In obedience to the command which the Earl of Rothes has received from their Excellencies the Lords Justices, it is his Lordship's orders that Major-General Kennedy's regiment of foot, now under your command, do hold themselves in readiness to march from their present quarters to Cork, according to routes which will be sent to them for that purpose, when they will receive orders to embark for foreign service. They are to carry along with them their tents and camp equipage. The usual number of carriages will be allowed them by the Government. The cannon, ammunition carts, and artillery stores which belong to the regiment are to be left at Galway, under the care of the troops which are to remain there.

"I am, Sir, &c., &c.,

"ROBERT CUNINGHAME.
"Adjutant-General.

"*To* Lieut.-Col. CROSBIE,
Or officer commanding General Kennedy's regiment in Galway."

From the foregoing, it appears that guns, stores, tents, and camp equipages were attached to each regiment; that in those days they were maintained completely equipped for foreign service, and to each regimental surgeon a set of capital instruments and chest of medicines were furnished gratis by Government.

At this date, Lieut.-Colonel Crosbie retired from the command, Major Demetrius James succeeding to the Lieut.-Colonelcy, and Captain Robert Elliott to the Majority.

Leaving Galway and reaching Cork, long detention, owing to contrary winds, supervened. The delay proved beneficial, as affording opportunity to the battalion, latterly sub-divided in cantonments, to be got together, completed by drafts from other regiments to 700 strong, and subjected to a course of drill and discipline; as well as enabling the officers to cater for the voyage.

On the 25th of April a fleet of men-of-war, under Admiral Holborne and Commodore Holmes, anchored in the Cove of Cork, bringing Major-General Hopson, who superintended the embarkation, Lord Charles Hay, Colonels Percy, Forbes, and Lord Howe, with other officers, and a detachment of Royal Artillery.

The 43rd mustered in great spirits, and embarked without confusion or accident in the transports, 'True Britain," 'Neptune,' 'Richard and Mary,' 'Liberty,'

'Brotherhood,' and 'Sharp,' averaging from 203 to 360 tons' burthen each. On the 8th of May they set sail, and towards the last days of June sighted Halifax.

Anchoring in Chebucto Harbour, the commanding officers landed and waited on the Earl of Loudoun and Major-General Abercrombie, who testified much satisfaction at their arrival, so long expected. The several detachments disembarked, encamping to the left of the troops from New York.

On the 18th of July the 43rd, in conjunction with the 17th, was reviewed by Lord Loudoun and other generals, who expressed great admiration of their regularity and martial bearing.

To inure them to the sort of warfare anticipated, as well as to foster and encourage discipline, the men were employed in constructing field-works round the camp, where intrenchments were thrown up. They were formed into distinct bodies, one half carrying on approaches, while the other defended, sallying out to obstruct the workmen, while the covering parties attacked, repulsed or pursued; making many prisoners, much to the diversion of spectators. This game of soldiers was persevered in until the end of August. Quantities of fascines, hurdles, and gabions were daily made by the troops, and put on board the ships, together with the artillery, stores, and heavy baggage of the army, except their clothing and camp equipage, and all ordered to hold themselves in readiness at a moment's notice.

The expedition for Louisbourg consisted of 11,288 men, exclusive of artillery, marines, and 500 rangers. It was formed in brigades, and embarked on the 2nd of September. On this day a boat full of 43rd men accidentally capsized, but they were saved with the loss of only a few arms and some ammunition. The admiral of the fleet was instructed to do his utmost to decoy the enemy out of their harbour while the transports and convoy of frigates remained at Halifax waiting events.

Every preparation was complete, when a French schooner was intercepted off the banks of Newfoundland, bound from Cape Breton to France. She struck to the 'Gosport' man-of-war, and pretended to throw a packet overboard, which arousing suspicion, a rigorous search was instituted, and a small bag found secreted under a pile of dried fish, containing letters addressed to the French Ministry announcing the arrival of their fleet at Louisbourg, consisting of 22 ships of the line, besides frigates, and detailing that not only had they a garrison of 3000 men, but an army of 4000 more, intrenched up to their necks, with 25 pieces of cannon and 3 mortars, all ready to oppose our descent. An intimation was appended that both fleet and army were in excellent spirits, and amply provided with all requisites for a prolonged defence.

Owing to this accidental insight into the enemy's tactics, the proposed expedition was relinquished. The 43rd, 27th, and 46th, were desired to keep themselves in immediate readiness to sail for the river St. John, from whence to proceed to garrison Annapolis Royal, Fort Cumberland, and Fort Edward, to be, with the troops at Halifax, under the command of Major-General Hobson. The abandonment of the Louisbourg scheme gave great umbrage in England, and the conduct of the commanders was even stigmatized as pusillanimous.

The remainder of the army sailed southward with Lord Loudoun. On the 12th of September a subaltern's party of the 43rd disembarked and marched to Fort Edward; and on the 16th Lieutenant Knox, with another detachment, was ordered on board the 'Success' to serve as marines.

Nothing resulted, as a fear arose that the enemy would

attempt during autumn to strike a blow in Nova Scotia, and try to recover Fort Cumberland. The 43rd therefore left for that place.

Fort Cumberland was a pentagon, beautifully situated on an eminence, and not inappropriately named by the French, who built it after the peace of Aix-la-Chapelle, "Beau Séjour." It was taken from them in 1755 by Colonel, afterwards General Monckton. The fortress, however, was but a miserable affair; the bastions formed of square timbers, and round the scarp below the parapet was a frize or row of pointed pickets laid horizontally. There was but one gate, with a drawbridge and sally-port, and on the curtain looking towards an advanced block-house on the Gaspereau and Baye Verte country was a long battery *en barbette;* but so weak and puerile was the rampart, that its own guns if discharged for two or three hours successively, must have caused its total annihilation and laid all open for an enemy.

During its occupation by the 43rd, an additional piece of ground was taken in and encircled by stout palisades, with loopholes for musketry, and the glacis extended. This was called a spur, and formed a tolerable barrier against an Indian enemy. In the interior, good barracks, with workshops and storehouses, were erected for the better accommodation of the troops. From this and similar forts, an officer with only thirty men could make a capital defence against comparatively overwhelming numbers, provided he was not attacked by artillery, and that the enemy did not attempt to fire with lighted arrows, a dodge practised by the Indians when guns were not mounted.

On the east side of Fort Cumberland stood the ruins of St. Lawrence, destroyed on our taking possession. When the 43rd arrived, the country appeared one complete swamp, neither town nor village being discernible, the enemy having burnt every habitation between Baye Verte and Gaspereau, together with the chain of forts formerly existing.

While the French were in possession of Fort Cumberland they had no artillery, but hit on the ingenious device of imitating guns. Out of large trees they shaped and fashioned representations of cannon, securing them by cords from end to end, and morning and evening fired a salute therefrom. On the reduction of the place and special inquiry after the guns, they were obliged to confess their crafty stratagem of "seeking the bubble reputation e'en at the cannon's mouth."

Until the middle of October, the 43rd, in conjunction with the 28th, were daily employed in strengthening the fort, by which time they had rendered it sufficiently secure against all invaders, the most dreaded of whom was M. Bois-Hibbert with his lawless band. He was a notorious partisan and lieutenant for the French king. He had arrogated to himself for his crest, "Trois canards *regardant*." By all accounts three scalping-knives proper would have been more appropriate.

While employed on the works, the men received one shilling per day, and the non-commissioned officers and officers in proportion. Some of the latter, experienced in the Netherlands, received three shillings per day as overseers or assistant engineers.

The troops were supplied with spruce beer. This liquid was deemed an essential preservative of health, especially when feeding on salt provisions, being an excellent anti-scorbutic. The decoction is of the most simple kind, composed of tender shoots of spruce-fir boiled for three hours in water, then strained off into casks with a certain proportion of molasses, and as soon as cold ready for consumption. Molasses were then issued gratis. Of this beverage the soldiers were obliged to draw five pints per diem, for which they were mulcted in pay 9½*d*. per week currency. According to the accounts of the paymaster of the 43rd, the spruce deductions amounted to 80*l*. currency in seven weeks.

On the 13th of October six companies of the 43rd embarked for Annapolis on board the 'True Briton' and 'Neptune;' and four, under Major Elliott, in the 'Richard and Mary,' for Fort Edward. On the 17th the headquarters arrived.

Annapolis belonged to the French previous to 1714, but through the treaty of Utrecht was ceded to the British crown. The fort, quadrangular, was on an artificial height, and with the ramparts was raised by loose earth faced with square timbers. At each angle was a bastion, with a ditch, covered way, and good glacis. The curtains east, west, and south, were flanked by demilunes, and to the north by the river. The town ran eastward, protected by a block-house built on a peninsula called Hog Island. On the level of the covered way was a barbette battery mounting six 24-pounders and a 13-inch mortar pointing down the river. Behind this stood the powder-magazine, with which the garrison communicated by means of a sally-port. The works were in a wretched condition.

The detachment relieved by the 43rd presented a very shabby appearance. Discipline had been entirely neglected, and even uniform disregarded. The men had been permitted to work for civilians, while the officers had become so socially intimate with the surrounding families that all soldier-like duties were forgotten, and they neither attempted to set an example of regularity themselves, nor to quell any subordination that arose in consequence. The spirit and characteristic of the soldier were utterly merged in sloth and inanity. All grades were to be found clustered of an evening in the public-houses, where the general *refrain* of their orgies rang forth—

> "A lass is good, and a glass is good,
>   And a pipe to smoke in cold weather;
> The world is good, and the people are good,
>   And we are all good fellows together."

Very little time elapsed, however, before, under Lieut.-Colonel James, all was restored to propriety. He issued the most stringent orders for the restoration of a strict system of discipline. Patrols were established; the gunner of the main guard was directed to be very punctual in reporting all vessels to the commanding officer so soon as sighted. No one was permitted to suttle or sell any sort of liquor in the fort. No fires or lighted pipe were allowed to be carried from barrack to barrack.

Annapolis had, until then, been actually supplied with fire-wood from Boston and other ports in New England, although the fort and a margin of cleared land around were an oasis in the "Bush;" said bush being composed of excellent fire-wood of all kinds. The fact was, that the French and Indians disputed the country inch by inch, even to within range of our artillery; consequently, the troops, few in number, durst not venture beyond their lines, and importation of fire-wood became a necessity.

When the officer of the guard requested lights for his own use and that of his men, an angry refusal was returned by the Fort Major, who asserted he "had been there many years, and such a monstrous demand had never before been made, the officer of the guard passing his time in his own quarters or elsewhere, and that he possessed no funds for such a contingent." Colonel James quickly caused a new light to dawn on this functionary's views, and candles were produced and henceforth systematically issued.

During the previous summer, the enemy had stolen various horses from the inhabitants, and they were now observed quietly grazing on an eminence. A party of soldiers and volunteers sallied forth, and, after much manœuvring, managed to catch eight. As they returned triumphant, random shots were fired at them. The ex-proprietors waited on Colonel James, and claimed the horses. He deemed it right and politic to comply with their demand, in order that no pretext for preferring complaints against either officers or men under his command should arise.

On the 1st of November a contract for winter provisions was concluded. Beef and mutton stood at 4d., pork and veal at 6d. per lb.; milk (very scarce) at 3d. per quart; and eggs 1s. per dozen. Neither bread nor butter were obtainable. Sea biscuits soaked in water, redivided and rebaked, formed the substitute. Spirituous liquors were abundant and reasonable.

Men off duty were detached to the carefully planted French orchards, to lay in apples. Two captains, two ensigns, and the chaplain also volunteered, under an armed party of fifty. An advanced guard felt the way. The armed men were ranged so as to prevent surprise, whilst the others filled hampers, sacks, and baskets. The fine fruit proved no small luxury to the poor fellows so long rationed on salt provisions minus vegetables. Subsequent raids proved equally successful.

Frequent fires glimmered by night, showing that an enemy was nigh. On the 6th of December a party of soldiers and artificers crossed the water to cut wood. They were without a covering party, as it was imagined no molestation would be attempted within range of the fort guns. However, while at dinner, they were surprised and fired at by a party of French. Being unarmed, they were forced to beat a retreat to the water's edge. Grenadier Miller was killed, and six others, with master carpenter Eason, taken prisoners. Instantaneous pursuit was ordered, to recover the prisoners. Townsmen also volunteered, and tracked the French for two miles by blood from the prisoners' wounds. Having been enjoined by the Colonel not too rashly to penetrate the fastnesses of the woods, they returned upon finding the corpse of the grenadier stripped of everything but his breeches. They had not had time to scalp him.

Towards evening the enemy returned to the same spot, fired a *feu de joie*, and set up a yell of defiance; whereupon two captains, two lieutenants, two ensigns, four sergeants, two drummers, and 100 men, with four guides, were ordered out to scour the country. Night set in so dark and tempestuous, with rain falling in torrents, that the guides had great difficulty in making way, and at one time the rear of the detachment got lost, when a couple of shots were fired to halt the advanced guard. After some delay, the rear closed up, and the whole party waded the Saw Mill Creek, reformed, advanced, and halted at Josen's Village, distant seven miles from Annapolis. Intense frost suddenly set in; fires durst not be lit for fear of alarming the enemy, so wet and cold they walked about, arms in hand, until daybreak, when moving on, Barnaby's Ford was crossed. The descent was narrow and winding, and here they hoped to fall in with the enemy, but none was visible.

Marching on by Renne Forêt they encamped at Gôdet's Village, when an unsuccessful attempt was made to wade the river. They secured, however, thirteen sheep, roasting them after Indian fashion. Next A.M. they started for Bernard Grotêt, six miles higher up, where the current still proving too rapid, many officers and men, lame and fatigued, the guides ignorant of the roads, already thirty miles from the fort, and short of provisions, it was resolved to turn back.

On reaching Renne Forêt River they were saluted with a shower of balls and buck-shot, accompanied by horrid yells. Captain Pigou, in command, was shot dead on the spot, the advanced guard cut off, and the remainder fell back about one hundred yards. It was then decided to force the pass. Before doing so, Sergeant Cockburn, a brave Scotchman, was sent forward to recover the deceased officer's property. This he performed in the teeth of the enemy's fire, bringing back his captain's laced hat, watch, sash, fusil, cartouch-box, pistols, and purse, containing thirty guineas. His gallantry was justly rewarded with five guineas and the laced hat.

Captain Maitland then assumed command, exhorting all to be cool and steady, and moved towards the pass, which the enemy had fortified. Trees were so thickly matted as to be almost impenetrable. As the advance mounted the hill, the enemy was observed skulking and running from right to left. They thereupon gave chase into the woods, routing and firing on them as they fled.

Having gained the eminence, they reformed, and found the enemy had totally disappeared. Wading Barnaby's River, and turning the dangerous defile at the mills, they reached Commeau's Village, where the wounded begged an half-hour's halt. In this interim, they were agreeably surprised by being joined by an officer—a volunteer—and twenty men, who had separated themselves during the skirmish, to make a flank or rear diversion while the main body engaged in front. In the evening all reached the garrison, worn and harassed, with the loss of one captain, one sergeant, and 22 rank and file.

On the 9th of December the day's order contained the following notice:—" A Court of Inquiry to sit this day.

at 11 o'clock, to take an inventory of the late Captain Pigou's effects. As the Hon. Captain Maitland, and the rest of the officers of the party, have acquainted the Lieutenant-Colonel that the men behaved extremely well yesterday, he takes this opportunity of returning them his thanks, and makes no doubt they will always evince equal bravery on every such occasion."

On the 10th a grenadier, who had deserted when attacked by the enemy on the 8th, came into camp and surrendered. He was arraigned by court martial for cowardice, and pleaded guilty. The following award was the result:—" It is the opinion of the Court, that the prisoner is a notorious coward, and they sentence him to *ride the wooden horse* half-an-hour every day for six days, with a petticoat on him, a broom in his hand, and a paper pinned on his back bearing this inscription, '*Such is the reward of my merit.*'"

The sentence was carried into execution, to the inexpressible mirth of the whole garrison, and of the women in particular. On subsequent occasions this man proved himself to be a remarkably gallant soldier, and the captain of his company declared, that when any dangerous or difficult service was imminent, he only wished all under him could be as surely depended on.

Riding the wooden horse was a punishment formerly much in vogue in the service. The horse was formed of planks, nailed together so as to form a sharp ridge or angle, about eight feet long. This ridge represented the back of the horse, supported by four posts or legs, about six feet high, placed on a stand made moveable by trucks. To complete the resemblance, a head and tail were affixed. The culprit was placed with his hands tied behind him; and frequently, to increase the punishment, muskets were tied to his feet, to prevent, as it was jocularly said, his horse from kicking him off. Subsequently it was found that riding the wooden horse had a tendency to injure the men, and induce rupture; it was in consequence abolished. The last reminiscence of this durance vile was to be seen on the parade-ground at Portsmouth in the year 1780.

1758.

On the 27th of April, to the great mortification and annoyance of all, orders arrived that three companies from Annapolis, with three from Fort Edward, under command of Lieutenant-Colonel James, were to relieve the 28th Regiment at Fort Cumberland, in lieu of proceeding to Louisbourg. Instructions from England desired that one entire regiment might garrison Annapolis Royal and the other forts in Nova Scotia. His Excellency made choice of the 43rd for this service, as being the most complete in numbers, and the youngest corps in the province.

On the 7th of December news of the fall of Louisbourg reached the garrison, which event they celebrated by bonfires, salutes, and *jeux d'artifice*.

In October twelve recruits joined from New York. From the suspension of active employment, garrison life now became exceedingly tedious. Seniors and subalterns framed a memorial to Colonel James, begging him to apply to the Commander-in-Chief to grant permission for their regiment to join the army in spring, for whatever service destined.

1759.

Early on New Year's morn some excitement was caused by a huge bear rushing in between the Gibbet and the Block House. The garrison turned out, and for nearly an hour had excellent sport in hunting and firing at Bruin; but he skilfully parried all attacks, and eventually escaped by swimming across the bay.

Before the severe frost set in, the marshes had overflowed, thus affording capital sleighing and skating, of which the officers took constant advantage. One morning two of the 43rd discovered a dead man lying on the road to Gaspereau. The circumstance being reported, a party at once was despatched to bring in the corpse,—that of one of the finest grenadiers in the regiment. He was stripped of everything save his shirt and breeches, and two parts of his skull were scalped. The rolls of the companies were instantly called, when it appeared that one sergeant and three privates of the Rangers, and seven of the 43rd, were missing. They had been seen going out in the morning to cut wood,—though in direct defiance of repeated orders,—and it was immediately suspected that they had either been killed or made prisoners.

The whole company of Rangers consequently scoured the country, and returned towards evening, bearing the dead bodies of four men of the regiment, and one Ranger, not only barbarously murdered, but scalped in the most horrid manner. The victims had been fired upon and wounded through the breast, and each was shot in the same place save one, who was evidently killed by a tomahawk across the neck. The Ranger was stark naked, and his body marked by means of a stick and blood in hieroglyphics.

The following afternoon, all officers attending, the men were buried, or sunk in a pit of snow, the ground being so frost-bound that it could not even be broken with pickaxes.

The Irish officers of the garrison celebrated their patron saint's day, St. Patrick (March 17th), by entertaining their brethren in arms at dinner, and by bestowing half a dollar on each Irish private.

In April Colonel James received an order for the regiment and one company of Rangers to hold themselves in immediate readiness to join the proposed expedition up the St. Lawrence, then assembling at Louisbourg, under General Wolfe. Directly this intelligence was bruited, loud and protracted huzzas rent the air. Soon after, Colonel James was directed to select one captain, one lieutenant, one ensign, three sergeants, one drummer, and seventy rank and file, to form a light company.

A simultaneous attack on all the French strongholds was arranged. General Wolfe, already so distinguished, was, supported by a strong fleet from England, to ascend the St. Lawrence with 8000 men, and besiege Quebec. General Amherst, Commander-in-Chief in North America, with 12,000 men, was to reduce Ticonderoga and Crown Point, cross Lake Champlain, follow the course of the Richelieu to the St. Lawrence, and join Wolfe in his attack. Brigadier-General Prideaux, with a third army, reinforced by a body of provincials and friendly Indians, under Sir William Johnson, was to invest the then important fortress of Niagara, which in a manner commanded the back settlements of the Upper Country. It was further proposed that these troops under Prideaux, after the reduction of Niagara, should fall down the St. Lawrence, besiege and take Montreal, and then join or co-operate with the combined forces under Amherst and Wolfe.

When this plan was formed, the French had 5000 veteran troops in the neighbourhood of Montreal under the Marquis de Vandreuil, Governor of New France. His lieutenant-general, Montcalm, whose reputation as a skilled soldier stood high in the military world, was at Quebec with an army of 10,000 Europeans and Canadians, and M. de Levis, an active officer, was at the head of a flying detachment, both strengthened by a large body of trained Indians thoroughly acquainted with the woods and defiles. The garrison of Niagara numbered 600 men.

Ticonderoga and Crown Point were in a respectable condition; while the city of Quebec, strong in its natural configuration, the bravery of its inhabitants, and the number of its garrison, had received every practicable additional fortification that the art of man and war could devise.

The 43rd now made the most of their time at drill and target practice. Great attention was bestowed on the light company, to get it into tip-top order and fit for any service to be performed.

Sailing on the 12th of May they anchored off Louisbourg on the 24th, when orders were given to furnish twenty light infantry to complete Captain Delaune's company, and also to lay in a large stock of shoes as all future supply would be precarious. The Grenadiers of Louisbourg, under General Wolfe, had been initiated into his new system of drill, and were in the highest state of efficiency.

Never having had any prior opportunity of seeing the 43rd Regiment, Wolfe desired them to be reviewed before him by Brigadier Monckton, directing that in their firing they should expend ammunition cartridge. He was pleased to say he "never saw greater regularity, closer fire, arms better levelled, or less disorder, in any other regiment since he had the honour to be an officer," &c., &c.

On the arrival of some new corps, their commanding officers expecting to be similarly reviewed, apologised, owing to long cantonment, for not being thoroughly *au fait* in this novel exercise, and were met by the reply, "Pooh! pooh! new exercise—new fiddlesticks! if they are otherwise well disciplined and will fight, that's all I shall require of them."

Here the officers of the 43rd had their heavy, inconvenient, common firelocks exchanged for fusils. General Wolfe daily landed the regiments for drill, not merely to secure continued efficiency, but to render them adepts in the use of the flat-bottomed boats specially constructed for this service.

On the 1st of June each regiment was supplied with pickaxes, spades, shovels, and billhooks, as well as fishing-tackle to amuse them during the voyage. On the 5th the fleet set sail amidst great enthusiasm. Entire confidence was reposed in the admiral and generals, and the universal toast was, "British colours on every French fort, post, or garrison in America!"

On the 18th the transports bearing the 43rd hove to off the Islands Bic and Barnaby, where they learnt that Admiral Durell had taken possession of the Island of Coudre and proceeded to that of Orleans. On the 27th they landed on the Isle of Orleans; Wolfe, accompanied by Major M'Kellar of the Engineers, proceeding alone to reconnoitre. He found the French encamped on the north side of the river, their right extending close to Quebec, and their left to the Falls of Montmorency. The ground chosen by the French general was high and strong, and they were evidently adding every kind of work that ingenuity could suggest to render it impregnable.

During the next six weeks our troops were diligently employed in throwing up earthworks, strengthening their position, and pushing forward every sort of preparation. The enemy twice made ineffectual attempts to destroy our fleet by sending down on the 28th of June, and again on the 28th of July, fireships and long fire-rafts freighted with grenades, swivels, &c., to be discharged as they floated along.

Little or no damage ensued, as some ran ashore and others were towed away clear by our seamen, who exhibited great spirit and alertness.

Wolfe now determined upon an attack of the French

lines at Montmorency, selecting a particular point at the mouth of the river. On the 31st of July the Louisbourg Grenadiers, with those of the 15th, 43rd, 48th, 78th, and a detachment of Royal Americans, along with the 15th and 78th Regiments, under Brigadier Monckton, embarked and rendezvous'd at Point Levi. Orders were given as to signals, and the 43rd desired to hold themselves in immediate readiness. The colonel and major determined that the regiment should embark, land, and fight by companies under their own officers, which afforded peculiar satisfaction to the men.

In the afternoon a brisk cannonade was kept up from every quarter. Owing to the gloominess of the weather, several of the boats struck in attempting to land, retarding operations, while some confusion was caused by the French shot and shell. The enemy then abandoned the right of their camp, and with their whole force lined their intrenchments from the centre to the left. At half-past five our first division, consisting of all the grenadiers of the army, landed at Point de Leste, obliging the enemy to relinquish the detached battery and redoubt below the precipice. By this time the troops to the eastward of the Fall were in motion to join and support the attack, but the grenadiers, too impatient to wait for reinforcements, rushed up the hill, making vigorous though impracticable efforts to gain the summit.

In this predicament they received a volley of musketry from the enemy's breastworks, but which our brave fellows would not return, preferring to reserve their fire until they might reach the top of the precipice. Notwithstanding their unparalleled valour, and the good conduct of their officers, they were forced to retire in disorder, owing to the continued heavy counter fire, and seek shelter in the redoubt and battery on the beach where Monckton's corps, with those under Townshend and Murray, were at hand to sustain them. Their mortification was much enhanced by the consciousness that the mistake was attributable to their own impetuosity.

In this state of things, with night approaching and the ammunition damaged by a severe thunder-storm, Wolfe sent to stop Townshend, and ordered Monckton to re-embark his division with the shattered corps of grenadiers as best he might. By excellent management all were got off with as many wounded as were recoverable, and the enemy did not risk pursuit. Our loss on this occasion was 443 killed, wounded, and missing, amongst whom were two captains and two lieutenants killed; one colonel, six captains, nineteen lieutenants, and three ensigns wounded.

The casualties in the grenadiers of the 43rd were nine rank and file killed; Captain Maitland, Lieutenant Clements, and thirteen rank and file wounded.

Our position then appeared to grow desperate, while Wolfe's health began to fail. In a letter to Pitt, dated headquarters, Montmorency, of the 2nd September, after saying he had been suffering from fever, he added:—

"I found myself so ill, and am still so weak, that I " begged the general officers to consult together for the " public utility. * * * * To the uncommon strength " of the country, the enemy have added for the defence of " the river a great number of floating batteries or boats. " By the vigilance of these and the Indians round our " posts, it has been impossible to attempt anything by " surprise. * * * * We have almost the whole force " of Canada to oppose. In this situation there is such a " choice of difficulties, that I own myself at a loss to deter-" mine. The affairs of Great Britain require the most " vigorous measures; but the courage of a handful of " brave men should be exerted only where there is some " hope of a favourable event."

When this despatch reached England, it created great

consternation and anger in the Cabinet. Pitt feared he might have been mistaken in his favourite general, in whose genius he had placed the utmost reliance, believing that—

> "Where the matter match'd his mighty mind
> Up rose the hero; on his piercing eye
> Sat observation, on each glance of thought
> Decision follow'd, as the thunderbolt
> Pursues the flash,"

and that the next news might be annihilation or capitulation. In the conclusion of his melancholy letter, Wolfe, however, had said that he would do his best; and that best turned out a miracle in war. In conjunction with Admiral Saunders, he conceived the plan of scaling the Heights of Abraham. On the 6th of September, the regiments began to move. The 43rd, the 15th, and 78th reached Goreham's Post, and at nightfall forded the river Etchemin, about fifty yards across, with a strong uneven bottom and rapid current. The enemy fired, but their shot fell short. Boats were found in a cove, and the regiments rowed to their respective ships. The 43rd were particularly fortunate in being named to the 'Seahorse' frigate, where Captain Smith and his officers entertained them *en prince*.

On the 7th Admiral Holmes's squadron weighed, doubled the mouth of the Chaudière, and came to anchor off Cape Rouge. At 2 P.M. the 'Seahorse,' 'Lowestoffe,' and two floating batteries lately taken, were ordered to edge into the cove and attack the enemy's armed craft. At the same time, to mislead the enemy who turned out in great strength, the troops were rowed up and down as if intending to land at different places, while Wolfe meditated another point of descent. Accompanied by two general officers, he went up the river to reconnoitre, returning at night.

On the 9th boisterous weather impeded all operations,

and so crowded were the transports that Wolfe ordered 1500 men to be landed on the south shore, and cantoned in the village and church of St. Nicholas. Being informed that two officers of the 43rd were invalided on board ship, he expressed the most kindly consideration, saying he would with pleasure lend his barge to convey them to Goreham's Post, whence they should have an escort to Point Levi camp. The offer was gratefully declined, both assuring the General that no consideration could induce them to leave until the event of the expedition should be decided.

On the 11th a fresh disposition of the forces was decided on. The 'Lowestoffe' and 'Squirrel' frigates were ordered to follow the flat-bottomed boats, and as it was necessary that some of the men should remain in them all night, a gill of rum extraordinary was served out.

The officer of the 43rd in command of the escort being asked in the General's hearing as to the state of a sick brother officer, replied, "He was in a very low, indifferent way," which the other lamented, adding, "He has but a puny, delicate constitution." This, as being a case similar to his own, struck his Excellency, who interrupted with, "Don't talk of constitution; that officer has good spirits, and good spirits will carry a man through anything." He was invariably socially kind towards young officers. On one occasion, having invited an ensign to dinner, the subaltern announced the distinction to his companions in the words, "I dine with Wolfe to-night;" when he was tartly pulled up by a senior for alluding thus familiarly to their leader. "Would you talk of *General* Cæsar? then why of *General* Wolfe?" was the ready reply, which being repeated at headquarters was very complimentarily acknowledged.

Every preparation was completed to surprise the enemy, and compel him to fight. All the large boats below were to be filled with seamen, marines, and such detachments as could be spared from Points Levi and Orleans, in order to make a feint off Beauport and Point de Leste, and engross Montcalm's attention while the army forced a descent on the upper side of the town. Such were the dispositions up to the morning previous to the battle on the Heights of Abraham, which eventually decided the fate of Quebec and of French rule in Canada. Towards evening the boats worked up and lay half channel over opposite to Beauport, while at break of day the ships attending them were to edge in as near as possible, without grounding, and cannonade the intrenchments. After dark the whole squadron moved up the river with the flood tide, and before sunrise fell down with the ebb.

BATTLE OF QUEBEC.

Before daybreak on Thursday, September 13th, 1759, a descent was made upon the north shore, some 120 yards eastward of Sillery. The debarkation comprised 1600 men in thirty flat-bottomed boats. This was a regular surprise, such an attempt never having suggested itself to the enemy, and consequently found them unprepared. Their chain of sentries from the summit galled our troops as they landed, and picked off several officers and men before the light infantry could dislodge them. In one of the boats three men of the 43rd were killed, and four others wounded.

Captain Donald M'Donald, of Frazer's Highlanders, commanded the advanced guard of the light infantry. On gaining the heights he was immediately challenged by a French sentry. Thorough master of their language and military tactics, he replied after their own *genre*. Being dark, he completely succeeded in hoodwinking the sentinel, saying he was there in command of a large party to take post, desired him immediately to join his guard and call off all his men stationed along the heights, while he would take care to give a good account of the English if they should persist. This *ruse* was perfect, and saved many lives.

Wolfe, with Brigadiers Monckton and Murray, landed with the first division, and so soon as the boats discharged their respective cargoes they returned for reinforcements. No time was lost ere the troops began to clamber up one of the steepest and most perpendicular imaginable precipices. On reaching the summit they reformed, and ere daylight gleamed their right extended to the town, their left towards Sillery, with the river and south country in their rear. Wolfe then detached the light troops to the left to dislodge the enemy from their batteries and to disable their guns. The main body then faced to the right and marched in files until they reached the Plains of Abraham, selected by Wolfe. While the troops were forming on the hill rain fell. About six o'clock the enemy made their appearance on the heights between our forces and the town. The column halted, and wheeling to the right formed in line of battle. Quebec was to the eastward in their front, with the enemy under its walls. The right of the British line was flanked by the declivity, and the main river with that of Charles and the north country on the left.

The first disposition of the troops placed the Grenadiers of Louisbourg and the 28th Regiment on the right, with the 43rd and 47th on the left. Part of the light infantry took post in Sillery, and the remainder occupied a chain of houses, so situated that they covered the left flank. Wolfe then advanced some sections of the Grenadiers and 28th below the height, to the right, to annoy the enemy and prevent their getting round the declivity and the St. Lawrence, which they had been observed to attempt. The 15th and 35th Regiments had now come up, forming a second line, and were quickly followed by the 48th, 58th, 2nd battalion of the 60th, and the 78th Highlanders. The forces were then distributed thus: first line, 35th to the right, in a circular form, on the slope of the hill; 58th, left; Grenadiers, right; 78th, left; 28th, right; 47th, left; with 43rd in the centre. Wolfe, with Brigadiers Monckton and Murray, commanded this line. The second, under Townshend, was composed of the 15th, 2nd battalion of the 60th, with a reserve of the 48th under Colonel Burton, in four grand divisions at large intervals.

The enemy likewise drew up in battle array, bringing guns to bear upon our lines with canister and round shot; but the most serious annoyance was caused by a steady fire kept up by a body of Indians, concealed in corn opposite the right wing and in a coppice in front of the centre. Some platoons from the 47th, under Colonel Hall, were sent to dislodge them, which being accomplished, the whole line was ordered to lie down.

About eight o'clock, two brass 6-pounders opened upon the enemy, obliging them to shift their position and reform into three large columns. At nine the two armies neared a little, when Montcalm's light cavalry made an attempt upon our party at Sillery, but were beaten off. Captain de Bougainville with his troops swooped down upon the left of the second British line, hoping to penetrate; but by a masterly manœuvre of Townshend they were forced to desist, and the third battalion of the 60th was then detached to secure communication between the beach and the boats.

At ten o'clock the enemy in three columns with loud shouts advanced, two inclining to the left, the third towards the right of the English line, firing obliquely from a distance of 130 yards until they came within forty. Our troops stood unflinchingly, and, in strict obedience to their officers, did not return a single shot. This steadiness, with the havoc caused by grape, made the enemy waver, when a volley broke them and they precipitately fled. Before the cloud of smoke could evaporate, our men had reloaded and hotly pursued them almost to the very gates of the town, taking many prisoners.

The weather now cleared, and a bright exhilarating sun replaced the morning drizzle. The Highlanders chased vigorously towards Charles River, and the 58th to John's Gate until checked by cannon fired from two hulks, while a gun, which the townspeople had brought up, simultaneously poured grape into the right advance. Colonel Walsh then cleverly wheeled the 28th and 43rd to the left, and flanked the coppice where a body of the enemy had made a stand as if desirous of challenging a renewal of the combat, but a few rounds from the two corps triumphantly completed the victory.

In forming the line of battle, Wolfe had ordered all to load with an additional ball. The 43rd and 47th, in the centre, being less exposed to the oblique fire from Montcalm's columns, poured in their volley with the same precision as if on parade. The French officers afterwards owned that on no previous occasion had they ever been opposed by such a fire, or ever seen such discipline and regularity; that they believed every bullet found its billet, and that the centre corps in particular levelled and fired "*absolument comme un coup de canon.*"

Great was the joy over this success, but it was inexpressibly damped by the loss of one of the greatest heroes of which any age can boast, that of GENERAL JAMES WOLFE, who, at the early age of thirty-three, received his mortal wound. When the fatal bullet pierced him he was carried to the rear, and forbid any surgeon being summoned. "It is useless," he said; "I feel all is over." When in an apparent state of stupor, the words, "They run! they run!" were suddenly echoed. He raised himself, earnestly questioning, "*Who run?*" "The enemy, sir. Egad! they give way everywhere." Upon which the dying chief exerted his failing powers to articulate, "Go one of you, my lads, to Colonel Burton; tell him to march the 48th with all speed down to Charles River to cut off the retreat of the fugitives from the bridge. Now, God be praised, I rest in peace," and immediately expired.

Brigadier Monckton, on the left of the 43rd, was seriously wounded. The command then devolved on Brigadier Townshend, who, with Brigadier Murray, at the head of every regiment, returned thanks for the extraordinary good behaviour which had prevailed. As soon as the corps had rested and refreshed themselves, intrenching tools were brought on shore, and the men set to work to throw up redoubts, to fortify the houses and to land guns and ammunition.

The strength of our army on the day of the battle on Abraham's Heights was as follows, including officers, non-commissioned officers, privates, and general staff:—

15th, Amherst's	406
28th	421
35th, Otway's	519
43rd, Kennedy's	327
47th, Lascelles's	360
48th, Webb's	683
58th, Anstruther's	335
60th, Monckton's and Lawrence's	862
78th, Frazer's Highlanders	662
Grenadier Companies	241
General officers and staff	13
Total	4829

The French army numbered 7520, and their loss was estimated at above 1500. That of the English amounted to 664 in all; 59 killed, including 9 officers; 600 wounded; and 5 missing.

On this memorable day the 43rd was commanded by

Major Elliott; Colonel James having remained in charge of the camp. The casualties in the regiment were 3 privates killed; ensign Levis Jones, 2 sergeants, and 18 privates wounded, and 2 missing.

The officers taken prisoners, conscious of their own inhuman behaviour to ours under similar misfortune, entertained strong apprehensions of being harshly treated; with raised hats they piteously sued for quarter, repeatedly asseverating that they were not present at the massacre at Fort Henry in 1757. They, as well as some deserters who came in after the action, declared that Quebec would surrender in a few days, and that General de Montcalm was suffering acute agony from a mortal wound. At night, Brigadier Townshend, accompanied by 200 men, visited the French General Hospital, a convent in which the wounded officers and privates were tended by nuns of the St. Augustine order.

The Marquis de Montcalm occupied one of the rooms. When the surgeons had dressed his wound, he demanded if it were fatal, and if so, how long he might possibly survive. Being told that his life could not be prolonged beyond a few hours, he ejaculated, "So much the better: I am happy I shall not live to see the surrender of Quebec." Officers pressed around him for commands as to their future operations; to which the warrior replied, "I will neither give orders nor interfere any further. I have much business to transact of greater moment than that of our ruined garrison and of this wretched country. My time is very short, therefore pray leave me. I wish you all comfort, and to be happily extricated from your present perplexities."

He then called for his chaplain, who, with the bishop of the colony, remained by his bedside until he expired. Shortly before dissolution, he paid our troops this compliment: "Since it was my misfortune to be defeated and mortally wounded, it is a great consolation to me to be vanquished by so brave and generous an enemy. If I could survive this wound, I would engage to beat three times the amount of such forces as I commanded with a third of their number of British troops."

> " The great Epaminondas conq'ring died,—
> Hist'ry, brave Wolfe! shall place thee by his side;
> While, e'en in death thy triumph to maintain,
> The vanquish'd Montcalm swells the victor's train."

The French regulars had fired slugs of lead and iron, and some being found in the pouches of the prisoners, when interrogated, the answer was, with a characteristic shrug of the shoulders, "*C'est notre usage, sans mauvais intention*"!

From the 14th to the 17th the army continued to strengthen their position, and the fleet moved into the basin preparatory to the attack on the lower town. On the 17th an officer was sent to our camp with proposals of surrender. The admiral was immediately summoned. The capitulation was to be contigent on the non-arrival of M. de Levis and M. de Bougainville with their forces.

The following day, however, the garrison formally capitulated; articles were duly ratified and exchanged, and the keys of the gates presented to General Townshend. The fleet and army took possession both of the upper and lower towns, and guards were posted. The Louisbourg grenadiers marched in, preceded by a detachment of artillery, and a gun with British colours hoisted on its carriage. The union-jack floated on the citadel, and flags were displayed on the declivity in view of the basin and the suburbs below Quebec.

On the 18th the mortal remains of Wolfe were embalmed and put on board ship at Point Levi for transmission to England. Colonel James with a detachment of the 43rd attended the corpse to the water side, when most sensible grief was apparent on every countenance.

A brother officer subsequently wrote the following monumental inscription:—

> "Underneath, a hero lies,—
> WOLFE—the young, the brave, the wise;
> No tombstone need his worth proclaim,
> Quebec for ever shall record his fame,
> Quebec for ever shall with wonder tell
> How great beneath her walls her conqueror fell."

The Canadians surrendered by whole sections, submitting themselves to the General's mercy, and many deserters came in from M. de Levis' army. On the 23rd a solemn thanksgiving took place on the late field of battle, and on the 24th the troops were reviewed by General Monckton, who then left on sick leave for New York. The Hon. Captain Maitland of the 43rd was appointed adjutant-general.

On the 29th the regiment mustered 1 lieut.-colonel, 1 major, 7 captains, 10 lieutenants, 7 ensigns, 1 chaplain, 1 adjutant, 1 surgeon, 1 mate, 1 quarter-master, 29 sergeants, 18 drummers, 2 fifers, and 585 rank and file.

A company of volunteers was ordered to be formed, and Ensign Crank Maw of the 43rd was appointed to it. Soon after, he sallied out with a party hoping to take a prisoner for intelligence; but "his sight not being equal in goodness to his spirit and ability," he was himself wounded and captured.

REVIEW OF THE WINTER CAMPAIGN IN CANADA, 1759-60.

When Brigadier-General Murray as governor, and Colonel Burton as lieut.-governor, marched into Quebec, our garrison was by no means secure against a *coup de main*, though our victorious troops consisted of ten regiments, two companies of royal artillery, and one company of New England Rangers, amounting to some 7300 men.

Six bastions, with curtains of slight masonry, forming

a chain from Cape Diamond to St. Roque, were the only defence and dependence. The city was in a miserable plight; one-third of the houses reduced to ruins, while those still erect were so perforated by our own guns during the first onset, as to be unavailable. The enemy's army consisted of five battalions of veteran troops, thirty companies of marines, *troupes de colonie*, two troops of light cavalry, 1200 Acadians, and about 12,000 Canadians, in all near 18,000 men, who had not undergone a tenth part of the fatigue and privations to which ours had been exposed. They had many advantages; being perfectly acquainted with the country, they obtained in abundance fresh provisions from the immense tract in their possession.

Our troops remained within the walls only long enough to render the houses habitable, and secure the ramparts against surprise, and then took the field. Six hundred men were marched out, two hundred going to St. Foy, the remainder to Lorette, and took post. When they were well secured, another corps of 700 marched to St. Augustine, brought off the enemy's advanced guard, with a great many cattle, and disarmed the proprietors.

These two posts were of great importance, as affording an opportunity of watching the enemy's movements whilst covering our own. They likewise controlled eleven parishes, whereby fresh provisions, wood, and every requisite for subsistence was secured. Two hundred men were set to work to construct hand-sleighs to draw firewood. Other parties were despatched across the St. Lawrence to disarm the *habitans*, and oblige them to swear fealty to King George.

The French had taken up their quarters at Point au Tremble, St. Augustine, and Calvaire, with detachments between Jacques-Cartier and Trois Rivières. Their general was informed that our garrison began to flag, owing to perpetual and unavoidable hardships. Relying upon his superiority of numbers, he therefore resolved to repossess himself of the place in the depth of winter. Snow-shoes were distributed, hundreds of scaling-ladders were constructed, and the men exercised in fixing and climbing them. This *grand coup* was to have come off at the end of February or middle of March at latest. Notwithstanding every endeavour to conceal their intentions, they oozed out. Some miscarriages in the practice of an escalade momentarily suspended the project, but it was never thoroughly abandoned.

A detachment was sent to Point Levi, to collect recruits from the south coast to reinforce their army and to form a magazine of provisions. Calvaire and St. Augustine were strengthened by companies of grenadiers. They were in quiet possession of Point Levi, when the light troops, supported by a portion of the 43rd, crossed and precipitately routed them.

In a few days they returned in greater force to recover the post; but Murray, having had notice, marched some battalions over the ice, cutting them off, and sent the light troops to attack in front. Finding themselves thus hemmed in, they made so hasty a flight that only part of their rear could be overtaken. Detachments were despatched to surprise the advanced posts of St. Augustine and Calvaire, yet notwithstanding the alertness with which the enemy retired, nearly 100 prisoners were taken.

The situation of affairs became critical. It was more than probable the French fleet and army would fall down the river as soon as navigable; while the ground being still frost-bound, intrenchments could not be thrown up. These considerations induced Murray to order the light infantry to Cape Rouge, with injunctions to fortify the port, and prevent any landing. The work was scarcely begun when the frost broke, the enemy's fleet fell down, and landed their army at Point au Tremble; whence they marched direct to Lorette, to surprise that post and cut off those of Cape Rouge and St. Foy. Murray by his vigilance and activity frustrated these designs. His detachments fell back on St. Foy, after entirely destroying those posts, as well as every bridge. At the same time, half the garrison marched out with field-pieces, and with little or no loss covered the retreat. This occurred on the 27th of April, and on the 28th was fought the

Battle of Sillery.

" 'Tis not in mortals to command success: we'll do more—deserve it." M. de Levis and his army occupied St. Foy, and his advanced posts possessed a coppice contiguous. Early on the morning our light troops pushed out and drove them to a greater distance. Our army marched to the Heights of Abraham, carrying their intrenching tools, when the enemy's van was descried on the eminences of Sillery, and the bulk of their forces marching along the road of St. Foy. Our troops were ordered to throw down their tools and advance, the moment being deemed propitious for attack. The 48th, 15th, and second battalion of the 60th formed the right brigade, under Colonel Burton; the 28th, 78th, and 47th, the left, under Colonel Frazer; the 58th, right centre corps; and the 43rd, commanded by Colonel James, left centre. Our second line consisted of the 35th, and third battalion of the 60th, drawn up two deep in order to appear more numerous. The right flank was covered by Major Dalling's light infantry, and the left by a company of volunteers and rangers. The artillery were placed in front at intervals or on the flanks, as circumstances required.

Our little army numbered 3140; that of the enemy 18,000. The field-pieces were well served, and as soon as our troops came within musket range, the light infantry attacked the enemy's grenadiers on the left, and routed them. Simultaneously, the volunteers and rangers engaged their right and possessed themselves of a redoubt. The enemy's centre, perceiving their right and left give way, fled without firing a shot. Their main body then advanced rapidly, formed in columns, and, in spite of all efforts to prevent it, one of their columns came directly to sustain the fugitive grenadiers, then pursued by our light infantry, who, thus overpowered, retired with great loss. The enemy then wheeled round on some rising ground, vigorously charging our right wing in flank, whilst M. de Levis with another division made a like movement on our left. The action now became obstinate on either side. The 35th was ordered from the second line to support our right wing, and the third battalion of the 60th the left.

Quebec being the grand object, the enemy, disregarding our centre, hoping to outflank and get between us and our garrison, supported their wings with fresh reinforcements. Fortune, trembling in the balance, seemed inclined to favour the more numerous army. The enemy possessed themselves of two redoubts on our left, thus obtaining a grave advantage, but "by an excellent movement of the 43rd, ordered by Colonel James from the centre to support the third battalion of the 60th on the left, both corps made a vigorous effort to recover the works, and succeeded. They maintained them for some time with admirable firmness, but at length, being reduced to a handful, they were compelled to yield to overwhelming numbers." In the course of the action, the British troops were insensibly drawn from their more advantageous situation into low, swampy ground, where they fought knee-deep in dissolving wreaths of snow and slush, from whence it was utterly impracticable to draw off the artillery. Under these circumstances, after performing prodigies of valour, having had the whole force of the country to contend against, and fearful lest communication with the town might be cut off, the contest was relinquished. So regularly and deliberately conducted was the retreat, that the enemy did not follow with either spirit or energy, which the vast importance of their success should have entailed. For two hours the fighting had been extremely warm. The English had 1100 of all ranks killed, wounded, and made prisoners. The enemy owned to above 1800. The casualties in the 43rd amounted to five rank and file killed, Captain Skey, Lieutenant Clements, and sixteen privates wounded; Captain David Maitland was taken prisoner.

On the evening after the battle, the enemy opened their trenches. Up to the 10th of May they were incessantly employed in landing artillery, ammunition, provisions, ladders, and tools. Civilities were interchanged between the hostile commanders. M. de Levis, under flag of truce, sent branches of spruce-fir to brew beverage for the General's acceptance, who in return presented him with a Cheshire cheese. An incessant and destructive fire was kept up from the English batteries with such effect that in nine days the enemy lost 500 men; but this was not achieved without occasional accidents on our side. Amongst these, a chest of ammunition blew up, which communicating with the men's arms, some of them went off, and was the cause of a lieutenant and several of the 43rd being shot and scorched. The spirit of the garrison never flagged, and on receipt of intelligence that on the 9th of May the enemy intended to storm the town, our gallant soldiers exclaimed, "They had better not, lest they should catch a tartar!" On the 11th the enemy unmasked their batteries and opened a tremendous fire, but with slight effect. Four officers of the 43rd were sitting in a tent discussing pease-porridge, when a shell fell amongst them. The had scarcely time to throw themselves on the ground ere it burst, but with no other damage than the loss of the porridge, which was upset in the *melée*.

On the 9th, the 'Lowestoffe' frigate had come into the basin, and on the 15th a ship of the line and another frigate anchored before the town. Early the next day this little squadron worked up with great spirit and engaged the French fleet, which instantly weighed anchor, but was so closely followed and so briskly attacked by our frigates, that all their ships were driven ashore in different places and destroyed. This acted like a thunderbolt on the enemy; they took flight the same evening, abandoning all their artillery, amunition, field equipages, provisions, and immense stores of every siege requisite. Our entire loss during this investment did not exceed thirty killed and wounded.

The Indians committed great irregularities in the French camp, getting drunk, plundering the officers' baggage, and cutting up tents. Falling upon a small guard of grenadiers in charge of officers' effects, they scalped every man but one, who contrived to make his escape. One hundred and fifty-two French officers were killed and wounded. They behaved with great inhumanity to our dead, scalping, and then leaving them unburied.

1760.

On the 18th of May Lord Colville's fleet arrived before Quebec. General Murray returned public thanks to the garrison for the great zeal, intelligence, and bravery they had shown during the siege. It may be noted here, although not officially recorded, that great credit was due to women, numbering nearly 600, attached to the different regiments, who rendered eminent service as nurses, laundresses, &c. In spite of the rigorous winter, not one had succumbed or been invalided, and of the sixty-three belonging to the 43rd, the orderly sergeant on presenting his morning state to the adjutant on the 12th February, touched his hat, reported them "all well: able to eat their allowance, and *fit for duty both by day and night.*"

On the 30th of May, the garrison numbered 5070 men—2517 fit for duty, 2553 sick or recovering. Scurvy had committed great ravages: one method of cure adopted was burying the victims up to their necks in sand.

Expedition against Montreal.

General Amherst was now in motion towards Montreal, as well as Sir William Johnson, with a large body of Indians. It was determined that the other troops should co-operate. The 'Porcupine' sloop of war, with two armed vessels, eight floating batteries, and twenty flat-bottomed boats with their crews, were under Captain Deane. Colonel Frazer remained in charge of the garrison at Quebec. The field force consisted of 2451 men, drafted from all the different regiments, and formed into seven battalions and two brigades.

The quota contributed by the 43rd amounted to thirteen officers, ten sergeants, ten corporals, and 207 rank and file. They were reviewed on the 2nd of August, and on the 13th embarked in great order. On the 14th they got under weigh with a flood tide and fair wind. As they passed the fortress of Jacques-Cartier they were shelled, but the breadth of the river protected them. On the 17th the division from Louisbourg, under Lord Rollo, came up, and all advanced together. General Murray detached from Quebec a force of recovered invalids under Colonel Frazer, to reduce Jacques-Cartier, which was effected on September 7th. During their progress the enemy harassed and impeded them on every possible opportunity; but on their appearance before the fort, the Marquis d'Albergotte surrendered at discretion.

On the same date the army landed at Point au Tremble, eleven miles from Montreal. The peasantry brought out teams to draw the artillery, saddle-horses for the officers, and waggons for the baggage. The march lay through a fertile country, but the enemy having destroyed the bridges, it was 9 P.M. before Longue Pointe could be reached. The night being dark the troops all halted, taking up their quarters in houses and barns. Some Mohawk Indians carried tidings to General Amherst that Brigadier Haviland and his forces had arrived within twenty-four hours' march of Montreal. Next morning they proceeded, and by noon took up encamping ground under Mount Royale. General Murray pitched his tent in the suburbs. So soon as Montreal found itself surrounded by our three armies, articles of capitulation were proposed and signed. War thus abruptly terminated—effectually dissolving the colossal power which France had so long and so assiduously laboured to erect in the American empire. Joy and triumph were diffused throughout the entire British dominions over this splendid and unexpected surrender.

After the capitulation of Montreal the 43rd returned to Quebec, and were cantoned at De Chambeaux, Lobinièrie, and De Gravien.

Muster taken at Quebec, 2nd Oct., 1760.

Colonel, Kennedy. (*Absent by permission.*)
Lieut.-Colonel, D. James. (*Resigned.*)
Major, Elliott.

Captains.

Boughey Skey.
John Carter.
Hon. Rd. Maitland.
Roger Spendlove.

Alex. Montgommery.
James Talbot.
David Maitland.

Captain-Lieutenant, William Dunbar.

Lieutenants.

Christopher Knight.
(*Adjutant.*)
John Knox.
Henry Clements.
Vernon Hawley.
Toby Purcell.

Blundel Dalton.
Robert Shaw.
Robert Molesworth.
William Spread.
Nicholas Lysaght.

Ensigns.

Walter Nugent.
Trevor Hall.
Lewis Jones.
(*Died 25th Nov., 1759.*)
Thomas Arthur.
Crank Maw.

John Hatfield.
Monsieur Mercer.
F. Lehaute.
Henry Knight.
(*Quarter-Master.*)

Surgeon, William Yonge.
Assistant-Mate, Ed. Tudor.

Strength of each Company on Paper, 2nd Oct., 1760.

Companies.	Sergeants.	Corporals.	Drummers.	Rank and File.
Talbot's	3	3	1	30
Kennedy's	3	3	2	40
James's	3	3	2	45
Elliott's	3	3	1	49
Montgommery's	3	3	1	37
R. Maitland's	3	3	2	44
Spendlove's	3	3	2	44
Carter's	3	3	2	48
Skey's	3	3	2	62
D. Maitland's	3	3	2	41
Total	30	30	17	440

1761.

In February an accident happened to one of the transports, by which Major Elliott and a detachment of the regiment were cast away on Sable Island, but were happily extricated, and reached Halifax with the loss of only two seamen. Singular to relate, after the interval of eighty-one years, relics of the disaster turned up. Near the governor's residence a large pyramid of sand, about 100 feet high, had long been an object of curiosity; but in 1842, after a violent hurricane, it completely disappeared, and a number of small houses, built of the timber and planks of a vessel became visible. On examination they were found to contain various articles of furniture, and stores in boxes marked "43rd Regiment." The boxes and cases were perfectly rotten, and their contents most miscellaneous. Bullets of lead, military shoes, bales of blankets and clothing, scabbards, beeswax, a small convex glass, a copper halfpenny of George II. anno 1749, military shoe-buckles, brass pins, bones, gold braid, and though last, not the least curious, a tiny brass dog-collar, with "Major Elliott, 43rd Regiment," engraven. Captain Darby took this relic to Halifax, and presented it to Captain Tryon, of the 43rd, then Brigade-Major in that garrison.

On the 25th of March Major Robert Elliott was promoted to the lieut.-colonelcy of the 55th Regiment. He had served with great credit and distinction in the 43rd, and had commanded it, as before stated, on the memorable 13th of September, on the Heights of Abraham.

The 43rd were now encamped on Staten Island, whither they had been sent to form part of a force destined for descent on the West Indian Islands, it having been determined to resume operations dormant since 1759. Our relations with Spain had again become equivocal, and it behoved us to assume an independent position, lest formal war with that kingdom should be proclaimed.

Here Lieut.-Colonel Dalling, having succeeded Colonel

James on his retirement, joined and took command. He was an officer of experience and merit, having served throughout the late campaigns at the head of the light infantry.

This expedition under General Monckton consisted of eleven battalions, besides rangers and artillery. The 43rd numbered 26 officers, 30 sergeants, 30 corporals, 18 drummers, and 394 rank and file. On the 19th of November they sailed from New York for Barbadoes, where being joined by drafts from the garrison of Belle-isle, together with reinforcements from various leeward islands, raised the whole to 12,000 men.

1762.

On the 7th of January they landed at Martinique, in a creek called Cas Navire. From the numerous ravines, intersected with rivulets, the country appeared studded with natural fortifications. The progress of the troops, particularly that of the artillery, was greatly impeded by guards posted and batteries erected wherever the ground permitted, and these obstructions were especially conspicuous on the locality chosen for the first attack.

The town and citadel of Port Royale are overlooked and commanded by two eminences—Morne Tortenson and Morne Garnier—each protected by formidable ravines. Morne Tortenson was first doomed. A corps was ordered to advance on the right along the sea-side, to take the redoubts in the low grounds. A thousand sailors rowed close by to assist. A body of light infantry moved to the left, while a centre attack was made by the grenadiers and general forces, under the fire of batteries which with great labour had been erected on the opposite side. The enthusiasm of our soldiers carried each work in succession, driving the enemy from post to post, till they eventually fled, leaving us masters of the Morne. Many escaped to Morne Garnier, a stronger and much loftier hill than that of Tortenson, which it overlooked and commanded. Nothing decisive could be achieved without possession of this superior height.

Several days elapsed before effective arrangements could be made to dispossess the enemy. Meanwhile, *en masse*, they left their eyrie, and attacked our advanced posts. Immediate repulse and pursuit followed. We improved a defensive into an offensive advantage, passed the ravines, mingled with the fugitives, scaled the hills, seized the batteries, and took post on the summit of Morne Garnier. The French escaped into the town, the militia into the country, and only waited until our defences were completed to surrender.

St. Pierre, a place of considerable strength and capital of Martinique, still remained intact. The reduction of Port Royale, together with the ill-luck which seemed invariably to attend French tactics, determined their leader, just as General Monckton was about to embark for St. Pierre, to propose terms for the capitulation of the whole island. Being the principal mart of trade, and seat of French rule and power in the Caribbees, its surrender naturally entailed that of other dependencies. Grenada, very fertile and with several good harbours, gave in her adhesion; St. Lucia and St. Vincent followed; and the English thus became undisturbed possessors of a numerous group of islands. The light company of the 43rd was present on their submission.

The regimental casualties on the 24th of January were two rank and file killed, Captain Spendlove, Lieutenant Nugent of the grenadiers, and six rank and file wounded; on the 27th, Ensign Knight, of the light infantry, wounded.

EXPEDITION AGAINST HAVANNAH.

War with Spain was now officially declared, and England, determined to aim at once such a blow as would subjugate that nation's power, and compel her to sue for peace, organized and despatched a strong force, military and naval, under Lord Albemarle and Sir George Pocock, to dispute her West Indian possessions. They sailed from Portsmouth, and on May 7th fell in off Cape Nicholas with the squadron—43rd Regiment inclusive—ordered from Martinique to join and take part. At this junction the armament amounted to thirty-seven ships of war and 150 transports, conveying some 10,000 men; 4000 more were advised from New York.

Anxious to push ahead, the admiral performed a most dashing though dangerous feat,—that of running along the north shore of Cuba and passing through the straits of Bahama.

Havannah now lay before them—the most opulent and flourishing city in the West Indies. The harbour is one of the finest in the world. Strong forts guarded the entrance. The Spanish fleet lay in the basin, evincing no desire to come out and fight, although little inferior to that of the English. They relied upon the internal strength of the place, and the great difficulties attending protracted operations in unhealthy climates. They were far from deficient in proper measures for defence. A strong boom was thrown across the mouth of the harbour, behind which three ships were sunk.

On the 7th of June, when all was in readiness, the admiral with part of the fleet, to distract the enemy's attention, bore to the westward; while Commodore Keppel and Captain Harvey, with a detachment of the squadron, effected a landing towards the east. The light infantry were formed into one corps, and the grenadiers into three battalions. The principal body of the army was divided into two corps: one under General Elliott advanced to Guarda Vacoa; the other, of which the 43rd composed a part, was occupied in the attack of the MORO. A detachment was also encamped to the westward, cutting off all communications between Havannah and the country, and diverting concentrated surveillance. The artillery was dragged over a rough, rocky shore. Several men dropped dead from heat, thirst, and fatigue. In spite of all obstacles, batteries were raised against the Moro, composed of sandbags filled with earth collected many hundred yards in the rear, and carried forward on the shoulders of the men. Others were also erected on the hill on which the Moro stood, in order to drive the enemy's ships deeper into the harbour, and prevent their molesting our troops in their approaches. Firing on either side was kept up with great vivacity.

On the 29th of June the Spaniards made a resolute sally in considerable force, but were beaten back, leaving 300 men *hors de combat.* Directly our batteries were complete, three ships under Captain Hardy opened with a tremendous cannonade against the fort, which was fiercely answered for some hours. But the Moro, situated upon a high and steep rock was bomb-proof, and the vessels reluctantly sheared off with considerable loss. Firing from the castle and batteries was continued for several days without intermission. The English had never been better matched, or military skill more severely tested.

On the 3rd of July our principal battery took fire, and was totally consumed. This mortifying accident rendered nugatory the labour of 600 men during seventeen days.

Sickness now prevailed and rapidly increased in that fœtid atmosphere. The army became reduced to half its original strength, and at one time no less than 5000 soldiers, with 3000 seamen, were down in fever or other distempers, their sufferings horribly aggravated by local malaria, great paucity of water, and want of good provisions. Still, by the spirit and perseverance of the effective officers and men new batteries arose; our fire by degrees becoming equal and finally superior to that of the opponents. By the 20th of July, the cannon of the fort was silenced, the upper works beat to pieces, and a lodgment effected in the covered way. Two days after, the Jamaica fleet, *en route* to Europe, landed siege material, and on the 28th reinforcements arrived from New York.

These cheering events infused fresh life and rekindled the besiegers' hopes, just as a new and serious difficulty presented itself. An immense ditch, cut in the solid rock, eighty feet deep by forty wide, yawned before them. Fortunately a ridge of rock had been left covering the ditch towards the sea, and, mining being the only feasible expedient, over this narrow ridge the miners passed, burying themselves in the walls.

The enemy caused 1200 men to be transported across the harbour, climbing the hills, and making three attacks on our posts. But the ordinary guards, though surprised, defended themselves so lustily, that the Spaniards were unable to destroy any part of our approaches, and were driven back with great slaughter.

This was the last effort to save the Moro, which, although undermined, held out with sullen resolution. On the 30th of July the mine was sprung. Half of the east bastion was blown down, leaving a breach, which, though narrow and difficult, was judged practicable. So great was the spirit and coolness with which the detachments ordered on this dangerous service mounted, that the enemy drawn up on the opposite side, paralysed by the sight of such gallantry, fled at once.

Don Luis de Velasco, the governor, collected 100 men round the colours, and the Marquis de Gonzales, second in command, fell while endeavouring to rally them. Don Luis, disdaining to retire or ask for quarter, received a mortal wound, and expiring offered his sword to the conquerors. Thus, at the end of fifty-three days' siege, the Moro became ours, and no time was lost in following up our advantage. A line of batteries was erected commanding the town, and the fire of the Fort directed against it.

On the 2nd of August a second division of troops arrived from North America.

On the 10th Lord Albemarle, by message, represented to the Governor the irresistible force of the attack he was about to make, but which, to avoid needless effusion of blood, he was willing to suspend if the Spaniards would surrender. The Governor returned a civil but resolute answer, that he was prepared to defend his trust to the last, and instantly opened fire. To convince him that the menaces used were no empty boast, Lord Albemarle ordered a general discharge from the batteries, which poured into the town on every side with such effect, that in six hours, to the heartfelt relief and triumph both of fleet and army, almost all the enemy's guns were silenced, and numerous flags of truce hoisted. Capitulation ensued, when the British undertook to respect the established religion, laws, and private property of the inhabitants, to award honours of war to the garrison, and reconduct them to Spain.

The booty accruing to the victors was estimated at 3,000,000*l.* sterling; but the distribution was shamefully jobbed, and caused such umbrage that for a time seamen fought shy of entering the service. The petty officers, seamen, and soldiers received a very unequal and inadequate recompense for the bravery they had shown and the multiplied hardships they had undergone.

The admiral and general each received 122,697*l*. 10*s*. 6*d*.; captains of ships each 1600*l*.; lieutenants R.N., each 234*l*. 13*s*. 3*d*.; sailors and marines each only 3*l*. 14*s*. 9¼*d*.; field officers, each 564*l*. 14*s*. 6*d*.; captains, each 184*l*. 4*s*. 7¼*d*.; and to each private, 4*l*. 1*s*. 8*d*.

Our loss at the Havannah was :—killed, 11 officers, 15 sergeants, 4 drummers, and 260 rank and file. Wounded, 19 officers, 49 sergeants, 6 drummers, and 576 rank and file. Died from wounds, 4 officers, 1 drummer, and 51 rank and file. Died from disease, 39 officers, 14 sergeants, 11 drummers, and 632 rank and file. Missing, 1 sergeant, 25 rank and file.

The 43rd, under Brigadier-General Reid, was in the third brigade. It consisted of ten companies, numbering 380 men, commanded by Colonel Dalling. Captain Spendlove was wounded, 10 rank and file were killed, 15 wounded, 4 reported missing, and 13 dead from fever. Upon the reduction they were sent—then only 240 strong—to Jamaica, where, by drafts from other battalions in the West Indies, they were completed to 500.

1764.

On the 19th of March they were relieved by the 36th, and sailed for England. In July the regiment reached Portsmouth, marched into Hilsea barracks, and from thence to Chatham, where Major Skey, with a party of recruits, joined.

In October they were inspected by Major-General Parslow. His report detailing the names, ages, country, service, &c., of all the officers and men is very complete, and his remarks thereon may be quoted in his exact terms.

The 43rd Regiment of Foot.—Remarks.

Officers	Armed with fusils, which they are desirous that they may be permitted to make use of instead of espoutons. Salute well. Uniform good, faced with white, and laced with gold.
Non-commissioned Officers	Properly armed and dressed.
Men	Good size, and in general young.
Exercise	Well performed.
Evolutions	Performed according to the new regulations, and surprisingly well for the time they had to practise; march well, both in slow and quick time.
Firings	The whole according to order, and well.
Arms	Good.
Accoutrements	Good, coloured white.
Clothing	Good, and well fitted.
Recruits	Appeared in the ranks.
Guetres	Black, not well fitted; white bespoke.
Accounts	Not yet settled, having received no pay but for effectives.
Complaints	The same as the King's own regiments in regard to the barracks.

For the numbers, a good regiment, well appointed, and fit for service.

(Copy)　JOHN PARSLOW,
Oct. 2nd, 1764.　　　　　　　　　　　Major-General.

N.B.—All the sergeants had halberds, and the ramrods were iron; and the grenadiers' *match cases* (50) were wanting; they had 18 drums.

In this year a board of general officers resolved that grenadiers should lay aside their swords, "as that weapon had never been used during the Seven Years' War" since when the arms of all British infantry soldiers have been limited to the musket and bayonet.

1765.

During July of this year the 43rd were reviewed in the neighbourhood of London by His Majesty George III. Small parties were detached to Deal, Ramsgate, and Dover, to assist the officers of the revenue in the prevention of smuggling.

1766.

In this year the regiment was stationed in various southern and western home districts, frequently changing quarters to suppress incidental riots and disturbances. During the assizes, contrary to custom, they were allowed to remain in the towns. The King again reviewed them at Windsor.

1767-69.

In June, 1767, they marched from Exeter to Newcastle-upon-Tyne, and detachments were sent to Morpeth, Sunderland, Tynemouth, and Berwick. From these stations they moved to Edinburgh, and in July the whole regiment mustered in the castle.

1770-73.

Early in the spring of 1770, the headquarters, with two companies, marched to Glasgow, and until 1773 the 43rd were cantoned in the principal military posts in Scotland, without any events of importance occurring.

1774.

War of Independence.

In April the regiment marched to Portsmouth to embark for North America, where serious colonial disputes had arisen.

After the peace of 1763, to 1773, our American colonies had prospered; but discontents arose. The colonists chafed at the supremacy of Great Britain, and when it was determined to prevent smuggling in America much angry feeling was engendered. Trade was injured, and the navy, in their zeal to obey the recent mandates, but ignorant of custom-house laws, made illegal seizures. At Boston a strong movement was set on foot to protest against the salaries of judges and employés of the crown. A committee was formed and resolutions passed claiming the sole right of legislation. This brought the Governor of Massachusetts and the General Assembly to loggerheads. The Assembly voted the ordinary salaries, arguing that such allowances accepted from the crown entailed dependence thereon. This vote for the ensuing year was reluctantly confirmed by the Governor, but he positively declined to agree to its extension.

The Home Government, at this epoch, thought it expedient to grant to the East India Company some indemnification against the grievances of Lord Clive's arbitrary rule. One was, permission to send tea to any part of the globe. That shrub "which cheers but not inebriates," being one of Lord North's pet *spécialités*, he determined to dispatch a large consignment to North America, convinced that the Provincials, attracted by the moderate figure affixed, would be ready to purchase, and no longer protest against the small duty chargeable on exportation.

The King was amusing himself at a naval review off Portsmouth, while the Massachusetts Assembly were denouncing their president and the seeds of civil warfare taking root. At the moment these agitations were lightly regarded, but ere long they assumed a serious aspect. Lord North's shipment of tea arrived; but the New Englanders—however in later days they may have clamoured for tea-totalism—would have none of it; and when the vessels came alongside the wharf at Boston, the Governor and Custom-house refused a clearance. On the 18th of December, 1773, to prevent the dreaded consequences of this importation, a number of men disguised as Mohawk Indians boarded the ships, and pitched it overboard without doing further injury. Parliament then framed the vindictive Boston Port Bill, and altered the constitution of Massachusetts. This measure fanned the flame for open rupture, so that the name of tea being associated with ministerial grievances, tea-drinking became almost synonymous with Toryism. Leaders soon sprung up amongst the malcontents, and diffused a spirit keenly subversive of British rule through the provinces.

Governor Hutchinson dissolved the Assembly, resigned, and was succeeded by General Gage. Although the latter's popularity with the colonists was great, he came in direct collision with the Assembly when he refused to receive an address animadverting on the conduct of Hutchinson and his predecessor Sir Francis Bernard. A resolution in favour of a congress was passed. The congress met at Philadelphia, and a petition for redress of grievances unanimously voted to the King. It enumerated the insults received, claimed the rights of Britons—*Peace, Liberty, and Safety*, and was signed by fifty delegates. Benjamin Franklin bore the despatch to England.

His Majesty refused to receive the petition. Ministers, under court influence, recommended coercing the colonists, and coercion was adopted. In the Upper House, Lord Chatham endeavoured to bring in a conciliatory bill, but failed; while Burke, in the Commons, was similarly defeated. Lord North then carried a resolution promising to "desist from all taxation except commercial imposts, whenever any one of the colonial assemblies should vote a reasonable sum as a revenue to be appropriated to the Parliament." The colonists regarded this as insidious and evasive. Two bills were subsequently introduced, debarring nine of the provinces from all foreign commerce, but leaving New York, the three Delaware counties, North Carolina, and Georgia unmolested.

Many petitions and warm debates ensued. Wilkes presented his address from the Corporation of London, but the King remained obstinately convinced that his American subjects were rebelliously disposed, and that the original vote of his parliament was correct. The Governor of Boston issued a proclamation for the encouragement of piety and virtue, for the prevention and punishment of vice. In proof of the spirit of discontent fostering amongst the people, on one occasion a zealous divine used in the pulpit the following emphatic language:— "O Lord, if our enemies will fight us, let them have fighting enough. If more soldiers are on their way hither, smite them, O Lord, to the bottom of the sea!" Every heart seemed to respond, "Amen; yea, let them have fighting enough!" All was discord. Rumours of an attack on Boston floated. Precautionary measures on the part of the General led to an assembly of delegates from every town in Suffolk, who passed resolutions, the sum total being that although they considered themselves oppressed by the late acts of the British Parliament, and were resolved, with Divine assistance, never to submit to them, still they had no inclination to commence war with His Majesty's troops. General Gage used every endeavour to calm them; but indications grew graver, and on the approach of winter, he ordered temporary barracks to be erected. The Boston carpenters declined to work, and none would come from New York. Eventually fifty were procured from Halifax. Winter clothing was imminently requisite, but every merchant refused to supply it, on the ground that they would not contribute any article for the benefit of men sent as enemies to their country.

In June, 1774, the 43rd, which had been the first corps that landed in America from England, was in camp at Boston in company with the 4th, 5th, 10th, 23rd, 38th, 47th, 52nd, 59th, and 64th Regiments, three companies of the 18th and two of the 65th, with six companies of artillery.

1775.

In February General Gage received intelligence of the deposit of some brass cannon in the town of Salem. A field-officer and some men were sent to seize and bring them to Boston, but failed. The next attempt to remove American property led to the first bloodshedding in this unhappy civil war.

COMBAT OF LEXINGTON.

Intelligence having reached Gage that a quantity of military stores were collecting at Concord, eighteen miles from Boston, he determined on their capture. On the night of the 18th of April, a secret expedition of about 800 of the Grenadiers and Light Infantry, together with some Marines under command of Lieut.-Colonel Smith, were ferried across the Charles River to East Cambridge. "They will miss their aim," was overheard from a voice amidst some bystanders. The affair had already got wind, and a couple of youths on fast-trotting horses were on the road before them, while the bells in Boston called the minute men. This looked bad for Smith's return, but he obeyed orders and commenced his march.

The troops had made good progress, when Colonel Smith sent forward six companies of Light Infantry under Major Pitcairn to secure the bridge he would be obliged to pass. On their reaching Lexington at 5 A.M., Major Pitcairn in the haze discovered about seventy militia drawn up on the village green for the purpose of inviting attack.

Narrators differ as to which party fired the first shot; for while some assert that the colonists, upon being ordered to throw down their arms and disperse, fired upon the troops, which was returned without waiting for orders, others have it that Pitcairn, having discharged his own pistol, gave the word. Be it as it may, the upshot was that Pitcairn's horse and one man were wounded; seven of the militia killed, and nine disabled.

About seven o'clock the King's troops, leaving one hundred Light Infantry under Captain Laurie of the 43rd to guard the bridge, reached Concord and destroyed what stores they could find.

Numbers of armed men now assembled, and it was noon when Colonel Smith began to retrace his steps, by which time the whole country had risen, and a shout was set up by the Americans that "the lobsters" had turned tail. The red coats then found themselves exposed to an incessant and galling fire from every available cover. It was in vain facing about, they could not induce their assailants to come to close quarters. Before reaching Lexington their ammunition began to fail, the wounded to drop, and the flanking parties to knock up. The Americans bore witness to the admirable behaviour of the British officers on this occasion; but had it not been that intelligence had reached Gage of the opposition first met with at Lexington, upon which he despatched Lord Percy with twelve companies, some marines and field-pieces, all their gallantry and efforts must have been abortive: they arrived just in time, finding Colonel Smith's men so fatigued as to be described "with their tongues hanging out of their mouths like dogs after a chase."

Having marched nearly thirty-six miles, weary and worn they reached Charleston, and passed on directly to Boston, minus 1 lieutenant, 1 sergeant, 1 drummer, and 62 rank and file killed; 2 lieut.-colonels, 2 captains, 9 lieutenants, 2 ensigns, 7 sergeants, 1 drummer, and 157 rank and file wounded. The grenadiers and light companies of the 43rd lost Lieutenant Hull, wounded,—he was taken prisoner, and died of his wounds; 4 rank and file killed, 5 wounded, and 2 taken prisoners.

The Lexington event showed how erroneous was the

belief of home authorities, that the appearance of a regiment, or even the sight of a grenadier's cap would be sufficient to put an American army to flight. The whole province rose to arms. The militia, amounting to 20,000, surrounded Boston, fixed their headquarters at Cambridge, and formed a line of encampment, strengthened with artillery, from Roxbury to Mystick, a distance of thirty miles. Colonel Putnam, an old and brave provincial officer, with a large reinforcement from Connecticut joined. The Americans regarded Lexington as a glorious victory, and declared their intention of driving the King's troops from Boston. This caused a crisis.

Congress, which now assumed the appellation of "The United Colonies," adopted resolutions for raising an army, for the establishment of a paper currency, a post office, &c. So directly did they oppose the Government that General Gage, in a final effort at reconcilement, issued a proclamation, by which pardon was offered, in the King's name, to all who should lay down their arms and return to their occupations—while those who refused should be treated as rebels and traitors.

Charleston had been neglected by both sides; but as the Provincials, on the 16th of June, sent a body of men to throw up intrenchments on Bunker's Hill, and by daybreak had constructed strong works (which being discovered by the men-of-war), a continual fire was opened upon them.

BATTLE OF BUNKER'S HILL.

Preparations were instantly made for landing ten companies of grenadiers, ten of light infantry, the 5th, 38th, 43rd, and 52nd battalions, with a proportion of field artillery, under command of Major-General Howe and Brigadier-General Pigott. It was past three o'clock in the afternoon when they landed without opposition, under cover of guns of the fleet. The troops formed with the light infantry on the right, the grenadiers on the left, the 5th and 38th in the rear, and the 43rd and 52nd as a third line.

This was the first occasion upon which the 52nd acted in unison with the 43rd, afterwards honourably and fraternally linked during the Peninsular War, and singularly enough, in the early formation of the corps both had been numbered "the 54th," though eventually changed to "the 43rd" and "52nd."

The Americans in force were strongly posted on the heights, their right flank covered by a large body occupying houses in Charleston; their left by a cannon-proof breastwork. The attack began by a heavy discharge of cannon and howitzers. The enemy did not return a shot until the troops approached close to the works, and evinced a resolution which would have done credit to old soldiers. They then opened with deadly effect. Nearly the whole front rank of the British fell at the first discharge, and volley after volley was poured into them until the bravest began to waver and fall back. Encumbered with their knapsacks, containing three days' provisions, advancing up a steep hill, knee deep in long tangled grass, and clambering over zigzag fences to attack brave men behind intrenchments, momentarily reinforced by hundreds, and under a burning sun, few soldiers but staunch British infantry could have been persuaded to renew the conflict—but again they returned to the charge, and were again, in spite of many heroic attempts of their officers, obliged to retire.

General Clinton, witnessing this state of things from Copt's Hill, took a boat and was ferried over as a volunteer, bringing a small reinforcement. A new mode of assault was then organised. General Howe, having discovered a weak point between a breastwork and a rail fence, led the left wing and resolved to apply the main strength against the redoubt and breastwork, and to rake the latter with artillery, which he disguised by a feigned show of force at the fence. The men took off their packs, some even their coats, being ordered to stand the American fire and rely on the bayonet alone.

The artillery then opened, raking the breastwork, and driving the enemy into the redoubt, where, after a ferocious hand-to-hand struggle (in which at one time General Howe was left alone), the Provincials, fighting desperately, were driven out and retreated over Charleston Neck. The loss on our side was:—Killed, 1 lieut.-colonel, 2 majors, 7 captains, 9 lieutenants, 15 sergeants, 1 drummer, 191 rank and file. Wounded, 3 majors, 27 captains, 32 lieutenants, 8 ensigns, 40 sergeants, 12 drummers, and 706 rank and file.

The 43rd sustained severe casualties. Major Spendlove, Captain Mackenzie, Lieutenants Dalrymple and Robinson, dangerously wounded; 2 sergeants, 10 rank and file, killed; 3 sergeants, 2 drummers, and 77 rank and file, wounded. Major Spendlove expired from the results. For upwards of thirty years he had served with unblemished character in the regiment. Four times previous he had been seriously wounded in action, and his bravery elicited especial approbation from the Commander-in-Chief. He had been nominated to a brevet majority in July, 1772, and became regimental major in February following.

Thus ended the sanguinary affair of Bunker's Hill, in which the bravery of the Provincials had been so conspicuous as to compel men present at the most remarkable actions of the last war to admit that the engagement was the hottest they ever witnessed. Even the battle on the Heights of Abraham, with all its glory, and the guerdon of half a continent, did not cost the lives of so many distinguished and honourable officers as this attack of an intrenchment cast up in a few hours.

Dr. Warren, who had relinquished the medical profession to lead his countrymen, was killed fighting bravely at their head. He was greatly regretted by all who served under him. His *costume de guerre* was composed of a light coloured coat, white satin waistcoat lined with silver, and white breeches with silver loops.

The British troops kept possession of the peninsula, fortified Bunker's Hill, and had two garrisons to maintain. Surrounded and insulted by an enemy they had been taught to despise, cut off from fresh provisions, confinement and heat of climate added, soon filled the hospitals, and rendered their position truly critical.

The Provincials used every endeavour to foster discontent and cause desertion. Printed circulars found their way into our camp. One of these, addressed to the British soldiers, bore the following contrasted bills of fare :—

Prospect Hill.	Bunker's Hill.
1. Seven dollars a month.	1. Threepence a day.
2. Fresh provisions in plenty.	2. Rotten salt-pork.
3. Health.	3. The scurvy.
4. Freedom, ease, affluence, and a good farm.	4. Starving, beggary, and want.

The arrival of a regiment of light cavalry from Ireland increased their wants. Such was the predicament of the camp that enormous quantities of provisions, even to vegetables, firewood, and minor necessaries, were shipped from England. Through contretemps and storms, only a few of the vessels, with their cargoes in the most miserable condition, reached Boston, and they had the mortification of seeing others taken at the very mouth of the harbour. The loss of coal ships added severely to their hardships, as they were obliged to lie in tents exposed to driving snow and cutting winds.

General Washington was appointed Commander-in-Chief of all the American forces. With other generals and large detachments of volunteers he arrived before Boston in July. This served to inflame all classes of the people, including young Quakers, who, forgetting their principles of non-resistance, enrolled in large numbers. The aggregate force under arms and training throughout the American continent was, at one time, computed at 200,000.

While the enemy were hoping that ice would shortly enable them to cross the harbour, a copy of the King's Speech with the rejection of their petition arrived. This aroused the most poignant indignation. The document was publicly burnt. They changed their colours from a plain red ground to a white flag with thirteen stripes, symbolic of the number and union of the colonies.

1776.

The winter proved milder and passed over more tranquilly than anticipated. In the beginning of March a battery at Phipps's Farm waged active hostilities against the town. General Gage had gone on leave to England. Washington, with a strong detachment under General Thomas, took possession of the Heights of Dorchester, and so diligently did they work that, in a few hours, a strongly fortified battery appeared. Howe, who had succeeded to the command, ejaculated, " I know not what I shall do ; the rebels have done more in one night than my whole army could have accomplished in months." Before the British had time to recover their surprise, Thomas opened on the town, obliging the ships of war to shift their moorings. Howe had but two possible courses open,—either to dislodge the enemy, or evacuate Boston. He chose the former ; but, on closer inspection, discovered that another and much stronger work had been thrown up, and accordingly deemed his position no longer tenable.

On the 8th of March a flag of truce was sent to Washington from the "Select Men" of Boston, informing him it was Howe's intention to evacuate the city, but that he would leave it intact, provided he were permitted to withdraw unmolested. This communication not being official, Washington returned no reply, but at the same time caused it to be intimated that if properly put, with Howe's signature, he would treat. Howe refused, but without any opposition embarked his men and baggage, together with all woollen and mercantile goods they could carry off, and sailed for Halifax accompanied by 2000 Royalists.

As the men embarked, Washington marched in with drums beating, colours flying, and all the triumph of victory.

For want of room, Howe left behind many pieces of ordnance, horses, and large quantities of provisions. He was severely censured for omitting to destroy the ammunition he could not embark, and for leaving an insufficient harbour guard. In consequence of this negligence, various ships, ignorant of the evacuation, ran into Boston. Amongst others, the 'Hope,' having Colonel Campbell of the 71st, with 700 men and 1500 barrels of gunpowder, besides carbines, bayonets, and artillery stores on board, —all of course captured.

After stormy home parliamentary debates, it was decreed that 13,000 Hessians, Brunswickers, and other German auxiliaries, should be subsidized, and in April set sail from Spithead. Generals Burgoyne and Phillips followed. Letters patent constituted Lord Howe and General Sir William Howe his Majesty's commissioners for restoring peace in the American colonies. Active operations recommenced in June. On the 12th, the forces, under Howe and Admiral Shuldham, sailed from Halifax, landing on Staten Island by the 4th July, where the regiment (Lieut.-Colonel S. Clarke in command) was placed in the 5th brigade, under Brigadier-General Smith.

Lord Howe arrived some days later. His first act was an unsuccessful attempt to obtain interviews with Washington.

In August, more Hessians joined; also Sir Peter Parker and General Clinton with the squadron and troops from North Carolina, and some regiments from Florida and the West Indies.

In the affair of Charleston, the admiral having had a material part of his breeches torn away, besides being otherwise wounded, an American paper thus commented on his disaster :—

> "If honour in the breech is lodg'd,
> As Hudibras hath shown;
> It may from thence be fairly judg'd,
> Sir Peter's honour's gone!"

The generals resolved to attack Long Island. General Putnam was at that time in command of a strong force encamped and intrenched at Brooklyn. On the 27th Howe carried his lines, after a gallantly contested action. The Americans lost 3000; the British, 350 men. In the 43rd one man was killed, Lieutenants Mair and Weir were wounded. This signal defeat palpably cowed the spirit of the Provincials.

On the 15th of September General Clinton and a large force proceeded to Keff's Bay, three miles north of New York, and effected a landing. This unexpected movement caused the Americans to abandon the city, and retire to the north end of the island, leaving their artillery and stores. A British brigade took possession of New York, and the rest encamped in the centre of the island. A few days after, some incendiaries, who had concealed themselves for the purpose, set fire to the city in several places, reducing a third of it to ashes.

Howe then attacked and defeated the American army under Washington, at White Plains, on October 28th; at Fort Washington on November 16th; and New York Island on November 20th; the 43rd Regiment, still in the 5th Brigade, under Clinton, taking part in each action. In this last series of operations, the British loss reached 800 men killed and wounded; but the loss in the 43rd cannot be ascertained. That of the Americans amounted to 3300. The year closed with a succession of triumphs on our side.

1777.

A ray of sunshine gleamed on the American arms with the opening of this year. Washington surprised our post at Trenton on the Delaware, and took 1000 Hessians prisoners. Lord Cornwallis, with a force in which were the flank companies of the 43rd, marched to their succour. Several skirmishes took place. Washington shrank from a battle, kept up his fires and retired during the night. Cornwallis then fell back on Brunswick. His force wintered there and at Amboy. Their privations were rigorous and unremitting, and their ranks thinned by frequent collisions while searching for provisions and forage. By unaccountable lack of tents and field equipage, Cornwallis was unable to take the field before the 23rd of July, but managed to keep possession of the hills commanding the Rariton and the Amboy.

Seventeen battalions were left to protect New York, and the 43rd occupied Rhode Island. Howe landed at Elk ferry, and made for Philadelphia. On the 3rd of September, Washington advanced to the Brandywine

River, with 15,000 men, and on the 11th the two armies encountered. The enemy sustained a crushing defeat, but darkness checked pursuit; an hour or two more of daylight would have utterly annihilated the American army. They acknowledged a loss of 300 killed, 600 wounded, with 400 prisoners, and eleven field-pieces. The victors lay that night on the field of battle, having lost 100 killed and wounded, amongst whom were several officers, but none higher in rank than a captain. The grenadiers of the 43rd came up too late to participate in the engagement, but the light company attached to the second battalion, commanded by Captain Charles Maclean, with Lieutenant Alexander Mair and Ensign Weir, were present.

America had now become so conspicuous and interesting a theatre of action that bold and enterprising spirits from various parts of Europe, either in search of glory and excitement, or in quest of military experience and improvement, constantly dropped in. Amongst these, the Marquis de la Fayette was sufficiently enthusiastic as to purchase and freight a ship with military stores dedicated to the American service. He himself held a command, and was wounded at Brandywine.

After this victory it was necessary to follow up cautiously, as it was expected Washington would exert himself to repair his defeat. The British troops took possession of Philadelphia, which the enemy quitted and encamped at Germantown. It was ascertained that General Wayne, with 1500 men, upon some scheme of enterprise, was lying in the woods. Major-General Grey, with two regiments and a body of light infantry, was detached to surprise them. They arranged measures that the business should be done at the point of the bayonet, without firing. At dead of night the outposts and pickets were forced; the troops, guided by the light of the camp-fires rushed in, and killed or wounded about 300, taking many prisoners.

Batteries were thrown up round Philadelphia, to keep the Americans at a distance. Two of their frigates opened fire on the town, when the 'Delaware,' of thirty-two guns, grounded so effectually that a party of grenadiers brought their battalion field-pieces to bear upon her, and she was boarded and taken.

Contrary to all expectation, Washington, after shunning everything that might lead to general action, on the 3rd of October suddenly quitted his strong post at Skippach Creek, and marched all night to surprise the Royal army in camp outside Philadelphia. The attack began upon the 40th Regiment and the battalions of light infantry, who were at length overpowered by numbers. Colonel Musgrave held on most gallantly until the arrival of General Grey with a great portion of the left wing, supported by Brigadier-General Agnew and his phalanx. For some time the fighting was very warm, but the enemy then fell into total disorder, and were driven off. Towards the close of the engagement, Lord Cornwallis arrived with a squadron of light horse, and joined in the pursuit. Three battalions of grenadiers, those of the 43rd inclusive, ran themselves out of breath in their ardour to succour their fellow-soldiers, but were too late for any share in the action. Our loss amounted to 535, but the proportion of slain scarcely exceeded seventy. In this number were unhappily some brave and distinguished officers, particularly Brigadier-General Agnew and Lieut.-Colonel Bird. Lieut. Weir, 43rd, was wounded. The American loss amounted to nearly 1300. General Nash was killed, and amongst the captives were fifty-four officers.

After this affray the enemy retired to Skippach, and

the Royal army occupied Philadelphia, chiefly with the view of reducing Mud Island and removing obstructions in the River Delaware, in which service the fleet was to co-operate. Batteries were erected on the western bank, and when completed, Colonel Dorrop, with a strong body of Hessians, attacked the redoubt of Mud Island, and also that of Red Bank, containing a force of 800 men. After forcing the outwork with the utmost gallantry, he found them much better armed in the body of the redoubt. They fought with obstinacy, but Colonel Dorrop being wounded and taken prisoner, and the whole party having suffered severely in the approach and assault, were finally compelled to retire. The grenadiers of the 43rd, engaged on the western shore, under Captain Hatfield, had two men killed. The 'Augusta' man-of-war, and 'Merlin' sloop, had drifted up the river to assist, but unfortunately ran aground, and being ignited by the enemy's fireships, lost a considerable part of their crews. This check by no means damped the resolution of the commanders to open up the Delaware. They set to work to construct an overpowering array of batteries. On a second attack, the redoubts were completely destroyed, and the enemy dreading another assault, abandoned them, setting fire to all they could, but still leaving a profusion of munition. Although the British arms were everywhere ascendant, save in the mishap at Red Bank, yet no tangible results were derived from these victories, beyond securing in Philadelphia a good winter lodging for our army.

Washington removed his camp to Valley Forge, a very strong position upon the Schuylkill, about fifteen miles distant.

While the battalion companies of the 43rd occupied Rhode Island, and the grenadiers and light infantry were engaged in the Jerseys; a large and gallant army, under Generals Burgoyne and Carlton, was employed upon the side of Canada and the Lakes. After many hardships and reverses, Burgoyne finally surrendered on the 17th of October.

1778.

The hostile armies passed the remainder of the year 1777 within a few miles of each other, and in perfect inaction. Our troops were well supplied and healthy. Successful predatory expeditions into the Jerseys were the only operations which marked the concluding administration of Sir W. Howe, who in May ceased to command, and was succeeded by Sir Henry Clinton. Meanwhile, Washington and Congress were active in preparations for a new and vigorous campaign. Fresh commissioners accompanied our new Commander-in-Chief, but the hour for peaceful negotiation had long passed. Simeon Deane arrived at York Town from Paris, bringing for ratification by Congress copies of two treaties of close alliance, which had been concluded between France and the United States.

It was now determined to evacuate Philadelphia, no longer a post of military or political importance, and to retire on New York. Under the excellent arrangements of Admiral Lord Howe, though Washington did his utmost to impede their march, the British army passed the Delaware without interruption or danger. Sir H. Clinton, well aware that the hostility of the country would cut off every source of subsistence from his troops, was too sagacious to put the fate of a whole army in hazard, and provided accordingly: so that the British trains of baggage, provisions, and line of loaded carriages and horses, extended for twelve miles. Verging to the right, they pushed on to Sandy Hook, where Clinton sent General Knephausen forward in charge of the baggage, and covered his line of march with a body of troops not easily equalled; and thus free for action, he assumed command in person. They comprised the 3rd, 4th, and 5th brigades, the Hessian grenadiers, a battalion of light infantry, the Guards, and 16th Light Dragoons. Seizing the critical moment, he turned on several corps of the enemy which were endeavouring to surround and outflank him and cut off the baggage column. This attack was made at Freehold. The British Grenadiers and the Guards began the action with such spirit that the enemy soon gave way. Their second line made a more vigorous resistance, but before long were completely routed. Sir Henry Clinton now feeling convinced that his object—the preservation of the convoy—was achieved, returned to his former position. Our loss in slain was very small, but grievously enhanced by that of the brave Colonel Monckton, while fifty-nine soldiers dropped dead from sunstroke; and here again, with the exception of one grenadier returned as killed in the muster-roll, that of the flank companies in this harrowing march cannot be ascertained. On the last day of June the British army reached Neversink, and passed over to New York.

During summer the Americans, in co-operation with a formidable French fleet under Count d'Estaing, determined on an attempt to take Rhode Island. After a demonstration, the French were driven off by a violent storm; but the Americans, under General Sullivan, with a force of 10,000 men, landed at the north end of the island, and moved towards Newport. Sir Henry Clinton, apprehensive for the safety of his troops, sent considerable detachments to reinforce Major-General Pigott in command there, bringing up his garrison—of which the 43rd formed a portion—to 6000 effectives.

State of the Regiment in Rhode Island:—
  Lieut.-Colonel, Marsh.
  Major, D. Ferguson.

Captains.

J. Gunning, *staff.*   Dn. Cameron.
Thos. Innes.   R. M'Kenzie.
H. Knight.   Wm. Miller.

Captain-Lieutenant, Wm. Thorne.

Lieutenants.

J. Losac.   Jas. Rivers.
A. P. Skeyne.   A. Malcolm.
Jas. Dalrymple.   S. Murray.

Ensigns.

J. M. Clark.   C. Vignoles.
O. Dowling.   J. Affleck.
J. Dorrington.   Wm. Wansfold.
Wm. Roach.   Wm. Sherlock, *not joined.*

  Chaplain, C. Taylor.
  Adjutant, Wm. Miller.
  Surgeon, D. Mackintosh.
  Mate, R. Waigh.

	S.	C.	D.	F.	P.
8 companies—effective strength as per roll	24	24	13	0	457
The Grenadiers at Long Island, under command of Captain Hatfield. Dunbar Todd	3	3	2	2	34
The Light Company under Captain M'Lean at Philadelphia. Mair Weir	3	3	1	0	35
Total	30	30	16	2	526

By this muster it appears there were but two fifers on the regular establishment, and that they were both with the Grenadiers.

When, however, the French fleet withdrew, Sullivan, not feeling secure, resolved also to retire. This being discovered, General Prescott was ordered, on the 29th of September, to detach a battalion from the second line towards the left flank of the enemy's encampment, while

Brigadier-General Smith, with the 22nd and 43rd Regiments, and General Losberg with the Hessians and Anspach Chasseurs followed. The enemy was now reported in large force at Quaker's Hill. The 54th and Hessians were directed to advance; but before they could obey, the spirited behaviour of the troops under General Smith had gained possession of the strong post, and obliged the enemy to retire within their works. At dusk an attempt was made to surround and cut off the Chasseurs, extended on the left. Two regiments were ordered to their support, and after a smart engagement the enemy retreated. That night the troops lay on their arms, it being intended to follow up operations next day; but the Americans departed across Howland's Ferry, completely evacuating the island.

In referring to these details, Sir H. Clinton remarked:— "Amidst the general tribute due to the good conduct of every individual leader in command, I must particularly distinguish Lieut.-Colonel Campbell and the 22nd Regiment, and with great applause the spirited exertions of the 43rd, under Colonel March." In Pigott's report he used these words:—"Nor can I conclude this account without expressing my sincere acknowledgments to every officer and soldier under my command, and to the several departments for their unwearied exertions to counteract so many difficulties."

The troops engaged were the 22nd and 43rd Regiments, the Royal Artillery, the flank companies of the 38th and 54th, the 1st and 2nd battalions of the regiment of Anspach, the Hessian Chasseurs and Artillery, the King's American Regiment, and some seamen. The return of loss amounted to 1 captain, 1 volunteer, 4 sergeants, 31 rank and file, 1 driver, killed; 2 captains, 5 lieutenants, 7 ensigns, 13 sergeants, 1 drummer, 180 rank and file, 2 drivers, wounded; 1 lieutenant, 1 sergeant, 10 rank and file, missing. Of the 43rd, 1 sergeant, 2 rank and file, were killed; Ensign Roach, Ensign Affleck, 2 sergeants, 14 rank and file, wounded; 1 rank and file, missing.

1779.

From the autumn of 1778 until that of 1779, all active operations were suspended. It then became evident that a plan was concocting between Washington and d'Estaing for a formidable attack by sea and land on New York; and Colonel Campbell having been detached with a force to besiege Savannah, thus weakening the garrison, it was deemed advisable to withdraw the British troops from Rhode Island, and to allow that post to fall into the hands of the Americans. Accordingly, in the night of the 25th of October, the island was quietly evacuated, and the 43rd were transferred to New York.

1780.

This year was passed by the regiment in garrison in New York, with the exception of the grenadiers and light companies employed in the siege of Charleston and the taking of Washington's dragoons. On the conclusion of the siege, Captain John Hatfield was appointed Governor of the Forts in Sullivan's Island.

1781.

After a series of heavy operations in Virginia, Lord Cornwallis's army had become so weak that Sir H. Clinton thought it necessary to reinforce him with two regiments, the 43rd being one. On the 26th of May they landed at Brandon on the James River, and marched to Meades, where they joined the field force.

CAMPAIGN IN VIRGINIA.

La Fayette, the general then immediately opposed to Cornwallis, abandoned Richmond, crossed the Chickahominy, and marched with celerity towards Bolton Bridge. On the 6th of June Lord Cornwallis's outposts were assailed by skirmishers and riflemen. At 4 P.M. the pickets were allowed to be driven in, his lordship not believing a regular attack would be hazarded. At sunset, however, a body of Continentals, with some field-pieces, began to form in front of the British camp. Cornwallis then ordered his troops under arms, directing an advance in two lines. The onset of the first was conducted with great spirit; our light infantry soon put an end to the business on the right, but the left wing, composed of the 43rd, 76th, and 80th Regiments, under Lieut.-Colonel Dundas, were opposed to the Pennsylvanian regulars, combined with a detachment of La Fayette's Continentals, and two six-pounders. A smart action was kept up for some time, but finally the enemy gave way, abandoning their guns. Darkness prevented the cavalry from following up the victory. The Americans lost 300 in killed and wounded; the English, 5 officers and 70 privates disabled.

Lord Cornwallis, on his rapid marches from Charleston to Camden, through North Carolina to Wilmington, from thence to Richmond, and from Richmond to Williamsburg, made a route of more than 1100 miles as the crow flies.

After the affair at James Town, La Fayette retired to repose, and Cornwallis crossed the river, upon which the Commander-in-Chief wrote expressing surprise that he should have quitted Williamsburg without consulting him, and directed him to repossess it, and establish a defensive post and place of arms, which he supposed could be easily found at Old Point, Hampton Road, or York Town. Old Point being recommended by the admiral, Cornwallis ordered its capabilities to be examined. They were pronounced defective for the purpose required, and the other points named, even more so. Acting under the spirit of his despatches, he saw no option left but to select

York Town and Gloucester, of which he accordingly took possession. By the 22nd of August the British force, numbering 7000 men in excellent condition, began to fortify the posts. Under various pretences, La Fayette sent the Pennsylvanian troops to the south of James River, entering into future dispositions with the French Admiral Le Gros.

Washington and Rochambeau then proceeded to Williamsburg, where La Fayette was encamped, the French fleet lying in the bay. A council of war was held on board the admiral's ship 'Ville de Paris,' the result of which was a plan for the reduction of York Town with all despatch. Rumours were scattered to induce belief that New York was the fancied goal. Their force combined amounted to 16,000 men, and the militia of Virginia were also called out. On the 27th of August, Washington gave out in general orders :—" If the enemy should be tempted to meet the army on its march, the General particularly enjoins the troops to place their principal reliance on the *bayonet*, that they may prove the vanity of the boast which the British make of their peculiar power in deciding battles with that weapon."

Next morning the army marched and halted within two miles of York Town. On the 30th, Cornwallis was closely surrounded by the enemy, but still hoped that Clinton, by the arrival of Admiral Digby, would be able to co-operate and bring round to the 'Chesapeake' a sufficient force in men and ships to turn the scale in his favour.

Siege and Surrender of York Town.

York Town was nothing but a small village on the peninsula between York and James rivers. On an opposite tongue of land stood Gloucester, the other village which Cornwallis occupied and fortified. Colonel Dundas, with 600 or 700 men, was in command of the fort at

Gloucester Point, while Cornwallis with the main body was encamped on the high ground over York Town. An express arrived, stating that a council of war had decided to embark at least 5000 troops, and every exertion be made to relieve them: that the fleet consisted of twenty-three sail of the line; and a postscript added that Admiral Digby, with three more vessels, were at Sandy Hook.

Upon the receipt of this despatch, Cornwallis, under cover of night, withdrew from the outer works and concentrated close around the town, in full belief that he could hold both York and Gloucester until the expected succours should come up. The following day, his abandoned works were occupied by strong detachments of the enemy and the town regularly invested; while 2000 men, under the Duke de Lauzan and Weedon, took up a position in front of Gloucester Point. As De Lauzan approached, Dundas sallied out and made a brilliant charge upon the French, costing them many lives. He then, joined by Tarleton, retreated within his lines, and remained blockaded by the French and Americans, who contented themselves with having thus hemmed him in. On the 6th of October, the enemy constructed their first parallel at 600 yards from the British works.

Cornwallis, writing on the 11th, stated:—"On the evening of the 9th their batteries opened, and have since fired without intermission with about forty pieces of cannon, mostly heavy, and sixteen mortars, from eight to sixteen inches. We have lost about seventy men, and many of our works are considerably damaged. With such works on disadvantageous ground, against so powerful an attack we cannot hope to make a long resistance.—P.S. 5 P.M. Since my letter was written we have lost thirty more men." And on "October 12th, 7 P.M.:—Last night the enemy commenced their second parallel at a distance of 300 yards. We continue to lose men."

To retard the construction of this second parallel, the garrison kept up an incessant fire. Two redoubts erected in front particularly annoyed the assailants; but on the 14th they were carried by storm, one by the French, the other by the Americans, in true spirit of emulation. A sortie was ordered under Lieut.-Colonel Abercrombie, with 250 men. They succeeded in forcing the redoubts, spiked eleven heavy guns, and killed and wounded about 100 French. They regained their lines with but trifling loss, though closely pursued by an overwhelming force. Unluckily, the men who spiked the guns did not, in their hurry, perform the work effectually; the cannon were soon again rendered serviceable, and the second parallel seemed completed, and unassailable by any future sorties.

On the following day Lord Cornwallis could hardly show a mounted gun, and his shells were nearly expended. As a climax to his calamities, sickness had broken out, and a considerable portion of his men, besides the wounded, was in hospital. Reduced to extremity, he attempted by midnight to pass the garrison over to Gloucester Point, but a violent storm prevented this plan from being carried into execution. At break of day the enemy's batteries opened on York Town; and as on the last remnant of our bomb-shells being counted they were found not to number above one hundred, the only alternative was to surrender or consign the brave men who still survived to inevitable destruction should an assault take place. Terms of capitulation were granted, on himself and forces becoming prisoners of war, and General Washington took possession of Gloucester. The American and French army consisted of 22,000 men; 13,000 Americans, and 9000 French. The amount of the British force was under 5000.

Sir Henry Clinton had made arrangements to embark

with about 7000 men. He had hoped the fleet would leave New York on the 5th of October, but unfortunately it did not sail until the 19th, the very day that Cornwallis had capitulated. The vexation experienced on arriving off the Capes of Virginia may be conceived, when the mortifying fact was intimated. Knowing that the French fleet exceeded that of the British, he decided on returning to New York, the relief of York Town and Gloucester having been his only object.

The effective strength of the 43rd, in rank and file fit for duty, under Lord Cornwallis, stood as under:—

June 1st	285
July 1st	280
August 1st	292
September 1st	192
October 1st	185

Present and fit for duty on the day before the surrender (October the 18th), 94 rank and file; sick and wounded, 168; losses in the field, between the 28th of September and the 19th of October, amounted to 1 sergeant, 9 rank and file, killed; 1 sergeant, 1 drummer, 16 rank and file, wounded; 1 captain, 11 rank and file, missing.

Never had greater courage and energy been displayed than in this expedition. Through varied difficulties and trials the brave men, led by Lord Cornwallis, and animated by his example, had conquered all obstacles, so far as human exertion could conquer in a country the nature of which rendered it impossible to subdue the resistance of the inhabitants so long as they remained united. Both French and Americans, the first especially, confessed that no troops could have better deserved a happier fate than that met with by the English. They acted to the last with an intrepidity and discipline which won the admiration of all judges of military merit. The place they defended with so much courage against the combined armies, was, not only in the words of Lord Cornwallis, but in the opinion of the enemy, no more than an intrenched camp, subject in most places to be enfiladed. In Andrews' History of the War appears a paragraph so much to the credit of the Americans that impartiality demands its insertion. "All due care was taken for the good treatment of the British captured by the Americans. They were distributed in the three provinces of Virginia, Maryland, and Pennsylvania, as much by regiments as practicable. Their allowance of provisions was the same as that of the American soldiers. One officer to fifty men resided near them for the purpose of inspecting and providing for their proper treatment. When departing for their respective places of confinement, they were completely clad; and arrangements were also made for their being regularly and abundantly supplied with all reasonable conveniences."

1782.

General Sir Guy Carleton succeeded Sir Henry Clinton in the chief command. No event occurred between the hostile armies in the vicinity of New York. In this year the 43rd received the title of the MONMOUTHSHIRE REGIMENT, and was directed to cultivate a connection with that part of the country to facilitate the procuring of recruits. It was a fancy of His Majesty that all corps should be told off to specific counties, and they have ever since so appeared in the 'Army List.'

Probably contemporaneous with this, transformation in the items of dress took place, the ornaments on the officers' uniforms being altered from gold to silver, which they continued until the whole of the regular army were changed back into gold in 1830, when silver were apportioned to the militia. In the 'Army Lists' from 1769 the lace worn by the rank and file is described in italics, above the "Succession of Colonels." That of the 43rd was then white, with a red and blue stripe. In the edition of 1783 no reference whatever is made; but in the following issue the men's lace is again annoted, and the 43rd commenced to wear "white, with a red and black stripe," which remained in vogue until the introduction of the tunics, when all superfluous embroidery was abolished.

On the 30th of November provisional articles of peace were signed at Paris between England and America; and on the 3rd of September following, the definitive treaty was ratified. The thirteen States were declared independent. English students of history will not find much to gratify their national pride in the details of these ill-starred bickerings. On our side, it must be owned, the war was begun unjustly, carried on unskilfully, and closed humiliatingly. But lessons of reverse, if judiciously applied, are often more profitable than those of success.

1783.

The men of the regiment included in the surrender of York Town returned to England early in this year, and landed at Southampton. Captain Duncan Cameron, for his general services, was on the 19th of February promoted to a brevet majority; and soon after, Captains Maclean and Hatfield received the same, for having commanded the grenadier and light companies in the several combats and heavy skirmishes in the Jerseys, and elsewhere.

In June one company was at Jamaica under Captain-Lieutenant Losack and Lieutenant William Mackerell. Captains J. Bulkeley, J. Innes; with Ensigns Stuart, Abernethy, J. Fenton; 5 sergeants, 4 corporals, 4 drummers, and 10 privates, mustered at Monmouth. Many officers were out recruiting. Major Skene was Brigade-Major in Canada.

1784.

On the 8th of August a muster of eight companies was taken at Hilsea Barracks.

1785.

On the 4th of January the eight companies, still skeletons, were mustered at Deal.

1786.

By midsummer the eight companies had been augmented to ten. The regiment was at Chatham, whence on the 30th of October it moved to Windsor. As it approached the town it was met by King George III., who, struck with the order and regularity presented on march, expressed his desire to inspect it as early as convenient. Lieut.-Colonel Marsh, commanding, proposed the following day, to which His Majesty assented, and, being then even more forcibly impressed with their fine appearance and discipline, declared his unqualified approbation and admiration. The Colonel, in reply, intimated that the high state of regimental efficiency was owing to the exertion and merits of Major Hewitt rather than his own.

This honourable and disinterested assurance naturally brought Major Hewitt's name prominently forward, and upon Colonel Marsh being shortly afterwards appointed Colonel-Commandant (of the newly-raised regiment, 77th), His Majesty himself bestowed the Lieut.-Colonelcy of the 43rd on Hewitt, with many gracious and flattering remarks, and three years later evinced his continued recollection by spontaneously desiring his nomination as Deputy Adjutant-General in Ireland, though other officers of rank and character were applicants.

1787.

The regiment was encamped at Fern Hill, and employed in making roads in Windsor Forest. Towards the end of the year they received orders to embark for the West Indies, and in consequence marched to Portsmouth. Their number was then identical with that of the previous year, save an increase of sixty-four privates. Before sailing, however, counter-orders desired their return to Hilsea Barracks, from whence they were despatched to Ireland.

1788.

On the 15th of January they landed in the Cove of Cork, and on the 20th marched to Dublin. Here they were brigaded with other corps, and encamped in the Phœnix Park for instruction in the new system of military movements, recently introduced by Colonel (afterwards Sir David) Dundas, whose book of tactics, sanctioned by the Horse Guards, became standard authority.

1789-90.

During these years the regiment was quartered and distributed at many country stations throughout Ireland, including Mullingar, Granard, Enniskillen, &c.

1791.

They returned to Dublin.

1792.

Moved to Youghal and Kilkenny.

1793.

The peace of 1783 had given a long rest of ten years; but the French Revolution, now dawning, brought orders for the 43rd to embark on the 17th of November for the West Indies, under command of Lieut.-Colonel Drummond.

Having been augmented on 8th May by 10 sergeants and 70 privates, their strength was 22 officers, 35 sergeants and corporals, 22 drummers and fifers, and 565 rank and file.

1794.

In the latter end of January they reached Barbadoes harbour, and, joining the squadron already assembled there under Sir Charles Grey, proceeded at once for the reduction of Martinique, Guadaloupe, and St. Lucia. The force employed on this service was as follows:—A detachment of white and black dragoons, 3 battalions of grenadiers, 3 battalions of light infantry—the 6th, 9th, 15th, 39th, 43rd, 56th, 58th, 64th, 65th, and 70th regiments. Divided into three brigades, the first was commanded by Lieut.-Colonel Prescott, the second by Major-General Thomas Dundas, and the third by H.R.H. Prince Edward, until whose arrival from Canada it was placed under Lieut.-Colonel Sir Charles Gordon.

On February 3rd all sailed from Carlisle Bay for Martinique, and on the 5th the troops landed under a heavy fire. The French defended the forts, which were numerous and strong. The 3rd brigade under Sir C. Gordon landed on the 8th, to the leeward, on the side of Cas Navire, under cover of a division of the fleet. The enemy being master of the grand road and the heights above, the English commander made a movement towards the mountains, and turning them unperceived with part of his force, gained the most commanding post in that part of the country. By daybreak on the 9th Colonel Myers descended the cliffs and occupied La Chapelle, while Sir C. Gordon advanced to a position affording easy communication with the transports. On the 12th he observed the works at St. Casse and the forts guarding the first ravine to be abandoned, on which he took possession, while Colonel Myers with five companies of grenadiers and the 43rd Regiment crossed four ravines higher up, seizing all the defending batteries. This movement was completely successful, the enemy flying on every side, and our troops soon mastered the five redoubts between Cas Navire and Fort Royal. They then occupied the posts of Gentilly, La Coste, and Crichet, within a league of Fort Bourbon.

In the meantime the admiral sent a fleet to co-operate with the forces under General Dundas in the Bay of St. Pierre, where on the 17th a body of soldiers and sailors made good their landing. On their approach the enemy decamped, leaving their guns primed and loaded and their colours flying, which were hauled down and the British substituted. Dundas then marched in, took possession of Government House, and established quiet and good order. A drummer caught in the act of plundering one of the peaceable inhabitants was instantly hung at the gate of the Jesuits' College, by order of the provost-martial. St. Pierre being captured, the enemy's strength then became concentrated on Forts Louis and Bourbon.

An active siege was commenced, the forts being completely invested by the 20th of March; on the 22nd, terms of surrender were signed, and on the 23rd H.R.H. Prince Edward, who had arrived on the 4th and assumed command of the 3rd brigade, took possession of both gates of Fort Royal. On the 25th the garrison to the number of 900 marched out of Fort Bourbon with honours of war assigned for their gallant defence; they descended the hill with colours flying, and, laying down their arms on the parade of Fort Royal, embarked immediately for France.

Five stand of colours and the two flags of Fort Bourbon were brought to England by Major Grey, and presented with the despatches to the King, who with great pomp and ceremony himself conducted the trophies to St. Paul's

Cathedral, and consigned them to the custody of the Dean and Chapter.

From the time of landing at Martinique until the reduction of Fort Bourbon, a period of forty-seven days, the British officers shared all the hardships of the men, sleeping in their clothes without shelter, exposed to the heavy rains and nocturnal damps which in a tropical climate so severely try the constitution.

Leaving General Prescott with five regiments to garrison Martinique, Sir Charles Grey embarked the grenadiers, the light infantry, the 6th, 9th, and 43rd, with engineers and artillery, for St. Lucia, which, after a mere show of resistance, surrendered on the 4th of April. Two regiments remained, while the rest proceeded on an expedition against Guadaloupe.

This French colony has been the theatre both of British victory and defeat. Captured in 1759, under the administration of the first William Pitt, it was restored on the peace of 1763, and held by France until 1779. During the American struggle it was retaken, but again relinquished in 1783, and continued under the Bourbon and Republican rule till 1794.

Sir Charles Grey, with a portion only of his force landed under a severe cannonade from Fort Fleur d'Epée. Orders were given and strictly obeyed, not to return fire, but to use the bayonet alone, by which they carried all before them. One company only of the 43rd was with this detachment. The remainder of the battalion subsequently landed to occupy fortified posts, and with the capture of Guadaloupe active operations were temporarily suspended. Between Martinique and Guadaloupe the British loss amounted to 71 killed, 193 wounded, and 3 missing.

Captain Fenton and Lieutenant Crofton were killed, and Captain Burnet and Lieutenant Graham, of the 43rd, severely wounded at Fort Bourbon. The former while leading was actually blown up. His clothes being on fire were dragged off by those nearest, leaving his person entirely discoloured by the explosion. In this state he received a musket shot which broke his arm, and, being mistaken for a French Black, was bayoneted in various places by his own grenadiers before he could discover his identity. Notwithstanding the dreadful condition to which he was reduced, Captain Burnet survived to the joyful relief of his horror-stricken assailants.

On the 23rd of April Major James Drummond succeeded to the lieut.-colonelcy, *vice* Hewitt, promoted, and Captain George Dennis became Regimental-Major by purchase.

Major-General Dundas, commanding in Guadaloupe, died of yellow fever, and Lieutenant-Colonel Blundell succeeded as next in seniority. The garrison, originally too weak for the duty, was much reduced by insular distemper, so that early in June a French naval and military expedition of 2000 contrived to make good their landing, and after two repulses carried the post of Fleur d'Epée by storm. Their success was greatly accelerated by the treachery or cowardice of the French Royalists, then in the fort, who, after volunteering to sally on the besiegers, no sooner approached them than they turned and fled. The British merchants and sailors had thrown themselves into the fort to assist the decimated garrison, and this little band, headed by Lieut.-Colonel Drummond, did all that gallant mortals could, but, opposed to so many French regulars, at length were obliged to retreat.

So soon as this intelligence reached Sir Charles Grey, at Martinique, he started with such forces as he could collect, but his means were inadequate to the emergency. Victor Hughes, the French commissioner, a man of talent and activity, but of cruel and remorseless temperament, liberated the negro slaves, armed and urged them, as well as the mulattoes, to strike for the chance of permanent freedom, stimulating them with promises of unlimited plunder and division of the spoils. Skirmishes took place, but nothing decisive occurred until the 2nd of July, when three battalions of British, with a battalion of seamen, were despatched under command of Brigadier-General Symes, to attempt the surprise of Point à Pitre. The guides betrayed the troops, leading them to the strongest part of the French position, where it was impossible to scale the ramparts, and whence they were assailed with a heavy fire of round and grape shot, exposed also to a flanking discharge of musketry from houses in the town. Neither courage nor discipline could avail under such posers, and retreat was imperative. The Brigadier received a severe wound, and Colonel Gomm, and Captain Robertson, R.N., were amongst the killed.

Sir Charles Grey then abandoned his attempt to expel the French from Guadaloupe, and sailed for Martinique, leaving Major-General Graham with headquarters at Berville. The noxious effects of the climate and fens told rapidly and fearfully; sick or convalescent composed the majority in camp, and several companies were unable to produce a single effective file. The 43rd could not afford a corporal and three privates for patrol. On September 1st their strength was, rank and file fit for duty, 23; sick, 176.

On the 26th of September the enemy, with a large body of troops, landed on the southern part of Guadaloupe. One portion marched on Petit Bourg, where Lieut.-Colonel Drummond, with some convalescents and a party of Royalists, met them; but perceiving their great superiority of numbers, found it necessary to retreat and take post at a battery called Point Bacchus. The French, on entering Petit Bourg, committed outrageous cruelties, putting to death all the sick in the hospitals, including many women and children, and otherwise mutilated the bodies.

Their next move was to Point Bacchus, where Lieut.-Colonel Drummond and his detachment, being surrounded, were compelled to surrender. As some of the prisoners, enfeebled by exhaustion and illness, fainted on the march, they were instantly bayoneted; and many civilians of all ages and conditions, regardless of sex, were condemned to the guillotine.

Brigadier-General Graham, at Berville, cut off from communication with the shipping, and hopeless of relief, was also constrained, after a gallant resistance, to submit to the inexorable vicissitude of war, and capitulate. He and his officers were cruelly and ignominiously treated. After these disasters, the only British hold on Guadaloupe was Fort Matilde, which was soon invested by the French, but held out until reduced to a mass of ruins. A reinforcement of 3000 having joined the enemy, it became worse than useless to prolong the unequal contest. The fort was during night silently evacuated, and the operation so conducted that most of the garrison had embarked before the alarm was given. The total loss amounted to sixteen killed and seventy-five wounded.

During this year of mortality the following officers of the 43rd died of fever, or other incidental disorders, in the West Indies:—Captains Vignoles, Bayard, Affleck, Spencer, M'Dowal; Lieutenants Butler, Graham, Dennison; Ensigns Daniel, Kirwan; Quarter-masters Burnett, Bruce, and Surgeon Hodkinson. There were surviving at Point à Pitre, and prisoners to Victor Hughes, on the 31st of December, Lieut.-Colonel Drummond; Captains Thompson, Cameron, Thorley; Lieutenants Hull, Cameron, Tidy, De Yonge; Ensigns Desborough, Delisle, and Surgeon Samson.

1795.

Very early in the year these officers, with others of the 35th Regiment, resolved to attempt escape from the hulk in which they were imprisoned. Seizing the felicitous moment when a boat was alongside, they overpowered the guard, leaped in, and rowed off. Luckily there was no vessel to pursue, and once beyond the reach of the guns they were safe.

Before long the British prisoners were exchanged on cartel. The officers, non-commissioned officers, and a few privates of the 43rd forming the *skeleton* of their once numerous battalion, returned to England and joined the section which had remained at home to recruit, under Major Dennis, while the greater portion of the men were drafted into other regiments remaining in the West India Islands.

In August the 43rd were stationed at Monmouth, about 300 strong. Moving to Exeter, they received a draft of 500 men from the Londonderry Fencibles. This addition was brought about by Captain (afterwards Major-General) Armstrong, who had taken great interest in the formation of that corps, and through whose suggestions His Majesty was induced to accept their services. From Exeter the 43rd proceeded to Maker Heights, Plymouth, embarked in smacks at Cawsand Bay, and proceeded to Portsmouth, disembarked at Gosport, and marched to Fareham, where the whole corps, except officers and a few sick men, were, by an order from the Commander-in-Chief, drafted into the 31st Regiment. Here a new set of colours was presented, and in the end of November the skeleton of the corps was sent back to Exeter to receive a draft from the 102nd Regiment, or Colonel French's levy as it was called.

1796.

During this year the regiment, under command of Lieut.-Colonel Dennis, was stationed at Hilsea, the Isle of Wight, Southampton, and Lymington, and received three additional drafts from the Irish levies.

1797.

In this year the office of chaplains of regiments was abolished. In February a draft of 600 was received by the 43rd from the 16th Regiment. These men had been raised for foreign service by parishes in and about London. On the 15th of March, the 43rd, upwards of 1000 strong, under command of Colonel Drummond, again sailed for the West Indies, disembarking and occupying Fort George in Martinique on April 23rd. In September they were relieved by the 14th Regiment from Barbadoes, and removed to Fort Edward, where they remained until the end of the year.

1798.

On New Year's Day they were sent round to St. Pierre. At this period regimental paymasters, at the daily pay of fifteen shillings, were established. The muster-roll of the 43rd at St. Pierre showed—1 lieut.-colonel, 2 captains, 10 lieutenants, 2 ensigns, 1 adjutant, 1 surgeon, 1 assistant-surgeon, 27 sergeants, 20 corporals, 14 drummers, and 181 privates.

1799.

The regiment remained at St. Pierre, and suffered terribly from the pestiferous atmosphere.

1800.

On February the 6th, removal to the town of Fort George, headquarters of the West Indies, took place.

At this date the entire strength of the regiment had dwindled below 300. Shortly after arriving at Fort George, an order was issued that the men might volunteer for the different corps in the West Indies preparatory to being sent home, and on the 25th of April 37 sergeants, 12 drummers, and 99 rank and file, with the following officers—

Captains.

J. Cameron (*in command*).　|　Ed. Hull.

Lieutenants.

Adrien de Yonge.
Rd. Elers.
Geo. Delisle.
J. Carroll.
C. Bygrave.

G. Grieve Gulliman.
Andrew Du Moulin.
R. Kippling (*Adjutant*).
Ewen Cameron.
Joseph Wells.

Ensign, James O'Donnel.
Surgeon, Rob. Salmon.
Assistant-Surgeon, Sullivan.
Quarter-Master, Thos. Loftus.

embarked from Port Royal on board H.M. ship 'Prince of Wales,' landing at Portsmouth late in June. They moved to Stroud, and in October to Tilbury.

This year His Majesty directed "that in future the use of hats is to be entirely abolished throughout the whole of the infantry of the army; and that instead thereof caps are to be worn, of which a sealed pattern has by order of His Royal Highness the Commander-in-Chief, been deposited in the office of the Comptroller of Army Accounts, there to be had recourse to as occasion may require.

"His Majesty is pleased to permit the colonels to engrave the number of their respective regiments on each side of the lion on the lower part of the brass fronting; and likewise to the regiments which are entitled to that distinction, His Majesty grants permission to bear their badges in the centre of the Garter. The Grenadiers, who are allowed to wear these caps occasionally, when they do not use their proper grenadier caps, may, if their colonels choose it, bear the grenade in the same manner as regiments entitled to them wear their badges. It is His Majesty's pleasure that the tufts used by the Grenadiers shall be white; those of the Light Infantry (who are likewise included in this order) dark green.

"All soldiers shall wear the button of their respective regiments in the centre of the cockade, except the Grenadiers, who will use the grenade.

"The caps are to be made of a sufficient size to come completely on the soldiers' heads; they are to be worn straight and even, and brought forward well over the eyes.

"The Field and Staff Officers, as also the Officers of battalion companies, are to continue to wear hats as usual. The Grenadier Officers are permitted to wear hats when their men do not parade in dress caps. The officers of the light companies are to wear caps similar to those ordered for the light infantry."

1801.

On New Year's Day a route was received for Portsmouth. On arriving there they were forwarded to the Isle of Wight, and after a few days' sojourn embarked for Guernsey, where the regiment remained three years, during which recruits came in from the English and Scotch Fencibles and the Irish Militia.

1802.

The Peace of Amiens being definitely ratified on the 27th of March, several corps were disbanded; amongst them the Tarbet and Loyal Irish Fencibles, from whence, being reduced in Jersey and Guernsey, men volunteered *en masse* into the 43rd.

1803.

On the 17th of July a decree notified that the 43rd should be forthwith formed into a corps of LIGHT INFANTRY. The regiment was then commanded by Colonel Richard Stewart, A.D.C. to H.M. George III.

1804.

On the 12th of January the regiment quitted Guernsey, landed at Dover, and marched to Ashford. In June they passed on to Shorncliffe, and were brigaded with the 52nd and 95th. Here that martial spirit and future historian William Napier joined, being on the 11th of August gazetted captain in the 43rd.

On their return, many men from the Militia and Corps of Reserve volunteered, and on the 25th of November the SECOND BATTALION was organised at Bromsgrove, consisting then of two companies only, under Captains Cameron and Gardiner; but its formal establishment was to consist of 1 lieut.-colonel, 2 majors, 10 captains, 12 lieutenants, 8 ensigns, 5 staff, 22 sergeants, 20 corporals, 22 buglers, and 380 privates. All standing orders and regulations of the first battalion were to be strictly observed, and Major William Sorel was appointed to the command.

1805.

On the 15th of February the second battalion received seventy-five men from the 9th Reserve, and twenty-eight recruits from other parties. It then consisted of four companies under Captains Cameron, Gardiner, Haverfield, and Dalzell. On the 9th of June the first draft, consisting of seventy-nine men, was given to the first battalion. A regimental school, under the auspices of Captain Gardiner, was established, of which Sergeant Crawley was appointed master. On the 28th of July the battalion was formed into eight companies, the four additional being under Captains O'Donnel, Scaafe, Gifford, and M'Lachlan. On the 26th of August H.R.H. the Commander-in-Chief reviewed the first battalions of the 43rd and 52nd at Shorncliffe. The effective strength of the 43rd was— 1 lieut.-colonel, 2 majors, 10 captains, 22 lieutenants, 8 ensigns, 6 staff, 54 sergeants, 20 buglers, and 970 rank and file. The majors were John Cameron and Edward Hull; adjutant, Abraham Shaw, formerly sergeant-major of the 52nd, to which regiment he returned as adjutant in 1806. On the 22nd of October the second battalion, 236 strong, marched to Dover, returning to Hythe on the 28th.

The regiment remained encamped on the Kentish coast, forming part of a force under Sir John Moore, watching the movements of the French troops at Boulogne destined for the invasion of Britain, and terming themselves "The Army of England." In fine clear weather the enemy's lines were visible, and contests between their gun-boats and ours repeatedly witnessed. During winter they were in barracks either at Saltwood or Shorncliffe, and on one occasion Brabourne Lees was occupied by the first battalion. At this time, in conjunction with the 52nd and Rifles, they were instructed in a system of drill and manœuvring which in after days caused them to be held up as models to the army. By degrees the whole of the British infantry was initiated into this method.

1806.

By the 1st of November the second battalion of the 43rd reached 500 rank and file. On the 1st of December thirty-two men were transferred to the first battalion, while seventy-two of the Reserve were sent to the first garrison battalion. Sergeant-Major Murphy received a commission, and was appointed adjutant to the 54th.

1807.

In January Major Cameron was promoted to a lieutenant-colonelcy in the 7th West India Regiment, but subsequently removed to the 9th British Infantry, which he commanded in many battle-fields with great distinction, and became K.C.B. He had served in the West Indies at the siege of Fort Bourbon, the capture of Martinique, St. Lucia, and Guadaloupe, and commanded the 43rd in the action of the 30th of September, 1794, and at the different attacks made by the enemy until the 4th of October, when he was severely wounded and taken prisoner. He was succeeded by Major (afterwards Adjutant-General) Sir John Macdonald. The battalion was told off for foreign service to Copenhagen.

EXPEDITION TO COPENHAGEN.

At the commencement of the present century this country stood almost alone against the influence of Continental despotism. The Emperor Napoleon, then in the zenith of power and ambition, seemed determined to ruin the commercial prosperity of England. A confederacy of the Northern powers of Europe was formed to exclude British vessels from navigation in Germanic waters. Denmark, still smarting under the attack by Lord Nelson in 1802, entered a strong adhesion. She had reconstructed a large fleet, fully equipped, and ready for action. The British Government determined to attempt the capture of Copenhagen and her navy.

Preparations on a grand scale for the execution of the design were carried out in the hope of rendering resistance and bloodshed improbable. The first battalion of the 43rd, under Colonel Stewart and mustering 1050 bayonets, was ordered to join the expedition. The armament consisted of forty-two ships of war, twenty-two of which were of the line, several frigates, and a forest of transports.

The land forces, commanded by Lord Cathcart, amounted to 20,000 effective men, while the naval operations were directed by Admiral Gambier. On the 1st of August they left the Downs, on the 16th the Danish coast was sighted, and the debarkation commenced under cover of gun-brigs. The 43rd landed at Wisbech, a small place in the island of Zealand, some eight miles north of Copenhagen, and in conjunction with the second battalion of the 52nd and the 92nd Highlanders, formed a brigade of reserve under the command of Major-General Sir Arthur Wellesley.

Lord Cathcart issued a proclamation announcing the object of the expedition, lamenting the cause and expressing a hope that the Danish fleet would be peaceably surrendered in trust to England, to be restored on conclusion of the war. He added that in case of refusal force would be used, and the inevitable loss of life chargeable on those who advised resistance to a measure dictated by imperious necessity. To this specimen of military logic the Danes gave no reply; they determined on resolute resistance. Hostilities immediately commenced. After a fierce struggle, and sustaining considerable damage, the English ships overpowered the batteries and flotilla defending the sea approaches to Copenhagen, and the main body of the army advanced to within four hundred yards of the ramparts, forcing one of the enemy's strongest redoubts then turned against them.

A detachment of four regiments, with a squadron of Hussars under Sir A. Wellesley, was ordered to march against a body of Danish troops assembled to surprise us. The attack was led by the 92nd Highlanders, well supported by the 43rd and second battalion of the 52nd. The Danes, much superior in number, were advantageously posted in front of the village of Kioge. On our side the onset began with the usual spirit. An impression being made on the enemy's line, the 92nd were ordered to charge. The movement was decisive, the shock irresistible. The Danes, throwing down their arms and accoutrements, fled in all directions, leaving many lifeless on the field, while many more were taken prisoners.

On the 31st of August the English batteries were ready to open fire. Lord Cathcart once more proposed terms, which the Governor, General Pieman, refused. Bombardment was then resorted to, and vigorously carried on until the 7th of September. By that time the city was much injured, many public and private buildings burnt and destroyed, and it became evident that if continued Copenhagen would speedily be reduced to ashes. Negotiations for surrender were proposed and entered on. On the A.M. of the 8th, articles of capitulation were drawn up, to be ratified at mid-day. By these the British were placed in possession of the citadel and dockyards, with all the flotilla and naval stores; a mutual exchange of prisoners to take place; all persons and private property to be respected; and within six weeks the citadel was to be restored to the King of Denmark, and the whole island of Zealand to be evacuated by the British army. These stipulations were carried out to the letter.

We were thus placed in possession of sixty-three ships of war, including sail of the line, frigates, brigs, and gunboats, all nearly ready for sea. A vast collection of implements of all kinds necessary to equip or build a fleet was found in the arsenals. Ninety-two transports were loaded to convey the plunder to England. The ordnance carried off was stated at 2465 pieces, including long guns, carronades, and mortars. The prize money due to the troops alone amounted to nearly one million sterling. The total loss sustained by our army amounted only to 50 killed, 79 wounded, and 25 missing. That of the Danes probably reached 1000, including, unhappily, some women, children, and old men; the Governor having declined to avail himself of the opportunity offered to send them out of the city. Napoleon expressed astonishment that the English did not appropriate the hardy Danish sailors along with their armada!

Dissenting opinions may prevail as to the moral justification of this enterprise, but none can deny that it proved a grand political stroke, attended by complete success.

On the 20th of October the 43rd re-embarked under command of Major Edward Hull, Colonel Stewart having been removed to the staff as brigadier-general. Upon the signal for sailing being given, the whole fleet stood out to sea, and the interminable line of shipping presented a magnificent spectacle. During the night previous to landing in England a violent squall arose, and at one time placed the 'Syren,' with seven companies and nearly as many hundred men of the regiment, in the greatest jeopardy. After ominous straining of her timbers, she struck on a sandbank, and it was feared all would perish. While dire confusion and alarm prevailed, Ensign Neale, with the utmost *sang froid*, produced his flute, striking up "The Dead March in Saul." His proclivities must eventually have undergone transformation, as in later life, after having fought with distinction at Vimiera, he sold out and entered the Church.

On arrival, the battalion proceeded to Yarmouth, and Lieut.-Colonel Giffard was appointed to the command of the second battalion.

1808.

At this juncture, Europe beheld with amazement the occupation by Napoleon of the greater part of Spain, and the subsequent coronation of his brother Joseph as king. Through the treachery of her prime minister, Spain was betrayed, and her king a captive in France. The royal family of Portugal had fled, taking refuge in Brazil, and, natural indignation surging in each country, both rose to arms. The British Government, resolved to aid the Spanish and Portuguese patriots, ordered troops to the Peninsula. Sir Arthur Wellesley was named commander.

Before sailing, intense satisfaction was diffused among the men by permission being received from the Horse Guards authorising the abolition of "hair-tying," a most irksome and absurd custom long prevalent.

They formed the advanced guard of that noble army, destined to cast dark shadows over Europe in a prolonged career of strife, bloodshed, honour, and glory. Portugal was their first field of action. Being joined at Mondego Bay by General Spencer from Cadiz with 4000 men, Sir Arthur advanced with a force of 13,000 infantry and between 400 and 500 cavalry, and on the 17th of August the first action between the French (under Laborde) and the English, near the village of Roriça, took place. During the night Laborde retreated upon Torres Vedras, leaving the road open for the victors. Wellesley followed him, keeping near the sea, and towards evening received intelligence that Anstruther's and Ackland's brigades, with a large fleet of store ships, were off the coast. He therefore sought an advanced post, and Vimiero being selected as eligible, he sent from thence a detachment to cover the landing.

The second battalion of the 43rd, though the younger in arms, was destined to be foremost on the field, and to take part in the first of the long series of brilliant actions which eventually led to the word 'PENINSULA' being emblazoned on their colours.

They landed in white duck trowsers and light marching order—and so fought at Vimiero—and proceeding found the army under Sir A. Wellesley in position; the 43rd and 52nd being placed in Anstruther's brigade, in front of the village, on a rugged height.

Early on the morning of the 21st clouds of dust became observable, and in another hour parties of the enemy's cavalry began to appear upon the hills, extending as they advanced, and covering dense columns of infantry, which, following the road, threatened our left. Junot's intention had been to surprise Sir A. Wellesley's army at daylight; but the ground proved so difficult that it was nine o'clock before he obtained a view of the British position. He immediately organized two simultaneous attacks; one directed against the left, the other against Fane's and Anstruther's brigades in the centre. Junot had a force close upon 14,000 infantry, with a regiment of cavalry, and 23 pieces of very small artillery. At 10 o'clock commenced the

Battle of Vimiero.

The advanced columns of the enemy were composed of Swiss regiments and French corps d'élite. From their embodiment victory had invariably attended them, so that, when Junot gave the word of command, adding—"Soldiers, you have only to march and meet these cowardly islanders and drive them into the sea," full of impetuosity and determined to carry everything before them, they rushed at our advanced pickets, charged the 50th, 71st, 9th, and other parts of our army posted on an eminence in the centre of the line. Astonished at not being fired upon, they halted for a moment, and were in the act of proceeding with their attack when the gallant "Half-hundred" first, and the other corps as they could find room, met them with loud shouts and a most resolute charge of the bayonet, driving and scattering them back in all directions.

Junot's next aim was to turn the British right flank, but with no better success.

Kellermann then rallied the fugitives behind his grenadiers, making a last effort to retrieve the day. A strong column was again sent forward to gain possession of the village of Vimiero. Anstruther being engaged in disposing of the enemy on the right, did not order the 43rd to the assistance of the 50th—whose left flank the French in some force had surrounded—until firing on both sides had commenced. When they took up position the assailants were literally within five yards under an embankment, and immediately directed a steady and destructive fire upon them. A desperate conflict then took place in some vineyards, the enemy pitching into the young battalion like mad, and many broken heads resulted on either side.

"Then, when the narrowness of the way and the sweep of the round shot was crushing and confounding the French ranks, the 43rd, rallying in one mass, went furiously down upon the very head of the column, and with a short but fierce struggle drove it back in confusion. In this fight the regiment suffered severely, and so close was the combat that Patrick Sergeant-Armourer of the 43rd, and a French soldier were found dead, still grasping their muskets with the bayonets driven through each body from breast to back."

The French immediately fell back along the whole front, while Kellermann threw the reserve into a pine wood to cover the retreat, leaving many of their guns behind. In this action 6 officers and 113 men of the 43rd were placed *hors de combat*; about one-sixth of the loss sustained by the whole British forces. The following is the list as per despatch :—Major Hearn ; Captains Ferguson,

Haverfield, and Brock; Lieutenant W. Madden and Ensign Wilson, wounded; 1 sergeant, 1 bugler, 38 rank and file, killed; 5 sergeants, 68 rank and file, wounded, 48 of whom died.

The other incidents of Vimiero may be briefly summed up. The division of Brennier made a fierce attack towards our left, which was as fiercely overthrown and the French General taken prisoner. Ferguson's brigade completely isolated Solignac's corps on the French right, and pressed them so closely that they would in all probability have surrendered, had not Ferguson been suddenly commanded to halt. This order proceeded, not from the victorious Wellesley, but from his senior and successor, Sir H. Burrard, who was on the field earlier as a spectator, and assumed the direction of affairs at this important moment. Solignac thus gained time to extricate his troops, and the whole French army retreated, leaving on the field thirteen guns, several hundred prisoners, and considerably above 2000 men killed and wounded. The following day their main body made a precipitate and most remarkable march into Lisbon, a distance of fifty miles, with only a halt at noon of a couple of hours—a circumstance, if the state of the roads and country be taken into account, hardly credible.

After the battle, the 43rd having reformed, a strong party was sent on fatigue duty to bury the dead and collect the arms and appointments of the slain and disabled. They were so employed for the remainder of the day, bivouacking on the night of the 21st, a little to the right and rear of their original position. Sir Hugh Dalrymple arrived on the 22nd, and superseded Sir H. Burrard in his short command—three generals-in-chief in twenty-four hours. The fact carries its own commentary. At Cintra a convention was ratified on the 30th of August, by which the French agreed to evacuate Portugal.

In the 'Wellington Despatches' we find the following, dated Torres Vedras, 29th of August, 1808:—

"SIR,—I have the honour to enclose herewith a letter from Brigadier-General Anstruther, covering a representation from Major Hull of the 43rd Regiment, respecting the inadequacy of the present establishment of subalterns and non-commissioned officers to carry on the duties of the 2nd battalion of that corps, in the field; and also a statement of the services of Major Hull, whom I am induced to recommend for the lieut.-colonelcy, for the reasons stated in Brigadier-General Anstruther's letter, should His Majesty be pleased to appoint an additional lieut.-colonel to the 43rd Regiment.

"I have the honour to be, &c. &c.,

"A. WELLESLEY."

On the 8th of September the 43rd moved from Porto Salvo to Quelus, where the battalion was encamped until the 12th of October. The men were paid up and necessaries supplied from Lisbon. For nearly six weeks the officers luxuriated in the beautiful villas or Quintas, with their richly laden gardens and vineyards. After the departure of the French they paid occasional visits to Lisbon, and partook of its amusements. Dysentery was very prevalent amongst the men, owing probably to the indiscriminate use of light wines, abundance of fruit, and exposure to the heavy night-dews. A return being called for, it was found necessary to leave behind 8 sergeants, 13 corporals, 2 buglers, and 190 privates. Lieutenant Brown (late General Sir George Brown, commander of the forces in Ireland) remained in charge.

Nearly two months after the convention of Cintra, the British army marched, under command of Sir John Moore, to the assistance of the Spanish patriots. The 43rd, with the 9th and 52nd, under Major-General Beresford, reached Coimbra on the 26th of October, and put up in a superb convent. On the 6th of November they joined Sir John Moore's force at Visac, and proceeded to Salamanca by way of Almeida. During the march they encountered heavy rains, and suffered much fatigue. Throughout Portugal the troops had been hailed with enthusiasm, the inhabitants vying with each other in hospitable attentions, so that on entering Spain they were proportionally disappointed to find themselves regarded rather as enemies than friends. Roads, however, were better, villages neater, and more general comforts to be met with.

Disaster upon disaster overtook the Spaniards. The French at last gained possession of Madrid, and obliged Sir John Moore to move to Ledesma, which place was reached by the battalion 5th December, where it remained about a week. Here Private John Clarke, of Captain Hull's company, while on sentry at the gate, was shot at by a Spaniard and severely wounded in the shoulder. The culprit was sentenced to be *garotted*, and underwent execution accordingly.

A division of British infantry, with artillery and cavalry, had marched from Lisbon by the circuitous route of Talavera, consequently our full force was not assembled before the 11th of December. During this time the enemy made no attempt to harass. They remained tranquil at Salamanca.

On the 12th the battalion marched to Zamora, and to Toro next day, where they were put up in Spanish barracks; on the 21st moved on Malgarde Seba, headquarters being established at Sahagun by the 23rd December.

From the period of leaving Toro the men suffered many privations, and were kept constantly on the alert, always with their arms in their hands. Heavy snow fell; but the men of the 43rd were strong and in excellent order. Want of fuel was much felt, the troops being obliged to cook with chopped straw.

Reverting to the first battalion of the 43rd, on arrival from Copenhagen they moved to Colchester and Malden, numbering 1080 bayonets, under Lieut.-Colonel Gifford; from whence they embarked at Harwich, then sailed for Falmouth, and joined the fleet with the force assembled under Sir David Baird, amounting to upwards of 10,000 men. Upon reaching Corunna they were brigaded with the first battalion of the 95th Rifles, under Brigadier-General Craufurd, and marched towards Salamanca, and on the 20th December effected a junction with Moore at Mayorga. The collected force, amounting to about 24,000 men, moved forward to Sahagun and its vicinity; the first battalion of the 43rd then enumerating 817, the second 411.

On the 21st Lord Paget, with the 10th and 15th Hussars, made a dashing charge upon a very superior body of the enemy's cavalry at Sahagun, killing and taking prisoners fifteen officers and 200 privates.

Moore intended to attack Soult, then posted at Saldanha at the head of 18,000 men, but had hardly arranged his plan when he received information that Napoleon was advancing from Madrid with overwhelming numbers. Immediate retreat was the only alternative.

The first battalion of the 43rd formed part of the rearguard under Brigadier Robert Craufurd. The French armies, numbering in the aggregate 60,000 men, were endeavouring to hem in and crush Moore; and so closely was he pushed that the French advanced guard entered Tordesillas on the very day he left Sahagun. At Benevente another cavalry skirmish took place, again terminating to the great credit of Lord Paget and his light dragoons.

Sir John Moore, instead of being aided, was much impeded by the Spaniards. Although he had given Romaná strict injunctions to leave the road to Astorga open, he found it completely occupied by Spanish troops, and only by dint of extraordinary exertions was he enabled to get his own away before the French entered. Napoleon, now finding that he could not come up with Moore before he reached Benevente, made over the command to the three Marshals of France with their three divisions. The light brigade, with two guns, reached Castrogonzalo, on the Esla, and took up a position to protect the passage of the river, as the British cavalry had not yet arrived. Soult was pushing rapidly forward; some chasseurs of the Imperial Guard, hovering about, at last rode up to the bridge and captured some women and baggage. The enemy was evidently bent on a surprise.

Accordingly, John Walton and Richard Jackson, privates of Captain Napier's company, were posted in a hollow beyond the bridge, and at a distance from the picket, with orders to give immediate alarm. "It was directed that one should stand firm while the other fired, and ran back to notify whether there were few or many. Jackson fired but was overtaken, receiving ten or twelve sabre cuts in an instant. Nevertheless he went staggering on and gave the signal; while Walton, with equal resolution, stood his ground, and wounded several of the assailants with his bayonet, who retired, leaving him unhurt, but with his cap, knapsack, and belts cut in about twenty places. His bayonet was bent double, and his musket, covered with blood, was notched like a saw from muzzle to lock. Personal courage could hardly be more brilliantly exemplified. Jackson escaped death during the retreat, and finally recovered of his wounds."

The cavalry and stragglers having passed, the destruction of the bridge at Castrogonzalo was commenced, half the brigade being employed while the other protected them. At ten o'clock at night a party of the enemy attempted to pass the pickets. A short skirmish ensued, and they were repulsed. For two days and nights, Captain Napier's and Lloyd's companies were without relief on this service until accomplished, when the brigade marched to Benevente, where the cavalry and reserve still remained.

They found the convent which had previously sheltered them now occupied by several thousand infantry, and the lower galleries so densely packed with horses of the cavalry and artillery, that it was hardly possible for one man to enter. On two of the officers returning and opening the only door, a large window-shutter appeared on fire. The flames were spreading towards the rafters. A few moments more, and the straw under the horses must ignite, and 6000 souls and animals perish. Captain Lloyd, of the 43rd, a man of prodigious activity, strength, and presence of mind, signalled to his companions to maintain silence, and, springing on the nearest horse, he ran along the backs of the others, reached the blazing shutter, tore it from its hinges, and threw it out of the window. Returning in like manner, he quickly awakened a few of the men, clearing a passage without any alarm, which would have been almost as disastrous as the flames.

From Benevente the British retired to Borillas, where Craufurd's brigade separated from the main body, and, marching by cross roads towards Orenze and Vigo, embarked for England.

The sick of the first battalion had been left behind, under charge of Lieutenant Pollock, to follow by Calcabellos and Bitanzos to Corunna. The men were placed in bullock-carts, which travelled so slowly that much apprehension existed lest they should be taken prisoners. On approaching Calcabellos, skirmishing was distinctly heard. The carts stuck in deep mud at the foot of a hill near the town. It was impossible for the animals to move them while occupied. Pollock, therefore, ordered the men to get out and walk up. All complied save two, who declared their total inability to stir. Expostulation failing to convince them that such refusal might cause the capture of the whole party, they replied, they "did not care, for walk they could not a single step." Determined to fulfil his duty, and—if possible—deliver all safely at Corunna, Pollock desired the nearest to get on his back, carried him up the hill, and, returning, brought up the other in like fashion, although having himself one arm in a sling; still suffering from the effects of a broken arm.

He then proceeded to an adjacent village, to try if any better sort of conveyances were attainable. Kicking open an out-house, he found seven fine mules ready saddled. Of these he took possession, placing two men upon each, the rest following in the carts while he himself walked. Soon after, they came upon a place containing extensive wine-vaults. The temptation was irresistible, and when he came up he found all hands filling their canteens. Even the two men he had carried up the hill had suddenly found the use of their legs, and were as active as the rest. Naturally indignant, he instantly threw the contents away. Upon reaching Corunna and delivering up the men, it was discovered that the mules belonged to the commissariat, and had been stolen by some of the Spaniards. Upon Lieutenant Pollock reporting himself to Colonel Hull, that officer advised him at once to join the second battalion, which accounts for his obtaining the clasp for Corunna, although legitimately belonging to the first battalion.

The second battalion, in General Beresford's brigade, attached to General Hope's division, had endured many privations after leaving Toro. It was kept constantly on the alert, with arms in hand, ready to act at a moment's notice. Kits had failed, and the wretched shoes served out at Salamanca were all but useless. The battalion was formed into a flank patrol, covering Frazer's and Hope's divisions as the army marched by Benevente, Astorga, and Bembibre. Many men during the last leagues fell out from fatigue.

1809.

On the 3rd of January Villa Franca was reached, and a ration of bread, the first for many days, obtained. Part of the rearguard was attacked by the French cavalry, when General Colbert and some dragoons were killed by our riflemen, and the following day, finding themselves pressed by the enemy, were forced to abandon military chests containing upwards of 25,000*l*. They were flung over deep ravines in hopes of preventing misappropriation. At Lugo Sir John Moore drew up his army, numbering nearly 19,000 men under arms, and offered battle a league in front of the town, but Soult declined. After remaining a whole day in position, and finding that his wily opponent would not fight, he judged it no longer safe to show an offensive front, so quitted his ground at night, leaving camp-fires burning. He thus deceived the enemy, gained a good start, and reached Corunna on the 11th.

The following letter, addressed by Lieut.-Colonel Hull, to the "Committee of Management of the Patriotic Fund," reflects honour on a meritorious sergeant of the Regiment:—

"GENTLEMEN,—I beg to state for your information an instance of gallantry and conduct in a sergeant of 2nd battalion of the 43rd Regiment of Foot, which I believe has seldom been exceeded by one in that rank. On the retreat of the British army through

Spain, Sergeant William Newman was left at a village about four miles from Betanzos, to collect and bring in some stragglers and sick of the regiment, at which time there were about four or five hundred of that description belonging to different corps in that place. Some time after the troops had marched, an alarm was given that a party of French cavalry was approaching, and the men were all endeavouring, in the greatest confusion, to make off as fast as their weak state would admit, when Sergeant Newman pushed on a little way to a narrow part of the road, where he continued to stop nearly one hundred of those not able to march, and sent on the rest to join the main body. These men so collected, he formed into one corps (there being no officer present), and withstood and repulsed repeated attacks of the French cavalry; regularly retiring and facing about for four miles, when they were relieved from their perilous situation by the rear-guard of our cavalry. The officer commanding the cavalry reported the behaviour of the sergeant to General Frazer, who commanded the division, and who, having ordered an enquiry to be made, and finding the circumstances proved as before stated, recommended him for promotion. The Commander-in-Chief has been pleased to appoint him to an ensigncy in the 1st West India Regiment. As, however, there must be a great expense in fitting himself out, and preparing for his voyage, I beg to recommend him in the strongest manner to your favourable notice.

"I am, Gentlemen,
"Your most obedient humble Servant,
(Signed) "E. HULL,
"Lieut.-Colonel, 43rd Regiment.
"*Commanding 2nd Battalion.*"

Extract from the Proceedings of the Committee:—

"Resolved that the sum of fifty pounds be presented to Ensign William Newman, in testimony of the high sense which the Committee entertain of his gallant and meritorious conduct."

BATTLE OF CORUNNA.

Until the battle fought on the 16th of January, the battalion occupied the suburb of St. Lucia. During the interval, stragglers actually crawling upon their hands and knees, so fearfully lacerated were their feet, came in, to enable them to join the ranks. On the 14th the transports from Vigo entered the harbour. The artillery, with the exception of one brigade, the dismounted cavalry, which were numerous, the sick and all other encumbrances, were immediately embarked, so that the army could at any moment retire without inconvenience. An order to shoot the horses had previously been issued, which was obeyed with great regret.

The battalion was engaged in raising mortar batteries. The enemy attacked our position in three strong columns, covered by numerous skirmishers and a powerful artillery. Our pickets were driven in, and the village of Elvina gained, but quickly retaken and the French repulsed in all their attacks. The brigade to which the 43rd was attached, on the extreme right of the army, covered the retreat of our troops to their shipping, which took place during the night with great deliberation and regularity. The covering battalions then retired within the works of Corunna before daybreak, and held them during the 17th. The enemy opened a battery from the Heights of St. Lucia upon our transports, some of which were slow in getting under weigh. They cut their cables and ran for it. In the confusion two vessels went ashore, which our marines therefore set on fire, and their blaze enabled the 43rd, who retired in small detachments from the works after dark, to reach the boats in safety, leaving Corunna to be defended by the Spaniards.

The loss of Sir John Moore, who received his mortal wound during the carrying of the village of Elvira, caused profound grief. The soldiers adored him, while his social and amiable qualities endeared him to all ranks and classes. His funeral, which took place in the most perfect silence of stilly midnight, has formed the subject of lines unequalled for pathos in the British poetical *répertoire*.

"Not a drum was heard, not a funeral note,
    As his corse to the rampart we hurried;
Not a soldier discharged his farewell shot
    O'er the grave where our hero we buried.

"We buried him darkly at dead of night,
    The sods with our bayonets turning—
By the struggling moonbeam's misty light,
    And the lantern dimly burning.

"No useless coffin enclosed his breast,
    Not in sheet or in shroud we wound him;
But he lay like a warrior taking his rest,
    With his martial cloak around him.

"Few and short were the prayers we said,
    And we spoke not a word of sorrow;
But we steadfastly gazed on the face that was dead,
    And we bitterly thought of the morrow.

"We thought as we hollowed his narrow bed
    And smoothed down his lonely pillow,
That the foe and the stranger would tread o'er his head,
    And we far away on the billow.

"Lightly they'll talk of the spirit that's gone,
    And o'er his cold ashes upbraid him,—
But little he'll reck, if they let him sleep on
    In the grave where a Briton has laid him.

"But half of our heavy task was done,
    When the clock struck the hour for retiring,—
And we heard the distant and random gun
    That the foe was sullenly firing.

"Slowly and sadly we laid him down,
    From the field of his fame fresh and gory;
We carved not a line, and we raised not a stone,
    But we left him alone in his glory."

Of the second battalion 2 sergeants, 3 corporals, 2 buglers, and 174 privates were lost during the retreat from Sahagun. The casualties in the first battalion amounted to 1 captain (Carruthers, died), 1 sergeant, and 65 rank and file. Many of these perished of fatigue, or were taken and retained by the enemy until the peace of 1814, when a small number returned from the French prisons. Some found their way into Portugal, and joined the forces under Sir John Cradock. They were subsequently incorporated in a company of the 1st battalion of detachments formed with many others left sick and wounded after the battle of Vimiero.

The battalion was shipped for England on board the 'Resolution' and 'Elizabeth,' and after a tempestuous passage, landed at Plymouth, where the inhabitants loaded the men, women, and children, with kindness, gratuitously supplying clothes and other comforts. On the 23rd of March they entered Colchester Barracks, where the first battalion was already stationed, and in the happiness of reunion quickly forgot all the trials and hardships of the late campaign.

Recruiting went on briskly, many militiamen and volunteers joined, and before the second battalion had been located one week in Colchester Barracks it was augmented by upwards of 500.

Expedition to Walcheren.

On the 18th of June the vast armament, under Admiral Sir Richard Strachan, composed of 35 ships of the line, 2 of 50 guns, 3 of 44, 197 sloops, bombs, and other armed small craft, intended for a descent on Holland, assembled in the Downs. The land forces, under General the Earl of Chatham, including officers, numbered 39,219. All were in a high state of spirits and discipline. On June 20th, the second battalion of the 43rd, with other corps, left Colchester and moved to Shorncliffe Barracks, where, until the 17th of July, they remained brigaded with the second battalion of the 52nd and 95th, under command of Major-General the Hon. W. Stewart. On that day they marched through Dover to Deal, where they found innumerable boats ready to convey the soldiers, streaming into the town by every available road, to their ships, from whose mastheads floated—

> "The flag that 's braved a thousand years
> The battle and the breeze."

In incredibly quick time the men were pulled off by the blue-jackets in the presence of countless fair daughters of Albion, gathered from afar to watch their departure.

The strength of the battalion on embarkation amounted to thirty-five sergeants, twenty-two buglers, and 605 rank and file. They were placed on board the 'York,' seventy-four, and on the 31st July were in East Kapelle roads off Walcheren. Little opposition was offered, and the troops were immediately employed in the reduction of Flushing. The object of the expedition was to destroy or capture the enemy's ships afloat, on the Scheldt, as well as those building at Antwerp and Flushing; to destroy the arsenals and dockyards; to reduce the Island of Walcheren, and render, if possible, the river no longer navigable for ships of war. Should this programme prove impracticable, the commanders were to return to England, leaving a force sufficient to maintain the future possession and protection of Walcheren.

On the arrival of the battalion at East Kapelle roads, a heavy fire was observed from the mortar and gunboats directed on the town of Terverre. Part of the fleet had already entered the Veergat, and landed a large force, together with 300 sailors. The army advanced and occupied the place, taking some field-pieces, and driving the enemy into Flushing. Hope's division took possession of Fort Balzon. The French fleet retired behind a chain drawn across the Scheldt, near Fort Lillo. On the 5th of August, Zandolist, opposite Fort Bathz, was attacked with twenty-eight gunboats, but were driven off by the batteries. The weather had become so boisterous that the sea blockade of Flushing could not be accomplished until the 7th. The enemy threw a thousand men across the Scheldt, to reinforce the town, and made a sortie from Flushing on the right of our line, but was repulsed.

Meanwhile the 43rd had been placed in small craft in the Sloe Passage between Walcheren and South Beveland. The light brigade was composed of the second battalions of the 43rd, 52nd, and 95th Rifle corps. On the 13th the batteries below Flushing were completed, and some frigates and bombs having taken their station, a fire was opened from upwards of fifty pieces of heavy ordnance, and kept up during the night, vigorously returned by the enemy. In the morning seven line-of-battle ships, anchored in the Deserlo Passage, got under weigh and ranged along the sea front, led by Sir R. Strachan, plying a furious cannonade until the town presented one vast conflagration. Firing from the ramparts having nearly ceased, General Monnet was summoned to surrender. An evasive answer was returned. Hostilities were recommenced and continued until the following day, when the enemy craved a suspension of arms, and the governor and entire garrison became prisoners of war, while all the valuable stores fell into our hands. The loss of British killed, wounded, and missing during the siege amounted to about 720, including officers.

Offensive operations were at an end. The troops found themselves in the midst of abundance. Pay was issued with punctuality, and recreations of all kinds were indulged in. The British army was suddenly roused from this state of peaceful enjoyment by the approach of a foe more terrible than that of French myrmidons. A pestilential fever broke out, from which men staggered, fell, and dropping, almost instantaneously expired. With such fearful rapidity did this scourge prey upon its victims that in fourteen days 12,086 soldiers were struck down, and so virulent were the seeds of the disorder that even convalescents rarely in any case ever wholly recovered their former vigour of constitution. This destroying angel was long remembered with awe-struck terror by the name of "Walcheren" fever.

On the 10th of August, headquarters, with the right wing of the 43rd, marched for South Graven Polder, where they were cantoned until the 15th; the other wing, under Major Elers, remaining at Turgoes. Headquarters and right wing moved on the 16th to the parish of De Groa, and were cantoned in the neighbouring farmhouses until the 30th, when, just as they had sat down to dinner, a sudden order desired them to move to the coast. The meal was instantly abandoned, everything packed up, and the beach gained in two hours, where embarkation began without delay. Next morning, 200 of the sick, officers and soldiers, were removed on board small craft for England. The headquarters of the battalion were removed from the 'Ganges' to His Majesty's ship 'Salsette,' but by this time every man was ill, and many had died. At Harwich there disembarked 32 sergeants, 35 corporals, 21 buglers, 566 privates, nearly all prostrated by the fever. As they crawled on shore, an honest countryman, pointing, observed to his companion, "I say, Bill, there goes the King's hard bargains." 1 sergeant and 7 privates were left at Walcheren.

The battalion marched to Colchester. Those at all able to move were sent to Sudbury for change of air, which in some cases proved highly beneficial; but from first to last their loss was 126 men by the epidemic. The final evacuation of Walcheren took place towards the end of December.

This expedition can only be regarded as a disgraceful record of the incompetency of the ministry then in power. To their errors in judgment, combined with the jealousies and recriminations existing between the naval and military commanders, may be ascribed the loss of 7000 brave

British soldiers by fever and ague, ingloriously sacrificed in an unhealthy climate, while their services would have been invaluable in Spain   The miserable event gave rise to a caustic epigram :—

> "Lord Chatham, with sword *un*drawn,
> Stood waiting for Sir Richard Strachan;
> Sir Richard, longing to be at 'em,
> Stood waiting for the Earl of Chatham."

After Walcheren, the second battalion of the 43rd remained in England to recruit for the first in the Peninsula.

Napoleon, on quitting Spain at the close of 1808, left the task of complete subjugation to his delegated marshals. This will prove that so arrogantly secure did he make of Soult's immediate progress in Portugal that he fixed the 5th of February for the arrival of his troops at Oporto, and the 16th instant for his own triumphant entry into Lisbon. This army consisted of 23,000 men, of which 4000 were cavalry, with 56 pieces of cannon.

Early in spring the British Ministry, convinced that the Spanish and Portuguese cause was not hopeless, despatched General Beresford with twelve or fourteen officers to re-organize and form the army of the latter nation. The English troops left in the Peninsula on the withdrawal from Corunna consisted of a brigade under Brigadier-General Cameron, the 14th Dragoons, with the sick, convalescents, and stragglers of Sir John Moore's army; the whole amounting to some 7000 men, under command of Sir John Cradock at Lisbon. From this body was formed the first and second battalions of detachments. The first of these had, besides the 43rd company, one from the 29th, another from the 52nd, and a third from the 95th, commanded by Colonel Way of the 29th. The 43rd were in charge of Lieutenant George Brown, with whom was Lieutenant Brockman. Reinforcements reached the Tagus in March and April, increasing the army to 13,000 men. This enabled Sir J. Cradock to take up a position out of Lisbon, and to cover the great roads leading upon that city. Government determined to intrust the defence of Portugal to the general who had so successfully distinguished himself in the year previous. Sir J. Cradock was therefore superseded and appointed Governor of Gibraltar.

On the 16th of April Sir Arthur Wellesley sailed from Portsmouth in the 'Surveillant,' Captain Sir G. Collier, nor did he again touch English soil until 1814 as F.M. Duke of Wellington, at the very moment that the Prince Regent was exhibiting the arsenal, dock-yard and fleet to the Emperor of Russia and King of Prussia. Sir Arthur reached Lisbon on the 22nd of April. His reception was an ovation. The city was illuminated, the people hailed him as their former deliverer, and testified intense gratification and delight. On the 25th he was introduced to the regency in the palace of the Inquisition, when the rank of Marshal-General of Portugal was conferred, and he joined the army at Coimbra on the 2nd of May. Each town through which he passed was brilliantly illuminated in his honour, while ladies emulated each other in bestowing "wreathed smiles" and offering magnificent bouquets.

Sir Arthur determined to advance with his main body on the enemy's front. A division under Marshal Beresford was directed on Viseu and across the Douro to co-operate with Silviera. The British troops were in excellent order, and the Portuguese regiments, although less soldier-like in *ensemble* than their allies, came out better than was expected. Great credit was due to Marshal Beresford, for upon being appointed Generalissimo of this army, he first clothed them in English fashion, doubled their pay, dismissed the service two of their general officers as ignorant and incompetent, and instituted such regulations and drills, that what was like a country rabble became metamorphosed into a respectable body of regular troops.

It was intended to surprise the French under General Franceshi, on the 10th; but the neighing of horses and stupidity of the guides caused a failure. On the following day the enemy was observed on the skirts of a wood. Sharp skirmishing ensued. The four battalions of the German Legion marched diagonally to turn the left, which appeared the weak point—meanwhile—the French managed to push a column of infantry down the road, through the village of Grijon, which being reported to Sir Arthur, he replied, "If they come any further, order the battalions of detachments to charge them with the bayonet." This alternative was unnecessary, as finding our whole force in their front, they retired.

On the 12th a hair-dresser, escaped from Oporto in the night, brought intelligence that the French had destroyed the bridge of boats over the Douro, and had secured all those on the other side. Sir Arthur ordered Colonel Waters to proceed directly to the river and procure boats, *coûte qui coûte*. Passing up the left bank he at length, two miles above the city, descried a small old boat embedded in the mud. Others were seen on the opposite side, and some peasants consenting to accompany the Colonel and ferry back four boats, the troops were conveyed over. Soult discredited the possibility until incontestably proved by our firing. The enemy then issued from the town, in great numbers bringing guns to bear, but being tamely served, did little mischief. Suddenly they began to retreat. On their deserting the quays, the Portuguese jumped into the boats amidst vociferous cheering. General Charles Stewart pursued.

At the passage of the Douro the British loss did not exceed 120 men, while the French, besides 500 killed and wounded, left in our hands many prisoners, many sick in hospital, and various pieces of cannon. The 43rd company had about 10 killed and wounded. Sir A. Wellesley in his despatch wrote:—" I cannot say too much in favour of the officers and men. They have marched in four days over eighty miles of most difficult country, have gained many important positions, and have engaged and defeated three different bodies of the enemy's troops. I have also to request your Lordship's attention to the conduct of the flank companies of the 29th, 43rd, and 52nd Regiments under Major Way of the 29th."

On the 29th of May the first battalion of the 43rd, complete in officers and numbering 1072 bayonets, marched from Colchester to Harwich, under command of Lieut.-Colonel Gifford. In conjunction with the first battalion 52nd and first battalion 95th Rifles, they embarked for Portugal. These two regiments had each upwards of 1000 effectives, and with the 43rd were as fine and efficient a body of men as ever took the field. The Tagus was made on the 28th of June. On the 2nd of July the rifle corps and right wing of the 43rd proceeded up the river and the left followed. All went well until within a league of Villada, when some of the boats got aground, and the men were disembarked and took the road, reaching Villada on the evening of the 5th. After leaving Abrantes they crossed to the left of the river; but finding only bad roads, a barren country, and little or no food, they recrossed. At Villa Velha the country improved. At Castel Branco they rested for two days, understanding that Sir Arthur was not so much in want of them. From thence a short cut was made to Zebreira, on the frontier of Spain, where they heard of Sir Arthur having reached Orobispo, in the neighbourhood of Talavera, at that time occupied by a part of the French army under Victor. Either this piece of intelligence, or a direct order from Wellesley, induced Craufurd to push forward by forced marches to Coria by way of Zarza Maior. At Coria it was absolutely necessary to give the division a day's rest, after which they proceeded pell mell night and day, allowing but a few hours in the meridian heat for cooking, and arrived about three miles in front of Talavera at nine o'clock on the morning of the 29th, just one day after the battle. Of this celebrated march Napier wrote:—"That day General Robert Craufurd reached the English camp with the 43rd, 52nd, and 95th Regiments, and immediately took charge of the outposts. These troops, after a march of twenty miles, were in bivouac near Malpartida de Placenzia when the alarm caused by the Spanish fugitives spread to that part. Craufurd, fearing that the army was pressed, allowed the men to rest for a few hours, and then withdrawing about fifty of the weakest from the ranks, commenced his march with the resolution not to halt until he reached the field of battle. As the brigade advanced crowds of the runaways were met with, and although not all Spaniards, all propagating the vilest falsehoods—" The army was defeated;" "Sir Arthur Wellesley was killed;" "The French were only a few miles distant;" nay, some blinded by their fears, affected to point out the enemy's advanced posts on the nearest hills. Indignant at this shameful scene, the troops hastened rather than slackened the impetuosity of their pace, and leaving only seventeen stragglers behind, in twenty-six hours crossed the field of battle in a close and compact body; having in that time passed over sixty-two English miles in the hottest season of the year, each man carrying from fifty to sixty pounds' weight upon his shoulders. Had the historian Gibbon known of such a march, he would have spared his sneer about the 'delicacy of modern soldiers.'"

Discussion having arisen as to the correct data furnish by the foregoing extract, a leaf out of Lieutenant Pollock's—43rd Regiment—pocket diary may be likewise quoted :—

"Left Coria on the 24th (July, 1809) for Galesta; on the 25th to Malpartida, a distance of four leagues, under soaking rain. Next A.M., 26th, about three leagues, crossed the river Pietar, and after marching two leagues found we had taken the wrong road; obliged therefore to cross the country about two leagues, where we halted, having marched upwards of seven leagues; next morning marched for Naval Moral, four leagues. Next A.M., 28th, the brigade marched at 1 o'clock with the intention of only going four leagues, but before we had got so far we met the Spaniards running away in all directions, with baggage, &c., and who reported an engagement; proceeded therefore about six leagues to Oropesa, where we filed off to a wood and stopped until 4 o'clock, when we again continued the march at a very quick pace until 11 o'clock. The brigade then lay down with their arms in their hands, and after remaining in that situation for three hours again marched and reached the ground where the action had been fought the day previous—a harrowing march of *sixty-six miles in thirty hours.*"

Great was the disappointment and disgust in the brigade at finding they were but a few hours too late to take part in the battle, but as in close column they passed over the field, they were cheered by the whole army, and their arrival at this particular moment was hailed as an auspicious omen. Although as a regiment the 43rd were not present at Talavera, their company of detachments, under Lieutenants Brown and Brockman, formed on a hill to the extreme left of the position, greatly distinguished itself by repulsing at the point of the bayonet a formidable attack. This company, consisting of 4 sergeants and 100 rank and file, lost 10 privates; Lieutenant Brown was wounded, and Captain Gardiner of the regiment, brigade-major to General Stewart, killed.

The Spaniards behaved infamously, refusing the slightest assistance in burying the dead, and although sufficient corn to support the army for a month was secreted in Talavera, declined to produce it. This conduct sowed the first seeds of contempt and dislike, never after wholly eradicated, in the hearts of the British towards their allies. Provisions were scant, water stagnant, and the enemy concentrating in the vicinity. The French had continued a rear-guard on the Alberche until they retired through Santa Olalla. An anecdote was related highly creditable to King Joseph. In the house where he had lodged, a caricature was discovered of 'El Reye Pepé,' which created great indignation in those around his person. On his departure next morning, H.M. tendered his host a snuff-box, remarking that he would do well to be more careful of the contents than of the caricature. On being opened it was found to contain the King's miniature.

At this time the 43rd, 52nd, and 95th Rifles, were ordered to "compose a Light Brigade under command of Brigadier-General Robert Craufurd."

The Duke of Dalmatia, at the head of an imposing force, had entered Placenzia. The fate of the Peninsula seemed now suspended on a thread, and the peril of the British army extreme, owing to their great numerical inferiority. In this alarming attitude of affairs, the General abated not one whit of his usual calmness and fortitude. He occupied himself in visiting the hospitals, procuring all attainable comforts for the wounded and dying, while he neglected no possible precautions against surprise.

On the 3rd of August the 43rd, with the light brigade left Talavera for Oropeza, crossing the Tagus at Arzobispo, and reaching Almaraz on the 8th. During the march, grievous privations from want of food and water were undergone; even a breakfast of acorns was deemed a luxurious repast. Within a few days, Major Proctor and Captain M'Lachlan of the 43rd succumbed from fever contracted on the march. The latter had distinguished himself at Vimiero. Major M'Leod now commanded the regiment, Colonel Gifford being on the staff.

Meanwhile, Sir Arthur had taken up a position on the other side of the Tagus, by the bridge of Arzobispo, thus baffling the combinations of the enemy. Craufurd's brigade, with six pieces of artillery, was directed to gain the bridge of Almaraz, lest the enemy discovering the ford below, should cross and seize the Puerta de Mirabete. This movement was effected, but the Spanish infantry under Albuquerque permitted Mortier to take advantage of their supineness, and the French cavalry, secretly assembled, with General Coulaincourt's brigade, suddenly entered the stream. The Spaniards running to arms, opened upon the leading squadrons; but Mortier, with a powerful concentric fire of artillery, overwhelmed them.

Sir Arthur and his army gained Deleytoza, and depositing the wounded in a large convent, proceeded westward. On the 11th of August headquarters were at Truxillo. Craufurd's light brigade was relieved at Almaraz by the Spaniards, and took the road of Caceres to Valencia de Alcantara. The pass of Mirabete disclosed how much they had suffered. With difficulty and many halts they were only able to reach Campo Mayor on September the 11th, where the pestilent fever of the Guadiana committed distressing ravages. Four sergeants and 106 rank and file of the 43rd perished from the epidemic. Dysentery also raged, and in a short space of time that scourge cost the British army 5000 men. Here the men of the regiment hitherto attached to the first battalion of detachments joined.

On the 3rd of September, Wellesley left Truxillo, gradually drawing towards the frontiers; passing through Medellin and Merida to Badajoz, where he established himself. The enemy had not followed the defeated Spaniards; but fearful of leaving the north of Spain without troops, and feeling secure of the capital, the three corps set out on their return towards Salamanca, and thus ended the campaign of 1809.

The actions of July had taught the enemy that their arms were no longer infallible; their repulse awakened some degree of energy in the Spaniards, while Europe began to recognise the possibility of beating the French. To this and the succeeding campaigns may be ascribed the resuscitation of the *morale* in European armies which the unbounded conquests and ambition of Napoleon had almost totally annihilated. In December Craufurd's brigade marched from Campo Mayor to Coimbra and Celorico.

At Coimbra the nuns invited the officers of the 43rd to a breakfast, at which they waited themselves. Placed inside a double grating, they turned round a table plentifully supplied with a great variety of chocolate, coffee, cakes, and other delicacies.

1810.

On the 3rd of January the 43rd arrived at Pinhel, close to the River Coa, where they were cantoned.

Sir Arthur Wellesley—now Lord Wellington—was regarded as the only general capable of directing the defence of Portugal, our ancient ally, and at the same time inspiring entire confidence both at home and abroad. Calculating that rations for a larger force might not be procurable, he demanded but 30,000 troops to prosecute the war. Success, he urged, could only be arrived at by combined earnestness and devotedness in purpose and action on the part of the natives. It was necessary to secure two points; first, to concert measures by which sufficiency of subsistence should be attainable for the British and Portuguese armies; secondly, to devise plans by which the enemy should be deprived of supplies. The inhabitants were ordered to destroy their mills, break down the bridges, remove the boats, abandon their dwellings, and carry off their property wherever the invader might approach; while the entire population, converted for the nonce into soldiers, should close on the rear and flanks and cut off all exterior resources. Stern as the mandate might appear, the exigencies of war rendered it essential for the preservation of the kingdom, and it was unhesitatingly obeyed.

Lord Wellington, in pursuance of his comprehensive plans, sought a position covering Lisbon, where the allied forces should neither be turned by the flanks, forced in front by numbers, nor reduced by famine. The mountains abutting upon Lisbon furnished the key to the arch of defence. Lord Wellington determined to convert these mountains into a gigantic and impregnable citadel. Hence the far-famed lines of TORRES VEDRAS.

Intrenchments, redoubts, and glacis, covered more than five hundred square miles of mountainous country, between the Tagus and the Atlantic. The defensive force may be computed at 80,000, of which the British contributed 30,000. The frontier to be protected from Braganza to Astramonte was 400 miles. Every probable or possible movement of the enemy was weighed by the acute and fertile brain of the English general, actively alive to the multiplied counter-combinations to be anticipated. In case of disaster a line of inner intrenchments was prepared to secure embarkation, and 24,000 tons of shipping were retained in the river to receive, if necessary, the British troops.

On the 6th of January the 43rd crossed the Coa, and were cantoned in villages. Every morning, one hour before dawn, they were under arms, and so remained until daylight.

On the 22nd of February, in a General Order issued by Lord Wellington at Viseu, the following notice appeared:—"The 1st and 2nd battalions of the Portuguese Chasseurs are attached to the brigade of Brigadier-General Craufurd, which is to be called The Light Division."

In March the whole brigade, except the 52nd, who remained with Craufurd at Pinhel, pushed its advance towards the Agueda, as a corps of observation on Massena, about to besiege Ciudad Rodrigo. The rifle corps occupied the post of honour in rear of the pass of St. Felices, in order to watch a French column, occupying the towns of St. Felices, Villa Nueva, &c.; and the 43rd in their cantonments extended from the right of the Rifles as far as Ciudad Rodrigo. The German Hussars, a very fine body of men acknowledged by all to be the only troops fit for the work, formed a chain along the banks of the Agueda for a distance of twenty-five miles.

Craufurd's division reached 4000 effectives, with six guns. While the hussars watched the distant bridges, the troops could always concentrate under Almeida, and on the side of Barba de Puerco the ravine was so deep that a few companies of the 95th were considered competent to oppose any number. Seven minutes sufficed at midnight for the division to get under arms and half an hour by day or night to assemble at the alarm posts, with the baggage loaded and stationed at a convenient distance in the rear. The troops evinced a celerity, promptness, and intelligence, never surpassed under any circumstances. At midnight on the 19th of March the Rifles stationed at Barba de Puerco had an affair with a very superior party of the enemy, who attempted a surprise, but, headed by the gallant Beckwith, they beat them off, and pushed the French column over the edge of a precipice.

On the 21st of April, seven companies of the 43rd were at Villa de Cierbo with the headquarters of the brigade, and three at Castellegos de Duas Casas. On the 27th the battalion marched to Almeida, headquarters moving to Gallegos, where the division was joined by Captain Ross' troop of horse artillery, two squadrons of the 1st German Hussars, and the 2nd Portuguese Caçadores. Ciudad Rodrigo was now being invested by the French, and on June the 11th the trenches were opened. The light division remained at Gallegos, observing the progress of the siege, and being stationed on a hill which overlooked the town, had a fine view of the operations.

At this juncture the French were most annoying, invariably watching the hours of cooking and meals, advancing at the very moment when all was prepared, obliging our men to empty their kettles and rush rapidly to arms, when they would immediately retire. Early in July the enemy appeared in great force. Ciudad Rodrigo capitulated on the 10th. On the 24th occurred the

COMBAT OF THE COA.

General Craufurd received positive instructions not to risk an action beyond the Coa. Carried away by his daring and ambitious spirit, he braved the whole French army, and brought on an ill-considered conflict which, although the result was glorious to the troops engaged, might have seriously compromised the deep-laid schemes of the Commander-in-Chief. Napier in his History gives a most graphic account of that bitter fight, where he himself was shot through the left thigh towards the close of the action, and his company lost one ensign killed and thirty-five men killed and wounded.

Lord Wellington wrote of this action near Almeida that it was one of the most brilliant of the exploits of the Light Division during the war: "I am informed, that throughout this trying day the commanding officers of the 43rd, 52nd, and 95th, Lieut.-Colonels Beckwith, Barclay, and Hull, and all the officers and soldiers of those excellent regiments, distinguished themselves."

To these public accounts we add a private letter from Lieutenant (afterwards Lieut.-Colonel) Henry Booth of the 43rd, to his brother in England:—

"Camp at Celorico, July 30th, 1810.

"We are both (alluding to his brother Charles, in the 52nd) as well as possible, quite clear out of all the scrapes, thank God! But to the point. Our gallant, I wish I could say *wise*, General Crauford, after having been driven from his position near Gallegos, about three leagues in front of Almeida, posted his division a little to the right of that fortress, amongst rocks, walls, and vineyards, on the slope of the hill which descends to the river Coa—a worse position, every one allows, could not have been chosen. However, after a dreadful stormy night, with incessant rain, thunder, and lightning until day-break, our men and officers thoroughly drenched —I may say half-drowned—and fire-locks nearly unserviceable, we waited patiently the attack of the French on the morning of the 24th. Our pickets were soon driven in, and the French fired on our line with musketry, shot, and shells; we returned the fire, and were ordered to retire *in line—very wisely and properly ordered!* But unfortunately, from the vast quantity of high walls, six feet high generally, the number of rocks, vineyards, and broken ground which continued down to the water's edge, our *line* was very soon broken, past all chance of being formed again, till we had crossed the bridge. In this manner the whole divison retired down this tremendous hill. This was fine fun for the French skirmishers, who were following us closely from rock to rock, pelting us pretty handsomely down to the river! However, in all this confusion, our fellows behaved nobly, and retired fighting inch by inch, which in the end proved our misfortune; for had we made the best of our way over the bridge, and occupied the hills on the other side as soon as possible, we should have suffered less, and precisely the same position would have been gained. But why did our General wait for the attack in so infamous a position? It was impossible for us to keep our ground, nor was it intended that we should. We remained, as it were to be fired upon, without the means of defending ourselves till we could cross the bridge. Would it not have answered the purpose if General Craufurd had *at first* occupied the hills on the other side of the bridge, advancing his pickets some distance in front, which could have retired on the approach of the French, covered by the fire of our line on the hills, and then defend the bridge, as we might have done against a much superior force? Every one asks the same question. The General is universally blamed, and Lord Wellington is said to have expressed to him his disapprobation. In proof he has given Sir Brent Spencer the command of the Light Division, which has caused no little satisfaction amongst us. To continue my tedious, and I am afraid, confused account, we defended the bridge against three attempts of the French to force it, in all of which they failed, suffering heavy loss. At last the firing mutually ceased, on account of the torrents of rain that fell, after five hours' hard peppering at each other. Towards night we retired, and have been gradually falling back on this place. The main body of the army is still more in rear, and we have only a few cavalry in our front. We *must* retire when the French advance. Where the army will halt and fight, of course we are ignorant. It depends entirely on the force they bring against us. We have had a good share of fag, and shall be glad to have a reprieve. Things are now, I assure you, coming to a crisis. All depends on the force of the French. It is the general opinion that the enemy will bring on such numbers as to leave little doubt of the issue of a battle. Happen what may, we have lads who will do their duty. The people of England, I dare say, are looking to us. Well they may. Now, my dear Tom, with much sorrow, I lay before you a long list of killed and wounded of the 43rd. Killed—Colonel Hull, who had joined us to take command the preceding day; Captain

Ewen Cameron; and Lieutenant Mason, a fine young lad of seventeen. Wounded—Captains Lloyd, J. W. Hall, W. Napier, Shaw, Deshon, the four first severely; Lieutenant M'Diarmid, Harvest, Johnston, Stevenson, Frederick, Hopkins. Poor Frederick, a fine young boy, has since lost his leg; it was amputated yesterday. Hopkins commanded the company I am attached to, and was wounded in the first fire. The command afterwards fell to me. I was not sot so unfortunate; I came clear off. Sergeants, drummers, and privates killed, wounded, and missing, 130.

The 95th has suffered almost as severely as ourselves in officers and men. The loss of the 52nd, I am happy to say, is comparatively trifling. Two officers wounded, and a few men killed. They were not so much exposed as ours and the 95th. We regret the loss of Colonel Hull; in short, of all who fell. Major M'Leod, who has succeeded Colonel Hull in the command, distinguished himself. Is not this a pretty loss for one regiment, owing entirely to the blunders of ———? I hope we shall be better managed for the future. We only wish for a fair chance; there is then no fear of our lads gaining distinction. Is it not a pity such fine fellows should always be obliged to fight *retiring*? Yet this must be the game now for a while. The French force in our front, in the neighbourhood of Almeida and Rodrigo, is stated to be about 80,000. It is said they are also advancing in other directions. This is a camp letter; pray excuse faults."

On the 4th of August, orders were issued that the Light Division should be divided into two brigades—the 43rd, 3rd Caçadores, and four companies of the 95th, in the first; the 52nd, 1st Caçadores, and four companies of the 95th, in the second. On August 27th, Almeida suddenly surrendered, and the brigade retired to Martagao.

Battle of Busaco.

In the beginning of September, the Light Division slowly retrograded towards Busaco, waiting the enemy's approach, Lord Wellington having there resolved to offer them battle. On the 26th they advanced by Martagao, and fell back skirmishing with the French. During the night the 43rd and 52nd, forming the left brigade of the division, were drawn up in line on a small plateau just behind a steep portion of the mountain range. The position was in front exceedingly strong, and the direct approach almost inaccessible. Notwithstanding, before daybreak on the 27th, the enemy's columns appeared in the woods below, and rapidly advanced. Loison's division, headed by Simon's brigade, led the attack. They soon drove in the English skirmishers, and scrambling up the rocks crowned our position. The artillery were obliged to fall back from their guns, and the summit was for a few moments actually in the possession of the French, when Craufurd, who, hidden by the crest of the hill, had keenly and anxiously watched their proceedings, waving his hat, gave the signal for the 43rd and 52nd to charge. With a cheer, they dashed at the enemy, overthrew their columns, strewing the hill with their dead and wounded, and secured many prisoners.

The enemy's attack on the 3rd division at first was more successful (Regnier's corps was employed there, Ney's against the Light Division). In this attack some of the Portuguese were overthrown, and the right of the division turned, and the French were in possession for a short time, when the 45th and 88th Regiments charged, and Colonel Cameron at the same time attacking with the 9th Regiment drove the enemy from their position, which finished the battle of Busaco. Lord Wellington, in his despatch after the action, said :—" On the left, the enemy attacked with three divisions of infantry of the sixth corps, that part of the Sierra occupied by our Light Division, commanded by Brigadier-General Craufurd, and by the brigade commanded by Brigadier-General Pack. One division of infantry only made any progress to the top of the hill, and they were immediately charged with the bayonet by Brigadier-General Craufurd, with the 43rd, 52nd, and 95th Regiments, and the 3rd Portuguese

Caçadores, and driven down with immense loss. In this attack, Brigadier-General Craufurd, Lieut.-Colonels Beckwith of the 95th, and Barclay of the 52nd, and the commanding officers of the regiments engaged, distinguished themselves. The loss sustained by the enemy in his attacks of the 27th has been enormous."

The casualties in the 43rd were slight:—1 captain, 1 sergeant, and 7 rank and file wounded. The officer was Captain Lord Fitzroy Somerset, on the staff of Lord Wellington.

The following letter addressed by Lieutenant Charles Booth, bearing on the action, is replete with interest:—

"Camp near Aruda, about fifteen miles from Lisbon, 9th Nov., 1810.

"Never did a military man commit so great a blunder as Massena in attacking the position of Busaco. Without any previous reconnoissance of our force or the nature of our position, he attacked what was far from being its weakest points with a force unequal to make the slightest impression. We lost certainly some brave fellows, but, compared to their loss (especially in *killed*), ours was a mere trifle. In the part of the line occupied by the Light Division and about 200 yards immediately to its front two columns of the enemy—supposed about 5000 each—were met by the two left-hand companies of the 43rd, and the right two of the 52nd. The front of their columns alone—chiefly composed of officers—stood the charge; the rest took to their heels, throwing away their arms, pouches, &c. Our men did not stand to take prisoners; what were taken were those left in our rear in the hurry of pressing forward in the charge. The flanks of the 43rd and 52nd in their charge met only the enemy's skirmishers who had by superior numbers driven in the 95th Rifles but a few seconds before the charge of the division. These poor fellows were all glad enough to give themselves up as prisoners, our men not being allowed to fire a shot at them. The advanced part of the charging line—the four companies first mentioned—after throwing themselves into the midst of the enemy's retreating columns, killing, wounding, and in short felling to the ground lots of them, were with great difficulty halted, and then commenced from the flanks of the whole division the most destructive flanking fire that I believe was ever witnessed. Not a tenth part of their whole force would have escaped had not the four companies, by precipitating themselves too far in front of the general line, exposed themselves to the fire of their comrades, and thus prevented more than 300 firelocks on each flank of the division from being brought into action. The flanks, and in fact every other part of the division (except the four centre companies), had to pass over in the charge some very steep rugged ground, where, not meeting with anything but the enemy's skirmishers, they pushed on head-over-heels, until the descent became almost perpendicular. At this time they were halted, and had a fine view of what was going on in the centre.

"I was in the left wing of the battalion, and am sure, though we were not five minutes in the charge down the hill, it cost us more than half an hour to get up into our first position again. I have often had described to me what is called a '*hot business*,' and where confusion 'tis said 'reigns triumphant on all sides.' If this be true, then I have only to say that I have never been in a general action, or what is termed 'hot business.' It must indeed be a terrible sight if it exceeds what we experienced at Busaco, where, to all those who had their eyes open and not poking their way with a bayonet, everything appeared to be carried on with the greatest possible regularity, considering the ground we had to act upon. Orders, to be sure, could only be communicated by sound of bugle, or by the stentorian voice of a company officer. Great was the screech set on foot by our fellows during the charge. Poor Barclay was shot twice in front of the four companies, at a very few paces from the enemy; he was cheering the men at the time.

"You will see by the 'Gazette' that the 52nd took General Simon, two or three field officers, and some of inferior rank. Some one has had the audacity, rascality, I should say, to contradict this in the newspapers; if this gentleman is wise, he will not give the slightest hint of his name to any of the Light Division. It was said, too, that he was actually engaged with the division on that day. General Simon was both wounded and taken by the same person—a private soldier of the 52nd. He had been much in advance and on the right of their column in coming up the hill, and at the time he was wounded was reconnoitring in their line of skirmishers. Harry I reckon as having narrowly escaped on several occasions during the retreat. At Busaco he was in Captain Lloyd's—the left-hand company of the 43rd—in one of those who met the head of the French column in the charge.

His captain, who was close to him at the time they reached the enemy's columns, was on the point of being bayoneted, but knocked down the fellow attempting it. Harry must have had a shave or two, as he could not prevent himself from being in the very thick of them, but he speaks only of the actions of others. At the Coa, near Almeida, his was one of the companies that covered the retreat of the division across the bridge; and had it not been for the gallant manner in which this detachment— principally 43rd—behaved, most of the division would certainly have been taken prisoners, or forced into the river, where they must inevitably have perished. Lieutenant Hopkins, in command of this company, had been wounded in the early part of the day, whilst in conversation with Harry respecting their unfavourable position. Harry, of course, took command of the company for the *rest of the day*, which was by far the most trying part of it, having been amongst the last of the few who escaped over the bridge after the retreat of the principal body of the covering party. Had any person of interest been inclined to have taken proper notice of his conduct, and that of a few others on that day, and represented it *properly* to Lord Wellington, a company would have been the least he could have rewarded them with.

"The day of the retreat to our present position, Harry's (Captain Lloyd's) company was on the rear-guard on the most stormy disagreeable day I ever witnessed. The enemy had come upon us rather unexpectedly whilst snug at our dinners at Alemquer. Considerable confusion ensued on our leaving the town, for the enemy's riflemen were actually entering it before the 43rd had assembled. Harry was in rear of all with a section of the company, and obliged to blaze away in all directions in order to keep them in check, so great was their impudence and spirits at seeing us retreat in so confused a manner. The town withal contained excellent plunder, and, what they most wanted, shelter for the day."

On the 1st of October a rapid file over the bridge at Coimbra was made. The enemy pressed on so fast that many dragoons were sabred in fording the river. Sir J. Fergusson wrote:—

"It was a distressing sight to see the inhabitants of that large town obliged to abandon their houses and property, and fly for their lives; many of the better class, accustomed to every luxury, obliged to travel on foot night and day, suffering every description of misery, until they arrived at Lisbon: many died from want and fatigue. The miseries of war never struck us so forcibly; we felt for the poor creatures, but it was not in our power to relieve them. We were hard pressed by the crowd, and with difficulty made our way through them to Condeixa, and escaped.

"The Light Division occupied a position in rear of Condeixa during the night, and the cavalry pickets to the front were employed in destroying our extensive magazines there—cavalry equipments, hospital supplies, tea, brandy, shirts, shoes, trowsers, and tobacco—and after a most disagreeable service, without rest, had to resume their march at daybreak. The division continued to fall back by Pombal, Buenavista, Batalha, Rio Mayor, Alcantara, and Sobral, to Alemquer. At this last place we were nearly surprised, through neglect in not posting pickets as they ought. The men were accoutred, ready to move in a moment, and no bad consequences occurred, with the exception of some officers losing their baggage, and several their dinners, which were left cooking at the fires for the French to regale themselves with.

"By a flank movement during the night, Aruda, below our station in the lines and the picket post of the division, was entered. This was the first knowledge we had of the famous lines of Torres Vedras. The pretty little town of Aruda was beautifully situated, and a favourite retreat of the rich merchants of Lisbon—their quintas being splendidly furnished, and made as luxurious as possible. It was altogether a little paradise; but how soon was the scene changed! It was plundered, burnt, and utterly destroyed; all the valuable furniture of the houses thrown into the picket fires, to the disgrace of our army; for unfortunately we did not permit the enemy to get possession of it, even for a moment to have shared the stigma."

From the 10th of October to the 15th of November the British army remained in the lines, when the enemy, finding them impregnable, retired to Santarem. Lord Wellington then deemed it expedient to remain on the defensive, and even to strengthen the lines. The Light Division, supported by a brigade of cavalry, occupied Valle and the heights overlooking the marsh and swamp below the French position. The bridge on the intervening causeway was mined; a sugar-loaf shaped hill, looking straight down the approach, was crowded with embrasures for artillery, and laced in front with a zigzag covered way. Lord Wellington fixed his headquarters at Cartaxo, to watch the further operations of the French, and in such close proximity the armies remained during the winter. Flags of truce were interchanged, and mutual civilities tendered.

1811.

The French Marshal, having with consummate skill and secresy arranged all for a retreat, which could no longer be delayed, on the night of the 5th of March, withdrew his divisions from Santarem. His army had suffered much from very short supplies, owing to a protracted demonstration in front of the British lines. At that time he was unaware of the advance of Soult, who had defeated the Spanish forces south of the Tagus. He partially succeeded in deceiving Lord Wellington with respect to the line of his retreat, by indicating a disposition to occupy Thomar, while he continued his march by the river Mondego to Pombal. Lieuts. Pollock and Taggart of the 43rd, with their companies, being on outlying picket, observed a change in the enemy's position, and that the fires looked low. Lieutenant Pollock desired one of his sergeants to come forward and aid him in investigation. Cautiously crossing the causeway and abattis which divided the camps, they were soon within a few yards of what appeared to be a sentry carelessly leaning against the wall. From his rigidity of attitude, they concluded he was asleep, and rushing forward to seize him, found the apparition but "a man of straw," dressed in up an old French uniform, and armed with a stick representing a firelock! The figure had been placed against the causeway before Massena decamped.

The Light Division was immediately ordered in pursuit. A slight skirmish took place at Pombal on the 11th.

Combat of Redinha.

In front of Redinha was an open plain, surrounded with wood; the enemy occupied the village at the extreme end, with a river in front and a timbered country in rear. By daybreak of the 12th of March both armies were in movement. The Light Division—then under Sir David Erskine (in Craufurd's absence)—was ordered to attack a wooded slope on Ney's right, while a like movement was made by the 3rd Division on the left. These exposed Ney's position entirely, but he held his ground until the heads of our columns shewed themselves at different openings from the wood, debouching into the plain. Upon a signal given, they rapidly deployed into line and advanced in beautiful order, supported by strong columns in reserve, with large masses of cavalry ready for a charge,—but Ney, under cover of the smoke from a volley of artillery, disappeared; firing the village, where some of his wounded perished, and retired by Condeixa.

The British had 12 officers and 200 men killed and wounded. Ney lost as many, but he might have been totally destroyed. Napier says, "Lord Wellington paid him too much respect."

The French were strongly posted. The Light Division planted pickets close to the enemy, but at night the French divisions stole out, and passing the British posts, made for Miranda de Corvo: owing to the darkness of the hour, they managed to execute this movement unchallenged.

The enemy intended retreating on Coimbra, but finding that town occupied by Trant and the Portuguese, suddenly took the mountain by the Puerta da Murcella, where the Light Division had a hard day's work to dislodge them. Commencing at daybreak, they skirmished across those mountains until 3 P.M.; the country was most difficult, but the men of the Light Division were excellent light troops, and experienced little loss. It was the sharpest day's lesson in skirmishing they had had during the war.

Combat of Cazal Novo.

So dense was the fog on the A.M. of the 14th, that the 52nd, unconsciously passing the enemy's outposts, had nearly captured Ney himself. The regiment was completely buried in mist; and as the vapour slowly rose, the 52nd was observed in the midst of the enemy's army, "appearing like a red pimple on the face of the country, black with the French masses"! At this juncture Lord Wellington came up and pushed the Light Division forward to sustain the 52nd, led by Captain William Napier, with six companies of the 43rd. The fight was vigorously carried on amidst numerous stone enclosures.

The right of the enemy was partially turned; but the main position could not be shaken until our left attack, under Picton and Cole, had developed itself. Ney then retired from ridge to ridge, and for a long time without confusion and little loss. Towards noon, however, the British guns and skirmishers got within range of his masses, and the retreat was concluded in confusion.

The loss on this occasion in the Light Division was 11 officers and 150 men, killed and wounded. Captain W. Napier of the 43rd was shot in the spine, and fired upon when down. He miraculously escaped death by dragging himself on his hands towards a heap of stones. He was in consequence gazetted to a brevet-majority.

In relating the occurrences of the 14th, Lord Wellington wrote—

"In the operations of this day, the 43rd, 52nd, 95th Regiments, and 3rd Caçadores, under the command of Colonels Drummond and Beckwith and Major Patrickson, Lieut.-Colonel Ross, and Majors Gilmour and Stuart, particularly distinguished themselves."

The Allies did not reach Ceira till late on the following day, when just as the men had lighted fires and were ready for the night bivouac, Wellington, taking a rapid glance at the position, determined to attack the French, who were encamped near the village of Foz d'Arronce.

Affair of Foz d'Arronce.

Lord Wellington directed the Light Division to hold the right wing in play while the horse artillery sharply and suddenly opened on the left. The first charge had so paralysing an effect on Ney's left wing, that it dispersed and fled in immediate confusion towards the river, and many were drowned or crushed to death upon the bridge.

Darkness caused the French to fire on one another in mistake for the foe. Their expulsion was so sudden and unexpected, that they were obliged to leave their kettles boiling over their fires, to abandon their entire stock of provisions, among which was a supply of excellent biscuit,—a great prize to our men, who, having outstepped their commissariat, had received no bread for four days.

The 43rd remained in the village during the night. The enemy retreated on Celorico, closely followed by the British army, of which the Light Division formed the advance, and almost daily skirmishes occured.

The British loss at Foz d'Arronce was four officers and 60 men killed and wounded. That of the French 500, of which one half were drowned. An eagle was afterwards found in the bed of the river. Lord Wellington, in a General Order, dated Lusao, the 17th of March, 1811, returned thanks to the generals, staff, officers, and troops, for their excellent conduct in the operations of the last ten days against the enemy.

He further requested the commanding officers of the 43rd, 52nd, and 95th Regiments, to name a sergeant of each for promotion to an ensigncy, in testimony of his particular approbation of these three regiments. Sergeant-Major J. Kent of the 43rd was selected from that corps and promoted into the 60th. The regiment, since quitting the lines, lost 1 Captain, 1 Ensign, and and 40 rank and file, killed, wounded, and missing. Captain Napier and Ensign Carroll were the officers wounded.

The French continued to retreat, occasionally taking up a strong position, to be invariably abandoned on approach of the English. On the 28th of March they had collected in such force on the Guarda, that Lord Wellington thought proper to concentrate his army in the neighbourhood of Celorico, for the purpose of an attack. The necessary arrangements were hardly concluded before the enemy disappeared without firing a shot, retiring to Sabugal on the Coa.

Meanwhile the blockade of Cadiz was prosecuted by the French, the battle of Barrossa had been fought, and Badajoz treacherously given up by Ismas.

Battle of Sabugal.

This action was not prearranged by Lord Wellington, but brought on by accidental circumstances.

Sir James Fergusson (then Captain in the 43rd) thus wrote:—

"On the 3rd of April we had an affair with Regnier's corps at Sabugal on the Coa, in which our regiment, the 43rd, displayed great gallantry and discipline.

"The morning was foggy, with rain; the advanced cavalry and Light Division were under Sir William Erskine, and owing to want of correct orders, the columns of attack were not properly directed. The cavalry and Elder's Portuguese corps were separated from us. The companies of the 95th Rifles attached to our Brigade crossed the ford and were soon in action with the enemy's pickets. The 43rd took the same direction and crossed the ford about half a league to the right of Sabugal, and as soon as each company gained the opposite bank of the river it moved rapidly forward in support of the riflemen, each company getting into line as it arrived. We had been scarcely formed when the riflemen were driven in and passed silently through our line; immediately two strong columns of the enemy approached. We were aware (by the peculiar noise of musketry when near) that they could not be far off. The 43rd Regiment stood alone to defend the ground; our 2nd Brigade not having yet passed the river, the whole of Regnier's corps being in our immediate front, but the fog prevented our relative situations from being seen. Immediately, with a British cheer, we charged, routed the columns and threw them back in confusion on the main body. Having gained the low ground in our charge, we discovered the enemy's main body strongly posted above, and cautiously retiring to our original ground, had scarcely gained it when three fresh columns of greater strength again advanced against us. The fog at this time in a degree clearing away, we discovered a wall in our front lined by a battalion of the enemy, with a howitzer in rear which had been dealing destruction in our ranks. We remained firm and steady under a heavy fire of grape and musketry until the enemy's columns neared us, when we again charged, routed, and drove them from the wall, taking the howitzer. Our soldiers were so much excited and advanced with such rapidity that our front was rather scattered; their cavalry took advantage, and imperceptibly gaining our flank, charged along our front. The greater part of the battalion took shelter behind the small wall and formed up, others behind some trees that afforded a certain protection, and we drove them from the field, preserving the howitzer from being retaken.

"About this time the 2nd Brigade arrived; the 2nd battalion of the 52nd formed on our right and the remainder a second line, when we again charged and drove the enemy before us.

"Another division of the army showed themselves on the left, and the enemy retired in columns. Colonel Sidney Beckwith commanded our Brigade, and showed during the action great coolness and firmness.

Colonel Patrickson commanded the 43rd in this gallant and distinguished action, as brilliant as any during the war."

Napier, in his 'Peninsular History,' relates the distinguished conduct of Lieutenant Hopkins of the 43rd, now Major Sir J. P. Hopkins, K.H., who on his own sole responsibility, and with much presence of mind, took possession of an eminence, repulsing various attacks of the enemy, and greatly conduced to the success of the day. A descriptive letter, written by himself, may be introduced:—

"Early on the morning of the 3rd of April, during heavy rains, the 43rd Regiment was formed in column of companies at their alarm post, close to the miserable Portuguese village in which they had passed the night. They were kept a considerable time under arms, awaiting orders for crossing the river Coa. At last an officer of the Staff rode up, and in a hasty, petulant manner asked Colonel Beckwith, who commanded the Brigade, why he had not marched to the ford. The Colonel replied that he had not received any instructions from the General, Sir William Erskine, for that movement. On this, however, the Colonel marched us rapidly towards the ford. We advanced right in front; four companies of the 95th led. We all crossed the Coa, which from incessant rains had become so swollen as to render the passage difficult and dangerous. The bank on the further side of the river was steep in ascent, covered with thick underwood. We soon gained its summit, halting in front of the brow of the hill to avoid the torrents of rain, fast pouring down, with the wind at our backs. The officers sat themselves, with their backs against a low stone wall. The enemy in position at Sabugal discovered us, and fired several shot. Colonel Beckwith laughingly said, 'Gentlemen, you have an extraordinary taste, to prefer shot to rain.' He ordered the 95th to advance to the town, which was some distance to our left front. They advanced in skirmishing order, under a sharp fire from the enemy, many of the shot reaching us. The atmosphere was greatly darkened by the bad weather.

"The firing on the Rifles became incessant, but they gained their ground up to the French position. Colonel Beckwith sent the 43rd forward in support of the Rifles; they descended towards the river, into a sort of plain, interspersed with trees and underwood. As we approached, the heavy fire of the French marked their line of battle, and the riflemen retired upon us in good order. Colonel Beckwith having gone some distance towards the left, in order to reconnoitre the position of the enemy, Colonel Patrickson was left in the entire command, and close upon the enemy. He gave orders for an instant advance and charge against the line in our front, which was on an eminence. At this moment a slight clearance from the rain enabled me, who was in command of the company on the extreme right of our line, to perceive that at some distance, towards our right rear, a strong detachment of the French from Rovena were directing their march to the ford. I saw all the danger of our being so turned, and immediately requested Captain Duffy, commanding the next company, to allow me to take mine to oppose the attempt of the enemy, who were gaining fast upon our rear. He replied that he could not take upon himself such a responsibility as allowing the separation of my company from the regiment. I said no time should be lost, and that I would take the responsibility at such a moment on myself; and instantly I marched off the company, by bringing up their left shoulders, advancing rapidly to the right towards an eminence at some distance, on which I placed the company in position, fronting the enemy, who were marching round the right flank. I was now quite separated from the Regiment, which was fiercely engaged with the French. I had above 100 men in the company, as several of Duffy's men had followed. The two subalterns with the company were William Freer and Henry Oglander, both most excellent officers.

"The body of French, who were marching towards the Coa, halted on seeing us, and despatched a body of infantry against us. I reserved my fire until they neared the summit of the hill, when I opened upon them, causing them to retire in some disorder to the plain. They again formed, and advanced as before, but were checked, retreating to a greater distance. At this time Colonel Beckwith rode up; I reported all that had occurred, and that the French had brought up two guns in rear. I requested his instructions. He spoke most handsomely to me, approving and thanking me for what I had done, and said that he should give me no orders, but leave me to act entirely on my own judgment, in which he had perfect confidence; that he would not forget me, and that he would bring me to the notice of Lord Wellington. On his leaving, Sir John Elly, who commanded the cavalry came up, when I begged that some dragoons might reinforce me. He made no reply, but rode off, shaking his head as if unable to comply. During this time the enemy were forming in greater strength, they advanced with the drummer beating the *pas de charge*; the officer in command, some paces to the front, leading his people to the hill. William Freer asked permission to go forward and personally engage him; this I of course refused, as his presence with the company was more important.

"The French bravely stood our fire, and their two guns were brought to bear upon us. I ordered a charge, which was done with great spirit, driving the enemy to some distance. Whilst these attacks were made, the Regiment was constantly engaged at

Sabugal. The firing was severe and continuous, never receding nor slackening, thus affording me the utmost confidence; for had not the French left been so severely attacked, they would have been able to detach a body against my rear or on my left flank, which would have compelled me to retreat upon the troops now advancing to our support.

"It was at this time the captured howitzer was left under command of the fire of the 43rd and Rifles, as every attempt of the French to carry it off was ineffectual, causing severe loss both in cavalry and infantry.

"The enemy were still at some distance, and appeared to be reinforced, and intending another attack; and I perceived the 2nd Battalion of the 52nd advancing rapidly. I went to the commanding officer, pointing out the enemy near, and we agreed it would be best for him to form his regiment on the right of my company, and make an immediate advance upon the French, which we did. As we advanced they retired, forming themselves into the line perpendicular to our left, and in continuation of their line to Sabugal, where their chief body was posted. I therefore brought up my right shoulders to front them, extending all my men as skirmishers; the 52nd doing the same to my right, we all commenced skirmishing amid the trees in unabated rain.

"The French showed fight, in their new line, mingling several dragoons with their skirmishers; their sudden debouch from behind the trees at first shook ours and severely wounded several. One man, close to me, was cut in the face, but he would not leave the field. A Manksman, of the name of Cassan, was taking his aim at a dragoon riding towards him, when another horseman appearing suddenly on his right, he turned his firelock and shot him dead, the other dragoon instantly galloping away. Colonel Mellish, of the Staff, rode along the line; he was to be seen in every post of danger, loudly and gallantly cheering the men. Colonel Beckwith, also with the blood streaming down his face, encouraged the men to stand fast against the enemy. Our whole line preserved their ground for some time, until a few of the horsemen getting amongst the skirmishers on the right, a sudden cry, 'The cavalry! the cavalry is in the midst of us!' caused the 52nd to retreat in confusion.

"I was with the skirmishers on the left, and did not retire my men, seeing that the horsemen who had got into the line were so few. Some men of the 52nd remained on the left with my company. It was fortunate that we remained skirmishing, as it prevented one of the colours of the 52nd falling into the hands of the French, owing to the firmness of the men. The officer bearing the colour came up to thank me, at the same time highly praising the gallantry of my men.

"The enemy, perceiving strong reinforcements marching up, commenced a hurried retreat. Seeing that the 52nd were now in line, with an opening between the wings, we forming in the centre, I directed William Freer to wheel the company into sections, as I intended to rejoin the Regiment. He was struck down by a shot in his face, but persevered in marching.

"The French, though fast retreating, were not pursued by the divisions of the army which had joined us; instead of which, the staff officers employed their time in complimenting the regiment for their conduct in the combat, and the pursuit was given up.

"I marched to my regiment along the line leading straight to Sabugal, on which we had last engaged, and came upon the howitzer, at the point where it had been posted by the enemy and where it had been compelled to remain.

"The Combat of Sabugal never having been faithfully rendered, justice has therefore been long withheld from the troops, who so greatly distinguished themselves in that action. Every writer on the subject, with the exception of Sir William Napier, only notices the affair of that day as but little more than a sharp and successful skirmish. Napier's account, however, is too diffuse, and rather inexact in some parts. Brialmont, the Belgian writer of the 'Life of the Duke of Wellington,' in his statement of Sabugal, is evidently led astray by the partial reports of the French generals. As he remarks,—'The French passed the Coa and established themselves at Sabugal. It was here that on the 3rd April Wellington fought the action, of which he says, with some touch of exaggeration, " This was one of the most glorious British troops were ever engaged in." We only know that if glorious to one party it was equally glorious to the other, for Regnier's troops showed themselves by no means inferior to those of the enemy.'

"Regnier, commanding in a chosen position at Sabugal, did not display high generalship, for, having at that point a force of 12,000 infantry, supported by cavalry and artillery, he failed in defeating the attack of 1200 British infantry, who nobly proved themselves the decided superiors of the French.

"Napier was mistaken in ascribing to General Beckwith the

merit of the attack, as Beckwith was then away on the left, which was threatened by a strong force of the enemy. The charge was entirely ordered by Colonel Patrickson of the 43rd. I was close to him when he gave the order, and also when he led the men to the charge, and it was during that advance that I found it requisite to move my company to the right, on the appearance of the French troops threatening that flank.

"It was well known that the Duke of Wellington was the most truthful of men, totally incapable of exaggeration; and it has ever been admitted that he never bestowed praise but where justly due. His report of Sabugal, therefore, that 'this was one of the most glorious actions that British troops were ever engaged in,' ought to be cherished and registered in history, as a lasting tribute to the honour of the British soldier."

Sir W. Napier, in a letter to Colonel Gurwood, wrote:—

"Sir Sidney Beckwith often spoke to me about Hopkins, describing him as one of the finest soldiers he ever beheld; and that so far as a man commanding one company could decide a battle, Hopkins decided the battle of Sabugal; not once, but many times he said this to me."

The loss of the Allies in this fierce conflict amounted to nearly 200 killed and wounded. That of the enemy was enormous. The 43rd had 1 lieutenant, 2 sergeants, 11 rank and file, killed;—2 captains, 2 lieutenants, 1 ensign, and 40 rank and file, wounded. The officers were Lieutenant McDiarmid, killed; Captains Dalzell and O'Flaherty; Lieutenants T. Rylance and Creighton (who died subsequently), and Ensign Carrol, wounded.

Lord Wellington's despatch contained the following paragraphs:—

"Colonel Beckwith's brigade of the Light Division was the first that crossed the Coa, with two squadrons of cavalry upon their right. Four companies of the 95th and three of Colonel Elder's Caçadores drove in the enemy's pickets, and were supported by the 43rd Regiment.

"They were, however, again attacked by a fresh column with cavalry, and retired again to their post, where they were joined by the other brigade of the Light Division, consisting of the 1st and 2nd battalions of the 52nd and 1st Caçadores.

"These troops repulsed the enemy, and Colonel Beckwith's brigade and the 1st battalion of the 52nd again advanced upon them. They were attacked again by a fresh column supported by cavalry, which charged the right, and they took post in an enclosure upon the top of the height, from whence they could protect the howitzer which the 43rd had taken, and they drove back the enemy.

"I consider the action that was fought by the Light Division, by Colonel Beckwith's brigade principally, with the whole of the second corps, to be *one of the most glorious that British troops were ever engaged in*. The 43rd Regiment, under Major Patrickson, particularly distinguished themselves."

Again Lord Wellington, writing to Captain Chapman of the Royal Engineers, on April the 8th, 1811, said:—

"We have given the French a handsome dressing, and I think they will not say again that we are not a manœuvring army. We may not manœuvre as beautifully as they do; but I do not desire better sport than to meet one of their columns *en masse*, with our lines. The poor 2nd corps received a terrible beating from the 43rd and 52nd, on the 3rd."

The French retired on Ciudad Rodrigo and Salamanca. The Light Division advanced towards Gallegos in pursuit, while the rest of the army remained in reserve, on the Coa. On the 5th Massena crossed the frontier of Portugal, exactly thirty days since the evacuation of Santarem. It must be conceded that the French General evinced great military ability in conducting his retreat.

Discussions have arisen as to the capture of the howitzer at Sabugal. Lord Wellington distinctly says in his despatches, that it was taken by the 43rd. Napier as distinctly claims it for the same regiment. He says, "A strong column of infantry, rushing up the hill, endeavoured to retake the howitzer, which was on the edge of the descent, and only fifty yards from the wall; but no man could reach it and live, so deadly was the fire of the 43rd."

> "Sabugal's Bridge and Coa's gory flood,
> The hill beyond, where *one* * brave band withstood
> A host, and seizing, heedless of its roar,
> The hostile gun away in triumph bore."

* *Note in the Original.*—" The 43rd Regiment."

After many years, Colonel Gurwood attributed the exploit to the 52nd, and circulated a pamphlet in corroboration, which also impugned the credibility of Napier on other points. Every officer, however, of the 43rd present during the action, confirmed the original statement, and General Sir G. Brown, G.C.B.—at that time Captain of the 43rd—in a letter to Napier, dated, " Horse Guards, June 21st, 1845," wrote, " The howitzer was as safely deposited under the fire of the 43rd, when the 52nd, or a portion of it, came up, as if it had been drawn to the rear of the regiment. Neither was this point ever questioned at the time, or as far as I know, for five-and-twenty years afterwards. The 43rd never retired further than behind the stone wall to renew their formation, which had been somewhat broken in driving the enemy over the hill and taking the said gun on the crest of it."

In Captain Moorsom's 'Record of the 52nd,' published in 1860, he again claims the capture of the howitzer, alleging that though it first fell into the hands of the 43rd, it was retaken by the enemy, and eventually recaptured by a company of the 52nd, commanded by Lieutenant Love. General Sir J. Fergusson, late Colonel of the regiment, repudiated this tale, desired it might be erased from the regimental records, and accredited where due—to the 43rd—their gallant and united brothers-in-arms.

Massena's sudden retreat from Sabugal, left Almeida to its fate, and it was immediately invested by the British.

On the 2nd of May, the French threw a large convoy into Ciudad Rodrigo. The Light Division fell back from Gallegos, towards the plains of Fuentes d'Onoro, and next day filed through the village, and took post on the high ground behind Almeida, the left of our army resting near Fort Conception, while our right was at Fuentes, with the river Dos Casas in front.

FUENTES D'ONORO.

On the 3rd of May the enemy attacked with great vigour, and drove our troops from the village of Fuentes, but it was soon regained by a determined charge, and our antagonists forced across the river. In these struggles both sides suffered severely; our troops continued to occupy the village during the night, and next day, upon Massena assuming command, some changes of position took place, and he made preparations for a grand attack.

On the 5th he was observed moving troops towards their left, and in consequence the Light Division, with the cavalry, were sent to support our right, where the French had already made some cavalry charges. The regiments of the Light Division were then thrown into squares. Norman Ramsay's troop of horse artillery was for a moment cut off, but reformed in a most dashing manner, and driving through the French, regained our lines in full view of the 43rd's square. Our right being outflanked in consequence of the position being too extended, the Light Division retired in squares under a heavy cannonade, every moment threatened by cavalry; but quickly concentrating in a closer and more compact body, the enemy abandoned their plan of forcing the right. Hard fighting took place in the village of Fuentes; the lower part being taken and retaken several times, and finally our troops retained the upper part.

In the evening the 1st brigade of the Light Division

occupied the village. Being well accustomed to outpost duty, they quietly occupied all the advanced posts, directing the men not to fire excepting under great emergency, and by this well-timed precaution quiet was soon established. They exchanged the dead and wounded strewn around, and strongly intrenched themselves. On the 10th of May the enemy retired across the Aguada, relinquishing farther idea of a second invasion of Portugal, and at midnight Regnier blew up the works of Almeida. In a compact column he managed to pass the English pickets and lines, and carried off his entire garrison, with the exception of three hundred of his men, who were taken prisoners. This brilliant exploit reflected little credit on the blockading force. Lord Wellington issued severe orders in consequence.

In the action of Fuentes d'Onoro the British had 1500 killed and wounded, and 300 taken prisoners. The loss of the French was more than double.

The French withdrew to Salamanca. The Light Division formed part of the force left with Sir Brent Spencer, while Lord Wellington, with two divisions, moved south to the relief of Beresford, and for the purpose of attacking Badajoz. It had been invested on the 5th May, and on the 12th the siege was raised. On the 16th the battle of Albuera was fought and won by British valour; the Fusileers covered themselves with glory.

The Light Division again occupied its old station, taking possession of Gallegos, Alameda, and Espeja, where they continued until the 6th of June. On that day Marshal Marmont (who had succeeded Massena in command of the French army), having introduced a convoy into Ciudad Rodrigo, moved out and directed his march upon Gallegos and Espeja, when the division retreated across the plain upon Alfyates, and General Spencer withdrew behind the Coa. Finding the French moving by the pass Barros, his route was directed by Sorto, Penamacour, across the pontoon-bridge at Villa Velha, arriving at Arronches on the 22nd, and took up ground at Monte Reguengo, on the Ceira, ready to move into position, if necessary, behind Campo Mayor.

While stationed at Campo Mayor, the 43rd received a splendid draft from the 2nd battalion, consisting of 1 major, 3 captains, 12 subalterns, 12 sergeants, and 345 rank and file.

Lieutenant Cooke, of the regiment, now Lieutenant-Colonel Sir J. H. Cooke, Lieutenant of Her Majesty's Yeoman of the Guard, who accompanied this draft, gives the following animated account of his first impression of the far-famed Light Division :—" On the 20th of July we descended into the valley, and at the edge of a wood awaited the coming of the division, from an advanced camp on their way to Castello de Vida. Every eye was on the stretch, and in the distance we descried a cloud of dust rolling towards us, the bright sparkling rays of the sunbeams playing on the soldiers' breast-plates, when suddenly the leading regiment of the Light Division burst forth; their bronzed countenances and light knapsacks, and their order of march, all united to inspire a conviction that their early discipline had not only been maintained amidst privations, battles, and camps, but had become matured by experience. They had traversed mountains and forded rivers; the grim and icy hand of death had grasped many in the unhealthy marshes of the Alentejo, and with sure effect had scattered balls amidst their ranks without distinction : yet the remainder of these veterans were still bent onwards, to gather fresh laurels in the rugged and uncertain paths of fortune. Seven battalions of light infantry and riflemen defiled before us with their threadbare jackets, their brawny necks loosened from their stocks, their wide and patched trowsers of various colours, and brown-barrelled arms slung over their shoulders, or carelessly held in their hands, whilst a joyous buzz ran through the cross-belted ranks, as their soldier-like faces glanced towards us, to greet many of their old comrades, now about to join in their arduous toils after a long separation. A cloud of dust alone marked their further progress as they receded from our view. Following in succession, we brought up the rear. At the expiration of an hour's march, we entered a wood, formed column, called the roll, and the whole division was then dismissed. The assembled multitude of voices, the tearing and cutting down of branches of trees, crackling of fires, rattling of canteens, shooting of bullocks through the head, and the hurrying of parties of soldiers for rum and biscuit for rations, the neighing of horses, braying asses and rampant mules, all resounded throughout the forest, giving new life and many echoes to its most intricate recesses. Groups of officers stood in circles; every countenance seemed decked in smiles, and a hearty welcome greeted us from all hands.

"Under the wide-spreading branches of a venerable cork-tree, decorated with pack-saddles, accoutrements, and other military trappings, dinner was served up and laid out on a pair of hampers, which served us instead of a table. Beef, biscuit, tea, rum, and wine, composed our fare; it being a usual custom to join breakfast and dinner, so as to make one meal serve for the twenty-four hours, the troops merely halting to cook and refresh themselves during the heat of the day. A more happy meal, I can safely say, I never partook of; and with infinite satisfaction did I regard the purple jackets and battered epaulettes of my companions. Our small keg of wine being emptied, the word passed to pack up and accoutre; and, in an incredible short space of time, the column re-formed.

"The 'assembly' sounded—the signal for march,—threes, from the right of companies, the bands struck up, and at the end of two hours' march, and towards nightfall, we entered another wood. The same ceremony gone through as already described, the blankets were spread out, the earth our bed, knapsacks our pillows, and the overhanging trees our canopy; the busy hum of life no longer vibrated through the bivouac, and thousands of soldiers slumbered and reposed their weary limbs, lying scattered through the forest or around the embers of expiring fires. My companions insisted on stretching themselves on each side of me, protesting that they ought to do this, as a protection against cold, for the first two or three nights, since a very heavy dew fell, so as almost to wet us through the blankets, notwithstanding the great heat of the weather by day."

Towards the end of July, Marmont retraced his steps to Salamanca, and the Light Division theirs to the banks of the Aguada, where they arrived on the 9th of August.

On the 29th, Major Hungerford Elers, of the 43rd, died at Celorico, of a fever brought on by unremitting exertions in his professional duties. The following memorandum was inserted in the orderly-book:—" Sept. 5th 1811. The Commanding Officer is much concerned to communicate to the regiment, that he has received accounts of the death of Major Elers, at Celorico, on the 29th ult. The mournful fate of an officer who had so long served in the regiment, who was so sincere a friend to the honour and interest of the corps, must be lamented by officers and soldiers. As a mark of respect for the memory of one so justly esteemed, it is requested that such officers as have it in their power will put on mourning, to be worn for three days."

All had remained tranquil until the 23rd September, when the French advanced with a strong convoy for the relief of Ciudad Rodrigo, and the division retired to Castel Branco. Two affairs with the enemy took place; one at El Boden, the other at Aldea de Ponte.

When Marmont had accomplished his object of succouring Ciudad Rodrigo, he returned to Salamanca, and the Light Division once more to their old cantonments, where they remained until the end of the year.

1812.

STORMING OF CIUDAD RODRIGO.

The campaign of 1812 commenced early. On the 8th of January the Light Division assembled from its cantonments, and invested Ciudad Rodrigo. During the night, six companies of volunteers—including Captains Ferguson's and Duffy's of the 43rd—carried by escalade, in a most masterly style, the outwork of St. Francesco. The 43rd lost one sergeant, and a few privates were wounded. With the exception of one man, the entire garrison was captured, and the first parallel, under heavy fire, commenced against the town. The duties of the trenches were taken by the Light 1st, 3rd, and 4th Divisions, relieving each other every twenty-four hours; the Light returning to their quarters — a distance of four leagues. The weather was severe, with sharp frosts, and the Aguada had to be forded going and returning.

On the 19th, two breaches having been pronounced practicable, the place was carried. The Light Division, ordered to assault out of its turn, was formed behind the Convent of St. Francesco at about 8 P.M. The storming party consisted of 100 volunteers from each British regiment. The 43rd was led by Captain James Fergusson, with Lieutenants Bramwell, Steel, and O'Connell; the 52nd contingent by Captain James; that of the 95th Rifles by Captain Mitchell, and the forlorn hope, by Lieutenant Gurwood; all under Major Napier of the

52nd, who directed that when the breach was carried, the 43rd party should clear the ramparts to the right, and the 52nd to the left, towards the great breach.

The forlorn hope led, and the storming party followed immediately. They hurried rapidly on, hearing the fire from the 3rd Division—ordered simultaneously to attack the great breach—and passing over the glacis, descended into the ditch near the ravelin, under a heavy fire. The forlorn hope were placing ladders against the face of the work, when Lieutenant Elliott of the Royal Engineers exclaimed, " You are wrong! this is the way to the breach in the *fausse braie*." The breach in the body of the place was then reached and carried in a moment. A gun was stretched across the entrance, near which some of the enemy were bayoneted.

Israel Wild, a private of the 43rd, was the first to mount the breach in the *fausse braie*, but no man could claim being the first to enter the great breach in the body of the place, as it was a neck-and-neck rush of from thirty to forty. The forlorn hope having gone too far to the left, were not actually the first, though amongst those to claim the honour,—Lieutenant Steel of the 43rd and Lieutenant Gurwood inclusive.

Before carrying the little breach the 43rd party cleared the rampart to the right, driving the enemy from their different traverses, until reaching the great breach. At this time the great breach had not been carried, and was obstinately defended by the enemy. Houses bearing upon it had been loopholed, and the descent into the town from the top of the rampart was considerable. The moment the storming party of the Light Division arrived at the spot, they made a determined attack upon the hostile defences, taking them in flank. At the same time the 3rd Division storming party entered the breach, and Ciudad Rodrigo was won.

The French had 300 killed, and 1500 made prisoners. The English lost 90 officers, and 1200 soldiers; of these, 650 men and 60 officers were slain or hurt at the breaches. The casualties in the 43rd were:—1 lieutenant, 1 sergeant, and 13 rank and file, killed; 1 captain, 1 lieutenant, 2 sergeants, and 35 rank and file, wounded. The officer killed was Lieutenant Bramwell of the storming party, who died of his wounds; those wounded were Captain Ferguson and Lieutenant Pattenson. Generals Craufurd and Mackinnon were killed; the former, shot through his lungs, survived until the 24th. Above 150 pieces of artillery were taken, including Marmont's battering train.

After the assault, the regiment returned to its cantonments for some six weeks.

SIEGE AND STORMING OF BADAJOZ.

After the fall of Ciudad Rodrigo, Lord Wellington moved south, to attempt the capture of Badajoz, a strong fortress on the left bank of the Guadiana, with a garrison of 5000 men, commanded by General Philippon, a first-rate engineer, and reputed in all respects a man of great ability. On the 16th of March the place was invested, trenches were opened, and the first parallel completed. As the 43rd fell in before daylight on the 18th, to relieve the 88th, who had first broken ground, one of the Connaught Rangers exclaimed with an oath, "Och! boys, SOUDRADRODRAGO was but a *flay-bite to this*." The stupendous nature of the undertaking was already recognized by the soldiers.

On the 19th the garrison made a sally, when a hot fight ensued. The enemy was beaten back in confusion, losing above 300 men. On the 25th, Fort Picurina, an important outwork, was carried by assault. On the 6th of April two breaches were reported practicable, and on that night the great conflict took place. Desperate it was expected to be, and most desperate it proved.

The day had been fine; all the soldiers, in high spirits, were cleaning themselves and accoutrements as if for a review. At half-past 8 P.M., the ranks were formed, and the roll called in an undertone.

Before the 43rd joined the division, Colonel McLeod long and earnestly addressed his men, expressing entire confidence in the result of the attack, and concluded by impressing that he trusted to the honour of all listening, to preserve discipline, and to refrain from any species of cruelty on the defenceless inhabitants.

As at Ciudad Rodrigo, the 43rd, 52nd, and 95th Regiments furnished each one hundred volunteers, with officers. The 43rd party was again commanded by Captain Fergusson, notwithstanding his having at the time two unhealed wounds; with him were Lieutenants Duncan Campbell and Alexander Steel, while Lieutenant Harvest was to lead the forlorn hope. In the most profound silence the division drew up behind a large quarry, about three hundred yards from the breaches made in the bastions of La Trinadad and Santa Maria. A small stream separated the Light from the 4th Division. A voice was suddenly heard giving orders about the ladders in that direction, so loud that it might have reached the ramparts. Everyone was indignant, and McLeod sent to say that he would report the circumstance to the Commander-in-Chief. Luckily, nothing beyond croaking of frogs responded to the ill-timed voice. At 10 o'clock, a carcass was thrown from the town, which illuminated the ground for many hundred yards. Two or three fire-balls followed.

Soon after, a suppressed whispering announced that the forlorn hope was stealing forward, heading the storming parties, and in two moments more the division followed. One single French musket-shot resounded from the breaches. All with great regularity gained ground leisurely but silently; the 43rd, 52nd, and a part of the Rifle corps gradually closed to columns of quarter distance. The ladders were placed on the edge of the ditch, and they were descending in wrapt stillness, when suddenly an explosion took place at the foot of the trenches, and a burst of light disclosed the exact position. The ramparts were crowded with troops, who, well prepared, let loose every possible implement of destruction, while all beneath seemed convulsed. A succession of explosions, with unceasing roar of musketry, soon levelled the party, very few escaping. Captain Fergusson, amongst the foremost, was wounded in the head.

But three ladders were placed down the counterscarp for the Light Division to gain the ditch, and were exactly opposite the centre breach. With amazing resolution, the whole division rushed to the assault. The soldiers swung themselves down, cheering lustily. At the bottom of the ladders, Lieutenant Pollock, 43rd, who was in command of Lord Fitzroy Somerset's company, with Cooke, Considine, and Madden, met Captain Duffy of the regiment, who exclaimed, "Pollock! they," meaning the storming party and the forlorn hope, "are all wrong; they have gone to the 4th Division breach," pointing at the same time to the small one. Thus undesignedly this company were the first up to the sword-blades. To get into Badajoz by that breach was impossible. The men repeatedly tried and failed; the French soldiers stationed behind the bristling *chevaux-de-frise*, deliberately killing every one who approached. Cannon shot alone could have levelled or destroyed them. The left breach, at the Santa Maria bastion, was not attempted until near twelve o'clock, when Lieutenant Shaw, of the 43rd, with great difficulty collected about seventy men of different regiments, and made an effort to gain the top. The whole party was prostrated by two rounds of grape and musketry, "and the intrepid Shaw stood alone."

Meantime the 3rd Division carried the castle by escalade, and the 5th, under Walker, entered the town by the San Vincente Bastion, and thus Badajoz was won. At midnight the 4th and Light Divisions retired, but many soldiers remained in the ditch, unable to ascend the ladders owing to the heaps of dead and wounded. The troops, excited beyond control by the desperate service in which they had been engaged, sacked the place, plundered the houses, ripped up furniture in search of treasure, and appropriated all they could find.

Generals Picton, Colville, Kempt, Harvey, Bowes, Walker, Champlemond (Portuguese), and almost every officer commanding a regiment, besides more than 300 other officers, and nearly 5000 gallant veterans, fell in the breaches and round the walls. The 43rd had to mourn the loss of their chief, the gallant M'Leod, who was killed while trying to force the left corner of the large breach. He received his mortal wound within three yards of the enemy. The three British regiments of the Light Division, as brave and well disciplined soldiers as ever stood under arms, suffered dreadfully in the assault, nearly half their number perishing. The loss of the 43rd, as shown by Lord Wellington's despatch, exceeded that of any other regiment employed in the operations. They lost 20 officers and 335 sergeants and privates, killed and wounded: killed, 1 lieut.-colonel, 3 lieutenants, 4 sergeants, and 74 rank and file; wounded,

1 major, 3 captains, 12 lieutenants, 1 ensign, 18 sergeants, 1 bugler, and 238 rank and file.

Officers Killed.

Lieut.-Colonel Charles McLeod.
Lieutenant Horatio Harvest, forlorn hope.
    „   Charles Taggart.
    „   E. L. Hodgson, died of wound, 8th April.

Wounded.

Major John Wells, severely.
Captain James Fergusson, ditto.
    „   George Johnston, slightly.
    „   L. Strode, ditto.
Lieutenant S. Pollock, severely.
    „   G. Rideout, ditto.
    „   Thos. Capel, ditto.
    „   W. Freer, right arm amputated.
    „   H. Oglander, left arm ditto.
    „   Wyndham Madden, severely.
    „   Edw. Freer.
    „   Jas. Considine.
    „   A. M. Baillie.
    „   John O'Connell.
    „   John Cooke.
Ensign Wilkinson.

Lieut.-Colonel Charles M'Leod of the 43rd had early given proofs of ardent military attachment. His services commenced under his father's friend, Lord Cornwallis; upon whose death in India he was the bearer of despatches to England announcing that event. He was next employed at Copenhagen, and subsequently in the Peninsula; and succeeded to the command of the regiment at the affair on the Coa, when Hull was killed. His character and services are best epitomised in the words of the illustrious commander who, with the glory of his own deeds, has transmitted to posterity the name of M'Leod. The following is an extract from Lord Wellington's despatch, announcing the fall of Badajoz:—

"In Lieut.-Colonel M'Leod, of the 43rd Regiment, who was killed in the breach, His Majesty has sustained the loss of an officer who was an ornament to his profession, and was capable of rendering the most important services to his country."

M'Leod, who had only attained his twenty-seventh year, was buried amid springing corn, on the slope of a hill opposite to the regimental camp. Six sorrowing hearts, the only officers of the 43rd able to stand, laid him in his grave. His brother officers, desirous of recording their affection and respect, erected a monument to his memory in Westminster Abbey, on which is engraved the above extract.

The day following the fall of Badajoz, as Lieutenant Pollock lay suffering in his tent, a private of his company brought him an offering of three fine fowls, remarking that they would make good broth. This man had been rather a disorderly character, and Pollock had on many occasions administered punishments. He was therefore surprised by the act, and said, "Howard, you are the last man in the company from whom I should expect such attention." "Sir," replied Howard, "I have gratitude. You might have had me flogged twenty times; but, Sir, you always punished me yourself, and I have gratitude."

This anecdote proves the fallacy erroneously held by many, that the British soldier is a mere machine, devoid of susceptibility and generosity of feeling towards his officers. Let officers but treat their men as brethren, with compatible kindness and consideration, and no attachment will be closer knit or more enduring. Such was the system inculcated in the 43rd.

The British camp at Badajoz broke up on the 11th, leaving a corps to repair the defences, under General Graham, afterwards Lord Lynedoch.

Soon after Brevet-Major William Napier joined and

assumed the command. Major Hearne succeeded to the lieut.-colonelcy of the lamented M'Leod, and Napier became regimental major.

While the British army was engaged before Badajoz, Marshal Marmont entered Portugal, having masked Ciudad Rodrigo, and threatened an assault on Almeida. On the 12th of June the British army, in concentrated force, crossed the river Aguada, the Light Division leading the centre column, and after a long march took up a position in front of Salamanca—the French, under Marmont, being about two miles distant. On the 16th July the Light Division, by a night march, moved to Castrijon. The French retired from Salamanca, leaving 800 men to garrison the three forts, when the 6th Division took possession of the town, and St. Vincente being in flames, the enemy permitted our troops to ascend the breaches without opposition.

On the 18th of July, Marmont, with his whole force, appeared before Castrijon, making a very determined attempt to cut off the Light and 4th Divisions. So resolutely did he press forward that frequently during the day the advanced columns were marching abreast of each other within musket range, yet so steadily was the retreat conducted, that little loss resulted.

On the 19th Lord Wellington rode up to Lieutenant Wilkinson of the 43rd, on picket, and asked, "What are the enemy doing?" Wilkinson replied, "The French are in motion." The Commander-in-Chief said, "Yes,— to the right, now," and ordered the 1st Brigade of the Light Division to make a corresponding movement.

On the 21st both armies crossed to the left bank of the Tormes. This movement was made after dark, under an appalling storm of thunder and lightning, of which the flashes were so vivid as to daze and blind the men for minutes together. The British again took up the position of St. Cristoval, when the Light Division formed the extreme left, as a check upon the attitude assumed by the right Division of the French army.

On the afternoon of the 22nd Marmont made a sudden movement to the left, and attempted to cut in on the British communications with Portugal. Wellington instantly seized the opportunity, and gave the signal for a general attack.

BATTLE OF SALAMANCA.

This was the first general action in the Peninsular War where Lord Wellington attacked. The battle began on the right, where the 3rd Division, under Major-General Pakenham, carried everything before them. The 4th and 5th Divisions assailed the French centre, while Pack's brigade of Portuguese, more to the left, followed the example, but was repulsed. By 6 o'clock the battle was at its height. The Prince of Orange, A.D.C., then rode up, and ordered the Light Division to move on the left attack, in open columns, which they did, and then closed to quarter distance. The shades of evening were beginning to fall when the enemy made their last effort, amid flashes of cannon and small arms. Lord Wellington was within fifty yards of the front when the advance commenced firing. As he passed the 43rd, he called out, " Come, fix your bayonets, my brave fellows," which they instantly obeyed, and were upon the point of charging, when the enemy, having fired a volley or two, which passed mostly over their heads, disappeared.

" In the battle of Salamanca the 43rd led the heavy column employed to drive back Foy's Division and seize the ford of Huerta, and on that occasion the Regiment made a very extraordinary advance in line for a distance of three miles under a cannonade, which, though not heavy was constant, with as clear and firm a line as at a review. What renders the march more remarkable is that it was made after dark; the Regiment kept its line simply by the touch to the centre; and the late General Shaw Kennedy, who commanded the left centre company on that occasion, declared that the line was so well kept as to have been able at any moment to fire a volley and charge with the bayonet. Major Napier rode during the whole time in front of the left centre company, and from time to time joked with Captain Shaw on the safety of the humble pedestrian compared with the lot of a mounted officer, as the round shot all flew over the heads of the men on foot."

The advance and bearing of the regiment on this occasion so delighted Lord Wellington, that the following morning, during breakfast, it was the theme of his repeated encomium and admiration.

As night advanced firing ceased, and the French made no further resistance. Marmont being severely wounded, Clausel assumed command and conducted the retreat.

This battle served to show the decline of the French power and prestige in Europe, and placed for the first time our army in a position free to pursue the enemy at pleasure. It was fought on a Sunday, and lasted six hours. The inhabitants of Salamanca crowded the churches, offering up prayers and thanksgivings for the success of the British arms.

The Light Division continued its movement, and bivouacked at midnight round a village. The loss of the French exceeded 12,000. The allies had 694 killed, and 4270 wounded; of which numbers, 2714 were British, 1552 Portuguese, and the large balance of *four* Spaniards. The proportion of officers was very great. The 43rd had 1 Captain, 1 Lieutenant, 2 Sergeants, and 13 rank and file, wounded. The officers were Captain William Haverfield and Lieutenant George Rideout.

As morning dawned the Light Division advanced,

formed *en masse*, while the heavy German dragoons made a brilliant charge, breaking the enemy's rear-guard, posted on the heights of La Serna, and took several hundred prisoners before they had time to complete their squares. Clausel then carried his army off, marching fifty miles in thirty-six hours. On the 28th the Light Division bivouacked round Olmedo, where Lord Wellington gave a ball, a general invitation to all officers being issued.

The enemy continued his flight over the Douro. While the impedimenta of the 43rd was crossing, an officer's bâtman of the regiment, with a pony, got out of his depth, and both were quickly carried down the stream. The soldier disdained, even at the risk of life, to quit his charge, and held on until a rope was thrown to him, by aid of which he conveyed the little animal and his master's portmanteau safe on shore. On the 30th Lord Wellington entered Valladolid, Clausel clearing out rapidly on his approach, and in his hurry leaving behind seventeen pieces of artillery, considerable stores, with 800 sick and wounded. The heads of our columns were now directed towards Madrid, but want of necessary supplies retarded operations, and only by dint of stringent exertion were partial provisions provided.

King Joseph, who, hoping to support Marmont, had advanced, now rapidly fell back, literally flitting through his capital. On the 9th of August Wellington's headquarters were at St. Ildefonso, and on the two following days his victorious troops, defiling by the passes of Guadarama and Naval Serrada, crossed the mountains and gained the plain in which Madrid is situated. The Light Division bivouacked in the park of the Escurial, from whence the 43rd, commanded by Major Napier, marched into the city. On the 12th Lord Wellington entered Madrid at the head of his army, and was received with intense and natural excitement. He proceeded at once to reconnoitre the defences of the Retiro, where Joseph had left a garrison. On the following evening the outer fortification of a triple line of defence was forced and next morning the French commandant surrendered; his garrison, amounting to 2000 men, being taken prisoners of war. An arsenal containing 20,000 stand of arms, 180 pieces of artillery, military stores of every description, and two eagles, rewarded the victors.

The troops were quartered in various convents and monasteries, while the officers luxuriated in splendid palaces and villas; rather a contrast to their previous sixty nights' quarters, where the heavens had been their only canopy, muddy fields and wet blankets their only couch, and covering. One of the young subs. of the 43rd found himself told off to a bed of down hung with white satin curtains and long gold-bullion fringes, the whole surrounded by a gilt helmet and waving plumes of ostrich feather.

As the Madrilenos began to reflect on the possible restoration of French rule, their goodwill cooled, and their *vivas* grew fainter when called upon to furnish supplies. Supplies of all kinds in Madrid were at that time exorbitantly dear,—an hypothesis not easily explained, seeing that the inhabitants lived almost entirely on fruit and vegetables, regarding Gaspachio — *soupe maigre* — composed of water, garlic, and onions, as a sumptuous repast.

On the 22nd a detachment from the 2nd Battalion joined. Its strength on landing at Lisbon was—4 captains, 7 lieutenants, 5 ensigns, and 200 rank and file; but, whether owing to the intense heat or the injudicious marching in the sun, only 3 captains, 2 lieutenants, 1 ensign, 2 sergeants, and 18 rank and file reached Madrid. Many perished from fever and ague, and 1 captain, 5 lieutenants, 4 ensigns, 2 sergeants, and 182 rank and file, were left sick at various hospital stations between Lisbon and Madrid. Lieutenant Fidlor expired at Madrid from the effects of the march. War carries many destroying adjuncts in its train beyond the deadly casualties of the field.

An empty money chest, difficulty in procuring sustenance, combined with a menacing concentration of French troops, determined Lord Wellington on the capture of Burgos as a *point d'appui*. Accordingly he sent forward three divisions, with some Portuguese and cavalry, following in person on September 1. The attack failed, and Soult now approaching in force from the south led to a retreat towards the frontiers of Portugal.

Hill, in command of the division at Madrid, left the capital, retiring slowly towards Salamanca, in order to keep communication open with the main body. On the 8th of November a junction was effected at Alba de Tormes, and by the 12th the whole British army, with a considerable number of Spanish troops, was assembled at Salamanca.

Soult had arrived and taken supreme command on precisely the same position occupied by Marmont on the 22nd of July. Lord Wellington wished and waited for a great battle there; but the French Marshal hesitated. Corunna had taught him of what stuff an English army was composed, when they turned and stood at bay on ground of their own selection. On the 14th Nov. all left Salamanca and moved towards Alba de Tormes, the enemy having crossed two leagues above that town. Under a fire of cannon, Wellington made a reconnoissance, and found them strongly posted on the left of the Tormes, at Mozarbes. The English advance fell back, the baggage animals were ordered to the rear, and all moved towards the forest in dense columns by echelon of divisions. The Light Division acted as rear-guard.

COMBAT OF THE HUEBRA.

Next A.M., as the men were roasting acorns to satisfy the cravings of hunger, after passing a wretched night of unmitigated rain under the trees, an officer suddenly espied French heavy cavalry stealing through the wood, who would have taken him prisoner, but for the speed of his English horse. Passing at full gallop, he exclaimed, "The enemy's cavalry! fall in!" Instantly the division seized their arms, debouched, and formed in contiguous columns, horse artillery filling up the intervals. In the afternoon, a report spread that the baggage had been captured, and Lieut.-General Sir Edward Paget, second in command, taken. This last rumour proved correct, and happened on the road the division was compelled to traverse. Lord Wellington now joined, and rode on the left flank of the column. The enemy's infantry, mixed with cavalry, began to come up in force. Wellington made a sweep round the column to look for the best fighting ground, and when the division emerged from the forest they were saluted on the left by a number of the enemy's guns posted on a high hill just above San Muñoz.

They at once broke into double time across the plain, and made for the ford of the river Huebra. The 7th division was already formed in close column on the opposite side, suffering terribly from the effect of round shot. Two squadrons of heavy dragoons protected the brigade of the Light Division. All plunged into the water under sharp artillery practice, scrambled up the steep bank on the other side, causing momentary confusion. Lord Wellington rode up in front of No. 1 company of the 43rd, and regarding them placidly, simply said, "The enemy must not cross here." At that moment a round shot carried off one of the legs of Lieutenant George Rideout of the regiment, and knocked a German hussar from his horse.

Lieutenant Rideout died from the effect of the shock.

LIGHT DIVISION THEATRE.

GALLEGOS.

On Saturday Evening, the 6th. of March, 1813.

WILL BE PERFORMED.

FORTUNE'S FROLIC.

MEN.

Robin Roughead,	Lt. Hennel, 43d. Regt.
Snacks,	Lt. Pattenson, 43d. Regt.
Mr. Franks,	Lt. Pemberton. 95th. Regt.
Rattle,	Lt. Havelock, 43d. Regt.
Clown,	Lt. Hopewood, 95th. Regt.
Servant,	Lt. Hamilton, 95th. Regt.

WOMEN.

Miss Nancy,	Lt. Lord C. Spencer, 95th. Regt.
Dolly,	Lt. Hble. C. Gore, 43d. Regt.
Margery,	Lt. Grubbe, 43d. Regt.
Villagers, &c.	

TO WHICH WILL BE ADDED THE FARCE OF

RAISING THE WIND.

MEN.

Plainway,	Lt. Pattenson, 43d. Regt.
Fainwou'd,	Lt. Hopewood, 95th. Regt.
Diddler,	Capt. Cator, Royal Artillery.
Sam,	Lt. Hennel, 43d. Regt.
Richard,	Lt. Considine, 43d. Regt.
Waiter,	Lt. Hamilton, 95th Regt.

WOMEN.

Peggy,	Lt. Ed. Freer, 43d. Regt.
Miss Durable,	Capt. Hobkirk, 43d. Regt.

NO ADMITTANCE BEHIND THE SCENES.

VIVAT WELLINGTON.

[PRINTED AT FRENEDA.]

At the battle of Salamanca he had been struck by a ball, and also slightly wounded at Badajoz. He was much liked and esteemed in the regiment, and was afterwards buried by the side of General Craufurd at Ciudad Rodrigo. Three companies of the 43rd, which had been left in the wood, crossed the Huebra at full speed pursued by the enemy, with the round shot of both armies flying over their heads; but they at last withdrew, and the division bivouacked for the night, entering on Ciudad Rodrigo the following day, and thus ended what is termed the retreat of Burgos.

The loss of the 43rd at the passage of the Huebra consisted of Lieutenant Rideout and Baillie, wounded; 1 sergeant killed, and 1 sergeant and 10 rank and file wounded; 3 sergeants and 22 rank and file were missing, of whom some were taken, and others died of wounds, fatigue, or privation.

Many men of the regiment, who had been with Sir John Moore, declared that the retreat from Salamanca, though shorter, was quite as severe as that to Corunna. There they were amply provisioned; here neither bread nor biscuit was forthcoming, owing to the culpable neglect of the commissariat. In consequence, the commissary-general of the Light Division was dismissed, and the underlings tried by court-martial.

The British army then went into winter cantonments. The Light Division remained near Rodrigo; the headquarters of the 1st Brigade, to which the 43rd was attached, being at Gallegos. Lord Wellington established his headquarters at Frenada, within the frontiers of Portugal. During the winter both men and officers, among their relaxations, amused themselves by getting up private theatricals. The 43rd came out particularly strong, evincing unrivalled talent in the histrionic art. The appended play-bill is a fac-simile of one of their programmes:—

It must be owned that considerable dissatisfaction reigned in England that greater results had not been achieved by the eventful campaign of 1812. Dazzled by its opening brilliancy, the nation anticipated an uninterrupted series of decisive victories. Ballasteros, the Spanish General, whose disobedient and wrong-headed conduct rendered the retreat from the capital imperative, and whose pride and jealousy went far to imperil the whole of the British army, had the hardihood to reflect upon the Commander-in-Chief for relinquishing Madrid, and failing to capture Burgos. The Government Opposition papers caught up the protest, and inserted many trenchant and strong animadversions. Lord Wellington's own brief and ready words offer the most terse and truthful commentary on his adopted policy. "I am much afraid," he wrote, "from what I see in the newspapers, that the public will be much disappointed at the result of the campaign, notwithstanding that it is, in fact, the most successful in all its circumstances, and has produced, for the common cause more important results than any in which the British army has been engaged for the last century. We have taken Ciudad Rodrigo, Badajoz, and Salamanca, and the Retiro has surrendered. In the mean time the Allies have taken Astorga, Consuegra, and Guadalaxara, besides other places, In the ten months elapsed since January, this army has sent to England little short of 20,000 prisoners, and they have taken and destroyed, or retained for their own use, the enemy's arsenals in Ciudad Rodrigo, Badajoz, Salamanca, Valladolid, Madrid, Astorga, Seville, and the lines before Cadiz, &c. Upon the whole we have taken or destroyed, or we now possess, little short of 3000 pieces of cannon. The siege of Cadiz has been raised, and all the country south of the Tagus has been cleared of the enemy."

1813.

The Russian catastrophe not only prevented Napoleon from reinforcing his armies in Spain, but obliged him to recall Soult, with 20,000 men; 70,000 remained, besides those under Suchet in the eastern provinces, and were then placed under command of General Reille, having headquarters at Valladolid. The army of the centre, under Drouet, was distributed round Madrid, while that of the south had its headquarters at Toledo. Nominally, these forces were under King Joseph, but practically handled by Marshal Jourdain. Clausel and Foy commanded separate divisions in Arragon and Biscay. The Spanish Government nominated the Marquis of Wellington their Commander-in-Chief. But his reliable forces only consisted of about 36,000 British and Portuguese infantry, with 6000 cavalry.

Early in April the 43rd received a draft from England of 1 captain, 6 subalterns, 6 sergeants, and 180 rank and file. On the day of their arrival the Light Division, commanded by Major-General Alten, formed in line and passed in review before Lord Wellington. The 43rd mustered 10 captains, 29 subalterns, and 80 men per company.

Active operations commenced in the middle of May, and in less than five weeks the main army of the French, under Joseph Buonaparte, was driven from Portugal to the Pyrenees. On the 26th of May the division halted in a wood below Salamanca. Next day the 43rd went into the town, and although the French had only left the previous night, the inhabitants appeared quite tranquil, with their shops open and trade stirring. Te Deum was performed in the cathedral, before Lord Wellington and the principal civil and military authorities; the former appearing in a grey frock coat, white tie, old sword, and cocked hat, while Castaños and another Spanish general by his side were *en grande tenue*.

On the 1st of June the Light Division passed the Douro, and encamped by Toro. The whole army moved forward from Braganza in three columns, and on the 12th the Light Division arrived at Hormillas. The day after, a loud explosion was heard, which proved to be the blowing up of the works of the castle of Burgos by the enemy before retreating. On the 15th the Division reached the valley of the Ebro, where, encountering a party of sturdy swarthy peasant women laden with supplies of fresh Asturias butter, the 43rd—not having tasted that luxury for upwards of two years—purchased largely, calculating on thus securing a rare evening banquet. As ill-luck would have it, they reckoned without their host, for the commissariat again proved deficient, and neither bread nor biscuit was attainable.

During the Peninsular War the peasantry living on the line of march were put to desperate straits to preserve their poultry. The moment a detachment marched into a village, fowls, ducks, geese, and turkeys were demanded. At length the owners of brood-hens and patriarchal ganders used, as soon as the drum was heard, to lock them up in chests and presses where darkness ensured silence, and in reply to inquiries protested that their last visitors had eaten up the whole. For a time this device succeeded; but one day a shrewd old campaigner carried a live duck he had contrived to borrow into a farm-house where it had been solemnly declared not a feathered denizen remained. He then pinched the creature until loud repetitions of "quack! quack!" were extorted, and directly a simultaneous reply resounded from all the boxes and cupboards in the room, to the utter despair of the Spanish farmer. In a twinkling the test became general.

On the 18th the Light Division suddenly came upon two brigades of Maucane's division, inflicting upon him a severe loss. The 43rd managed to secure the baggage and stores belonging to the French medical department.

The Division arrived at Subijana de Morillas, and on the 20th the allies halted between the Bayas and the Zadorra, that the columns might close up before the premeditated attack on Vittoria. Lord Wellington examined the ground, but high ridges of hills intercepted the view of the city and of the enemy's position.

Battle of Vittoria.

On the 21st of July the Light Division moved forward. Before dawn a heavy shower of rain fell, but with daylight the clouds dispersed, and the sun rose in splendour. On ascending a rising ground the whole French army became visible, drawn up in two lines. The river Zadorra was in front, and it was necessary to carry several bridges before action in the centre could be commenced.

At half-past eleven o'clock, Wellington led the way by a hollow road, followed by the Light Division, whom he placed unobserved amongst some trees exactly opposite to the enemy's centre, and within two hundred yards of the village of Villoles, proposed to be carried at the point of the bayonet. A Spanish peasant now reported that the enemy had left one of the bridges unprotected, and offered to conduct the Division. The right brigade, preceded by the 1st Rifles, instantly moved for the bridge indicated, which was passed at a run, and a steep road ascended, where a heavy column of French was descried on the principal hill commanding a bird's-eye view of the brigade. Luckily, however, the formation of the ground presented a sort of natural *tête-de-pont*, behind which the regiments formed.

Two round shots came amongst them, the second of which severed the head from the body of their guide; but so well concealed were the soldiers that the enemy ceased firing. The situation of the 43rd and the 1st Brigade was most extraordinary; at the elbow of the French position, isolated from the rest of the army, within a hundred yards of the enemy's advance, and absolutely occupying part of their position on the left of the river. No attempt was made by the French to dislodge them. El Rey Joseph, surrounded by at least 5000 men, was within a few hundred paces. Sir James Kempt, alarmed at the critical position of the brigade, sent for the 15th Hussars, who galloped forward singly up the steep, and dismounted in rear of the centre. The French dragoons then advanced within fifty yards to examine the strength of our force, but a few shots from the Rifles sent them to the right about.

This state of affairs lasted for half-an-hour, when the centre of the enemy drew off towards Vittoria, and the 3rd Division debouched rapidly from the rocks about Mendoza.

As General Graham reached the neighbourhood of Reille's position, the French flanks being threatened, they retired. So soon as the 3rd Division had closed up, Picton placed them, supported by the 4th, exactly opposite to the French centre. The 7th Division crossed above Tres Puentes, supported by the 2nd brigade of the Light Division, and forced the heights of Margarita.

The enemy having taken up a second position, upon Gomecha, the battle recommenced by a discharge on the 3rd Division as they deployed into line. The 43rd closed up in support, when they carried the village of Ariyez, the enemy's artillery being at that time within 200 yards of the 43rd, ploughing up the ground in their rear.

The first round shot was a spent one, which hit the ground near the centre of the regiment, bounded over the men's heads, striking the Colonel on the arm, but doing no mischief beyond that of a momentary blow.

Soon after, a shell burst, about six yards from the centre, but the men lay down and no harm accrued. The next round shot struck the 17th Portuguese, in close column, not a yard from the spot which the 43rd colours had just left, and only ten or twelve off them, killing a sergeant and taking a leg from each of the ensigns.

By six o'clock the centre of the British army had gained five miles from their starting point, vigorously driving the enemy, and by half-past the advance reached within one mile of Vittoria. There the French made a third stand, and showed such an imposing front that the left centre of the Allies remained at bay. Night approaching, Lord Wellington determined to win the battle before dark, and ordered the 4th Division on the right of the Light forward. With a rush they broke a dense French corps, who quickly retired in one confused mass.

The scene then presenting itself has been graphically described; the valley crowded with red bodies of infantry and smoking artillery, while the cavalry eagerly looked for an opening to gallop into the town. The enemy withdrew the right of their army behind the left as the only chance of retiring in anything like a compact body, sacrificing all their cannon, with the exception of two pieces taken in the subsequent pursuit. The road to Pampeluna was crowded by carriages freighted with terrified women and children, waggons laden with specie, wounded soldiers, and ammunition, and interspersed by droves of oxen, sheep, pigs, and mules. One figure was ludicrously conspicuous; the diminutive French paymaster-general, attired in most fantastic garb and powdered wig, offered gold doubloons to our dragoons as they passed, beseeching their protection. King Joseph left his carriage and baggage in the streets. The wife of the French general Gazan was taken a short distance from the town.

Various excesses were committed, but the greater part of the booty was appropriated by the camp followers. The 1st Brigade of the Light Division, in which was the 43rd, marched steadily through the strange and stirring scene, and not a man attempted to quit the ranks. They bivouacked a league beyond Vittoria; and laying aside their arms and packs, the weary and half-famished soldiers immediately set to work to capture the sheep and goats running wildly about, and to secure sacks of corn and flour lying by the road side.

Night ended the battle of Vittoria. The British loss was returned at 3308; Spanish and Portuguese, at 1602; the French at upwards of 6000; 143 brass cannon were left on the field. All who read the details and look on a plan of this battle will see that it was one of continuous movement; much ground being passed over on both sides between sunrise and sunset. At Salamanca the French sustained a great overthrow, and abandoned the field in haste and confusion :—at Vittoria—they were utterly routed and scattered like a flock of sheep.

The casualties in the 43rd were comparatively trifling: 1 bugler, and 2 rank and file, killed; Brevet-Major Duffy, Lieutenant Houlton, and 20 rank and file, wounded.

On the 20th the Light Division pursued the French towards Pampeluna, and as they went along, some officers of the 43rd observed a gun with eight horses and mules lying in a ditch. With exertion and difficulty it was rescued, and—as is usual—the animals sold by auction for the benefit of the Division. The only remaining gun carried off by the enemy from Vittoria was captured on this same day by Lieutenant Fitzmaurice and three men of the rifle corps. Villalba was reached on the 25th, when the baggage came up. All were in high spirits anticipating an early entry into the renowned city of Saragossa, when the line of march was unexpectedly changed, and the Division passing Pampeluna advanced towards Vera by a narrow road blocked up by large stones detached from overhanging cliffs, running along the right bank of the Bidassoa. Suddenly they were hailed by some Spaniards posted as sentinels, while a vidette of the enemy's chasseurs à cheval appeared on the brink of the crags.

Part of the division had been already sent to keep a look-out up the road leading to the heights of Echalar; before the mouth of the defile was reached a murmur from the head of the column proclaimed the enemy at hand, and rattle of musketry resounded. Lieutenant Baillie of the 43rd, who had been amusing himself with a volume of Gil Blas, could hardly tuck it into his breast pocket before a ball buried itself in the middle of the book, and knocked him off his horse. The bullet was afterwards shown as a curiosity, from the fact that the silk braiding of the pelisse was indented in the leaden surface; a fragment had been carried into the compressed leaves and remained tightly twisted round the ball. The 43rd attacked the enemy stationed behind orchards and stone walls, and driving them out, then supported the Rifles in their advance upon the heights of Santa Barbara, which they compelled the French to abandon; and the front being now cleared, the Division halted within half a mile of Vera. In this affair, which occurred on the 15th of July, the 43rd had 12 rank and file wounded.

The right of the enemy immediately opposed to the Light Division rested on a rock nearly perpendicular at an elbow of the Bidassoa overlooking the market-square of Vera. Their centre crowned the heights on each side of the Puerta de Vera; their left extending to the base of La Rhune. Our troops then re-entered the mouth of the pass. The 1st Brigade ascended the heights of Santa Barbara; the 2nd occupied a rising ground to protect the entrance of the defile leading to San Estevan, and pickets were pushed close up to Vera. The whole allied army took up the lofty chain of the Pyrenees, to cover Pampeluna and St. Sebastian. The position extended for thirty-eight miles as the crow flies, but nearer sixty for troops to traverse.

Napoleon was at Dresden, after his victories at Lutzen and Bautzen, when, on the 4th of June, tidings reached him that Wellington had crossed the Ebro. He immediately ordered Soult to the south to endeavour to retrieve matters. On the 13th of July the Marshal arrived at St. Jean Pied de Port, having collected nearly 40,000 men, issued a stirring proclamation, and prepared for a grand offensive movement. Three divisions more, amounting to 20,000 under Count d'Erlon, were destined to force the passes of Maya. His double object was to raise the blockade of Pampeluna and relieve St. Sebastian. On the 25th Sir Thomas Graham's attempt to storm that fortress failed, and on the same day Soult commenced his series of operations against Byng's brigade and Cole's division, amongst the rocks of Altobiscar. Lord Wellington turned the siege of St. Sebastian into a blockade, and put his whole force in motion to resist the machinations of the French.

The Light Division remained in front of Vera, until the morning of the 27th of July, when finding that the 7th Division had quitted the heights of Echalar, by which their right flank was exposed, the 1st Brigade descended quietly from Santa Barbara, and all concentrated behind the defile on the road to Lazaca. They crossed the Bidassoa and encamped on the mountain of Santa Cruz, from whence they still had a view of the French bivouac. On the following day the battle before Pampeluna was fought, thirty miles to the rear of the Light Division; but, from its entangled situation amongst the mountains, the result was unknown until three days after.

The Light Division having completely lost trace of the army, continued, during the 28th, in position at Santa Cruz; but at sunset, not without misgivings, began to descend a rugged pass, in hopes of cutting in upon the high road between Pampeluna and Tolosa. To increase their perplexities, night set in so dark that the men could no longer see each other as they floundered and stumbled over the jagged rocks and brushwood. Daybreak re-revealed the greater part of the 1st Brigade scattered over the steep. They then grouped together, taking the only discernible path, and luckily soon fell in with a mounted officer sent to direct them towards Leyza, where the rest of the Division were already in bivouac.

The French, who had suffered terribly in what are called the Battles of the Pyrenees, continued to retreat by the roads of Ronçesvalles, Maya, and Donna Maria, followed by five victorious divisions of the British. On the evening of the 31st, although obliquely to the rear of the pursuers, orders were given to overtake the enemy, and to attack wherever practicable. Accordingly, the Light Division got under arms in the middle of the night, and began to move.

Towards mid-day on the 1st of August, having already marched twenty-four miles, the regiments descended into a deep valley, and drew up in column to reconnoitre the right flank of the French, still hovering in the neighbourhood of Estevan. After halting one hour, the movement was continued, and for three more the Division continued to clamber up rugged acclivities, by still more rugged paths. By four o'clock, P.M., a flying dust was observed, glistening with the bright vivid flashes of small arms, on the right of the Bidassoa, and in the valley of Lerins. A cry instantly resounded, "The enemy!" By seven o'clock the Division having marched nearly forty miles in nineteen hours, it was absolutely necessary to halt the 2nd

Brigade near Aranza as a rallying point. The gallant 1st Brigade still held on, and reached the summit of a lofty precipice overlooking the enemy, within a stone's throw of the river which separated them. The French were wedged in on the other side by a narrow road with inaccessible rocks. They no sooner descried the brigade than a panic seemed to seize them, indescribable confusion prevailed, and they made a rush up the pass of Echalar, throwing down and trampling upon their own wounded and dying, while many of their cavalry, horses and riders, were precipitated into the river.

Some fired vertically at the British, while their wounded prayed for quarter, pointing to their dead and dying. Orders were given to support the Rifles while they repulsed the enemy, who had crossed over by the bridge of Yanzi in order to enable the tail of their columns to get off. The bridge being seized, the whole of the French baggage, with many prisoners, fell into the hands of the British columns following from San Estevan. Thus ended one of the most harassing marches ever performed.

Next morning the brigade filed across the bridge, and a small force was detached to guard the road towards Echalar, until the 2nd Brigade came up, when the Division again ascended the heights of Santa Barbara. As the pickets could not enter the valley until the right was cleared, and the enemy pushed from the mountain of Echalar, the 1st Rifles, supported by five companies of the 43rd clambered up. The soldiers, having been for two days without sustenance, were so weak they could scarcely stand. Fortunately an excellent commissary overtook the Division, and rations were served out, which the men devoured in the act of priming and loading for the attack.

Invisible firing commenced, all being enveloped in fog,

and as the combatants were literally contending in the clouds, it was impossible to ascertain which side was getting the best of it. As daylight waned all firing ceased, and the French Light Infantry were dislodged from the mountain.

Second Assault and Storming of St. Sebastian.

The first unsuccessful attempt to carry St. Sebastian cost the British 56 officers and 570 men, killed, wounded, or prisoners. Lord Wellington regarded the capture of the fortress as imperative; the French were equally determined to hold it. Another desperate struggle was therefore inevitable. The 5th Division, with some Portuguese brigades, resumed the close investment on the 31st of July. The long-previously demanded battering train only arrived from England on the 19th August; and so great was the supineness displayed by the home authorities, that when it was tardily received, all ammunition had been omitted. Breaches were made in the rampart on each side of the tower of Mésquitas, and in the curtain between the Tower of Los Hornos and the demi-bastion of St. Elmo, assault being fixed for noon on the 31st.

Fearing that the troops already engaged in the siege had become disheartened, Lord Wellington gave orders that the storming party should consist of 750 volunteers from the 1st and Light Divisions. In a highly complimentary letter to Baron Alten, commanding the Light Division, he begged "he would send 1 field officer, 2 captains, 4 subalterns, and 100 men to show the 5th Division how to mount a breach."

As soon as the communication was made known, whole companies volunteered, and consequently much difficulty was experienced in the selection. Of the 43rd, Major William Napier, Captain Brock, and Lieutenants Cooke and O'Connel were most earnest to be of the party, and had actually been told off, when it was discovered that seniors refused to waive their right of precedence. Lieutenant O'Connel was therefore the only officer from the regiment permitted to respond to the call. Hopkins, Murchison, James Considine, H. Baillie, and Cooke were present as spectators. Major Napier, having been expressly accepted to lead the Light Division stormers, proceeded to the market-place of Lesaca, where they were to parade, in order to assume command. Upon arriving, he was informed that Lieutenant-Colonel Hunt of the 52nd was to lead, and that his services would be dispensed with. He remonstrated with the General on the injustice, but without avail. He then appealed to Colonel Hunt to forego his claim. Hunt replied that, having gained his rank and been on several previous storming parties, he had no intention of offering himself for this, and did not know that Napier had volunteered; but being informed that another field officer was the man selected, whom he believed incompetent to do the Division credit, he then came forward; but consented to waive his claim if Napier could procure permission to that effect from Lord Wellington, who, however, met the application by a flat refusal, saying that he disapproved of volunteering, although necessary at times, as in that way he lost his best officers. Napier then determined to take a musket and march with the men who had come forward at his call; but some inkling of his design having reached General Alten, he desired him forthwith to return to his regiment.

The men of the 5th Division, naturally indignant at the stigma supposed to be attached to them, became so enraged that they declared they would bayonet the soldiers of the detachment, if they got into the town first. Major-General Leith, commanding the 5th Division, fearful of such collision, and participating in the feeling thus generated, would not permit the volunteers to lead the assault, but disposed them along the trenches of the hornwork. At 11 o'clock A.M. on the 31st, the storming party, led by Lieutenant Macguire of the 4th Regiment, filed out of the trenches, and shortly after, a mine exploded, destroying many of the enemy and not a few of the men at the head of the column. Here Lieutenant O'Connel, 43rd, was killed by a grape-shot in his thigh, speedily followed by a musket-ball in his abdomen. He had been one of the storming party at Ciudad Rodrigo, and at Badajoz, where he was badly wounded—a ball passing in at the top of his shoulder and coming out at the elbow joint. He was a great favourite, and a very gallant officer. Upon his death being reported to Lord Wellington, he ordered his commission to be sold for the benefit of his mother, a widow of slender means. Sergeants Kilpatrick and Thomas Blood of the regiment, were wounded—one being shot through the nose, the other losing his right hand.

The batteries on the besiegers' side were ordered to fire over the heads of the British, and at the end of half-an-hour the defence was evidently weakened. Fresh troops then filed out of the trenches, and the volunteers from the Light Division advanced together with the 2nd Brigade of the 5th Division. After some desperate fighting, the volunteers effected a lodgment, when an accidental explosion took place, annihilating many of the besieged. Major Snodgrass of the Portuguese service, under a tremendous fire of grape and canister, led his men through water breast high to assault the lesser breach, and effected a successful entrance simultaneously with that of the more powerful force at the greater breach. The British by degrees forced their way over the ramparts, and by 3 o'clock the town was theirs. A portion of the garrison managed to retire up to the Castle, where they held out until the 8th of September. Next day they marched out with the honours of war, leaving 500 wounded in the hospital. Thus, after sixty-three days of open trenches, the siege terminated.

Of the detachment of the 43rd present, consisting of 33, only 5 escaped unhurt. Lieutenant O'Connel and 5 rank and file were killed; 2 sergeants and 20 rank and file wounded.

About this time, the honourable distinction of "colour-sergeant" was introduced into the British army, by orders from the Commander-in-Chief. The following ten sergeants of the 43rd, who had particularly distinguished themselves, were selected as nominees by Major Napier, then in command:—

William Fitzpatrick, volunteered at the storming of St. Sebastian; lost an arm.
Richard Griffiths, volunteered at the storming of St. Sebastian.
Aaron Loveman, stormer at Badajoz.
Moses Loveman, stormer at Badajoz.
Samuel Rand, stormer at Badajoz; afterwards Quarter-Master of the regiment and Knight of Windsor.
Morgan Jones, distinguished at Badajoz.
Ewan Cameron, received a commission in 1815.
Thomas Blood, stormer at St. Sebastian, wounded severely. Received a commission in the 6th Regiment, 10th of November, 1813; his Lieutenancy on the 8th of September, 1814.
Samuel Armitage, stormer at St. Sebastian.
William Pardoe, stormer at St. Sebastian.

On the 31st August, the same day that the assault of St. Sebastian took place, Soult, with the right wing of his army, crossed the Bidassoa opposite St. Marcial, while another division forded the river two hundred yards below Vera, and immediately moved on to attack the heights occupied by part of the 7th Division. They frequently, without success, endeavoured to climb the eminence; so perpendicular was the ascent, that the Spaniards alone by their fire managed, in Lord Wellington's presence, to drive the enemy back.

Ensign Folliott, who had only arrived with a detachment of the 43rd from England a few days before, was suddenly surprised in a wood, on his way to join, and mortally wounded in the stomach. He expressed perfect resignation to his early fate, touchingly saying his only ambition was to have seen the regiment. Mortification supervened, and in a few hours the poor boy passed peaceably away, his comrades laying him beneath the wide-spreading boughs of an adjacent oak. Four of his men were also killed; but the rest, under Sergeant Loughlin, succeeded in joining.

During September the enemy worked hard in felling and sawing timber to form abbatis, and in the construction of intrenchments. The 43rd remained at Santa Barbara. An attack was arranged for October 7th, and the plan of operations communicated to all officers commanding companies. The redoubts were to be carried by repeated assaults of the 43rd and 52nd, while the 95th and Caçadores were to act as tirailleurs.

THE PASSAGE OF THE BIDASSOA.

The extreme left of the army was personally directed by Lord Wellington. At daybreak the 5th Division crossed near the mouth of the Bidassoa, and the 1st Division commenced the attack. Lord Aylmer's brigade, and a corps of Spaniards, covered by some pieces of cannon stationed on the heights of St. Marcial, also forded the stream at various places. A sharp contest then took place, particularly against the 5th Division, while ascending the steep and difficult slopes. The enemy, attacked simultaneously at different points, was finally beaten off. The 4th Division, in reserve behind Vera, deployed on the heights of Santa Barbara to support the Light.

The enemy, who had batteries and trenches in every place likely to be serviceable, occupied these with eight battalions, two of them Light Infantry. The morning was heavy, but it cleared off, and was a fine day.

The pickets of the Light Division, in front of Vera, began the attack of a detached ridge called the "Boar's Back," from its hogged up, protruding outline. Before they could debouch through the town of Vera, for the assault of the main position, covered by forts and abbatis, it was necessary to carry this jagged summit. The 43rd began to skirmish up one end, while the 3rd Rifles followed suit at the other, and being defended by only a small body of French troops, was speedily won. The 2nd Brigade, under Sir J. Colborne, then attacked, but unsuccessfully, as the enemy held a fort with great resolution, and not only beat them back, but in turn sallied from their works, and drove many of the assailants, principally Portuguese, over the precipices. At this critical moment the 52nd advanced in column, impetuously pushed back the French, driving them into the fort on one side and out at the other.

The 2nd Brigade then advanced, but the ground was so difficult that they were kept at bay for a considerable time. Meanwhile, the 1st Brigade pushed through Vera to support the skirmishers, who moved parallel with the 2nd Brigade,—the enemy pelting them with bullets from a small fort. So soon as a sufficient number of men could be got together, that post was carried, and between 300 and 400 men surrendered. After three hours' more hard toil, and clambering from rock to rock, there remained but 200 yards to the summit of the Puerta de Vera, when the skirmishers, grouped together in a compact body, forced the pass at the point of the bayonet. The French ran in all directions; and so elated were the victors, that about 300 of the 43rd descended the mountain with loud hurrahs, and chased the enemy for a league and a half into France. The 1st Brigade then took possession of boarded and well-roofed huts, constructed by the French as their winter quarters.

The 43rd lost in this attack on "The Heights of Vera:" 1 bugler, 6 rank and file, killed; 20 rank and file wounded. During the night fatigue-parties arrived from Santa Barbara with the knapsacks. The men of the Light Division had invariably fought with their packs on except when storming breaches or escalading forts, and this was the only occasion on which the rule had been departed from.

The following letter of Lieutenant Hennell of the regiment gives some interesting details relative to the " Passage of the Bidassoa," as it is called:—

"13th Oct., 1813.

"I shall now give you some particulars of the taking of the position. On the evening of the 6th I returned from Passages, where I had been on detachment, when orders were issued to take the position in front on the following morning. The principal force of the enemy was on the main road at top of the hill, and on a higher hill to the right. They had made trenches and batteries in every possible place. I learn by prisoners they had six regiments, two of them light, with two battalions each; in all eight battalions, and between four and five thousand strong. Had they fought as French troops *have* fought, and as they *ought* to have fought, we should have lost a great number, if not repulsed. The morning was very heavy, but it cleared up. Nothing could have been finer than our movements. The Division moved down into the valley close to Vera at daylight, and stayed there near two hours. The enemy, seeing every man of us move, sent out their light troops to fill the trenches and forts, and a small body attempted to defend the first hill with their skirmishers in front. A company of the 95th opened the business. About twenty men, with twenty supporting, marched coolly up the hill, when the French, who delight in a long shot, began directly our men showed their heads. However, the 95th moved regularly up the hill to within thirty yards of the top without firing, and then by way of breathing gave a volley, loaded, and advanced to the top, the support just behind them. The French did not attempt to defend it, but moved to their left, not without music, and in quick time.

"I firmly believe there are no better troops in the world than the 95th; they take things so coolly and deliberately, and seem to know their business so well. You have no idea with what glee we saw them, and how readily we fell in to advance as soon as our pickets had cleared the first hill, which they did soon; though it is said by many officers that there scarcely ever was a stronger position attacked. So well were the arrangements made, that our regiment was under cover almost all up the position. The 95th, with one company of ours, were thrown out to skirmish, and the pickets flanked all their trenches, and made them run in all directions; so that we marched nearly straight up this hill, one and a half mile from Vera, to the pass over it, in little more than an hour. The other brigade had not the advantage of ravines, and had to charge several redoubts and forts, which they did most gallantly, and this accounts for their loss being greater than ours. It was very interesting to examine all the works, &c., which we had been looking at through glasses for months. The Spaniards on our right behaved admirably. The hill they had to attack is at least twice as high as most here, and on the top of it a perpendicular rock, with the ruins of a chapel; it is the highest of any here, not excepting the Crown Mountain. They lost many men under it, and did not take it for two days. On the 7th Division moving round it, the French evacuated it in the night, leaving us in possession of all the Pyrenees. We can now go on any hill we please, and not only 'proudly survey them,' but send our bâtmen with covering party for corn. There has been a heavy firing from two o'clock till nearly this time (eleven o'clock). I hear they have attacked the Spaniards in the valley to our right. The 1st and 5th Divisions, and Lord Aylmer's Brigade are in the valley below us. The French are hard at work making their extended position as strong as they can. A general attack is expected. How far we shall go is uncertain. It will be a glorious battle. What a pity it is we have no John Bulls to see it from these mountains: you may see everything that takes place to Bayonne. St. Jean de Luz is a beautiful town, about a league from the bottom of the mountain, with a river running through it, and a small harbour. When at Passages I went to see the ruins of St. Sebastian. It was one of the most beautiful places in Spain; all the houses were large, built of freestone, with iron balconies; part of the walls are left with the balconies hanging down. Passages is very like Portsmouth—the harbour full of transports.

"Oct. 17th.

"The firing I mentioned was caused by the French taking back a hill with a fort on it. Two hours before daylight they took two companies of Spaniards prisoners. It was in France; as Lord Wellington did not send any English troops, I suppose he did not care for it.

"The following questions and answers have passed between the Governor of Pampeluna and Don Carlos:—

"'Q. Will you allow us to march out with baggage into France?
"'A. No.
"'Q. If you do not, the inhabitants will starve.
"'A. If I find any one inhabitant dies from want of food while a French soldier has a ration, I will hang the Governor.
"'Q. We will surrender if you do not send us to England, but have a Spanish guard.
"'A. If you want a Spanish guard over you, you have it, and cannot be in a better place.'

"So that it is likely to surrender soon; and I hear the Portuguese are gone round to Ronçesvalles, as the attack is to be made on their left. I have just come off picket on the mountain, and it has been the worst I have had. The Spanish troops have a longing desire to advance into France; it will require all Lord Wellington's management to prevent their murdering the inhabitants, plundering I am sure he cannot. I was on picket the day after the action. A young French soldier was mortally wounded in the side in running down the hill, and, although he was dying, they stripped him entirely naked, and left him on the long grass wet with the evening dew. Our picket found him, and told me when I arrived he was just dead. The Spaniards abuse the French prisoners, and the French theirs; declaring that, were it not for the red-coats, they would have thrashed them in millions. The French officers bear amputation much better than the English. One of our soldiers showed a French prisoner a French major wounded, 'Ah! and the devil go with him,' said the Frenchman, 'for he wanted us to charge you, but we knew better.' Some French prisoners in the rear were rejoicing in losing a leg or arm, saying they should now go home and have no more soldiering. The weather is now always either raining or blowing excessively hard. I bought a little pony from one of Longas' sweet youths the other day for thirteen dollars."

During the combat of the 7th, the right wing of the army guarded the mountains from Echalar to Ronçesvalles, while the left, after the action, held the ridge from the Rock of La Rhune to the Bay of Biscay. The 1st Brigade of the Light Division encamped in a forest at the base of the great Rhune, and the 2nd took post at the Puerta de Vera. The weather was cold and dismal, rain poured in torrents; wicker-work tents to protect the quadrupeds were constructed, and the month wore tediously away.

On the 9th of November the Light Division received orders to move and take up ground during the night preparatory to a general attack of the enemy's position in France; and before morning the 43rd got under arms, and marched silently by the north-east side of La Grande Rhune, through a narrow path, to within a few hundred yards of the French outposts. For six months they had been labouring at stone forts on the summit of La Petite la Rhune, which were now to be stormed; "but strong and valiant in arms must the soldiers have been who stood in that hour before the veterans of the 43rd." These are the words of Napier, who commanded the regiment on that day, when the rising of the sun above the horizon was to be the signal for commencing the

BATTLE OF THE NIVELLE.

No newer or better account of this action can be given than that contained in a letter written by Lieutenant Maclean of the 43rd—now Military Knight of Windsor :—

"Dec. 12th, 1813.

"On the night of the 9th we received orders to hold ourselves ready to march at an early hour the following morning, to assault the position of the enemy on La Petite la Rhune. Breakfast was ordered at 2 A.M., which we managed to eat most heartily; and having some remarkably thick American biscuits, Madden observed that their thickness would turn a bullet aside, at the same time putting one into the breast of his jacket. Never was prediction more completely verified, for early in the day the biscuit was shattered to pieces, turning the direction of the bullet from as gallant and true a heart as ever beat under a British uniform. Another bullet passed through Madden's left arm immediately afterwards.

"The regiment having moved off about 3 o'clock, ascended the side of the mountain, halting within a short distance of La Petite la Rhune, and close to our left we saw and passed the Rifles, lying down in close column, covered by their white blankets, in the faint light resembling a flock of sheep much more than grim warriors prepared for the strife. The most perfect silence had been enjoined, and the 43rd were directed to lie down in close column to await the signal of attack—the firing of a third gun from the right.

"We heard the French drums beating to arms, and even could distinguish voices, although not in sight of them; for being on the slope of a hill, we had no idea we were so near or about to attack. Sir James Kempt, who commanded the 1st Brigade of the Light Division, ordered that two companies of the regiment should lead in skirmishing order, followed by a support of four in line under Lieut.-Colonel Napier, and a reserve of three companies under Lieut.-Colonel Duffy. Major Brock's and Captain Murchison's companies were to lead the advance in extended order.

"The sunrise in those regions is most sudden, for darkness is dispelled by a burst of glowing light as the sun clears the head of a high mountain, and startles the beholder with its glorious brightness. Such was was its appearance as it glanced on the recumbent troops, and sparkled from their bayonets along the arms piled by companies that eventful morning. The next moment the sound of a gun followed by others was heard, and every ear was on the alert to count each shot. The men were on their feet in an instant, and the words 'Stand to your arms' being given, each soldier seized his Brown Bess. The Rifles folded their blankets, and moved off to their left. General Kempt mounted his horse, and said, 'Now, 43rd, let me see what you will do this morning;' and pointing to an intrenchment on a rising ground in front to the left of the regiment lined with French infantry, gave the order to advance and carry it; and then await the arrival of the support before an attempt was to be made on the stone redoubts on the ridge of rocks on the top of La Petite la Rhune.

"The companies then extending, and bringing their right

shoulders forward, were at once in fire, and after descending a short distance and crossing a piece of marshy ground, made a rush for the breastwork, which was quickly evacuated by the enemy; but not before they had by their sharp practice dropped a few of their assailants, who had scarcely returned their fire, so intent were they on rushing at the intrenchment. On clearing the breastwork, we brought our left shoulders forward to face redoubt No. 1, and as we were directed to wait for the four companies, we took such shelter as some scattered rocks afforded at about fifty or sixty yards from the first redoubt. The enemy made our quarters pretty hot, as they when firing were well covered, which our men perceiving were endeavouring to check by aiming at their heads when opportunities offered; but, to avoid exposing themselves, they preferred firing at the support and reserve, although not so close, for thus they had a far better chance of killing and not being hit by our men, and consequently could fire coolly. The redoubts were built of rough stones, but had no cannon.

"Captain Murchison and myself got alongside of a flat piece of rock within about forty yards of the redoubt, and as they could see part of us, they made the rock smoke with their shots. Captain Murchison raised his head to look over, and instantly his face assumed a livid appearance as if choking. I inquired what was the matter, when he with difficulty said, 'he was struck in the neck and must see a doctor!' but in the meantime, should the support arrive, he desired me to take on the company. Shortly after the surgeon examined him, and found that the bullet had got entangled in his neckcloth and had run round his neck. A sergeant pointed out better cover about twenty-five yards nearer the redoubt, to which we both went; and I borrowed his fusee and fired several shots at the heads of the French, the sergeant loading for me. While so employed, Colonel Napier and the support came sweeping up behind us, on which I gave the order to advance, and we all dashed forward with a cheer. Napier, boiling with courage, and being withal very active, attempted to scale the walls without observing the bayonet points over his head; and, being rather short-sighted, would certainly have been very roughly handled had not James Considine and myself laid hold of the skirts of his jacket and pulled him back, for which we received anything but thanks. We of course apologised to Colonel Napier for the liberty we had taken, for he was very wrath at the time. We then pointed out an easier ascent for him, and assisted each other over the wall. To show the danger he was in at the moment, I was even under the necessity of striking a bayonet up with my sword, though they were giving way, as a hint that we were coming over in spite of them. The hint was taken, and a free passage left.

"On getting inside I saw a French officer kneeling with his arm raised begging for quarter, and his head and face covered with blood. I told one of the men to take care of him, and proceeded through the gate at the rear, following the retiring enemy towards the second redoubt on the ridge of rocks, similarly constructed to the one we had just taken. I then met Cooke and Considine, and we consulted what was best to be done, as we had not a sufficient number of men with us to assault the second redoubt, most of them having joined the regiment below the rocks. We were then about 100 yards from it, and exposed to its fire. I proposed to Considine to follow a path leading along the face of the ridge of rock, which I expected would lead to the redoubt, and if I found it practicable would not return. I had judged correctly as to the direction of the path, for it led direct on the redoubt in question; but although the enemy must have seen me distinctly they did not fire in my direction: I suppose from seeing me alone, and being occupied by the others who were gathering for a rush. I quickly discovered they were about to quit the redoubt by the gate behind, for some were taking that direction, and before I could get close up they were off.

"On reaching the top of the ridge again, I found that I was on the flank of a long trench, filled with a regiment of French infantry, but high above it. The intrenchment was cut across a nearly level green, approaching which I perceived a portion of the 43rd advancing in column under General Kempt, and the French having fired a volley, I observed he had been wounded, and his A.D.C., Captain Gore (now Honourable General Sir Charles Gore), K.C.B., binding a handkerchief quickly round his arm.

"The order to charge was then given, a British cheer followed,— a line of levelled steel showed what the enemy might expect. I saw them waver, then spring out of the intrenchment and retire down the hill at a rapid pace.

"This had no sooner taken place than I observed on the other side, and also below me, a French officer waving his sword and encouraging his men to advance and retake the redoubt, but he could not induce them to follow. One of the 43rd skirmishers rushed at him with his bayonet at the charge, and in spite of his attempts to defend himself with his sword ran him through, and then returned to the level ground behind the trench the regiment had carried in such gallant style.

"Gore then rode up to me with orders from the General to stop the pursuit on which the men were eagerly bent; and it was with considerable difficulty that their ardour was checked and the men halted, for they were rushing after the enemy like greyhounds, so excited were they.

"The French, finding that they were no longer pressed, retired more tranquilly but still in confusion, our men firing on them as they descended the hill to some huts forming an old bivouac. I observed an officer on the way separate himself from the mob of fugitives, which removed him from our line of fire, and walk quietly along: on which a short stout soldier asked my permission to follow and take him prisoner. I consented, provided no one accompanied him; and although his musket had been discharged he would not wait to reload, but ran forward. He had not gone above 300 or 400 yards, when he overtook the officer and called on him to surrender. The Frenchman presented a pistol on turning round, which the 43rd man observing, and being then very near, poised his musket over his head, and pitched it with such precision that the bayonet penetrated his thigh and brought him to the ground, where he lay at the mercy of his adversary, who merely took possession of the pistol, and, what he considered of greater value, a flask of brandy. On rejoining his company, after offering it to me, he gratified his heated comrades with a sip as far as the supply would go. Both these French officers, who fell under our bayonets, were removed to Vera, and I was told were doing well.

"I now learned that Considine had his thigh broken by a bullet, and that Murchison, shortly after the doctor had examined him, was struck by another musket ball, which carried him off in twenty-four hours.

"After about a quarter of an hour's halt the Division moved on, the Rifles and 52nd leading: and some of the former were sent down the hill to drive the French from the bivouac to which they had retired. This was quickly done, but the French being reinforced again advanced; the drummers beating the *pas de charge* to retake the huts. The Rifles, however, were too wily, for, perceiving that the wind blew in the enemy's faces, they fired the huts, which with the straw therein blazed and smoked to such a degree that the French were obliged to relinquish their intention.

"The sight at this moment was truly grand: we looked from our vantage ground over an extent of about twenty miles occupied by two gallant armies, of which the Light Division composed the centre of the British. To the right the pass of Mayar and St. Jean de Pied de Port, to the left St. Jean de Luz, and from each extremity could be distinctly traced, by the flashes of fire and rising smoke, the advance of our troops and the gradual retreat of the French, offering an obstinate resistance at every favourable spot. But the British were not to be denied, and went in to win; and in short carried everything before them, notwithstanding the gallant resistance they met with.

"While looking around, William Freer came up and inquired anxiously for his brother Edward. Seeing that something was amiss, he turned round, saying, 'I see how it is,' and started off to the rear, where his worst fears were too soon confirmed: his brother having been shot through the head. Both brothers were fine courageous fellows, much liked in the regiment; each had been wounded, the elder had lost an arm at Badajoz. The younger frequently told me had a presentiment he would be killed in the attack of La Petite la Rhune. He happened also to be in the last company that went into action that day, when his presentiment was fulfilled, to the great sorrow of all his brother officers and the entire regiment.

"The Division then crossing a narrow valley ascended the nearest hill, driving in the French skirmishers, and at the top came upon a fine star-fort of earth, surrounded by a deep ditch containing about 700 men; and although the 52nd attacked it with their accustomed determination, they were repulsed with loss. The Commandant was then called upon to surrender, which he at first refused to do; but seeing that he could not defend the work for any length of time, he agreed: provided he was not to be marched to the rear by Spanish or Portuguese troops. This being accepted, the redoubt was given up and the French disarmed.

"This may be said to have ended the day's fighting."

On the signal being given for the advance, an incident of a very unusual character had occurred. The men were in the act of standing to their arms and "falling in," when the sergeant-major Russell placed himself in front of the leading company, drew his sword with a theatrical flourish, and facing about, violently threw his scabbard away, exclaiming with much gesticulation: "Soldiers! we have not had an opportunity of distinguishing ourselves since the siege of Badajoz. I must remind you in the words of the immortal Nelson, 'England expects that every man this day will do his duty,'—then follow me to victory!" All this was *muchio bellicio por nada*, and at the moment only excited a laugh of derision, but was not without inspiriting effect.

When reforming on the Plâteau, after the rocks of La Rhune had been carried, to the astonishment of the regiment they saw one of their privates, who in the confusion had got below the rocks on the right, endeavouring to lead on a Spanish regiment. This attempt he made several times before he discovered his own regiment.

Lord Wellington had directed the right attack against the French left, but by some oversight in his first despatch did but scant justice to the Light Division. On the 13th of November he, however, wrote from St. Pé:—" I have also to draw your Lordship's attention to the Light Division's conduct in the manner it deserves; these troops, under Major-General Charles Baron Alten, distinguished themselves in this, as they have on every occasion when they have been engaged. Major-General Kempt was wounded at the head of his brigade in the beginning of the day, in the attack on the enemy's works at La Petite Rhune."

In this action the 43rd lost 2 captains, 2 lieutenants, 2 sergeants, and 7 rank and file, killed; 4 lieutenants, 1 ensign, 8 sergeants, and 50 rank and file, wounded; Captain Thomas Capel and Lieut. Edward Freer were killed on the spot; Captain Robert Murchison and Lieutenant Angrove died of their wounds; Lieutenant James Considine had his thigh broken; Lieutenants Wyndham Madden (severely), William Freer, Hennel, and Ensign Rowley Hill, wounded. Major Napier received a clasp and the brevet of Lieutenant-colonel for his distinguished conduct.

On the following day the Light Division edged off to the right and crossed the Nivelle by the picturesque little bridge of Harastaqui. The whole army moved forward in three columns, and the right took post on the left bank of the Nive at Cambo. The extreme left of the British crossed the Nivelle, advanced to Bidart, and headquarters were established at St. Jean de Luz. Bayonne was strongly fortified. The enemy occupied farm-houses and villas around, and a morass, only passable at two points, covered an intrenched camp within cannon-shot.

The advanced posts of the 1st Brigade of the Light Division were placed in the churchyard of Arcangues, in the Château, and in a cottage close to a lake. The 2nd Brigade prolonged this line towards a deep valley which separated them from the 5th Division holding the plateau on the high road to Bayonne.

Since the passage of the Nivelle the weather had set in exceedingly disagreeable and wet. The regiment, after being much exposed in bivouac, was cantoned in the detached miserable cottages constituting the poor straggling hamlet of Arbonne. Matters went on quietly, and all field operations, with the exception of working parties intrenching the position of Arcangues, were apparently suspended.

Early on the morning, however, of the 29th of November, Kempt's Brigade was assembled in the vicinity of the Château d'Arcangues for the purpose, as they were informed, of making some change in the pickets along the line in their immediate front and in advance of the village of Bassussary; the outlying pickets consequently pushed forward,—the French sentries retiring, firing off their pieces and giving the alarm. Through some unfortunate misapprehension on the part of the officer in command of the advance, the whole body extended as skirmishers, acting almost independently of each other, regardless of what was occurring on their flanks and of the numbers opposed to them.

The French, seeing that our men persevered in boldly advancing, strongly reinforced their pickets, and were enabled to hold their ground. A fierce and violent hand-to-hand combat then ensued; the whole of Clausel's Division getting under arms, expecting a general action.

Cooke, of the 43rd, in his memoirs gives a graphic account of this "skirmish with a vengeance," and a letter written on the spot by Lieutenant Hennel, likewise of the regiment, is as follows:—

"Arcangues, Nov. 25th, 1813.

"The day after sending off my last, the left wing of our regiment was for picket, one and a half mile in advance. Two companies and a half halted at a large handsome house, and the other two and a half moved on a mile further to relieve the pickets in front. Since the 18th we have had very fine weather. Our sentries and those of the French were sufficiently near to converse. The country here is very hilly. I had the 'Times' with me and was reading it. I thought our opponents might like to see both sides of the question, so held up the paper walking down towards the ditch that divided us. The vidette immediately walked his horse down and met me; I asked him how he did. He said, 'Very well.' I gave him the paper and came away, wishing him 'good morning.' The picket got round him (the paper was the 8th Nov., General Stewart's despatch) and sent it to their officers. In half an hour an officer and six hussars came to relieve. The officer got off his horse and came down towards us. I immediately met him at the ditch, and he came over it without hesitation. We were very polite to each other: he came with me up my hill, and asked me if I spoke French; I told him 'no,' but that I would send an officer who could. Hobkirk came with two other officers, and on two more coming with blue great-coats, he asked if they were Portuguese. He stopped talking with us three-quarters of an hour, saying it was a pity we were fighting, as they esteemed us much as soldiers. I then walked back with him to the ditch and we shook hands. He was the chief of a squadron of 10th Hussars, dressed very handsomely, and seemed a shrewd man. Hobkirk and Baillie relieved us next day, and we went back to the château. The owner is a very handsome man, about twenty-five years old; his friends live in Bayonne. He talked to us without any reserve, and is very intelligent. He says the inhabitants are much less annoyed with our army than they were with the French; he confirms all that is said about spies watching political conversations, and also as to persons from the highest respectability down to the shoeblack, being employed as acquaintances, servants, &c., &c. Yesterday Soult allowed the inhabitants to return from Bayonne to St. Jean de Luz. Monsieur d'Arcangues told us that the people at Bayonne quite recognise the falsity of Buonaparte's accounts of the battles in Spain; as for instance, 'the road to Bayonne was crowded with English prisoners,' when not one was to be seen; but, he added, they believe what he tells them of the north, and though the people of the north know what he says of them is false, yet they believe what he says of the south.

"Next morning at daylight, instead of relieving us, the brigade came to drive the French back; of course the pickets led the way. We marched under cover to our range of hills in advance. Captain Hobkirk and Lieutenant Baillie, with their company and ours (Captain Simpson's), formed in the village opposite the French pickets; and when the firing commenced on our left, Captain Hobkirk's company got through the hedge, extended in skirmishing order, and moved on. I was immediately desired with a section (fourteen men) to move on his right, with orders to drive the enemy off the two first hills, and halt at a house pointed out.

"The whole country here is crowded with small woods, hedges, ditches, and houses. As we came upon the first hill, the French were running in a crowd upon the second. I opened a fire upon them as they passed. We ran down the hollow, and then moved up and displaced them there. I then had as fine a fire upon them as possible. We were upon a hill and in a ditch up to our shoulders, and they were crowding into a narrow pass to get into a wood close by a house, strongly intrenched behind which they had 9000 troops. I had this fire upon the men at the gateway about three-quarters of an hour, at 300 yards' distance. I then moved on, and found Hobkirk's and Champ's companies formed with General Kempt. I believe we had now accomplished all we wanted. General Kempt ordered us to move forward. I, being nearest to a gap, moved first; he called me back, and said, 'Now, mind, you are not to go beyond the wood.' We were now about 400 yards from their trenches: the first 100 yards was a close, the next a thick wood, the two next closes with a slight hedge between them, and with scarce any bank or ditch. Just as I came to the edge of the wood, Lieutenant Baillie following at the head of Captain Hobkirk's company, said, 'Here is cavalry! form up!' I turned round, and saw them and infantry, both much stronger than we were, entering the wood on the other side. We gave them such a fire as quickly sent them off, and then moved to the front of the wood, each man to his tree, and kept up a fire upon their trenches. They did not forget to return it, but it did little mischief as we were well covered by the trees; the boughs dropped fast around us, and the leaves were knocked up by our side.

"After being here half an hour, the advance was sounded (I afterwards found by mistake); Hobkirk and Baillie moved out of the wood at the head of their men, and I at the head of mine, under a tremendous fire to the slight hedge, not more than 90 or 100 yards from their trenches, in which were at least 2000 men on the three sides. As Baillie came up, he with three others was knocked over. Baillie was struck in the forehead, and instantly died. I was at the hedge first of my men, and instantly laid down flat; every man got as good a place as he could. The hedge and ditch scarcely afforded any cover. I ordered them to cease firing, as for every shot we gave they sent five or six in return, all striking within a foot or two of him that fired. At this time our other four companies kept up a fire upon them, and I thought they were going to storm the trenches.

"I lay here full an hour, having many wounded around me, when seeing no reserve coming up and our fire slackening much (five of us were lying together, and at one moment three of us were struck—one had the bottom of his chin knocked off within a few inches of my face, another was hit in the body, and the third in the arm), determined me to shift my quarters. I desired all around me to crawl on their bodies (if we had crawled on our hands and knees we should all have been knocked over) to our right into the hollow under cover. I collected about twenty men as I went along. As we began crawling, a man was killed just by me. When we had got thirty or forty yards we were under cover, and I stayed there about twenty minutes, setting a man to watch if they came out of the trenches, pointing out the road to retire by. The retreat sounded; they immediately rushed out, and I made the best of my way with my men over a little hill, under a tremendous fire, to some houses in rear where I found two companies. After leaving eighteen men under Lieutenant Steel, we retired to the rest of the regiment; as we left we learnt that Hobkirk, with twelve or fourteen men, were made prisoners. Lieutenant Steel was to retire to the position we wanted, and then halt. He had a shot in his leg, but it is not a bad wound. Thus ended, at two o'clock P.M., a skirmish which, but for the mistake, would only have cost us ten men wounded; as it is, we have 1 captain missing, 1 lieutenant killed, 1 wounded, 2 sergeants, 76 men killed, wounded, and missing. Thus I have passed the hottest fire I ever saw, Badajoz not excepted. I was in twenty times more danger than in either the battles of Salamanca or Vittoria, and I have not received the slightest injury; a loud call for gratitude—it shall not be unattended to. If I live to return, I shall have many remarks of a serious nature to make, that would be improper to place here. Baillie was a fine young man, had just come from England with Hobkirk, bringing a most superb kit. Hobkirk spends near 1000*l.* a year on dress. A flag of truce was sent to ask permission for his private servant and baggage to go to him, which was granted; and I hear Lord Wellington has sent the names of four French captains for them to choose one in exchange, so he will very likely return. Lord Wellington knows him personally. Major Napier called the officers together yesterday, delicately to point out to them the necessity of judgment and caution in the field; he said it was not necessary at this time of day for the officers of the 43rd to show themselves men of courage. By a deserter we learn the French have 9000 men on this side the Nive, and 1000 at Bayonne, and that they lost 100 men on the 23rd. We are intrenching the position we now have—Arcangues. We took a great deal of ground on our left by pushing them as we did. There is no reason why we should not advance. I find if I had remained with Hobkirk I should certainly have been taken prisoner, as full 200 men rushed out of the trenches and leaped over the hedge upon him."

It may not be uninteresting to mention that the Marquis d'Arcangues alluded to is still alive, and a remarkably fine specimen of the old French *haute noblesse*. During a recent excursion in La Basque, the writer of these records was hospitably welcomed at the ancient château, where M. d'Arcangues passes the autumn of his days, patriarchally surrounded by numerous children and grandchildren. His memory of the events of 1813—which rendered his estate historic ground—is acutely retentive. He related several anecdotes; among them, how one poor fellow of the 43rd, on being carried into the château seriously wounded, desired the surgeon to hand him the bullet just extracted, which he then placed under his pillow, saying it "should yet wing a Frenchman." The Marquis d'Arcangues remarked that he was well acquainted with various officers of the regiment, whom he characterised as a very gentlemanlike set, adding that he met Hobkirk at dinner at Soult's, the very evening of his capture, who from the richness of his dress was at first mistaken for a field-marshal.

Lord Wellington then determined to separate his army into two corps, to force the passage of the Nive. The Light Division remained on the left bank. Soult's position round Bayonne was far more compact and concentrated than that of the British. On the 9th of December the army was put in motion. The 2nd Division forded the river near Cambo; the Light Division advanced against the French in front of Bassussary and drove in some of their pickets; while the left, under Sir John Hope (who had succeeded Sir Thomas Graham), made way nearly up to the intrenched camp in front of Bayonne. Desultory skirmishing took place.

At daybreak on the 10th an advance of the enemy was observed within a hundred yards of the 43rd picket commanded by Lieutenant Cooke. About nine o'clock, a sentinel stationed on the highest ground informed him that he had seen a mountain gun brought on a mule's back and placed behind a bush. In a few moments, Soult with about forty staff-officers came within point-blank range to reconnoitre. During this short interval, Cooke, climbing up a tree, descried a column of the enemy lying down and in readiness to pounce upon his party.

Leaving the next senior officer in charge, he immediately gallopped off to acquaint the General, who desired him to despatch a mounted officer to Baron Alten, to delay firing until the latest possible moment, and at the same time sent part of another company to Cooke's support.

Soon after some French soldiers, headed by an officer—who feigning indifference made a bow to the party and carelessly looked about him—issued from behind the hedges and moved round within a hundred yards, while to the left a body of their cavalry appeared. Returning the civility of not being fired upon, the Chasseurs called to the men of the 43rd picket to retire. The French skirmishers then advanced, talking to each other, good naturedly allowing our sentinels to retreat without a shot. They expected by their superiority of numbers to win the post by a *coup de main*, and so to surprise more effectually the whole line. But when they were within twenty yards of the abbatis, Cooke called out, "Now fire away!" The first discharge did great execution; and thus commenced the

Battle of the Nive.

The enemy debouched from behind the thickets in crowds, and the flanks of the 43rd picket were turned, right and left; the French Voltigeurs shouting, "En avant, en avant, Français! Vive l'Empereur!" In the mean time the whole of the pickets of the 43rd ceased firing and retired leisurely, taking their station with the rest of the regiment, and formed in the churchyard of Arcangues, while the remainder of the brigade lined the breastwork of the château. One company of the 43rd having held its ground too long in front of Bassussary was surrounded. Duncan Cameron in command asked the soldiers if they would charge to the rear; upon this they rushed into the village with such prolonged huzzas, their sudden apparition so surprising a French brigadier that he halted his column; when they sprang across the single street and escaped.

The 2nd Brigade of the Light Division, previously in echelon to the left of the 1st and obliquely to the rear, now became sharply engaged. The plateau of Arcangues and Bussassary being gained by the enemy, became the pivot of Soult's operations, enabling his right wing to tackle the 5th Division on the high road to St. Jean de Luz. The attack opposite to the 43rd ceased, with the exception of the playing of artillery, which continued on the churchyard. This went on for some time, but the 43rd from the churchyard kept up so sharp and incessant a fire that the French gunners were at last glad to cease molesting them.

The enemy, collecting in force on the neighbouring heights, then seemed to meditate a closer attack. Two companies lined the interior of the church, round which ran wooden galleries; the walls were cannon proof, and water was carried into the building and a strong traverse erected across the door; so that if *par hasard* the enemy should gain possession, the fire from the galleries would drive them out. The rest of the battalion was stationed in reserve behind the stone wall encircling the churchyard, with fixed bayonets ready to charge. The enemy's advance was within two hundred yards, covered by cannon on the brow of the hill; the 43rd had two mountain guns, three-pounders, placed to the left of the church. The other intrenchments consisted of a few lightly turned shovels of earth, which the French Voltigeurs might have easily hopped over; and flank defences were wholly omitted.

On the 11th of December, it was conjectured the Duke of Dalmatia would break our centre by advancing against the church and château. Accordingly Sir John Hope detached the right of his force nearer to the left of the Light Division; but the enemy again attacked and obliged him to resume his original ground, when many brave men fell on both sides. Though the French advance was close to the 43rd, there was no firing, and the interregnum was used to strengthen the position. At this juncture, two battalions of German troops, men of Nassau and Frankfort, left the French lines and came over to the Allies.

On the 12th, firing continued through the greater part of the day. In the evening, on calling the roll of the regiment, a dozen men were reported missing, whereupon Colonel Napier despatched an officer with a sergeant and patrol in quest. The men were found in a small house filled with apples, on most amicable terms with about as many French soldiers—oddly enough belonging to the Imperial 43rd. The same object, that of securing the tempting fruit, had impelled both parties to the spot, and all had gone on the apple raid unarmed. The French, on observing that the English bore "43" on their breast-plates, examined them attentively, cordially shook hands, and expressed much pleasure in the accidental rencontre, asking many questions as to rations and allowances; and assured them if they would accompany them to a post a little way off they would give them some first-rate brandy. Upon the appearance of the officer, the Frenchmen, believing themselves prisoners, brought forth the whole of their spoil as a peace offering; but he merely pointed to the door, whence they effected their escape, while the English truants with crammed havresacks were escorted back to their quarters.

On the 13th Soult attacked Hill's corps at St. Pierre. It was a noble battle, nobly won by the British General. Both sides fought as if determined that the struggle should wind up, in brilliant style, the three days' combat of the Nive. The enemy, driven back at all points, never again resumed the offensive, nor was the British army further disturbed by petty affairs.

In the afternoon, Lord Wellington passing by the 43rd in conversation with Sir James Kempt was heard to say, "I have often seen the French well licked, but I never knew them get such a hell of a licking as Hill has given them to-day."

In the late various affairs the 43rd had 1 rank and file killed; 13 rank and file, wounded; 1 sergeant, 1 bugler, and 19 rank and file, missing. Lieut.-Colonel W. Napier was wounded, first by a musket-ball in the right hip, and again by the explosion of a shell which drove his telescope against his face. He received a clasp for having commanded the regiment. The year closed without further incidents, and national Christmas festivities were celebrated in due form.

1814.

Early in February the Light Division passed the Nive and occupied Bastide, but the 43rd were ordered to return to Ustaritz to bring on their new clothing which had reached that place from England.

Reaching Sauveterre they found the bridge had been blown up, and it was therefore necessary to ford the river upwards of a hundred yards in breadth. Although hardly three feet deep, so rapid was the current, and so stony the bottom, that it was deemed advisable for the strongest men to throw off their knapsacks, join hands, and form a close chain with their faces to the stream, in order to pick up any who might turn giddy or lose foothold. At night they bivouacked in a wood within three miles of Orthes, where they learnt that the battle of Orthes had been fought. Early on the 29th, the regiment got under arms, hoping to give the 2nd Division "the go by;" but the movement having been anticipated, strict orders were issued that they should follow in rear.

When within four miles of the river Adour, Wellington

rode up, and said, "Forty-Third, what are you doing here?" Napier replied that the officer commanding the column would not let them pass. In ten minutes the whole of the troops in their front were halted, the Regiment marched forward, and soon after formed column in the Grande Place of the town of St. Sever. From thence they were sent with Ross's brigade of Horse-artillery to Mont de Marsan to take possession of the stores in that town. When the bridge was reached, Picton declined halting the 3rd Division, and it was not until he received the most peremptory orders to do so that he consented. Soult having left Bordeaux to its fate, retired up the Adour to confront Hill's corps which had branched off to the right, and was moving in the direction of Aire to threaten the French Marshal's communication with Toulouse.

Instead of being received with hostility or sullenness at Mont de Marsan, the inhabitants flocked out to welcome the British troops. The new clothing was carried by the soldiers on the tops of their knapsacks, while nearly all their trowsers in wear were made from blankets. The French expressed much astonishment at seeing the troops of the richest nation in the world so thread-bare and poorly clad. The band struck up, and the women exclaimed, "Ma foi! Les Anglais ont de la musique! Et voilà de beaux jeunes gens aussi!"

The 43rd then took possession of the village of Brinquet, and social hospitalities were exchanged until the 19th, when the Division encamped on a ridge of hills east of Vic Bigorre: there they witnessed the attack on the town by the 3rd Division.

On the 20th, while 200 French cavalry blocked up the main road, a portion of the British army made a demonstration of crossing the Adour opposite the town of Tarbes. The 43rd formed column on the left, with a troop of the 10th Hussars below, facing the French detachment. Two of the enemy's videttes walked their horses to within a hundred yards of the 10th, and sarcastically challenged them to charge. The officers of the 43rd whispered them to avoid rashness and keep perfectly quiet until a company could creep along under a hedge to take the chasseurs in flank; when the main body instantly unmasked two pieces of cannon at half range, and began playing away. The 6th Division then attacked in reverse, obliging them to retire on Tarbes. Next morning, the enemy being in full retreat towards Toulouse, the Light Division cut in upon the high road of St. Gaudens, and eventually crossed the Garonne by a pontoon bridge, near Fenoulhiet, while the army marched in parallel columns on Toulouse. When within two miles, the enemy were seen in dense black columns filing out of the town, and forming in order of battle on the terre de Cabade, crowned with redoubts. Soult had arrived on the 24th of March, and his position was exceedingly strong.

Battle of Toulouse.

Lord Wellington remained on the left bank of the Garonne. On the A.M. of April the 10th, the enemy were to be forced near a large building in front of the *tête-de-pont* of Craniague by the 3rd Division. The 2nd Brigade of the Light Division branched off to the right to make a sham attack opposite the *tête-de-pont* of Les Minimes, and to keep up a link with the 3rd Division, while the 1st Brigade edged off to the left to support the Spaniards, then moving in echelon on that flank. While crossing a small rivulet, two of the enemy's guns opened from the detached eminence of La Borde de la Pugade. So soon as the Spaniards had crossed the stream and ditch they advanced rapidly, driving the French from their advanced posts, behind which they formed in column.

At 11 o'clock the Spaniards moved forward to attack the heights of Pugade, but suffered a terrible defeat; the French came round the left flank of the fugitive Spaniards, until stopped by the fire of a brigade of guns and an attack on their own left by the Rifles supported by the 43rd. The enemy, finding they had totally defeated the Spaniards, immediately moved a body of troops and cavalry to the right, to make head against the 4th and 6th Divisions; but after the repulse of the Spaniards the battle almost ceased on that side. About this time, an officer of the 43rd—Lieutenant Havelock,—extra aide-de-camp to Baron Alten, was seen riding at the base of the enemy's position, turning and twisting his horse at full speed, inducing a group of brother officers to imagine he was wounded and no longer able to manage the animal. Suddenly he fell, as it were, from the saddle to the ground, and the horse made a dead stop. Believing him killed, great was their surprise when he remounted, cantering towards them with a hare which he had ridden down.

By the middle of the day, the 6th Division gained the French position and took a redoubt. The 4th Division made an oblique march to the left to turn the enemy's right flank, which manœuvre greatly contributed to the victory. The French made a desperate attempt to retake the great redoubt in the centre, but without effect. Owing to this failure, they quietly evacuated those on their left, and the whole army retired to the faubourg of St. Etienne. Soult held the town on the following day, hemmed in on almost every side, but there was no firing, and during the night of the 11th retreated towards Carcassonne. Lord Wellington entered in triumph on the 12th.

On the 12th, a detachment from the 2nd Battalion

joined, consisting of 2 captains, 4 lieutenants, 3 ensigns, 3 sergeants, and 198 rank and file; only two days too late to share in the last laurels gathered in the six years' conflict.

For several days Soult declined negotiating with Lord Wellington, and the Division was for the last time put in motion, marching some leagues on the road to Ville Franche. Hardly had they taken up their ground, before General Count Albufera de Gazan, deputed by the Dukes of Dalmatia and Albuera to treat with Lord Wellington, alighted, and preliminaries for permanent peace were entered upon.

In consequence, the Division retraced their steps to Montech, where for six subsequent weeks the 43rd remained, passing the time most agreeably; the enjoyment of the hospitalities and gaieties lavishly offered by the leading residents doubtless greatly enhanced by long previous abstinence. On the regiment quitting Montech, great demonstrations of regret were made by the citizens, who in crowds accompanied them to the banks of the Garonne. The officers dismounted, walked behind the regiment escorted by the ladies of Languedoc, exchanging many tokens of mutual interest. The soldiers, too, had enrolled themselves in the good graces of the grisettes, and one, as her admirer entered the boat, flung herself into the river, but was fortunately rescued from a watery grave and eventually united to the sergeant for love of whom she had so nearly perished.

The whole British army then marched for Bordeaux, the Portuguese Caçadores detaching in order to regain their own country. They took leave of the Light Division with unfeigned sorrow, whom they would willingly have followed to any quarter of the globe. Having for several years fought side by side, they had themselves attained the same conspicuous state of discipline and efficiency.

"The training enforced by Moore was contrived to produce a perfect soldier. He did not merely teach striplings to move a hundred thousand men on paper, but put them in the ranks and made them practise the duties of privates. They thus acquired an inward, and not a mere outward knowledge of the functions they were to superintend.

"He also devised such improvements in drill, discipline and dress, arms, formations and movements, as would have placed him for military reforms beside the Athenian Iphicrates, if he had not had the greater glory of dying like the Spartan Brasidas.

"The material chosen by Moore to fashion after his own plan were the three infantry regiments—the 43rd, 52nd, and Rifles; and Sir William Napier records with pride that 'they sent forth a larger number of distinguished officers than any three regiments in the world. The men vied with their leaders in attaining excellence. They constituted Wellington's celebrated Light Division, and even before they had seen a battle were, according to Major Hopkins, looked up to as the veterans of the army by troops who had already been in fight.'

"'The greatest secret of war is discipline,' wrote the historian, and it was to discipline that the Light Division owed its supremacy; they were never negligent, never dismayed. Once, on their way to the lines of Torres Vedras, they started up from their sleep in the night, without an enemy being near or an alarm being given, and dispersed in every direction. A voice called out that the pursuing cavalry was amongst them, and immediately the whole of the scattered soldiers ran together to repel the attack.

"They are stated to have been no less orderly on the breach than in the line, and though they were always at the outposts, in the most hazardous situations, the only baggage they lost throughout the Peninsular campaign was on the retreat from Salamanca, when some horsemen got up to their rear in a wood and captured two mules.

"Six years of warfare could not detect a flaw in their system, nor were they ever matched in courage or skill. Those three regiments were avowedly the best that England ever had under arms. This is no idle boast. War was better known, the art more advanced under Napoleon than in any age of the world before, and the French veterans—those victors of a thousand battles—never could stand an instant before my gallant men."

Hardly had the Division sighted Bordeaux, and drawn up in an adjacent wood, before they were desired, with barely time to shake the dust from off their accoutrements, to form along the road, in order to be reviewed by their Chief—now created DUKE of Wellington. At the conclusion they moved on to Blanchefort Camp, and thence to Pouillac, where the final separation of comrades in arms, so long and gloriously associated, took place.

Brightly danced the sun's reflected rays on the glittering waters of the Garonne, as the greater part of the 43rd were rowed aboard the 'Queen Charlotte,' flag-ship of Lord Keith, Admiral of the Channel Fleet, for conveyance to Old England. The remainder embarked in the 'Dublin.' After nine days, the 'Queen Charlotte' dropped her anchor in Plymouth Sound. The battalion disembarked on the 23rd and 25th of July, and the officers gave a dinner at the 'Fountain' to the Admiral and his subordinates, in return for the kindness and courtesy shown them whilst at sea. Before the close of the month the 2nd Battalion arrived from Hythe Barracks, when an interchange took place.

After three months' rest and quiet at home, the 1st

Battalion, mustering 1050 bayonets, commanded by Colonel Patrickson, was ordered to form a brigade with the 7th Fusiliers, already on board ship, and take passage for the same destination—the New World. On the 10th of October, the regiment was placed in three transports, and, after remaining weather-bound for a fortnight, got under weigh. In six weeks Martinique and Dominica were sighted; Fort George was passed; and in twelve days the transports, convoyed by the 'Vengeur,' 74, made the delta of the Mississippi, thence steered for Lac Borgne, and on New Year's Day found themselves in the midst of a British fleet, the greater part of the ships from the 'Chesapeake' having arrived, with the troops which had captured Washington.

In the last great campaign of the American War there was no lack of courage, though an incredible amount of blundering. Not satisfied with ruining the trade of all towns on the Mississippi by blockading that river, it had been determined to attack New Orleans. The British commander finding that the intended *coup* was anticipated by the Americans, struck upon the bold idea of entering Lac Borgne in the season of short days and long nights, baffling winds, intense cold, and, withal, in a very difficult navigation—a daring enterprise, skilfully carried out. Before daylight on the 13th of December, the men-of-war's boats in three divisions had entered Lac Borgne; by the 21st, the land forces, commanded by Major-General Sir John Kean, were concentrated on Isle aux Poix; and on the 22nd, Captain Travers' company of the Rifles in advance, seeing a fire on the right-hand of the creek, landed and captured an American look-out picket without a shot being fired on either side. Early next day, 1600 British troops were landed within seven miles of New Orleans, and marching through a plantation the same company of Rifles quietly captured a major and twenty

American militiamen; but the officer contrived to escape, and spread the news of the British descent.

All difficulties had thus disappeared. A flat open plain with a cypress wood was on the right, the Mississippi on the left, with the city of New Orleans stretched in front. Up to this epoch General Jackson was virtually surprised; the troops however halted at the exact moment when they should have advanced, and no notice was taken of two American vessels of war anchored in the river. A staff officer—the present General Sir De Lacy Evans, K.C.B.—recommended that time should be taken by the forelock, but his seniors decided otherwise. Jackson thus gained breathing time, and, knowing that New Orleans was no place for defence, "Old Hickory" determined to show his generalship. The troops already landed were the 4th and 85th, five companies of the 95th Rifles, two light field-pieces, and a few sappers. Instead of being employed in throwing up some kind of cover, these soldiers were lounging about while the boats returned to fetch the remainder.

Fires blazed in the bivouac, arms were piled, and each soldier looked after his individual necessities. At eight o'clock the anchor of one of the sloops of fourteen guns—which had been observed up the river—was let go. The fires enabled the Americans to point their guns with precision, and then round and grape shot at once played amongst the astonished troops, knocking over the arms and boiling mess-kettles, and scattering logs of blazing wood far and near, maiming and killing many. Captain Hallen's company of the Rifles began a battle single-handed, against part of the 7th and 44th American regiments and a strong body of irregulars, led by Jackson himself; but they could not beat Hallen and his eighty men, wholly unsupported. There was severe hand-to-hand fighting, and prisoners were taken and retaken on both sides. The Americans failed in the great point of forcing the main road. Finally they gave way on all sides, after a contest of three hours, principally sustained by the Rifles and the 85th—in all about 1000 strong. Some companies of the 93rd Highlanders and 21st Fusiliers came up towards the close, and proved a most seasonable reinforcement.

Instead of following up his victory, the British General let slip his opportunity, although all his force was now landed.

Jackson continued to fire into the bivouac of the British, while he prolonged a broad ditch by a cut to the Mississippi, about one hundred yards behind his Crescent battery on the high road, in hopes of saving New Orleans for a day. Behind this, he constructed with the utmost despatch a barricade of near three-quarters of a mile in length—extending from the river to a wood, said to be impassable, on his left—composed of barrels and sugar-casks placed here and there along the edge of a ditch ten feet wide by three deep, the interstices filled with mud and all kinds of rubbish. Two heavy pieces of cannon were mounted on the original Crescent battery. From hour to hour, the Americans, unmolested, strengthened the barricade with bales of cotton and everything that came to hand.

On Christmas-day, Major-General Sir Edward Pakenham and Major-General Gibbs arrived. Pakenham at once declared that troops were never before in such a predicament, and although auguring badly as to the result, resolved to persevere in the attack. He made no instantaneous advance, but remodelled the small British force into two brigades; the dragoons, having no horses, were employed about the hospitals and other head-quarter purposes.

On the 27th, Jackson's schooner was blown up by red-hot shot from a battery hastily erected. On the following day a reconnaissance was made, by which we lost fifty men and made no way. The other American ship of fourteen guns was warped up the river nearer to the town. A battery was erected 700 yards from General Jackson's Crescent battery, and on the 1st of January, 1815, a second attempt was made on the American works with no better success. Such was the aspect of affairs fifteen days after the first landing of the British troops.

1815.

On the 5th of January the 7th and 43rd landed, both corps in splendid order, mustering upwards of 1700 bayonets. A grand attack being determined on, as a preliminary, at eleven o'clock P.M. on the 7th, 200 of the 43rd, with a proportionate number of officers, were ordered to the front to mend and guard a battery on the right of the enemy's lines, and endeavour to render it tenable before daylight. Water unluckily sprang up at the depth of a foot, obliging them to pare the surface for a great extent around; but they worked unflaggingly through the greater part of the night, when some cannon were dragged up and placed in the battery.

Two companies of the 7th and 93rd with one of the 43rd, a compact little column of 240, were to assault the Crescent battery, which now mounted twenty pieces. The working party of the 43rd had only just quitted the battery at which they had been toiling, when a rocket —the signal for attack—went whizzing aloft, falling into the Mississippi. For a minute or two all was silence; then a tremendous discharge from the British artillery opened upon the left of the American lines before they could even see upon what their fire was to be directed, and before the attacking column of the British was properly formed.

Light breaking disclosed the 7th and 43rd in echelon; the 85th had been detached across the river; the Fusiliers were within 300 yards of the enemy's lines. So great was the echo from all sides that each report seemed answered an hundred-fold. The assault had commenced, and the 200 men of the 43rd ran the gauntlet from the left to the centre, under a cross-fire, in hopes of taking part. But the attack had already failed, and companies were broken, driven back, and dispersed. Lieutenant Duncan Campbell of the 43rd was observed running about in circles, and at length fell on his face. When picked up, he was found to be blind from the effects of a grape-shot that had torn open his forehead. As he was borne insensible to the rear, with a convulsive grasp he clutched the hilt of his sword, the blade having been broken off by the shot, and then expired.

Three generals, 7 colonels, 75 officers, and 1781 soldiers had fallen in a few minutes. Pakenham was killed, Gibbs mortally wounded, his brigade dispersed, and Keane disabled. The command devolved upon Major-General Lambert. With the exception of the 200 of the 43rd in the centre, hardly a man was found all the way to the bank of the river, where Colonel Thornton had crossed. Lieutenant Rowley Hill of the 43rd remarked, "Look at the 7th and 43rd, like two seventy-fours becalmed. Why were they not led on?" Many old soldiers asked the same question, but in vain.

In conjunction with two companies of the 7th and 93rd, one of the 43rd, soon after the British artillery opened, had rushed forward under a murderous fire of cannon, rifles, and small arms, and although the Crescent battery was defended bravely, forced their way into it. But their ranks were nearly annihilated, as 8 officers and 180 men were killed or wounded. The remaining handful clung tenaciously to the battery; four pieces of cannon were taken, and the soldiers ensconced themselves in the exterior ditch, in hopes of succour. It was only when the grand attack failed that they retired, which was effected by some raising their caps on the points of their bayonets, and making a start inducing the enemy to fire a volley. Before the smoke cleared away, these men, at full speed, were almost beyond musket range. Only three officers of the whole detachment escaped unwounded. Lieutenant Steele of the 43rd alone got off scot free.

This company of the 43rd was commanded by Captain Robert Simpson. The subalterns were Lieutenants Duncan Campbell, Meyrick, and Alexander Steele—all volunteers. The loss amounted to 2 lieutenants, 1 sergeant, 1 bugler, and 11 rank and file, killed; 1 lieutenant, 2 sergeants, and 19 rank and file, wounded; 1 captain, 2 buglers, and 15 rank and file, missing and prisoners. The officers killed were Lieutenants Duncan Campbell and Meyrick; Captain Robert Simpson severely wounded and taken prisoner, and Lieutenant Darcy lost both legs by a round shot which entered his tent two days after. Captain Wilkinson—formerly of 43rd,—Acting Brigade-Major, had his horse shot under him, but observing that the Americans slackened fire, he rushed forward on foot: a ball pierced his body, and he fell into the shallow ditch. While gasping for breath, he said to the only officer who accompanied him, "Now, why do not the troops come on? the day is our own!" But it was too late, and the moment of probable victory eluded our grasp. The 7th and seven companies of the 43rd were still formed at within six hundred yards of the enemy's lines, full of enthusiasm, and waiting impatiently for an order to force the passage; but there they were kept, idle spectators of the defeat, after having been brought so many thousand miles to join in the combat and anticipated triumph. While the reserve were still anxiously looking for the result of Thornton's attack on the other side of the river, a volley was heard, then a few hasty discharges of artillery, and finally a round of lusty British cheers. The 85th had taken all the American works, batteries, sixteen pieces of cannon, and a stand of colours. On that side victory was complete: they were opposite to New Orleans, and enfiladed the enemy's lines.

Wonderful to relate, in this state of affairs, instead of renewing the main attack, a flag of truce was sent to General Jackson, asking leave to bury the dead—a request eagerly acceded to, on condition that no more troops should be sent across the river during the time so occupied. For the rest of that disastrous day, the reserve maintained their position. Two hours after dark they retired, on hearing that Colonel Thornton's party had been withdrawn from the opposite side of the river. Such was the sequel of a most inexplicable series of military tactics, and the failure was doubly galling when it became known that peace had actually been signed at Ghent, between England and America, a fortnight before this encounter; but in those days there was no submarine electric telegraph to flash intelligence with the rapidity of lightning from hemisphere to hemisphere.

On the 18th of January the British forces were entirely withdrawn from before New Orleans, and returned to the ships. In a few days they steered for Mobile Bay, and early in February landed on Dauphin Island, where they went under canvas, and on the 8th of April the 43rd with the 7th Fusiliers sailed for England. Off the Land's End a vessel hove to and distributed newspapers wherein long columns recounted Napoleon's invasion of France from Elba, with four small vessels, 800 infantry and 100 Polish dragoons, in an attempt to recover the Imperial diadem, at the very moment when the European plenipotentiaries were in solemn deliberation at Vienna.

On the 1st of June the 'Bucephalus' frigate, with part of the 43rd, let go her anchor at Spithead, and the transports, with the remainder of the corps, turned up a few days later, when all proceeded to comfortable quarters in Dover and Deal. A strong draft from the 2nd battalion, consisting of 1 captain, 3 lieutenants, 5 ensigns, 15 sergeants, and 190 rank and file, here awaited them.

On the 16th the regiment, mustering 1100 bayonets, was put aboard small craft for the purpose of joining the Allied army in the Netherlands. Landing at Ostend, they reached Ghent on the 19th, when their mortification may be better imagined than portrayed on finding that the great and decisive battle of WATERLOO, memorable for ever in all archives, military, political, or historical, had taken place, and the last act played out of the long, adventurous and stirring drama comprising the public life of one of the greatest yet direst of autocrats.

Joining the army near St. Denis, they were on July 4th placed in the 5th Division, under command of Major-General Sir James Kempt, and marched to Paris, where they encamped on the heights of Belville. On the 6th Louis XVIII. made his public entry into the French capital. On the 7th the 43rd moved to the banks of the Seine near Clichy, remaining until the 30th of October. They then went into cantonments at Melun and the adjacent villages. On the 30th of November a General Order fixed and formed into divisions and brigades that portion of the British forces intended to form the Army of Occupation in France.

The 43rd was placed in brigade with the 7th and 23rd Fusiliers, being one of the three comprising the 1st Division commanded by Lieut.-General Sir Lowry Cole, G.C.B. At Christmas they marched from Melun to Paris, and occupied the caserne in the Place Verte, doing duty at the barriers.

1816.

In January they marched for the north of France, followed by the 7th and 23rd. Early in February they reached Bapaume, the head-quarters of the battalion. Many fine soldiers, whose limited period of service had expired, left for England, and in October 100 undersized and worn men were also discharged and sent home.

1817.

On the 3rd of April, in consequence of the reduction of the 2nd Battalion, a detachment of 1 captain, 6 subalterns, 6 sergeants, 8 buglers, and 154 rank and file, joined the first. On the 12th the regiment moved from Bapaume to Valenciennes, thence to Cambray, and encamped on the glacis. On the 11th of October they broke up from Cambray; returning to Valenciennes.

1818.

Leaving Valenciennes in August, the 43rd returned to Cambray, and in September removed to Douchy. On the 23rd of October the whole of the British, Hanoverian, Saxon, and Danish contingents, under the command of the Duke of Wellington, were reviewed by the Emperor of Russia and King of Prussia, and went through a variety of manœuvres. It was a grand military display. The troops of each nation in different columns, having a supposed enemy in front, moved between Cambray and Valenciennes, threw their pontoons over the river, and crossed under a heavy cannonade, a large force of artillery and cavalry in the field, several good charges being made by the latter. Upon arriving at the open ground overlooking Valenciennes, the troops passed the allied sovereigns in review order, and the next morning they were all in motion for their different countries—some Cossacks having even to return to the walls of China. There was a grand ball given by the Duke of Wellington at the theatre at Valenciennes to the sovereigns in the evening.

On the 26th the British contingent of the Army of Occupation broke up and commenced its homeward route. The 43rd, still in brigade with the 7th and 23rd, arrived at Calais on the 31st, embarked for Dover, landed and marched to Canterbury.

1819.

During the following month, while there, the strength of the regiment was reduced to the peace establishment,

	F. O.	Capts.	Subs.	Staff.	Sergts.	Bugles.	R. & F.
From	4	10	30	6	55	22	810
To	4	10	20	5	35	22	650

Soon after this reduction, the regiment embarked for Ireland, and remained in barracks in Belfast until July, 1820.

In this year Lieut.-Colonel Napier left the regiment. On his leaving, all the officers who had served under him, even those who had quitted the service, or gone on halfpay, or into other regiments, subscribed to present him with a rich sword, bearing on its blade the following inscription :—

"Presented by LIEUT.-COLONEL PATRICKSON, C.B., and the Officers of the 43rd Light Infantry, to

LIEUT.-COLONEL WILLIAM F. P. NAPIER, C.B.,

as a testimony of their sincere regard for him, and their high admiration of the gallantry and conduct he ever displayed during his exemplary career in the 43rd Regiment."

1820.

In October of this year the 43rd removed to Dublin.

1821.

On the 7th of March a communication from the Horse Guards was received, bearing date the 2nd, stating that

"His Majesty had been pleased to approve of the regiment being permitted to bear on its colours and appointments, in addition to any other badges or devices, which may have heretofore been granted to it, the words—

Vimiero,	Salamanca,
Busaco,	Vittoria,
Fuentes d'Onoro,	Nivelle,
Ciudad Rodrigo,	Nive,
Badajoz,	Toulouse,

in commemoration of the distinguished services of the regiment at the Battle of Vimiero, 21st of August, 1808; at the action of Busaco, 27th of September, 1810; at Fuentes d'Onoro, 5th May, 1811; at Ciudad Rodrigo, 19th of January, 1812; at the siege of Badajoz, 6th of April, 1812; at the Battle of Salamanca, 22nd of July, 1812; at Vittoria, 21st of June, 1813; at Nivelle, 10th of November, 1813; at the passage of the Nive, on the the 9th, 10th, and 11th of December, 1813; and in the attack of the posts covering Toulouse, on the 10th of April, 1814." A communication was also received, dated the Horse Guards, 22nd of March, 1821, stating "that His Majesty had been pleased to approve of the regiment being permitted to bear on its colours and appointments, in addition to any other badge or devices which may have heretofore been granted to the regiment, the word

CORUNNA,

in commemmoration of the distinguished services of the 2nd Battalion, in the action fought near that town on the 16th of January, 1809."

In August, on occasion of His Majesty King George IV. visiting Ireland, the 43rd, in conjunction with others forming the garrison of Dublin, was passed in review; the full colonel, Lord Howden, G.C.B., in command. In the same month, an order was received for the further reduction of the army, and the regimental establishment was lowered

	F. O.	Capts.	Subs.	Staff.	Sergts.	Corps.	Buglers.	R. & F.
From .	4	10	20	5	35	30	22	620
To .	4	8	16	5	30	24	12	552

1822.

In December the regiment marched to Naas.

1823.

In February, 1823, to Limerick; in June to Galway; and in July to Fermoy, previous to embarkation for Gibraltar, when Major William Haverfield succeeded to the command, by purchase, vice Colonel Patrickson who retired. The 43rd reached Gibraltar on the 9th of October, and were inspected by the Governor, the Earl of Chatham.

1824.

Remained at Gibraltar. Here, for several months, General Don Miguel Alava was the honoured guest of the regiment. One of the finest specimens of the old Castilian nobles, his rare qualities both of head and heart rendered him beloved by all. Nephew of the Spanish Admiral Gravina, he was taken prisoner on board his ship and severely wounded at the Battle of Trafalgar. In 1810 he had been appointed Spanish Commissioner to the Duke of Wellington's head-quarters, which office he most efficiently filled until the close of the war, and had formed very intimate acquaintance with the officers of the 43rd. When the French invaded Spain in 1823, Alava, who had joined the Constitutional party, retired with their Government to Cadiz, carrying with them the King—Ferdinand. On the French storming the Rocadero they were obliged to submit, and deliver up Ferdinand. Alava was selected to hand over the King to the French outposts, and feeling that his life was no longer safe he got on board a vessel direct for Gibraltar. So soon as his arrival in the bay was reported the officers of the 43rd begged him to take up his quarters in their barracks—a proposal which, with warm expressions of pleasure, he accepted. Other regiments on "the Rock" were solicitous to show him similar attentions, but he used invariably to reply, " I like to live with my own family here—my old friends the 43rd."

Afterwards, during Lord Melbourne's administration, Don Alava filled the diplomatic post of Ambassador at St. James's.

1825.

Early in the year, General Foissac le Tour, the general commanding the French army in Spain, came to Gibraltar. Colonel Haverfield being absent on leave, Major Booth offered to show him the regiment. He replied he should be delighted, and came on the ground in full dress, a large crimson saddle-cloth embroidered in golden fleurs de lys, and attended by his aide-de-camp, nearly as richly caparisoned. On the conclusion of the field-day, General Foissac said, " Major Booth, you have well commanded your well-instructed regiment. This day has disabused me of an error of twenty years. I always thought the French infantry the quickest to move in Europe, but they are nothing to you, you move like cavalry!"

Singularly enough the French General thus unwittingly parodied the old Shorncliffe *refrain*—

"No cavalry in England can form a line so quick,
As the 43rd Light Infantry can—at the double-quick!"

A feat of surprising agility was at this time performed by Lieutenant Daniel Freer of the 43rd. Returning from a shooting-excursion with some brother officers, he was laughingly challenged, as they neared the saluting battery of twenty-one mounted guns on iron carriages, to jump one. To the astonishment of the spectators, he instantly jumped over the whole twenty-one, one by one, and turning back repeated the exploit without flagging.

A General Order was issued, directing that four companies of each regiment abroad—East Indies excepted—should be stationed at home, and also that the strength of such regiments should be augmented from eight to ten companies: the corps abroad to have six service-companies consisting each of 1 captain, 1 lieutenant, 1 ensign, 4 sergeants, 4 corporals, 10 buglers, and 82 privates. The four reserve companies at home to have each 1 captain, 1 lieutenant, 1 ensign, 3 sergeants, 3 corporals, 1 bugler, and 52 privates. A selection of officers and non-commissioned officers made for the purpose of joining the recruiting stations in England, arrived at Plymouth in July, where "THE DEPÔT" had arrived from the Isle of Wight; and in August the reserve companies consisted of 4 captains, 3 lieutenants, 2 ensigns, 1 assistant-surgeon, 14 sergeants, 4 buglers, and 84 rank and file. In October, the Depôt marched to Colchester, leaving a detachment of 1 captain, 1 lieutenant, 1 sergeant, and 44 privates, for embarkation to join the service companies.

1826.

In January the establishment of the reserve companies was completed, and they marched for Plymouth, where they remained until October, 1830.

1827.

Owing to the disturbed state of Portugal, and the hostile attitude of Spain, a British force of about 5000 men was despatched to the Peninsula, under command of Lieutenant-General Sir Henry Clinton, G.C.B. The service companies of the 43rd, being ordered to form part of that contingent, embarked from Gibraltar on board the 'Melville,' 74, for the Tagus.

On the 5th February they entered barracks at Lisbon, in brigade with the 23rd Fusiliers. Thence they marched by Coimbra to Leiria, remaining until the 19th, when they removed to Thomar, and on the 26th July made for Lumiar, which was reached on August 6th, after a fearfully harassing time, the heat being excessive, and many men expired from sunstroke. On the 11th the regiment marched to Belem for embarkation on their return to Gibraltar. This Portuguese episode furnished a strange contrast to the stirring incidents which had marked the footsteps of the 43rd over much of the same ground in 1810 and 1811.

A French paper related, as an incident of this *quasi* campaign, afterwards translated into the 'United Service Journal' of June, 1827, as follows:—

"*Military Punishment.*—A new kind of punishment has been inflicted in Lisbon upon an English soldier. Wishing to have his fill of port wine, and his finances being rather in a low state, he sold a pair of breeches to obtain the means of satisfying his thirst. This fact having been reported to his superiors, the soldier was compelled to stand sentinel two hours at the door of the barracks, in full uniform, but *sans culottes.*"

1828.

The 43rd, having returned to "the Rock," remained in barracks until the 17th September, when they were placed under canvas on the neutral ground, a mortal epidemic having broken out in garrison. The loss sustained amounted to 2 sergeants, 1 bugler, and 86 rank and file, including many of the finest and most athletic soldiers in the corps.

1829.

On the 10th January the regiment returned to their barracks, the scourge having been arrested.

1830.

On the 29th of June, 1830, by the death of Lieut.-Colonel William Haverfield, Major Henry Booth succeeded to the command of the regiment. By an order of the 2nd of August, the *Gorget*, as well as the "*black cockade*" of England, heretofore worn by every rank, was abolished, and a paltry gold crown substituted for the latter.

Disturbances of a serious nature having broken out in the manufacting districts at home, orders were given to stop the Admiral's flag-ship, the 'Windsor Castle,' on her course from Malta to England, and the whole of the 43rd, with little or no preparation—men, women, children, and baggage—were hustled on board, quitting Gibraltar the same night, the 17th of December.

Soon after getting under weigh, the weather became thick, and as the 'Windsor Castle' got abreast of Tarifa, all hands were surprised by a discharge from the batteries on the Mole. One round shot flew over the poop, another struck the ship just under the quarter-galley. Guns were ordered to be run out to return the salute, but the current carried the vessel past the Mole before they could be brought to bear. It afterwards appeared it was customary to fire at all ships approaching the land after dark, and the 'Windsor Castle' having drifted within the proscribed limit, Jack Spaniard boldly let fly into her. Notwithstanding the overcrowd on board, the greatest possible good humour and *bon-hommie* existed during the whole passage between the brave tars and their red-coated visitors.

1831.

The regiment disembarked at Portsmouth on the 2nd of January, marching on the 5th to Winchester Barracks, where, by express command, it was detained until the Duke of Wellington came down from London, accompanied by Lord Fitzroy Somerset, to inspect his old tried and favourite corps. Towards the end of the month they received a route for Manchester, and arrived there on the 14th of February. The reserve companies joined from Bolton. The whole strength thus consisted of 3 field-officers, 10 captains, 10 lieutenants, 10 ensigns, 6 staff, 42 sergeants, 36 corporals, 14 buglers, and 653 privates. The head-quarters, with six companies, were then, in aid of the civil power, detached to Wigan, and from thence to Haydock Lodge; while four companies, under Major Furlong, marched to Newcastle-under-Lyne, in consequence of insurrectionary ebullitions in the Potteries. Major George Johnson retired, and was succeeded by Captain Edward Walpole Keppel. Major Johnson had, throughout the Peninsular War and in the attack on New Orleans, served with the 43rd. He was slightly wounded at Badajoz.

1832.

In January the regiment moved to Dublin, and the Insurrection Act at that time being in force in Ireland, the captains were placed in the commission of the peace.

1833-34.

On the 8th of April the 43rd broke up from Dublin; the head-quarters proceeded to Castle Comer, the out-stations being Carlow, Castle Durrow, Maidenhead, Ballyragget, and Johnstown. At the end of May head-quarters removed to Kilkenny, with detachments throughout the country. In August the whole regiment moved to Cork, where they remained, under command of Major-General Sir T. Arbuthnot, until the 4th of June, 1835, the period of departure for New Brunswick, North America.

1835-36.

The service companies having been selected, the undermentioned officers embarked in the 'Prince Regent' transport, and proceeded up the St. John river to Fredericton, the capital and seat of government of the province:—

      Lieut.-Colonel Henry Booth, *in command*.
      Captains Charles R. Wright.
            " Samuel Tryon.
            " Hon. A. A. Spencer.
      Lieutenants J. Thomas.
            " J. Meade.
            " Jones.
            " Hon. C. R. West.
      Ensign Hoste.
      Surgeon Miller.
      Adjutant Priestly.
      Quarter-Master S. Rand.

The left wing sailed for St. John. The officers comprised:—

      Major E. W. Keppel.
      Captains W. Frazer.
            " W. Egerton.
            " W. Bell.
      Lieutenants F. Sanders.
            " J. A. Pearson.
            " Levinge.
            " W. D. Oxendon.
            " Lord William Hill.
      Ensigns J. C. Coote.
            " A. L. Cole.
            " H. Skipwith.
            " W. H. Herries.

Previous to anchoring, a steamer came alongside off Partridge Island, and carried away Lieutenant Pearson and twenty-five men to East Port, on the frontier of the State of Maine. The depôt companies left at Cork were under the command of Major Furlong.

1837.

On the occasion of Sir Archibald Campbell's resignation of the government of New Brunswick—the conqueror of the Burmese Empire — issued the following farewell address, after reviewing the 43rd for the last time:—

General Order.
"Head-Quarters, Fredericton, 19th May, 1837.

"His Majesty having been graciously pleased to accept Major-General Sir Archibald Campbell's resignation of the government of New Brunswick, His Excellency cannot leave the province without intimating to Lieut.-Colonel Booth, the officers, non-commissioned officers, and privates of the 43rd Regiment, the high opinion he entertains of the perfect discipline, general good conduct, and efficiency of that distinguished corps.

"Of no regiment with which it has been His Excellency's fortune to serve, during a long and varied course of service, has he had occasion to express himself more favourably, with none certainly has he ever parted with more sincere regret; and on making his report of the half-yearly inspection of this day, His Excellency will not fail to convey these sentiments to the General Commanding-in-Chief.

"By Command,

"J. CAMPBELL, Captain, A.D.C."

Sir Archibald Campbell was succeeded by Sir John Harvey, K.H., and soon after the rebellion broke out in Lower Canada.

THE CANADIAN REVOLT.

It has been pretty generally admitted that this wanton and wicked rebellion was alike unforeseen and unprovided for, both by the local and metropolitan governments; and though it may not have required the subtle spirit of a Fouché to fathom the conspiracy, it must be recorded that neither the authorities nor the very best men in the colony believed that all the united influence of Papineau and his colleagues would suffice to rouse his countrymen into armed resistance against the Queen's authority. Yet no doubt can be entertained that for three months previous to any overt act of opposition, there existed an extensive, if not a general system of organization, for the intimidation of government into an unconditional compliance with the wishes and demands of its leaders, and eventually, if deemed practicable, a determination to overthrow the regal power and erect a republic. Bodies of brigands, committed to open rebellion by Papineau—who, like all "patriots" of his class, shrinking from the perils and penalties he had provoked, had himself absconded—actually braved a collision with the Queen's troops, several of whom were killed or wounded in opposing overwhelming numbers. The local government at length adopted measures calculated to protect the loyal and constitutional inhabitants—French and English—comprising the majority of the province, and strenuously to support the British officers and troops.

Martial law was proclaimed. Sir John Colborne, afterwards Lord Seaton, had been watching the progress of the conspiracy, and devising means of meeting and defeating its outbreak. Collecting what troops he could of the scanty force at his head-quarters, he made Montreal—nearly the centre of insurrection—the pivot of his operations. He fortified the post, formed magazines, organized and armed the local militia, which, with two or three exceptions, included every man of British descent within the province. The regular force stationed in the two Canadas was extremely small, and distributed along an extended line of many hundred miles. To the talent, firmness, and ready capacity of Sir John Colborne, England was indebted for crushing out this rebellion with little loss or bloodshed.

Keeping a part of his force in hand, he directed two detachments simultaneously—one, under Colonel Gore, upon St. Denis, the other, under Lieut.-Colonel Wetherall, upon St. Charles. From unavoidable circumstances, that of Colonel Gore failed; but Colonel Wetherall, having admirably executed his instructions, fell back upon Chambly, from whence he had started. Colonel Gore subsequently re-advanced upon St. Denis, and occupied the place. In this state of affairs, the misguided *habitans* were abandoned by their leaders, who, leaving their dupes, sought their own personal safety in precipitate flight. Sir John Colborne, marching out of Montreal with all his disposable force, attacked St. Eustache and Grand Brulé, the focus of the revolt, and utterly dispersed or captured the insurgents.

While these events were passing in Lower Canada, a corresponding revolutionary movement, though of comparatively trifling import, was made in the Upper Province. Sir Francis Head, the Lieutenant-Governor, placed the troops of his district at the disposal of Sir John Colborne, declaring that he would confide implicitly in the loyalty of the inhabitants. This declaration, regarded as a rash bravado, was speedily put to the test with signal success. A Scotch agitator, named Mackenzie, connected with the incendiary press, taking advantage of the absence of a military force, assembled a few hundred vagabonds about Toronto, murdered several Royalists, including Colonel Moody—formerly of the British army—robbed the mails, and performed other characteristic feats. Sir Francis Head mustered the faithful volunteers, who from all quarters flocked to his standard, and, with the British pensioners, promptly marched upon the disorderly rabble, and scattered them to the winds.

Meanwhile, great anxiety prevailed, and the Governor of New Brunswick offered the services of the 43rd, of which one wing was at Fredericton, the other at St. John's. Engineers and Indians were sent into the forest, and preparations made to attempt a winter march across the Portage of the Madawaska to Quebec, "one of the most remarkable movements on record." The moral influence of this march was immense. It struck the heart of the disaffected, crushed every hope they had entertained from the sympathy of the sister provinces, and convinced the world that there is no season at which Britain cannot reinforce her colonies, while she possesses soldiers whose dauntless spirits never quailed before a foe, or recoiled from any trial or exertion, however rigorous or severe. During this march the thermometer ranged from 20° to 30° below zero.

This unique winter march through the wilds of New Brunswick and Canada is well described by Captain (afterwards Major-General) Mundy, of the regiment:—

" * * * I wish I could send you my 'Notes,' but this letter must go through the States, and a large packet would be inconvenient. A flying sketch of our 'Winter march through the Wilderness from New Brunswick to Lower Canada,' must therefore suffice. Our line of march was from St. John River, through Woodstock, Tobique, Grand Falls; thence on the ice to the Madawaska settlement, leaving the St. John River, crossing to the Tamiscauta Lake, along the right shore and its surface—then across the portage to the south bank of the St. Lawrence, near the Rivière du Loup—thence 110 miles along the river-side to Pointe Levi, and across to Quebec. And now for a summary of our progress:—

December 11, 9 A.M.—The head-quarters (viz., Colonel and Adjutant and my company), after much trouble in fitting the men and baggage into the sleds (fourteen in number), left Fredericton, and at the six-mile house bid adieu to a large party of the fair and brave of that place who had accompanied us thus far, and who had greatly assisted us by presents of every kind calculated for warmth and comfort. The cold was great, and the ground too bare of snow for good sleighing. At the River Tobique we encountered our first serious difficulty, being upwards of four hours crossing our eighty men over the stream, which was running blocks of ice. Beyond this a few sleds were smashed; no other mishaps worthy of mention. Left the Grand Falls on the 16th morning, and driving thirty-three miles on the frozen river reached the French settlement of Madowaska. Some horses knocked up—dreadfully cold—piercing wind with sleet. Here we found the commissary from Quebec with provisions, but he had failed in getting carrioles, and our New Brunswick drivers with great difficulty were bribed to continue the march. On the 17th, we fairly plunged into the eternal forests, from whence we did not emerge until the 22nd evening, on the banks of the St. Lawrence. From Madawaska the little track of the courier from Canada to New Brunswick had been roughly widened by cutting down trees; it was barely passable, and the men walked the whole way, the horses being capable of drawing the sleds and accoutrements only, and at many passes it required fifteen or twenty men to draw each sled. I brought up the rear always, and you may imagine the difficulties of our route when I tell you that three or four days I was from daybreak till dark getting my men over fifteen miles, and after all this excessive cold and fatigue, a wretched log camp (there were six of them on the route built for us), open at the top, smoking so dreadfully that we could not open our eyes; a bed of pine-branches, a supper of salt pork, biscuit, and unmilked tea in a tin pot, the heat of the fire singeing our moccassins, whilst our fur nightcaps were frozen hard to the walls of the hut, the snow on the roof, melted by the fire, dripping through on our luxurious couch. Many of the soldiers would not enter their camps, and slept out before a mountain of burning wood. The surgeon's thermometer went down two evenings to 24 and 30 degrees below zero, or 62 of frost. Pretty comfortable for one whom you have seen shivering in the drawing-room of ———, with the thermometer 100 degrees higher than this!

"At one of the camps, when we rose in the morning, the sleds and baggage were found entirely buried in snow, and one's strength could not fold the frozen blankets covering the poor horses. The drivers behaved with the greatest bravery and loyalty; without them we must have starved in the desert. They returned from the head of Lake Tamiscauta fairly worn out, and were relieved by the carrioles and French drivers of Canada. I can give no idea of the dreariness of our forest marches; but to the extreme thickness of the trees, covered with snow, we owe an efficient shelter from a wind that would have cut us in two. The lake is very beautiful, like Leman, but entirely covered with snow. We passed the thirty-six miles of the famous Portage (a track over the mountains, connecting the lake with the St. Lawrence) in two days. The first view of the St. Lawrence, in descending the hill range, was very grand and very dreary. The stream, twenty-four miles broad, half frozen over, though salt, and so blocked with piles of ice as to resemble the Arctic region. During our four days' strange march (150 men and baggage, occupying 100 carrioles) along the river, we were daily fed and lodged by loyal Canadians and priests. The thrashing which Colonel Wetherall had given the rebels prevented the resistance we were taught to expect—and fortunate, perhaps, for us it was; the country is very strong, the snow off the road very deep, and we had no artillery to drive them from their posts. The 26th was a day of great suffering from cold—nine hours going thirty miles. I was frost-bitten in the cheek, but not severely enough to break the skin. So was ——, and many of the men. It acts precisely like a scald from boiling water, raising a blister and leaving a vile sore. Several persons came from Quebec to meet us and offer assistance *en route*, and our passage of the river and arrival at the city were extremely striking and exciting—

nothing had been talked of for a month but the 43rd's march through the desert; and the 1st Division being, of course, the most adventurous came in for all the honours of the reception. The two companies were thrown across the river (one mile wide) in canoes at once—the paddlers singing merrily—the quays and wharfs crowded with spectators, and lined with the several corps of volunteers, and as the officers' boat touched the ice on which we landed all gave us a most terrific cheer. The police took charge of our baggage, and, my company in front (as it had been all the way), we marched through a lane of soldiers, preceded by two bands; and thus on the 28th December, the ragged, unshaven, smoke-dried, toil-worn, frost-bitten 43rd entered triumphantly their barracks—an ancient Jesuit convent."

This march—commenced on the 11th December, and performed in eighteen days including a halt of two—was a length of 370 miles. Colonel Booth and his officers had reason to be proud of their exploit; as when reported to the Iron Duke, he remarked that it was one of the greatest feats ever performed, and the only military achievement by a British officer that he really envied.

1838.

Reports of gatherings of rebels on the rivers Richelieu and Yamaska, backed by an application for troops from the Lieutenant-Governor of Upper Canada, reached Quebec. The 43rd, with the 85th, who had subsequently followed across the Portage, received orders to hold themselves in readiness, and an officer was despatched to hasten the 34th from Halifax. The head-quarters, with Captains Egerton and Mundy's companies escorting a large convoy of arms and ammunition for the volunteers of the Montreal district, trotted out of Quebec on the 5th of January in 114 carrioles—a cavalcade covering at least half-a-mile of road. The four remaining companies followed. They took the northern shore of the St. Lawrence, sleighing all the way over the most perfect ice. On the 30th, Captains Frazer, Egerton, and the Hon. A. Spencer's companies proceeded to St. John's on the Richelieu, and on the 1st of February the headquarters, with Captain Wright's, Tryon's, and Mundy's followed. The march from Fredericton to Chambly was 553 miles; the left wing from St. John's, New Brunswick, travelled 90 more. On the 1st of March the regiment moved upon Henryville to meet a large force of rebels assembled in that direction, who, however, on their approach retired, and the corps returned. In April they moved to Chambly, and in May to La Prairie, from whence on the 4th of June they crossed the St. Lawrence to Montreal, taking up quarters in the Quebec Barracks. Here a draft from the Depôt joined. Seventy-nine of the privates were volunteers from other regiments.

While at a field-day at 6 o'clock A.M. of 30th June, a sudden order reached the 43rd directing their immediate removal to Upper Canada. Precisely as the clock struck nine they left their barracks. The left wing proceeded by the Ottawa and the Rideau Canal, while the right took the line of the St. Lawrence, making a sort of amphibious march—by steam where the river was navigable, by land where the rapids rendered it impassable—and reached Kingston on Lake Ontario on the 3rd of July. On the 6th an order came to advance on the Niagara frontier, to occupy a line of country hitherto almost entirely defended by militia and volunteers. With the despatch which had lately characterised their movements the right wing, accompanied by Sir John Colborne, was embarked the same evening. A detachment of artillery with two guns, and a party of sappers and miners with camp equipage for 1000 men, were also shipped.

On one side the mouth of the Niagara stood the United States' Fort of Niagara—on the opposite shore the ruinous British Fort St. George; the Cross of St. George and the Stars and Stripes being within a short half-mile of each other. Under a burning sun a landing was made near the Canadian fortress, and the troops encamped. On the following day they were again embarked, landing at Queenstown. The cliffs at this point are 360 feet high, and the turbid stream—sole vent for the waters of the great western lakes, supposed to contain half the fresh water of the globe—rushes madly through the narrow gorge.

The route from Queenstown to Niagara was beautiful and exciting; the foliage of the solemn forests contrasting artistically with the luxuriance of the lower vegetation. Within a mile of their destination Lundy's Lane was crossed—a sandy ravine leading up to an elevation which formed the key of the British position in the battle of 1814. Reaching the pretty little village of Drummondville, and debouching from a straggling grove of chesnuts, a verdant plateau extended, scarped by a precipitous bank some 300 feet in depth, thickly clothed with magnificent trees. Far above their topmost boughs the mists and sunbow of the Falls spanned the heavens, and through the foliage sparkled the first glitter of the world's greatest wonder. The word passed to form open column of companies, the right wing 43rd reached the greensward just above the table rock; arms were piled, and all rushed to the edge of the soul-stirring and stupendous cataract,— "that 'almighty' fall of waters."

A few weeks later, all hands were put on the *qui vive* by the arrival of Lord Durham and household. Old Niagara probably never did, and never will again, see such a gathering of cocked hats and radiant uniforms as on this occasion, when His Excellency was met by Sir John Colborne and Sir George Arthur with their respective staffs. The Governor-General adopted the soothing system, and was most liberal in his hospitalities. Willing, perhaps, first to astonish, and afterwards to mollify the Yankees, he issued public notice of a review on the 17th of July—in which the 43rd were the principal actors—and cards for two hundred persons to dinner in the evening. An immense concourse, chiefly Americans, attended; the ground was kept by two companies of the 24th Regiment, and a troop of Her Majesty's Niagara Lancers—a most excellent and efficient corps.

The spectators had the enjoyment of a rapid field-day in Colonel Booth's best style, with a liberal allowance of blank cartridge. In the evening, all the *invités* betook themseves to the banquet—a feast chiefly remarkable for the strange *mélange* of guests, among whom were a considerable proportion of ladies.

1839.

The regiment remained before Niagara, interchanging agreeable sociabilities with the residents. Dancing, *fêtes*, and amusements of all kinds filled up their leisure hours.

1840.

In May the 43rd under Major Furlong moved from Drummondville to Amherstberg.

1841.

In May the regiment had to mourn the death of Lieut.-Colonel Henry Booth, who expired while on leave of absence in England. This was a heavy loss to the corps, in which for upwards of thirty-five years he had served with much honour to himself, and amidst the affectionate regards of all. By his unflagging exertions and devotion the 43rd attained the highest distinction. No sooner were the tidings of his death promulgated than the officers determined to raise a monument to his memory. The non-commissioned officers and soldiers voluntarily came forward requesting to be allowed to join, and so universal was the respect entertained that many men who had never known him added their mite to the subscription, simply from his character for worth and goodness. The memorial was placed in the church of Northallerton, and bears this inscription :—

NEAR THIS PLACE IS INTERRED THE BODY OF
LIEUT.-COLONEL HENRY BOOTH, K.H.,
OF THE 43RD REGIMENT OF LIGHT INFANTRY,
FIFTH SON OF THE LATE WILLIAM BOOTH, ESQ., OF BRUSH HOUSE,
IN THE PARISH OF ECCLESFIELD, IN THE COUNTY OF YORK:
HE DIED AT NORTHALLERTON, MAY THE 6TH, 1841; AGED 51.

HIS MILITARY LIFE WAS PASSED IN THE 43RD REGIMENT: HE ENTERED IT
AS ENSIGN, MARCH 6TH, 1806, WAS PROMOTED TO BE
LIEUT.-COLONEL, JUNE 29TH, 1830, AND RETAINED THE COMMAND OF
IT UNTIL THE DAY OF HIS DEATH.
HE SERVED WITH THE ARMIES IN SPAIN AND PORTUGAL,
UNDER SIR JOHN MOORE AND THE
DUKE OF WELLINGTON,
AND WAS PRESENT AT VIMIERO, CORUNNA, THE PASSAGE OF THE COA,
BUSACO AND SALAMANCA, VITTORIA, AND THE ATTACK
ON THE HEIGHTS OF VERA.

THIS TABLET WAS ERECTED BY THE OFFICERS, NON-COMMISSIONED OFFICERS,
AND PRIVATES OF THE REGIMENT WHO HAD SERVED UNDER
HIS COMMAND, TO RECORD THEIR RESPECT FOR
HIS CHARACTER AND THEIR ESTEEM
AND AFFECTION FOR HIS GALLANT, GENEROUS, AND AMIABLE QUALITIES,
BY WHICH HE WON THE HEARTS OF ALL WHO SERVED UNDER
HIM, AND INFUSED THROUGH EVERY RANK A HIGH
AND HONOURABLE FEELING.

1842.

From Amherstberg the regiment in July proceeded by wings through Toronto to Montreal.

1843.

In May the head-quarters moved to La Prairie; thence to Quebec in September.

1844.

In June the 43rd embarked for Halifax. Before leaving Quebec, General Sir James Hope, K.C.B., adverted in terms of high approbation to the discipline and conduct of the regiment; to the part they had formerly taken under Wolfe in contributing to the glory of the British arms, as well as the valuable assistance recently rendered while in garrison, to the saving of most part of the city from conflagration, and thereby earning the everlasting gratitude of its inhabitants.

1846.

In March the head-quarters sailed from Halifax in the 'Blenheim' troop-ship, arriving at Portsmouth on the 5th of April, and, leaving Gosport by railway, joined the depôt companies at Dover Heights, who since 1835 had been by various moves stationed in Clonmel, Bullevant, Cork, Devonport, Dover, Chatham, Dublin, Londonderry, Galway, Limerick, Cashel, Carlisle, Plymouth, returning to Dover, 18th July, 1845.

While here, several officers of the regiment pulled over from Dover to Boulogne in a racing gig. The crew was composed of Captains Meade, the Hon. T. Cholmondely, Lieutenants Primrose, Hon. Percy Herbert, Green Wilkinson, and Dennis, with a beach man to steer. Half-way across a squall came on; it was necesary to bale water without intermission, and only by a narrow squeak the French port was reached. On the Boulogne officials requesting to know the tonnage of their 'yacht,' they volunteered to carry up the little canoe. Its exhibition caused much astonishment; the Mayor and all the authorities made them forthwith great lions, and the following day they and their gig were triumphantly escorted on board the steamer for return to Dover. The incident, however, nearly cost them a reprimand; for the "Old

Duke," chancing to be at Walmer at the time, would have had them pulled up for leaving the country without leave, had not Lord Fitzroy Somerset interceded.

1847.

In January the whole corps returned to Portsmouth, occupying Cambridge House and Haslar Barracks.

On the 22nd of March new colours were presented to the regiment on Southsea Common by Lady Pakenham, wife of the Hon. Sir Hercules Pakenham, K.C.B., Lieutenant-Governor of the district and Colonel of the 43rd.

The Rev. Wyndham Carlyon Madden—who had been wounded at Badajoz and at the storming of the Rocks on La Petite la Rhune, and had served throughout the Peninsular War as an officer of the regiment, but now—Rector of Trinity Church, Fareham, having been invited by the Colonel and officers to consecrate their new banners, commenced by offering up an appropriate prayer, after which he addressed the Regiment as follows :—

"MEN AND BRETHREN,—The peculiar circumstances under which I here stand before you call for, and justify, I may hope, the few words I would now address to you. Though now invested with the sacred office of the ministry, I was once your comrade and companion in arms. The son of an old soldier, who bled in his country's cause: one of five brothers who all served in the war of the Peninsula, who all belonged to the glorious Light Division, who all shed their blood there—two of them their life's blood—I cannot but feel the most lively interest in all that concerns the welfare of the British army.

"But there are other circumstances which render my position here upon this day still more deeply interesting. I find myself in the presence of my own dear old regiment. Forty years ago, save one, I joined this regiment, a stripling of little more than fourteen years old, and for twelve years was associated with it in the perils and glories of that important period of its history. And though, at the close of the war, from considerations of a deep and solemn nature, I felt it to be my duty to retire from the army, with the view of preparing for the more arduous and holy service of the ministry, yet, believe me, I have never forgotten my dear old regiment. I have rejoiced in every opportunity of meeting with the few of my former comrades who have been spared, and I have marked with lively interest the high character for order and discipline, and high and noble bearing, which you have continued to sustain. These peculiar circumstances in my case give me boldness in addressing you; and in expressing a hope that both the officers and soldiers of this regiment will feel that they have a high degree of responsibility committed to them, in having to maintain the brilliant reputation which has been transmitted to them by those who have served and suffered before them. As to mere courage, if tried in the battle-field, we doubt not for a moment that this would be found in you. It seems to be a part of the very constitution of a British soldier—from the earliest records of our history the British infantry have been distinguished for that calm, serious, determined, and persevering courage, which has been able to withstand the most impetuous shock of assailing foes, and in its deliberate advance to overwhelm all resistance. But let me remind you, my brethren, that courage, mere animal courage, constitutes but one, and that not the most important quality in the character of a good soldier. Submission to authority, subjection to discipline, order, sobriety, fortitude, and patient endurance of privations and sufferings when called to them—these constitute the higher and more essential qualities of a good soldier, and may these, my brethren, ever be found in you. But I should be unfaithful to my sacred office, did I not also remind you that you have higher duties than these to fulfil; that you are, by profession, the soldiers of Jesus Christ, the King of kings, and Lord of lords; that in your infancy you were baptized in His name, and enlisted into His service; that you were then signed with the sign of the cross, 'in token that hereafter you should not be ashamed to confess the faith of Christ crucified, but manfully to fight under His banner against sin, the world, and the devil; and to continue Christ's faithful soldiers and servants to your life's end.' May you ever remember these vows, and have grace to fulfil them; may you never be ashamed of Christ crucified, who for you endured the cross, despising the shame. May you be strong in the Lord, and in the power of His might: may you put on the whole armour of God; may you fight the good fight of faith, and lay hold of eternal life. Hear the gracious and encouraging words of the great Captain of your salvation,—'Be thou faithful unto death, and I will give thee the Crown of life.' 'To him that overcometh will I give to sit with me on my throne, even as I also overcame and am set down with my Father on His throne.'"

Lady Pakenham then advanced, and placing the new banners in the hands of Major William Frazer and Major Wilbraham Egerton (who received them kneeling, as is the usual custom), said:—

"I have much pleasure in presenting these colours, as I feel persuaded they will be nobly borne, by a regiment that has always been distinguished for its valour abroad and by its good conduct at home. Receive these colours—in which *I* must feel the highest personal interest—with my earnest prayers for your prosperity as a corps, as well as for the realisation of my most sanguine hopes of your being blessed with success by the 'Giver of all victory' when called upon, in the defence of your Queen and country, to unfurl them in the day of battle."

Sir Hercules Pakenham then addressed the Regiment, followed by Lieut.-Colonel Furlong, when the new colours, preceded by the band, were marched down the front, reinstating the old, which were presented to Sir Hercules; after which all the men were regaled at the expense of the officers with a good substantial dinner.

On the 17th of June, in brigade with the 2nd battalion of the 60th Rifles, the regiment was reviewed in Hyde Park by his Imperial Highness Prince Constantine of Russia, in presence of her Majesty and Prince Albert, before marching to Newport in Monmouthshire, whence detachments were furnished to Pontypool, Carmarthen, Cardigan, Pembroke, and Cardiff.

1848.

Early in this year the 43rd moved to Templemore, in Ireland. Here the regiment lost Major Egerton, an excellent officer, who met his untimely end by the falling of the race-stand at Lismacrony. His body was removed to the head-quarters of the regiment, and interred with military honours at Templemore. The following was promulgated :—

"REGIMENTAL ORDER.

"*Templemore, April 11th*, 1848.

"It is with feelings of deep regret that Lieut.-Colonel Furlong has to communicate to the regiment under his command the very sudden and lamented death of Major Egerton, who expired at Birr Barracks, on the 10th inst., after lingering for a few days, from the effects of an accident which proved fatal. As a mark of respect to the memory of one so much regretted by every member of the corps, the Commanding Officer requests the officers will be good enough to appear with crape on their left arm, for six weeks, commencing to-morrow."

"The deceased was second son of Wilbraham Egerton, Esq., of Tatton Park, Knutsford, Cheshire, and brother of the present Lord Egerton. His several commissions bore date as follows :—Ensign, Nov. 4, 1824; Lieutenant, July 11, 1826; Captain, July 1, 1828; Major, Aug. 25, 1843 : all by purchase, and all in the 43rd Regiment. He served with the corps in Gibraltar, Portugal, and America. His amiable and gentlemanly qualities endeared him to all who had the pleasure of his acquaintance, his purse was at all times open to the wants of the needy; his death will be severely felt, and his memory will long be revered by every member of the 43rd Light Infantry."

His father afterwards presented a handsome piece of plate to the 43rd, "as a remembrance of his esteem and regard for a regiment to which his son, Major Egerton, was so much attached, and in which, after twenty-four years' service, he ended his life."

In April five companies, commanded by Major Frazer, went to Dublin, occupying Leinster House and Beggar's Bush Barracks; while the other five, under canvas at Tipperary, formed part of Major-General Macdonald's force, engaged in suppressing the rebellion got up by Smith O'Brien, of "Cabbage Garden" notoriety.

1849-50.

The regiment passed the latter end of this year and the following in garrison in the Royal Barracks, Dublin.

1851.

In May marched to Clonmel, and in September to Cork, for embarkation for the Cape of Good Hope. Colonel Furlong here retired from the command, owing to advanced age and frequent fits of suffering, induced by an unextracted bullet received at Quatre Bras. He was succeeded by Major Skipwith as Lieutenant-Colonel, under whom the service companies were formed on the 1st October. The officers appointed were as follows:—

Major, H. Skipwith—Lieut.-Colonel 17th Oct.

Captains.
R. N. Phillips—Major 17th Oct.

O. A. J. Gore.	D. C. Greene.
Hon. P. E. Herbert.	F. S. Bruere.
J. M. Primrose.	J Abercrombie Dick.

Lieutenants.

Hon. H. Wrottesley.	H. J. P. Booth.
Hon. H. W. C. Ward.	Lumley Graham.
A. C. V. Ponsonby.	Hon. L. W. Milles.

Ensigns.

F. G. Stapleton.	C. R. Mure.
H. Robinson.	Charles Calvert.
Hon. Barrington V. Pellew.	Hon. H. Annesley.

Paymaster, H. T. McCrea.
Lieutenant and Adjutant, W. Milnes.
Quarter-Master, Joseph Denton.
Surgeon, T. Davidson, M.D.
Assistant-Surgeon, John Madden.

29 sergeants, 25 corporals, 11 buglers, and 587 privates.

Sailing on the 12th, in H.M.S. 'Vulcan,' they reached Simon's Bay on Dec. 9, where the impedimenta was landed, and proceeding to East London, Buffalo Mouth, disembarked under most favourable auspices on the 17th, and immediately encamped.

THE KAFFIR WAR.

On the following day tents were struck, and a march of nine miles, resumed next morning, made. Being the Cape midsummer, the men, in heavy marching order, felt the heat severely, but by the 21st reached King William's Town, and joined the camp of the field force in British Kaffraria. The 43rd were received most cordially by His Excellency Sir Harry Smith, Governor and Commander of the forces, evidently delighted to meet a regiment with whom he was so long brigaded in the Peninsula. He complimented the corps highly on its general appearance and made the most minute inquiries about every officer. He discussed the principle of bush-fighting, and surprised many of his hearers by desiring them to discard anything connected with pipe-clay, adding that he required all officers to wear patrol jackets same as the men, with fustian trousers, dyed the colour of the bush, as being far more suitable to the description of warfare before them than the stiff unyielding uniform then in vogue. On the 30th three companies formed part of an escort to take supplies to Fort White, returning on New Year's Day.

1852.

On the 3rd of January four companies, under Lieut.-Colonel Skipwith, marched for the Great Kei river as escort with provisions for Colonel Eyre's force, and also to cover the passage. Baggage was restricted to what they could carry on one horse, from fourteen to eighteen stone weight, including cooking-pots, axes, blankets, change of clothing, and two or three bottles of brandy. Reserve ammunition was carried on ponies or mules. Each officer had a small tent, seven feet long by three high, with his saddle for a pillow. The only provision made for wounded was one stretcher per company. The men carried one blanket each, but had no tents nor any cooking utensils except the regulation mess-tin. The party, under Lieut.-Colonel Skipwith, comprised—

Sappers and Miners	30 rank and file.
43rd Light Infantry	200 ,,
60th Rifles	25 ,,
Cape Mounted Rifles	15 ,,
Fingoes	150 ,,
Montague's Horse	50 ,,

At night they halted at the Yellow river, breakfasted at Hangman's Bush, then over a fine level grass country to Old Fort. Next day, through a tremendous gorge, amidst the grandest scenery imaginable, they were on the near side of the river, bivouacking in a little copse of thorny mimosa. Towards evening great clouds of dust on the opposite plain were supposed to indicate the return of the force they had been sent out to meet. A party of the Cape Corps crossed the river, and brought word to Colonel Skipwith that General Somerset would cross in the A.M. with 20,000 head of cattle.

Two companies of the 43rd were sent to hold the wooded heights on their side of the Kei, and at eight General Somerset's advanced guard began to cross. The troops presented a miserable appearance, having been for six weeks exposed to heavy rains in the open field, during most part of which they had neither bread nor biscuit. Their clothes were so entirely worn out or disfigured that no one could have recognised traces of either the 60th Rifles or 73rd uniform.

The animals elicited much wonder and admiration. Their stature was enormous; the length of the horns of the oxen averaged between six and seven feet, but it was a curious fact that those of the bulls and cows were of ordinary dimensions. These cattle were driven by a party of Fingoes—the Kaffir slave race—some riding on trained animals. They were entirely devoid of garment, save a small pendant worn on the extremity of their persons. Many of the head men were ornamented with eagle's wings attached to the back of their heads, and reaching as far down behind as the calf of the leg—most singular appendages to their swarthy forms, giving an appearance quite Satanic.

Colonel Skipwith's command followed the rear of General Somerset's force up the heights, and next day the former marched with the cattle for King William's Town, the latter remaining to cover the passage of Colonel Eyre's party. Eyre's passage of the Kei was very striking. 8000 Fingoes rescued from captivity, and 30,000 head of captured cattle accompanied the force. It was the exodus of a tribe on a small scale, and many touching scenes in family groups, and other incidents, proved that domestic instincts, affections, filial respect, and love are not always wanting in the savage breast. Both forces returned to King William's Town on the 18th of January.

On the 27th five companies of the 43rd, under Lieut.-Colonel Skipwith, with the 73rd Regiment, the whole commanded by Colonel Eyre, proceeded into the Amatolas, for the purpose of destroying the growing crops of the enemy—a proceeding which in ordinary civilized warfare would be characterised as atrocious. It proved, however, a great success, for though the war was not for long afterwards wholly extinguished, virtually these measures terminated it, and broke the till then indomitable spirit of the Kaffir tribes.

The field force carried a small proportion of tents and pitched standing camps, from which they worked through the lovely valleys and forests of the Amatolas country, spreading devastation far and wide. Captain Bruère's company was sent to King William's Town on the 9th February for provisions. On their return they stopped at Fort Stokes, waiting for orders which never came. The officers with this party, besides Captain Bruère in command of the escort, were Lieutenant Hon. H. Ward, 43rd; Lieutenant Knox, 73rd; and Surgeon Davidson, who, though himself ill, replaced Madden on the sick-list. The convoy not arriving, a detachment was sent in quest, but returned without any tidings. The next day a Kaffir spy from Colonel Mitchell reported the company was halted in Old Fort Stokes. It then became evident that some order had miscarried; and as Colonel Eyre's command was short of rations, he despatched his D. A. Quartermaster-General, Faunce, with an escort of lancers, to bring the detachment as far as possible that night. The most dangerous point to be passed was a hill called Bailey's Grave. This ascent is short and steep, with bush on either side. The convoy approached the hill at half-past eight, and when fully committed in the pass, fire was opened from both flanks. The soldiers could only return the fire by the light of the flashes. Six oxen were killed in one team, and some delay ensued. Groups of armed Kaffirs could be seen in the distance seated round their fires. Suddenly a simultaneous flash appeared, evidently a signal, for at once a volley was fired into the convoy, killing two men of the 73rd and wounding another.

Surgeon Davidson of the 43rd, with his usual alacrity, hastened to tend his comrades, and was in the act of leaning over the pack-horse which carried the medical appliances, and getting out some lint, when he was shot dead by two balls entering his temple. None ever gained a higher place in the affection of brother officers or soldiers of his regiment. He was interred, along with his fellow-sufferers of the 73rd, in the Keiskamma Hoek, where a tablet records his worth.

Faunce finally extricated his party from the pass, and formed, after the custom of the country, a "waggon kraal" for the night. At daylight the march was resumed, with loose and distant skirmishing, in which two of the 43rd and two of the 73rd were wounded. The appearance of Colonel Eyre with a strong force on the summit of the Kabousie Pass put a stop to this work, and the convoy was brought in without further loss. Until the end of February the regiment was engaged in cutting the enemy's crops, when they returned to King William's Town. While the Division under Sir Harry Smith surrounded the "Water Kloof," all the available men of the 43rd with Lieut-Colonel Skipwith, proceeded on patrol to clear Fuller's Hoek occupied by the Chief Macomo and his followers.

Tidings of the loss of H.M.S. 'Birkenhead,' wrecked on the 26th of February off Point Danger, on her passage from Simon's Bay to East London, were here received. She carried drafts for nearly every regiment at the Cape. That for the 43rd consisted of 1 sergeant and 40 privates under command of Lieutenant Girardot. Her entire freight was computed to number nearly 700 souls.

Under a calm starlight canopy, she suddenly struck on a precipitous rock while going eight knots. The Captain —Salmond—rushed on deck, ordered the bower anchor to be let go, quarter-boats to be lowered, paddle-box boats to be got out, and a turn "astern" to be given by the engines. This last proved a fatal error, for as she backed water rushed into the large orifice made by the concussion, and the ship starting again, every plate of the foremost bilge was "buckled up," and the partition bulk-heads torn asunder. In a few moments, consequently, the foremost compartments and engine-rooms were filled, and a great proportion of the unfortunate soldiers drowned in their berths.

Captain Salmond begged Colonel Seton and Lieutenant Girardot to send men to work the chain-pumps. The surviving soldiers mustered with firm discipline, and did duty with heroic composure, implicitly obeying every order. Just before the ship broke at the bows, the horses had been pushed overboard, and the cutter held in readiness to receive the women and children, which was effected with the utmost regularity. The boats stood off about a hundred yards from the ship's side. The large boat in the centre of the ship was not available as the vessel was breaking up. The fore part sunk almost instantly: the stern end crowded with men, floated a few minutes, and then went down, leaving the main top-mast and top-sail yard only visible above water.

In this awful moment, the resolution and coolness of all hands were remarkable, "far exceeding," wrote an eye-witness, "anything that I thought could be effected by the most perfect discipline. Every one did as he was directed, and there was not a murmur or a cry amongst them until the vessel made her final plunge. All received and carried out their orders as if embarking for a world's port in lieu of eternity. There was only this difference, that I never saw any embarkation conducted with so little confusion." As the vessel was just going down, some twenty minutes after the first shock, the commander called out: "All those who can swim, jump overboard and make for the boats." Lieutenant Girardot, 43rd, and Captain Wright, 91st, implored the men not to listen to this suggestion, or the women and children must inevitably be swamped. Under this heroic appeal, the whole were engulfed in the waves. "Perhaps the annals of the world furnish no parallel to this self-devotion."

Very shortly before the 'Birkenhead' finally sank, Dr. Cullane, of the ship, got into one of the gigs, and, rowed by eight of the crew, made the best of his way to Butt

River. The absence of this boat was most deplorable, for had it returned nearly every man of the 200 who were on the drift-wood between the wreck and the shore might have been picked up before reaching the thick, tangled sea-weed which prevented them from reaching land. The boat could have made forty or fifty trips to and from shore, between daylight and dark, and thus landed all the survivors in a cove to the eastward of Danger Point.

Such as were not sucked into the abyss clung to the mast and yards, some struck out for the shore, others grasped floating pieces of drift-wood. The terrors of the sinking ship were nothing to the agony now encountered. Those on the mast and yard had little prospect but of a brief respite; those floating in the water had a still more horrible anticipation of being seized by sharks, or if sufficiently fortunate to escape the jaws of those monsters, to be condemned to slow but certain death by being caught and meshed in the impenetrable masses of sea-weed.

Captain Salmond was seen swimming strongly, but being struck on the head by a floating piece of wood, he sank, and Colonel Seton of the 74th likewise perished. As the last vestige of the ship disappeared, Lieutenant Girardot took a tremendous header, in hope of being clear of the wreck; but only to find a man's arms clasped round his legs, dragging him downwards. Managing to extricate himself, very much exhausted he again rose to the surface, obliged to turn on his back to rest and draw breath.

The night had darkened: owing to the electricity of the water land could not be seen, and therefore he was unable to conjecture in what direction to swim. Finding the jacket and shoes which he wore heavy, he took them off, and swam away from those still moving in the water.

At last he descried the top of one of the masts, with a swarm of men holding on. He made towards them to rest until it became lighter, when, observing some wreck floating in the distance, and in the direction of land now visible, he swam towards it; the others declining to accompany him. Girardot thus started alone, and securing what had been a cabin door, he placed it under his chest, and so propelled himself slowly along; while an intense sun glowered on his head, which he was obliged to wet continually. Still he persevered, though the coast was so rocky, and the surf breaking so heavily, that he beheld many dashed to pieces, while harrowing cries from others announced their fearful end by monsters of the deep. Upon reaching the weeds, he came up with and joined four or five fellow sufferers on a bundle of spars tied together.

On this raft they were providentially carried by the waves into a narrow creek, a hundred yards from the beach. One of the party could not swim—he had laid hold of the spars when the ship went down, by chance been borne in safety—and now, though so near shore, was helpless. On hearing this, Girardot desired him to rest his hands on his shoulders, and thus, though well-nigh exhausted, having passed ten hours in the water, swam in, and safely deposited his burden.

He remained for some time on the beach until twelve or fourteen men were collected, and seeing no prospect of further survivors, started with them and Cornet Bond, of the 12th Lancers, in search of food and shelter, of which they were deplorably in want. Great was their surprise to recognise in a horse, which came neighing up, Cornet Bond's charger, cast overboard with the other animals, but who had swum safely to shore. Some of the party were literally naked; and Girardot himself had only his shirt. They fell in with some Dutchmen, from whom, by aid of German, Lieutenant Girardot managed to extract that twelve miles off there was a farm; and, in the direction indicated, they proceeded over the burning sand, though, from exhaustion, when reached at last, only four arrived. The farm proved to be the property of Captain Smalls, late 7th Dragoon Guards. He was absent; but his wife, after hearing the story of the wreck, and of the poor fellows fallen on the roadside, immediately despatched a waggon to bring them all up, and provided clothing and food.

Early next morning Girardot visited the scene of the wreck, and fell in with Captain Wright, who with several more, had been rescued. They returned with him to Captain Smalls, where all remained until the 'Radamanthus' was sent to convey them back to Simon's Bay, whence Lieutenant Girardot and his men proceeded to join the head-quarters of the regiment. A severe illness, consequent on the exposure and sufferings, wherein he had displayed both moral and physical fortitude, entitling him to marked distinction, then laid him low. The Victoria Cross had not at that time been inaugurated, or Lieutenant Girardot, of H.M. 43rd Light Infantry, must have stood high in the list. As it was, neither reward nor honour was bestowed, although the late Sir William Napier, personally a stranger, recognising the hardness of his case, memorialised the Duke of Wellington for his promotion. Refusal was grounded solely on the irrevocable rule closing promotion to subalterns.

Reverting to the movements of the Regiment, on the 9th of March Blinkwater Post was reached. Until the 15th, from sunrise to sundown, they were employed in penetrating and scouring the fortresses of the Fuller's Hoek and Hermann's Kloof, during which the regiment lost Lieutenant the Hon. H. Wrottesley, shot in the thigh by a musket-ball, who died the same evening; 2 rank and file were wounded, 130 women, 1000 head of cattle, 130 horses were captured, together with a quantity of stores, arms, and ammunition. The loss of the enemy, in killed and wounded, was not ascertained, but supposed to be great.

The operations were conducted by various parties entering the forest at the same time, and working towards a common centre, while others pressed on through the bush to crown the heights. More difficult ground for troops to move in could not be found. The forest was very dense, interspersed with tangled rotten vegetation and pit-falls. The paths were very narrow, even for single file, and obstructed by rocks and steep precipices, under which the track frequently led. The enemy had nothing to do when one range of Kloofs became too hot to hold them, but slip over the table-land into another, and ring the changes from Fuller's Hoek to the Water Kloof, until the perseverance of the troops worried them out. Perched on their lofty Krantzes, overlooking the vallies, the Kaffirs could quietly select the particular detachment they deemed most advisable to attack. One plan was to assail the rear just as the men were retiring down the forest to their bivouacs in the plain below. It was thus Lieutenant Wrottesley was killed.

On the 18th a march was begun from Blinkwater Post. On the 19th, at Anatola Basin, they found Colonel Mitchell's division, and on the 21st Lieutenant Girardot, with the survivors of the 'Birkenhead,' reached King William's Town. The names of the fourteen soldiers rescued were as follow:—

Peter Allen.	Edward Ambrose.
George Blackley.	Love Daniel Bunker.
Francis Green.	Michael Harnet.
Michael Healey.	John Hearn.
George Harrison.	George Lyons.
George Peters.	William Sharp.
Joseph Corst.	John Woodward.

On the 24th the march was directed on Fort Cox, below which the camp was pitched; thence to Fort White, and again to the Debe Neck. The 28th was spent in scouring the Perie Bush, Murray's Krantz, and adjoining Kloofs. Late in the evening a party under Major Phillips ascended the forest. In the night a small detachment of the Cape Corps, with an officer, was despatched as a reinforcement. A picket of the 43rd was out, and the party seeing its fire, judging it to be Kaffirs, concluded to steal by it, which they accomplished, but only to find themselves in the centre of the bivouac. They instantly opened fire, and for a minute or so a terrible scene of confusion ensued. Luckily no one happened to be hit, though the clothes of some of the men of the 43rd were rent by balls. At daybreak they marched, accompanied by these men of the Cape Corps, through a thick fog, and with great difficulty formed a junction with Major Pinkney of the 73rd, all proceeding to Massacre Grove.

The head-quarters of Colonel Eyre's Brigade were meanwhile proceeding along the plains, and by the 31st every available man of the 43rd was on the march towards the Kei. After a very harassing night, the banks of that river were reached. Colonel Eyre then, with a strong detachment, and Captain the Honourable Percy Herbert's company of the 43rd, crossed the Kei, and, after three days' hard work, took 1200 head of cattle.

On the 31st Major-General the Honourable George Cathcart, with the local rank of Lieut.-General, arrived at Cape Town as Governor of the colony, in succession to Sir H. Smith.

Lieut.-Colonel Skipwith, with five companies of the 43rd, three troops of the 12th Lancers, and about 100 Fingoes, also proceeded to the junction of the Timo and Kei, and captured 150 head of cattle. They then, on April 4th, joined Colonel Eyre at the Kabousie camp.

Three men of the 43rd in charge of bât horses got lost, and were not found until long afterwards in the Boers' camp. While Colonel Eyre was over the Kei, his force made a most extraordinary march, in which Captain Percy Herbert and his company, together with Lieutenants Hon. L. W. Milles and Ponsonby, were greatly distinguished.

At the same time that Colonel Eyre crossed the Kei, Captain Armstrong, of Cape Corps celebrity, followed suit. On the 5th of April two companies of the 43rd under Lieut.-Colonel Skipwith, and two under Major Newton Phillips, marched in charge of captured cattle, and with provisions for the Brigade, to Keiskamma. On the 7th an attack on Anta's Hole took place. On this occasion Captain Bruère's company formed the rearguard, and having a sick man in charge, was sometimes out of sight of the column. Their march lay through thick belts of bush, and as they neared Mount Mac Thomas were surprised by a shower of bullets. In less than two minutes the ground behind them was perfectly dotted with Kaffirs, though previously it had seemed a complete solitude. They dashed from rock to bush, at once seeking excellent cover the moment after delivering their fire. Seeing the dilemma of the rearguard with their invalid, they aimed at the stretcher-men, who were then sent with their burden to the front for safety. The enemy next contrived to capture the staff pack-horse, and regaled themselves with the provisions, a ludicrous but vexatious sight to the troops, who could not attempt the recapture without useless risk of lives; the company retired in skirmishing order, keeping up a hot fire on their assailants. The first meeting with the column was truly distressing, as Captain Greene's company was observed emerging from the bush bearing the dead body of Captain Owen Arthur Gore. He was killed at "Anta's Hole," at the foot of Mount Mac Thomas, while advancing mounted at the head of his company, by two Hottentot balls. His death cast a great gloom over his brother officers, who idolized him; he was courageous and dashing to a fault.

The regiment went into camp at Keiskamma Hoek the same evening, where, after nightfall, a grave was dug, and a very large fire kindled. When the body had been laid in the grave and the soil replaced, the fire was raked over it and kept burning in order to bake the earth so as to prevent any upheaval, which might betray his resting-place to the Kaffirs, who invariably opened English graves, not with the sole object of insulting the dead, but to possess themselves of the blankets in which corpses were usually folded. Having observed the bones of some of their pre-deceased comrades blanching in the sun, induced the adoption of this precaution in poor Gore's case.

From the 8th to the 20th of April the 43rd were employed in patrolling the Amatolas, and lost only one man. On the 30th, the portion of the regiment from King William's Town joined at Keiskamma, when, being the winter season, all set to work to construct huts, and quickly a complete cantonment of wattle barracks sprang up. To give an idea of the size, it may be noted that, if fitted with boards and trestles, each room would accommodate thirty men, or sixteen if furnished with barrack bedsteads.

From the 6th to the 10th of May five companies, under Lieut.-Colonel Skipwith, patrolled the Chief Seyolos' country. Water was very scarce; the men began to suffer from inflamed eyes, and became thoroughly disgusted. Information was received that a permanent Laager of rebel Hottentots was established in the Buffalo mountains, under Hans Brander of the Cape Corps, who not long before had detached a mounted party of 100 down to the colonial frontier, and at the drift of the Kooness River waylaid a convoy of Minie rifles and ammunition escorted by Sappers. On the 13th of June, therefore, four companies of the 43rd, with Major Phillips, marched for the Keiskamma Hoek, and on the morning of the 20th, Captain P. Herbert's, Captain Greene's, and half of Captain Dick's companies, with Lieutenants Booth, Milles, and Ensign Mure, and 124 men, under Colonel Eyre, surprised the enemy in considerable force in their Laager, and with the trifling mischief of three privates wounded, routed them. For their conduct on this occasion, Captains P. Herbert and Greene were named in General Orders.

Major Phillips' detachment returned to the Keiskamma Hoek, where by the 31st the whole of the 43rd were collected. They were then employed in constructing brick houses for the officers, made from clay in the vicinity.

But the work was beset by many difficulties, especially want of cement, proper tools, and wood, as every tree had been cut in the adjacent kloofs, and all grass suitable for thatch had been burnt by the Kaffirs. In spite of all hindrances, before four months had elapsed, the Commandant's house and stables, the hospital, bakery, and fort were finished, and other buildings rapidly progressing. Races and other amusements were got up, and the Nimrods of the garrison contested the "Keiskamma Hoek" Plate with the utmost enthusiasm.

Early in October Colonel Eyre received a roving commission from the Governor to scour the Amatolas in search of the rebel chief Sandelli. From the 11th to the 26th every available man of the 43rd was employed on this patrol, under his surveillance; the companies coming to the Keiskamma Hoek at intervals for supplies. News here arrived that Moshesh, the chief of the Basatos beyond the Orange River, had failed to keep faith with the British Government, resolutely refusing to pay a fine of 10,000 oxen and 1000 horses, imposed by the former Governor, Sir H. Smith. Sir George Cathcart at once ordered an expedition to enforce the fine, and Colonel Eyre was summoned to join at Fort Hare with the following force:—3 companies 43rd, with Major Phillips, Captains Honourable P. Herbert, Primrose and Bruère; Lieutenants Honourable H. Ward, Ponsonby, Girardot, and Stapleton; Ensign Honourable H. Annesley; Surgeon Barclay, 12 sergeants, 8 corporals, 5 buglers, and 301 privates, with 3 companies of the 73rd Regiment.

The three companies of the 43rd, part of the expeditionary force to the Orange River sovereignty against Moshesh, chief of the Basutos, marched, with waggons and supplies, on November 6th, to join the main division under Sir G. Cathcart. The regimental band played, and the men were in high spirits at the prospect of coming excitement. They travelled slowly, the oxen being out of condition, but reached Fort Hare on the 8th, of which the cultivation and vegetation were refreshing. Oats and barley were plentiful—a great boon to the troops, as locusts had devoured all grass for miles around. On the 12th they encamped at Eland's Post, and were joined by three companies of the 2nd Queen's. On the 15th a General Order was read, giving well-merited praise to General Eyre's division, for service in the Amatolas. They continued their march, during which want of fuel was the greatest trouble. Not a bush or tree presented itself, and the only available substitute was dried cow's dung. The supply being very inadequate to the demand, men were seen, when opportunity offered, filling their havresacks with the commodity in an exulting manner truly ridiculous.

Upon entering the country of the Dutch Boers, Colonel Eyre assembled his brigade, and read out that portion of the Articles of War relative to martial laws on friendly soil. The Boers are an uncommonly fine race of men, and showed every civility to the troops. By the 22nd the town of Burghersdorp was reached; and on the 28th the Governor, Sir George Cathcart, arrived, when he divided his force into three divisions: 1 Cavalry and 2 Infantry. To the first division of the latter the 43rd were attached. On December 1st they were on the banks of the Orange River, and crossed that noble stream the following day, falling in with Sir George Cathcart and the Cavalry. On the 4th, the 2nd Division of Infantry, under Colonel Macduff, came up, and all were before Caledon River, expecting that Moshesh would now recognise the necessity of paying the promised fine. The troops encamped.

On the 17th Moshesh attempted a parley with the Governor, who replied, that unless the tribute were forthcoming within three days, he would invade his stronghold. A few droves of cattle were then ferried across, not amounting to one tithe of the exacted number, so that on the 20th the Governor determined to attack, seeing many herds on the adjacent hills. Captain Bruère and Captain Primrose remained with the guns, while Captain P. Herbert proceeded to ascend the mountain. The enemy fired the first shot from above, killing one, and wounding another, of the 73rd, and thus began the fight known as the *Battle of Berea*, the most considerable action in which the 43rd had been engaged since their arrival in South Africa. The two companies under Major Phillips proceeded to the foot of the heights scaled by Captain Herbert and his men, and secured 5000 head of cattle. Colonel Eyre and his staff were nearly surprised and taken by a party of Kaffirs, who having dressed themselves in British 12th Lancer uniforms—of which they had stripped our dead bodies—were not at first recognised as foes. They only escaped by hard riding.

Major Faunce, being an indifferent horseman, fell into the enemy's hands, and was murdered.

The loss of the 43rd was confined to 1 officer, the Honourable H. Annesley, and 6 rank and file wounded. Towards night the enemy attempted to close on the Infantry, but was repelled by discharges of canister from Major Faddy's battery. The contest was not, however, renewed, as next A.M. Moshesh sued for peace in the following characteristic letter, dictated to his secretary, and addressed to His Excellency Sir George Cathcart :—

"YOUR EXCELLENCY,—This day you have fought against my people and taken much cattle. As the object for which you have come is to have a compensation for Boers, I beg you will be satisfied with what you have taken. I entreat peace from you. You have shown your power, you have chastised; let it be enough, I pray you, and let me no longer be considered an enemy of the Queen. I will try all I can to keep my people in order for the future.

"Your humble Servant,

"MOSHESH."

Sir George Cathcart replied :—

"CHIEF MOSHESH,—I have received your letter; the words are those of a great chief, and of one who has the interest of his people at heart. But I care little for words, I judge of men by their actions. I told you that if you did not pay the fine, I must go and take it. I am a man who never breaks his word, otherwise the Queen would not have sent me here. I have taken the fine by force, and am satisfied. I am not angry with your people for fighting in defence of their property, for those who fought, and fought well, were not all of them thieves, and I am sorry that many were killed. This is *your* fault, for if you paid the fine it would not have happened. I now desire not to consider you, chief, as an enemy of the Queen, but I must proclaim martial law in the sovereignty, to give to commandants and field cornets power to make commands in a regular manner, and, with the consent of the resident, enter your country in search of plundered horses and cattle that may be stolen after this time, and I expect you to assist them; for though you are a great chief, it seems that you either do not or cannot keep your people from stealing; and among the cattle you sent as part of your fine, there were three oxen, the property of Mr. Bain of Bloemfontein, stolen since I crossed the Caledon River. Now, therefore, Chief Moshesh, I consider your part of the obligation fulfilled, and hope that you will take measures for preventing such abuses in future. In the mean time, as the Queen's representative, I subscribe myself,

"Your friend,
"GEORGE CATHCART,
"*Governor.*"

"*P.S.*—Chief! I shall be glad to see either yourself or your sons in the same friendly manner, and in the same good faith as before the fight, to-morrow or next day; but I shall now send away the army and go back to the colony in a few days' time."

On the 29th the expeditionary force departed, carrying with them the entire levy of cattle.

To revert to the station at Keiskamma Hoek, on the 1st of December, during a tremendous thunderstorm, two men of the 43rd were killed, and 19 others injured, owing to the explosion of ammunition in the pouches. The day had been very sultry, even for tropical midsummer. Just after dark the temperature suddenly changed to chilly cold, and large hailstones fell. A flash and detonation broke simultaneously, followed by the immediate ignition of ammunition, amid yells and shrieks of the men, imprisoned in their now prostrate tents, from which they could not extricate themselves. Captain Dick and Lieutenant Booth rushed out, and managed to drag up the pegs, and haul the soldiers—absolutely mixed up with the exploding pouches strapped to the poles—out, notwithstanding the terrific fury of the elements. Of all the 19 injured, few or none permanently recovered, although several served on for some years.

On the 11th a small party of the Bailey's Grave detachment, when on patrol, encountered some Hottentots, and lost one man. Lieutenant Lumley Graham, in command, had a dangerous personal scuffle, but contrived to shoot his antagonist, though not without a very narrow shave for life. Ensign Calvert, on a sporting excursion, accompanied by his servant, who had but one eye, was waylaid by five or six Kaffirs. Such adroit use did he make of his weapons, that he not only saved himself and man, but killed or wounded nearly all the assailants.

The following is the detail of the casualties in the 43rd since the Regiment landed in British Kaffraria:—

Killed in action, 3 officers, 2 privates.
Captain O. A. J. Gore, Surgeon Davidson, Lieutenant the Hon. H. Wrottesley.

Died of wounds	1
Killed by lightning	2
Lost in the 'Birkenhead'	28
Died of dysentery	27
Died of fevers	8
Other diseases	3
Wounded	14

„ Lieutenant the Hon. H. Annesley.

1853.

The three companies of the 43rd, under Major Phillips, returned from the Orange River expedition to Keiskamma on the 22nd of January. Two officers rode on to announce their approach; and their band played the brigade into the old quarters. Singular to relate, at that very moment a draft of the 43rd, consisting of 2 sergeants and 20 rank and file, under Lieutenant and Adjutant the Honourable Richard Monck, arrived from England. The contrast between the uniforms and accoutrements, thus placed in juxtaposition, was comical; the bright, clean clothes and smooth-shaved faces, cheek by jowl with tattered garments, shoeless feet, and unkempt heads.

A few patrols, devoid of any stirring incidents, only occurred until peace was concluded with the Kaffirs on

March 16th. On the 30th of April the Regiment was inspected by Major-General Sir C. Yorke; an ordeal it had not gone through since leaving Dublin in April, 1851.

Towards autumn orders were received that the 43rd should hold themselves in readiness for the Madras Presidency, and by a War Office letter its establishment was increased to 5 field-officers, 12 captains, 18 lieutenants, 6 ensigns, 7 staff, 58 sergeants, 50 corporals, 21 buglers, and 950 privates. On the 1st of November 9 men transferred their services to the Cape Mounted Rifle Corps.

On the 28th of November the Regiment, after having passed nearly two years in South Africa, embarked from East London on board H.M. sloop 'Baracouta,' and at Table Bay was transferred into freight ships. While the vessels were loading, the officers enjoyed a few days amidst the beautiful environs of Cape Town, probably the only pleasant part of their *séjour* in a country which all left without regret; an ungrateful land of "streams without water," "flowers without scent," and "birds without song."

The Kaffir War was a hard and discouraging service—often disastrous to the best troops; and though the combined and persevering efforts of an adequate body of disciplined soldiers must always prevail in the end against the dastardly and plundering warfare of savages, yet the immediate effect of their exertions is seldom or never apparent to the jaded and harassed spectators, who, passing their time in forced marches, unavailing pursuits, and useless skirmishes, are moreover discouraged by scandalous abuse from the colonists who do not fight themselves, and by the still more scandalous comments of strange writers in a stranger portion of the English press, who seek to depreciate the character and skill of officers and courage of the soldiers, and undertake to teach them how to fight in the Kaffir plains and forests, which they, the censors, never beheld. Such aggravations—added to the actual hardships of keeping the open fields in an immense extent of mountainous forest country, ill-clothed, ill-shod, and ill-fed, on one unvarying diet of beef as tough and leathery as hide, of biscuits which a stone would hardly break—made the Kaffir warfare—a service where no laurels were to be won—one for which few men indeed would willingly volunteer.

Some honourable exceptions there were to the assertion that the colonists would not fight. Individually they are brave and skilled in the use of firearms. It must be said, in excuse for their holding back, that their circumstances almost enforced it. On the outbreak of war, their first thoughts are naturally for their wives, children, flocks, crops, and herds—their only wealth and means of subsistence. They must remove from danger, and, banding together by several families, establish "Laagers," where water and forage are attainable. Their pleasant homesteads, engrafted by long toil, are abandoned to the torch of the savage; happy if, after years of strife and eviction, they return to find some portion of the blackened walls of their old house still standing, some clumps of their peach and orange trees still extant.

INDIA.

1854.

The battalion arrived in Madras Roads on the 30th and 31st of January, and went into quarters and camp on the esplanade of Fort George, thus commencing their first experience of India since enrolment. On the 24th of February the left wing, under Captain Primrose, marched for Bangalore, reached on the 15th of March. Cholera began its ravages: 1 sergeant, 1 corporal, and 5 privates succumbed *en route* to this Eastern foe. On the 1st of April, aided by drafts from different regiments in India, the muster-roll showed 52 sergeants, 43 corporals, 18 buglers, and 1005 privates. The head-quarters and two companies joined at Bangalore on the 26th, and the remaining portion of the right wing arrived soon after.

In September, disturbances being expected at Mysore, one company was detached from Bangalore and two from Fort St. George by rail to Vellore, to assist, in conjunction with the other forces, in disarming the mutinous 8th Native Cavalry. On the 20th of December, on a grand parade at Bangalore, medals for the Kaffir War were distributed. On the 24th the 43rd, in brigade with the 19th Regiment of Madras Native Infantry under command of Brigadier John Macduff, 74th Highlanders, marched to join Brigadier Whitelock's division for service in the Saugur and Nerbudda territory. Their strength was 30 officers and 969 men, including non-commissioned officers, buglers, and privates, under command of Lieut.-Colonel Primrose; Captain Dorehill was brigade-major. The Regiment was entirely composed of the finest description of seasoned soldiers ever remembered by the most veteran officers.

1855-58.

The interval between the close of 1854 and that of 1857 passed over in the ordinary routine of Indian service, without any particular incident or occurrence. In 1858 the first route received by the 43rd was for Kamptee, in the Nagpore country, a distance of 631 miles, completed on the 28th of March; being resumed for another 156 miles, Jubbalpore was reached on the 17th of April, where a detachment was left of 1 subaltern and 53 men. The march then continued by Dumoh and Banda, joining Whitelock's division on the 30th of May.

On the 3rd of June eight companies marched with the force destined for the attack of Kirwee under Brigadier Whitelock, which was reached on the 7th, when the Rajah Narrain Row surrendered in person, and his armed followers betook themselves to the hills. The Rajah's palace and treasures were seized. Forty-two lacs of rupees in coin, with an enormous quantity of gold and silver utensils and jewels, were captured, although it was conjectured that much had also been secreted or carried off by his troops, who had fled before the surrender. Three companies of the 43rd remained at Kirwee to form part of the garrison under Brigadier Carpenter of the Madras Army, while the head-quarters and remainder of the corps marched to Banda, taking with them forty-six prisoners. Two companies at once joined a detached force for that district under Lieut.-Colonel Primrose, and by July 1st all were together at Hernapore, when the Regiment marched to Calpee, and on the 7th went into temporary barracks.

On reaching Calpee, a march of 1300 miles—with only an occasional halt at large stations for a few days—had been performed by the 43rd; and these halts generally were for the purpose of laying in commissariat supplies. Some idea may be formed of the excessive exertion and fatigue undergone both by officers and men, when it is considered that this march was in most part performed during the hottest season of a year in which the mean temperature exceeded in heat that of any known during the fifteen preceding. The marches commenced before daylight, usually as early as 2 A.M., and it frequently happened that the rear of the column did not arrive in camp until 4 or 5 P.M. A mere country track constituted the only route, at times crossing chains of high, precipitous hills, cutting through rocks and jungles for days together, traversing and passing numerous rivers, many of great breadth, without bridges or boats. Now and again the entire Regiment was employed in dragging the carts—some hundred in number—containing ammunition, stores, &c., over almost insurmountable obstacles, where cattle were nearly useless.

The Monsoon, usually commencing in June, did not in this year visit Central India until the middle of July, consequently the acute sufferings of the Regiment under the burning and arid breezes of that inhospitable region were not only most exceptionally intense but protracted. At no point was this felt to such an extent as at Bisramnugger, one day's march north of Purneah. Three days were occupied in getting the carts down a ghaut by which the Brigade descended, during which time 2 officers and 11 men of the 43rd died from sunstroke. Even natives attached to the force succumbed from the same cause. Major Young of the 19th Madras Native Infantry with 12 Sepoys also similarly perished, and all lie buried in one spot close to the ground on which the camp was formed. During May and June the thermometer ranged at 120° in the Hospital tents, while in small ones this was usually exceeded by 8° or 9°.

In the first 950 miles only two deaths, and each accidental, occurred. The health of the Regiment had been most extraordinary; but later the amount of wear and tear endured began to tell on their constitutions. Sunstroke was of constant occurrence, and death generally most sudden; some of the stricken expiring in a few minutes, though others lingered on in a state of coma for hours. Three officers and 44 men of the 43rd died from this and miscellaneous causes. The officers were, Paymaster and Quarter-Master Denton (brothers), and Lieutenant Thomas Elwes. A finer body of men, well-grown, and averaging twenty-five years of age, had never before taken the field in India; all that were weakly had been left behind in Bangalore. On the Regiment reaching Calpee each company looked but the wreck of its former self.

Partial rest was imperative, and it was hoped that much good would result from the occupation of temporary barracks. In July there were 13 deaths; 8 from sunstroke. No more desolate place than Calpee could be found in the world, Aden not even excepted. It is situated on the banks of the Jumna, and for miles around the whole country is an intricate net-work of steep ravines, in which the baked, gravelly soil produces no sort of vegetation. On the 1st of August two companies with a force under Major Synge were sent to Jaloun, to rescue that fort, ignominiously surrendered by some local levies. On their appearance the rebels bolted.

A detachment under Captain Colville moved out with the force under Brigadier Carpenter, to engage the rebels occupying the hills. The head-quarters of the 43rd and two companies with Brigadier Macduff arrived at Jaloun, and encamped on the 31st of August. Incessant rain and the completely flooded state of the country prevented any attempt at active operations by Captain Colville until the 5th of September, when, having been reinforced by another company, they engaged the rebels at the village of Sahao, and continued on the move in the Calower district until the 24th, when they returned to Jaloun. After remaining there four days in camp, operations were renewed, directing on the Jumna, until the 12th of October, when the Brigade retired to Calpee. These movements took place in the height of the Monsoon. The country was a dead flat with no road of any kind through the greater part of the district, though many many miles of cultivated land were marched over.

On the 6th of September the detachment under Captain Colville was engaged at the Punghatten Pass, a village in the Punnah range. On the 11th November a company marched from Humeerpore to Banda for garrison; on the 17th two companies from Jaloun on field service; and on the 16th of December a company from Calpee with the force under Brigadier Macduff, moved to Jaloun. At that station they were joined by two more companies, and were engaged at Girnara on the Scinde. On the 22nd of December a small party of officers, 35 men of the 43rd, and 50 Sepoys, under command of Captain Woodlands, 1st Madras Native Infantry, occupying the palace at Kirwee, were attacked by a rebel force under Rada Govind, and beat it off after five days' fighting. They were not finally relieved until the arrival of Brigadier Whitelock.

On the 23rd of December two companies of the 43rd marched from Nagode to Kirwee to relieve that place. On the 24th a company proceeded from Banda to Kirwee as advance guard of Whitelock's force. They engaged the rebels at Purwarree, took four guns, and were mentioned with special praise in General Orders.

1859.

On the 2nd of January a subaltern and a few men were engaged in the Punnah Jungle. Private Henry Addison of the 43rd was severely wounded in rescuing Captain Osborne, political agent at Rewah, who had been worsted in a personal combat with a rebel Sepoy. For his gallant conduct Addison received the Victoria Cross. On the 5th the company that went to Jubbalpore was engaged at Bagowra. On the 19th three companies arrived at Calpee with Brigadier Macduff, from field service. On the 22nd head-quarters and five companies marched for Banda, and on the 29th were joined by three more. On the 11th of February head-quarters marched for Nagode, where they were joined on the 13th by a company from Kawah, and on the 14th by another from Kirwee, when, to the great joy of every one, the battalion was once more consolidated.

On the 15th the 43rd marched for Saugur, but on the 24th three companies were ordered back to Nagode. The hot season was passed in camp on the Maidan, at Nagode. On the 8th of July a General Order abolished brigade commands.

On taking leave of the 1st Brigade, of which the 43rd formed part, Brigadier Macduff expressed his warm thanks to Lieut.-Colonel Primrose "for the strong support and able assistance he had at all times given him," adverted to the good conduct of the Brigade both in action and pursuit, and also during the long and continuous marches of nearly 3000 miles, from Madras to the banks of the rivers Jumna and Scinde, and to the frontier of the Gwalior territory, enduring without a murmur the arduous labours and manifold hardships encountered. He also alluded to the large train of treasure, public stores, and ammunition entrusted to the Brigade, of which not even a single cartridge was missing. The Brigadier conveyed his special thanks to the following officers of the 43rd:—Captain William Dorehill, his Brigade-Major; Lieutenant the Hon. A. E. Harris, his A. D. C.; and Lieutenant H. C. Talbot, his orderly officer. Also to Surgeon A. Barclay, for his unvaried attention to the sick and wounded.

On the 14th of August two companies of the 43rd proceeded with a force under Lieut.-Colonel Nott, Madras Native Infantry, and fell in with and engaged Feroze Shah, routing his party, who abandoned their tents, horses, and equipments. On the 7th of October two companies, with a force under Lieut.-Colonel Oates, 12th Lancers, left Saugur. A patrol from this party, under Lieutenant D'Urban Blythe, 43rd, attacked the rebels near a village called Patourie, routing and pursuing them until they were completely dispersed. Two men of the 43rd were wounded, and Lieutenant Blythe was thanked in General Orders. Another detachment, under Captain Glover, attacked and dispersed a force near the village of Raisham, and two companies, with a force under Lieut.-Colonel Primrose, left Saugur for the district. This body, on the 23rd of October, attacked the rebels near the village of Gopalpore, killing many and taking several prisoners. On the 15th of November a company, with a force under Captain Currie of the 16th Punjaub Native Infantry, went into the district. The greater part of the Nagode detachment were in the field during October and November.

1860.

On the 18th of January the route was received for the Regiment to return to the Madras Presidency, and the head-quarters, with seven companies, under Major Synge, marched for Fort George. On the 2nd of February the three other companies, under Major Booth, joined at a halting-place, when the march was resumed, and Mirzapore reached on the 13th. On the 15th head-quarters and four companies, under Lieutenant-Colonel Primrose, embarked in steamers to descend the Ganges to Calcutta. The remaining six companies, under Major Booth, crossed the river and made for Benares. On the 6th of March all reached Calcutta, and were met by two officers and seventy-eight men from the depôt.

1861.

On the 15th of March the head-quarters and five companies embarked in the 'Sesostris,' towed by the 'Zenobia,' and on the 18th reached Madras. On the 28th the rest arrived, when the whole Regiment took up quarters in Fort George. On the 14th of May the 43rd paraded for review, and for the presentation of Indian

Mutiny medals, by Major-General M'Cleverty. On the 22nd of October the left wing, under Major Synge, embarked in the 'Sesostris' and 'Coromandel' for Calcutta.

1862.

On the 15th of February the head-quarter wing embarked for Calcutta, under command of Major (now Lieutenant-Colonel) Booth. This right wing remained encamped on the glacis of Fort William, joining the four companies of the left wing, the remaining company being at Dum Dum. In March three companies, under Major Synge, moved to Barrackpore, and in April Captain Mure's to Raneegunge; three companies and head-quarters, under Lieut.-Colonel Booth, and the four remaining companies, under Captain Colville, proceeded to Barrackpore. In November one company from Raneegunge joined the head-quarters, and the three remaining companies moved to Fort William, under Captain Mure.

1863.

In January head-quarters and three companies marched by road from Barrackpore to Fort William, although the river was open for their conveyance, and on each side a railway. This most useless and unnecessary march provoked much comment and criticism in military circles in Calcutta.

New Zealand.

In September the 43rd was ordered for active service in New Zealand, where fracas between the colonists, Maories and military were of perpetual occurrence. Arrangements having been made for leaving one company (Captain Mure's) to follow by first opportunity, on the 8th October the screw-steamer 'Lady Jocelyn' shipped head-quarters and the remaining nine companies at Calcutta, dropping down the river at once, and putting out to sea the following day for Auckland, and the numbers on board were—

Field Officers.	Captains.	Lieuts.	Ensigns.	Staff.	Sergts.	Corpls.	Buglers.	Privates.	Women.	Children.
3	2	9	4	3	43	35	18	556	51	88

The vessel proved in such crank condition as to excite serious apprehensions, and her commander, unwilling to jeopardise the lives of so many, changed his course and steered for Mauritius, reaching Port Louis on the 1st November, up to which time there had been casualties by death of 1 sergeant, 1 private, 3 women, and 1 child. Having taken in ballast, they left on the 6th, and arrived at Auckland without further mishap on the 11th December, where they disembarked and marched to Otahuhu to await further instructions.

1864.

On the 21st of April a force, under Major Colville, 43rd, was engaged with the enemy at Why-hee, about two miles from the Fort at Maketu. An ambuscade had been laid near the ford at Why-hee, and a party of rebels opened fire on Major Colville, Ensign Way, 3rd Waikato Regiment, and Private Key, 43rd, when crossing the river in a canoe. They were chased across the ford, and on their jumping out were followed by the Maories yelling and firing until they gained the bush and escaped. The rebels were not more than fifty yards distant, when the pursuit commenced, and Major Colville in his despatch describes their preservation as "most providential and wonderful." On arrival at the Fort a party of fifty men of the 43rd and 3rd Waikato Regiment (the former under Captain Smith, 43rd), was ordered out—Major Colville in command of the whole—to drive the enemy back across the ford. It was found that they had already recrossed, and, with augmented numbers, taken up a position at a distance of some 400 yards on the other side, from which, under cover of sand-hills and bush, they kept up a constant fire. A further reinforcement of thirty men, under command of Captain Hon. A. E. Harris, 43rd, was sent for, and a party of fourteen men of the Forest Rangers, with two officers, and various natives of the friendly Arawa tribe, also joined. As Major Colville's orders were very stringent not to go far from the settlement of Maketu, he was compelled to content himself with lining the side of the river, and firing, at upwards of 400 yards, at the rebels, who by this time were apparently above 300 strong, and gradually increasing.

This skirmish or interchange of shots lasted several hours. Three privates of the 43rd were killed, one of the Royal Engineers wounded, and the enemy afterwards acknowledged to having lost forty. Major Colville withdrew his men at dusk, and returned to the Fort. Slight tussles were of daily occurrence. On the 25th Captain Berner's company, under command of Lieutenant Hogarth, joined from Tauranga. At 4 A.M. on the 27th the Maories commenced a heavy fire on Fort Colvile, at Maketu, where our men were stationed, and H.M. ship 'Falcon,' and the steamer 'Sandfly' were despatched from Tauranga, bringing the Lieut.-General and staff. The 'Falcon,' on arrival, shelled the enemy out of their position and across Why-hee, the men-of-war following twelve miles up the coast, when they were pursued by Major Hay, with 400 loyal natives and some Forest Rangers and defence force, who killed upwards of fifty, many of whom were chiefs, took nine prisoners, over forty stand of arms, and a considerable quantity of ammunition, altogether achieving very good service.

Assault of the "Gate Pa."

Lieutenant-General Cameron, commanding the forces, having made a reconnaissance of the rebel intrenchments at Puke-hina-hina (Gate Pa), an attack was organized.

On the highest point of a neck of land, a quarter of a mile wide, of which the slopes fell off on either side into swamp, the Maories had constructed an oblong redoubt, well palisaded and surrounded by strong post-and-rail fence, difficult to bowl over with artillery, and an almost invulnerable obstacle to an assaulting column. The intervals between the side faces of the redoubt and the swamp were defended by an intrenched line of rifle-pits. The 68th Light Infantry, with a mixed detachment under Major Ryan, 70th Regiment, encamped on the 27th 1200 yards distant, and on that and the following day the guns and mortars intended to breach the position were brought up to the camp, augmented by a large force of seamen and marines from the squadron of Commodore Sir William Wiseman. Head-quarters and five companies of the 43rd, under command of Lieut.-Colonel Booth, joined. The composition and strength of the force assembled at Puke-hina-hina on the evening of the 28th, were as follow :—

General Staff.—5 officers.
Medical Staff.—3 officers.
Naval Brigade.—4 field officers, 6 captains, 7 subalterns, 36 sergeants, 5 drummers, 371 rank and file.
Royal Artillery.—1 field officer, 1 captain, 3 subalterns, 1 staff, 1 sergeant, 43 rank and file.
Royal Engineers.—2 rank and file.
Moveable Column.—7 officers, 6 sergeants, 4 drummers, 164 rank and file.
43rd Light Infantry.—1 field officer, 5 captains, 5 subalterns, 3 staff, 17 sergeants, 12 buglers, 250 rank and file.

68*th Light Infantry.*—3 field officers, 6 captains, 15 subalterns, 3 staff, 34 sergeants, 21 buglers, 650 rank and file.

Total.—16 field officers.
20 captains.
35 subalterns.
8 staff.
94 sergeants.
41 drummers.
1480 rank and file.

Artillery, viz :—
5 Armstrong guns.
2 howitzers.
8 mortars.

After dark a feigned attack was made on the front of the enemy's position, to divert their attention from a flank movement by the 68th, who had received orders to gain the rear and so surround them, which it was conjectured could be effected at low water by passing along the beach and outside the swamp on their right. The manœuvre succeeded perfectly, and in the A.M. the 68th, in extended order, was in rear of the enemy. The guns and mortars opened soon after daybreak, their fire being principally directed against the left angle of the centre work, regarded as the least impregnable point. At twelve o'clock a six-pounder Armstrong gun was taken across the swamp on the enemy's left to the high ground on the opposite side, from which its fire completely enfiladed the left of the position. The bombardment continued, with short intermissions, until 4 P.M., when a portion of the fence and palisading being destroyed and a practicable breach made, the assault was ordered.

One hundred and fifty of the 43rd with an equal number of seamen and marines under Commander Hay of H.M. ship 'Harrier' formed the assaulting column, led by Lieut.-Colonel Booth. Major Ryan and his detachment were extended as close to the work as possible, to keep down the fire from the rifle-pits. The remainder of the 43rd, seamen, and marines, amounting to 300 in all, followed as a reserve.

As Colonel Booth gave the word "inward face," the 43rd to the right, the Naval Brigade to the left, advanced by double files from the centre to where the breach had been made, which, protected in a measure by the nature of the ground, was gained with little loss, and an entrance effected into the main body of the work. A fierce conflict then ensued, in which the natives fought with the greatest desperation. Lieut.-Colonel Booth and Commander Hay, who led into the work with Captain Glover and Ensign Langsland, fell mortally wounded, and in a few minutes almost every officer of the column was either killed or disabled. Up to this moment the men, so nobly led by their officers, struggled gallantly and carried the position; but, finding themselves beset on all sides by a withering fire which had already laid low so many comrades, they suddenly wavered, and upon a shout being raised by the sailors, "They are coming into us in thousands, retire!" in spite of all Lieutenant Garland's entreaties to persevere, they fell back upon the nearest cover; he and three or four others alone remaining, until forced to make their escape from the Pa. These men were afterwards specially thanked by H.R.H. the Commander-in-Chief, and one of them, Colour-Sergeant W. B. Garland, received a medal for distinguished service in the field, along with an annuity of 15*l*. This disastrous retreat, commenced by the Naval Brigade, the Lieut.-General could only attribute to the confusion created amongst the men by the intricate nature of the interior defences, and the panic which the sudden fall of so many of their officers inspired, added to darkness setting in. Under these circumstances, the General hesitated to renew the assault by ordering up the reserve, and contented himself with throwing up a line of intrenchments within a hundred yards of the redoubt, intending to resume operations next day. An orderly was despatched to Tauranga for a reinforcement of all available men, and another company of the 43rd joined the same evening. The Maories, however, availing themselves of the extreme darkness of the night, abandoned their hold, and escaped through the lines of the 68th.

On taking possession of the work in the morning, Lieut.-Colonel Booth and some privates were found still breathing, and, to the credit of the natives, had not been maltreated, neither had any of the bodies of the killed been mutilated. The list of casualties in this sad affair was—

1st Battalion, 12th Foot.—Non-commissioned officers and men, 1 killed and 2 wounded.

2nd Battalion, 14th Foot.—Non-commissioned officers and men, 4 wounded.

40th Foot.—Non-commissioned officers and men, 1 wounded.

43rd Light Infantry.—Officers, 5 killed and 4 wounded; non-commissioned officers and men, 9 killed and 23 wounded. Afterwards died of wounds, officers, 2 : non-commissioned officers and men, 4.

65th Foot.—Non-commissioned officers and men, 1 wounded.

68th Light Infantry.—Non-commissioned officers and men, 2 killed and 18 wounded.

Total.—Officers, 5 killed, 4 wounded; non-commissioned officers and men, 12 killed, 49 wounded. Since dead, officers, 2; non-commissioned officers and men, 4.

Names of Officers, 43rd Light Infantry, killed and wounded :—

Captain R. C. Glover, killed.
„ C. R. Mure, killed.
„ R. T. F. Hamilton, killed.
„ E. Utterton, killed.
Ensign C. J. Langlands, killed.
Lieut.-Colonel H. J. P. Booth, died of wounds.
Lieutenant F. G. E. Glover, died of wounds.
Ensign S. P. T. Nicholl, wounded.
„ W. Clark, wounded.

The Naval Brigade had 4 Officers and 40 Seamen and Marines killed and wounded in this affair.

The loss of the enemy must have been very heavy, although not more than twenty bodies and six wounded were found in and about the position. The prisoners avowed that a large number of killed and wounded had been carried off during the night.

In General Cameron's despatch he wrote:—

"I deeply deplore the loss of the many brave and valuable officers who fell in the noble discharge of their duty on this occasion. The 43rd Regiment and the service have sustained a serious loss in the death of Lieut.-Colonel Booth, which took place on the night after the attack. I have already mentioned the brilliant example shown by this officer in the assault; and when I met him on the following morning, as he was being carried out of the work, his first words were an expression of regret that he had found it impossible to carry out my orders."

The following officers, non-commissioned officers, and men were brought to notice for good service in this engagement, and received the thanks of H.R.H the Field-Marshal Commanding-in-Chief, Lieutenant and Adjutant Garland being noted for promotion to an unattached company without purchase, for his gallant endeavours to rally the men. This officer was also specially mentioned in the General's despatch.

Lieut. and Adjt. G. Garland.	Sergeant W. B. Garland.
Ensign S. P. T. Nicholl.	Corporal Geo. Harrison.
" Wm. Clark.	Private Wm. Bridgeman.
" J. B. Garland.	" Chas. Maitland.

Engagement at "Te Ranga."

The rebels having become very audacious, and threatening an attack on Te Papa, frequent reconnoitring parties were sent out, and on the 21st of June Colonel Greer, commanding the forces at Tauranga, moved with a force of 3 field officers, 9 captains, 14 subalterns, 24 sergeants, 13 buglers, 531 rank and file, and found a body of 600 Maories, intrenched about four miles beyond Gate Pa. They had made a chain of rifle-pits of the usual form across the road in a position exactly similar to Puke-hina-hina, the commencement of a formidable Pa. Having driven in some skirmishers thrown out by the enemy, the 43rd and a portion of the 68th were extended, and kept up a sharp fire for about two hours, while a reinforcement of one gun and 230 men, comprising all the available men in camp, were sent for. When sufficiently near to support, the "advance" was sounded, and the 43rd and 68th at once charged and carried the rifle-pits in the most dashing manner, under a tremendous fire. For a few minutes the Maories closed savagely, and then were utterly routed. Sixty-eight were killed in the pits. The situation was favourable for their retreat, otherwise few could have escaped. The defence force pursued for several miles, but owing to the deep ravines with which the country is everywhere intersected, could not make much play. Major Synge, who on this occasion commanded the 43rd, had his horse shot under him. The bodies of 107 Maories were found and interred the following day; in the rifle-pits twenty-seven were brought in severely wounded, and ten prisoners. Many more perished and remained in the ravines. Among the killed were several influential Chiefs, one of whom, Rawhiri, was the leader of the rebels at the Gate Pa, while others of note were wounded.

Colonel Greer, in his report of the action, says that the enemy made a gallant stand at their rifle-pits; "they stood the charge without flinching, and did not retire until forced out at the point of the bayonet, which everywhere did its work." This defeat was a most stinging blow to the enemy, and doubtless influenced the large number who during the following month surrendered themselves and their arms.

The strength of 43rd Light Infantry present in this action was 2 field officers, 3 captains, 4 subalterns, 1 staff, 13 sergeants, 6 buglers, and 210 rank and file.

The British loss was small, considering the number engaged, the heavy fire to which they were exposed advancing to the attack, and the ferocious resistance encountered. The casualties in the 43rd were two officers wounded—Captain F. A. Smith, very severely; Captain H. J. Berners, severely.

The undermentioned officers and non-commissioned officers were brought to notice by Colonel Greer, on account of good service in this affair. Major Synge —commanding the line of skirmishers, horse shot under him in two places. Major Colville—leading the left of the line of skirmishers into the rifle-pits, himself one of the first in. Captain Smith—the first into the right of the line of rifle-pits, and whose gallant conduct was very conspicuous; severely wounded; recommended for Victoria Cross. Captain Berners—severely wounded when leading in front of his company close to the rifle-pits. Captain Hon. A. E. Harris—detached in command of two companies of the 43rd to the right to enfilade the enemy's position, brought the companies at the critical moment to assist in the assault. Lieutenant Hammick, acting Adjutant—who performed his duty with great coolness and courage under a heavy fire. Assistant-Surgeon Henry—who paid the greatest care and attention to the wounded under fire—and Sergeant-Major Daniels, who distinguished himself by his coolness and courage, were specially brought to notice by their commanding officer.

In forwarding Colonel Greer's despatch to His Excellency the Governor, Lieut.-General Sir Duncan Cameron remarked—

"The valour and discipline of the troops, and the ability of their commander were conspicuously displayed on this occasion, and the 43rd and 68th Light Infantry, on whom the brunt of the engagement fell, behaved in a manner worthy of the reputation of these distinguished regiments."

On the 7th of August headquarters and seven companies left Tauranga for Auckland, and marched to Otahuhu.

On the 22nd of November headquarters and four companies, under command of Lieut.-Colonel Synge, moved to New Plymouth.

On the 30th of November three companies, under command of Lieut.-Colonel Synge, proceeded on patrol fourteen miles beyond the Waitara River and burned some huts.

1865.

On the 2nd of March two companies of the 43rd, together with a detachment, 70th Regiment (Major Ryan, 70th, in command of the whole), proceeded from New Plymouth to Le Arei on patrol, and took some prisoners.

By 'Gazette' of March 21st, Major Colville was promoted to Brevet Lieut.-Colonel and Captain F. Smith to Brevet Major, for distinguished service in Te Ranga. Smith also received the Victoria Cross.

On the 12th of June a mixed force, under command of Colonel Warre, C.B., marched from Opunaki to Kopoaiaia, a distance of sixteen miles, over a flat and extremely wet and swampy country. A party of the 43rd Light Infantry, comprising 1 field officer, 2 captains, 4 subalterns, 1 staff, 5 sergeants, 3 buglers, and 125 rank and file, under command of Major Holmes, met for co operation. They destroyed the villages of Le Puru and Kekeria, for which Brevet Lieut.-Colonel Colville and Major Holmes were officially thanked.

On the 21st of July the War Office reduced the regimental establishment by 12 sergeants and 250 privates.

On the 28th a patrol of 1 captain, 1 subaltern, 1 staff, 2 sergeants, 1 bugler, and 51 rank and file, was sent, under command of Captain Close, from Warea. Turning a corner of the road, the party was surprised by a heavy volley from the natives, when Captain Close fell mortally wounded, and Private John Hallohan was shot dead by his side. Ensign O'Brien immediately ordered "fix bayonets" and "charge," but the aborigines escaped through the bush.

The undermentioned were brought to notice on this occasion by Ensign O'Brien, 43rd Light Infantry, who commanded the party when Captain Close fell:—

Sergeants Horley and Phelan, "who carried out the orders they received with great promptitude and coolness," and Bugler Peter Croughan, "who stayed by Captain Close's body, under a heavy fire, until he received assistance to remove it under cover."

On receipt of the above intelligence at New Plymouth, Colonel Warre, C.B., ordered out a party, under command of Brevet Lieut.-Colonel Colville, 43rd Light Infantry, for the purpose of chastising the Warea rebels. The column explored the track running inland between Tataramaka block and Warea, but came upon none. Le Aka and some other villages were destroyed. Private Samuel Boulton was killed. Captains Hon. A. E. Harris and Talbot, and Lieutenant Longley, were specially thanked for judgment and intelligence displayed.

Various moves of companies took place before October 22nd, when a party of—

F. O.	Capt.	Subs.	Staff.	Sergts.	Buglers.	R. & F.
1	1	2	0	4	2	85

NAMES OF OFFICERS:—
Brevet Lieut.-Colonel Colville.
Captain Hon. A. E. Harris.
Lieutenant Longley.
Ensign O'Brien—

left Warea to lay an ambush for the rebel Maories. About fifty were drawn on, and, fire being opened, they were soon forced to retire, but the regiment lost—

Brevet Lieut.-Colonel Colville, very severely wounded.
Sergeant M. Clifford, killed.
Private F. Pratt, died of wounds.
Sergeant J. Dyer, dangerously wounded.

On the 23rd Major-General Chute inspected the companies at headquarters, Lieut.-Colonel Synge in command. There were present on parade—

F. O.	Capts.	Subs.	Staff.	Sergts.	Corpls.	Buglers.	Privates.
2	3	4	3	13	5	3	89

1866.

On the 30th of January 100 rank and file, under Captain Livesay, and 100 under Captain Horan, joined a force under General Chute, and took part in the destruction of Waikowkow.

On February the 6th a party, under Captain the Hon. A. E. Harris, destroyed the villages of Peri Peri and Agakiki, with all standing crops.

On the 14th a party, under Colonel Synge, of 5 captains, 7 subalterns, 13 sergeants, 9 buglers, 230 rank and file, with one company of militia and some friendly natives, destroyed the villages of Agapukis and Suranga.

On the 19th orders were received for the regiment to be held in readiness to embark for England, and upon arrival at New Auckland, before departure was, on March 27th, reinspected by General Chute. There were present under arms—

F. O.	Capts.	Subs.	Staff.	Sergts.	Buglers.	R. & F.
1	10	16	5	40	18	521

Sailing for England on board the 'Silver Eagle' and 'Maori,' headquarters disembarked, on the 4th of July, at Portsmouth, and marched to Anglesea Barracks. The depôt companies, under command of Brevet Major Smith, V.C., had already arrived from Winchester. Strength of depôt was—

Capt.	Subs.	Sergts.	Buglers.	R. & F.
1	4	11	4	234

On October 20th the Regiment was inspected by

Lieut.-General Sir G. Buller, K.C.B., when there were on parade—

F. O.	Capts.	Subs.	Staff.	Sergts.	Corpls.	Buglers.	Privates.
2	9	21	2	36	30	18	458

1867.

On May 11th the establishment of the Regiment was reduced to—

Sergts.	Corpls.	Buglers.	Privates.
40	40	20	560

On June 10th the Regiment proceeded by rail to Aldershot, where it occupies the North Camp, and forms part of the 3rd Brigade, under Brigadier General Sir Alfred Horsford, K.C.B.

On December 24th, the non-commissioned officers and men entitled to the Banda and Kirwee prize money received their first instalment at Aldershot; a Private's share amounting to 50*l*., and a Sergeant's to 100*l*. About 120 received the above amounts, and in the afternoon of the same day 80 of the recipients went on furlough.

The annals of the 43rd are ended. Time alone can unravel future career and services. The traditions of the past are treasured as incitements to valour in the future. They have been recorded in the hope that veterans at their hearth-sides may be cheered by reminiscences of bygone days; while recruits will be inspired even more firmly to rally round the colours, bearing in mind that, as with men so with deeds, "the good they do lives after them."

True though it be that "The paths of glory lead but to the grave," yet from the grave of the soldier springs that patriotism which sheds lustre over victory and deprives defeat of dishonour; and, should our Regiment ever be called upon to choose between flight and death, "old corps" will prove undegenerate, and its ranks composed of stuff to whom might not be inapplicable the epigram of Simonides on those who fell with Leonidas:—

> "These won for Sparta fame through endless days,
> When death's dark cloud upon themselves they drew,
> But dying, died not, for their valour's praise
> From Hades' dwelling leads them up anew."

[*The enrolled names of the following Officers, with their Services, have been carefully culled from every attainable document; but as omissions and errors must—even with the most anxious scrutiny—arise, Sir Richard Levinge hopes any having reason to feel aggrieved, will credit to "his misfortune not his fault," where he has failed correctly to annote each individual date, merit, or honour.*]

SUCCESSION OF COLONELS.

Fowke, Thomas	January 3rd	1741
Graham, William	August 12th	1741
Kennedy, James	February 7th	1746
Talbot, Sharrington, *Honourable*	March 24th	1761
Noel, Bennet, *Honourable*	April 12th	1762
Carey, George, *Honourable*	September 26th	1766
Smith, Edward	April 26th	1792
Howden, *Lord*, G.C.B., K.C.	January 7th	1809
Keane, *Lord*, G.C.B. G.C.H.	August 1st	1839
Pakenham, Hercules Robert, *Honourable Sir*, K.C.B.	September 9th	1844
Fergusson, James, *Sir*, G.C.B.	March 26th	1850
Love, J. Frederick, *Sir*, G.C.B, K.H.	September 5th	1865
Garrett, Robert, *Sir*, K.C.B., K.H.	January 14th	1866

ALPHABETICAL ROLL OF OFFICERS.

Names.	Ensign.	Lieutenant.	Captain.	Major.	Lieut.-Col.	Remarks.
ABERNETHIE, Stewart	23 Jan. 1782	17 Jan. 1787	..	..	..	Out next year.
ABBOT, George Cary	26 Sept. 1787	..	..	..	..	Probably never joined.
ADAMS, P. Barwell	20 Nov. 1793	..	..	..	..	Died of fever in West Indies, 13th July, 1794.
AFFLECK, Edmund	..	26 Dec. 1785	30 Nov. 1792	..	..	Captain-Lieutenant, 30th April, 1792; died 1st May, 1793, in West Indies.
AFFLECK, *Sir James, Bart.*	29 Feb. 1776	9 Dec. 1778.	..	..	..	Severely wounded when in the 43rd at Rhode Island; promoted into the 26th Regt., 15th Sept., 1779; to Captain-Lieutenant 23rd Dragoons, 16th Jan., 1782; Major 19th Dragoons, 6th Dec., 1786; Lieutenant-Colonel 16th Light Dragoons, 25th March, 1795; Colonel, 1st Jan., 1798; Major-General, 1st Jan., 1805; Lieutenant-General, 4th June, 1811; General, 27th May, 1825; died 10th August, 1833.
AINSLIE, Henry	..	15 Aug, 1775	..	..	..	Out 1778.
ALDERSON, Jonathan	9 Sept. 1828	6 April, 1831	..	..	..	Retired 4th July, 1834.
ALLAS, William	24 Feb. 1813	3 Mar. 1814	..	..	..	On h.-p. 25th March, 1817; died 1818.
ALLARDICE, Rob. Barclay	29 May, 1863	..	..	..	..	To 93rd, 10th July, 1863; Lieutenant, 8th June, 1867.
ALLEN, William	31 Oct. 1804	..	..	..	..	Resigned April, 1805.
ANDERSON, Thomas	26 Oct. 1804	18 June, 1805	..	..	..	Expedition to Copenhagen; to 2nd Royal Veteran Battalion, 25th Nov., 1808; retired on f.-p. on reduction of the Battalion.
ANDOE, John Augustus	7 Feb. 1797	..	..	..	..	To 45th, 30th March; out in July.
ANGROVE, John	16 April, 1809	24 May, 1810	..	..	..	From Royal Cornwall Militia. Present at Vittoria and Vera; died of wounds, Nov. 13, at Nivelle.
ANNESLEY, *Hon.* Hugh, M.P.	18 April, 1851	29 July, 1853	..	..	..	Exchanged to Scots Fusilier Guards, 21st Oct., 1853. Lieutenant and Captain, 14th Aug., 1855. Captain and Lieutenant-Colonel, 18th May, 1860. Served with the 43rd Light Infantry in the Kaffir war of 1851-2-3 (medal), and was severely wounded. Served with the Scots Fusilier Guards in the Eastern campaign of 1854, including the battle of Alma (severely wounded); medal and clasps and Turkish medal.
ANNESLEY, Robert	8 Oct. 1796	19 April, 1798	..	..	..	To 62nd Regt.; out 1803.
ANTRIM, Hugh S., *Earl of*	25 June, 1829	..	..	..	26th July, 1833	To h.-p. 9th Dec., 1831; Lieutenant 7th Fusiliers, retired from the service, 1836; died 19th July, 1855.
ARBUTHNOT, John	13 Sept. 1776	..	..	..	..	To 82nd Regt., Jan., 1778; appointed Captain and Governor of Yarmouth, 1779; died 1810.
ARMFELT, Frederick Simon	17 Nov. 1863	..	..	..	..	Retired 6th Feb., 1866.
ARTHUR, Thomas	22 Nov. 1756	30 Aug. 1761	..	..	..	Served at siege of Quebec and different actions; expedition to West Indies; resigned Feb., 1765.

43rd Light Infantry.

Name				Notes
ATTY, John	8 July, 1851	..	..	Retired 5th May, 1854.
AUCHMUTY, Rob. Mulcaster	..	22 Sept. 1814	..	To 73rd Regt., 22nd Aug., 1816; h.-p., 25th March, 1817; out in 1830.
BAGOR, Milo	..	27 April, 1756	..	Ensign 17th Regt, 3rd June, 1752; out in 1757.
BAILLIE, Mackay Hugh	9 Nov. 1809	18 July, 1811	..	Served in the Peninsula, at Ciudad Rodrigo, Badajoz (wounded), Salamanca, Vittoria, and St. Muños (wounded); present at attack on the heights of Vera and at the Nivelle; killed before Bayonne 23rd Nov., 1813.
BAKER, William	9 Mar. 1785	..	..	Resigned 13th Feb, 1787.
BAMBRICK, Henry	13 Dec. 1809	12 Sept. 1811	..	Placed on h.-p. of the Regt., 25th Feb., 1817; appointed to 2nd Veteran Battalion, 3rd Feb, 1820; retired on f.-p. of the Battalion; died 1826.
BARHAM, Robert	2 July, 1812	..	..	From East Suffolk Militia. Retired 1813.
BARNETT, Thomas	6 June, 1795	..	..	Removed to 4th Dragoons, 28th Oct., 1795; out 1800.
BATEMAN, Hugh Osborne	6 Mar. 1856	24 July, 1857	1 May, 1864	Served in the New Zealand war of 1864–5.
BAXTER, Alex. Browne	5 Aug. 1813	22 June, 1815	..	On h.-p. of the Regt. 25th March, 1815; medal for Toulouse.
BAYARD, Wm. Shireff	24 Oct. 1781	1 June, 1785	30 April, 1792	Captain-Lieutenant, 31st May, 1791; died of fever in West Indies, March, 1793.
BAYLEY, William	28 Sept. 1815	..	..	Placed on h.-p. of the Regt., 25th Mar., 1817; out 1819.
BAYLY, William Prittie	2 Nov. 1815	..	..	Ensign in Army, 28th Sept., 1815; retired from Captain 92nd, Oct., 1841; died June, 1842.
BEAVAN, Samuel Phillimore	12 April, 1309	21 Aug. 1810	..	From Royal Radnor Militia; retired 2nd Sept., 1813.
BECKHAM, Horatio	..	..	25 Sept. 1813	From East Suffolk Militia to h.-p. of the 43rd, 25th Sept., 1814; medal for the British Legion of Spain; died 1856.
BECKHAM, Thomas	7 May, 1811	23 Feb. 1813	..	Captain 19th Regt., 3rd Dec., 1830; to h.-p., 8th March, 1845; Major, 9th Nov., 1846; Lieutenant-Colonel, Dec., 1818; Captain in 1st West India Regt., 8th June, 1854. 20th June, 1854.
BEDWARD, Thomas Bevan	24 Dec. 1796	..	..	From East Essex Militia. Resigned 24th April, 1797.
BELL, William	5 Nov. 1825	1 July, 1828	23 Dec. 1831	Was with the expedition to Portugal in 1862-7; and the suppression of the Canadian revolt, and was one of those to cross the Portage of the Madawaska; retired 21st Aug, 1840; died at Ipswich as Barrack-master, Aug., 1857.
BENNET, Vere Fane	9 Oct. 1855	26 Sept. 1856	..	Retired 22nd April, 1859. Was originally Vere Fane, assumed the name of Bennet.
BERESFORD, J. P. de la Poer	12 Oct. 1807.	..	..	Appointed to 1st Life Guards, 22nd Aug, 1834. Captain 1st Life Guards, 27th Dec, 1837; died 18th Oct., 1850.
BERESFORD, Lord William	14 May, 1829	4 July, 1834	..	
BERKELEY, George	10 Sept. 1807	6 April, 1809	26 Oct. 1815	Placed on h.-p. of the Regt., 25th March, 1817. Appointed 7th Fusileers, 11th Dec., 1817; to h.-p., 4th Dec., 1823. Assumed the name of Calcott. Served the campaign of 1808-9 with the 43rd, including the battle of Vimiero, the retreat under Sir J. Moore, and battle of Corunna; expedition to Walcheren in 1809; subsequently in the Peninsula, including the sieges and capture of Ciudad Rodrigo and Badajoz, battles of Salamanca, Vittoria, Pyrenees, Nivelle, Nive, and Toulouse (medal with ten clasps); expedition to New Orleans; campaign of 1815; and was present at the capture of Paris; retired as Major, 10th Jan., 1837.

Names.	Ensign.	Lieutenant.	Captain.	Major.	Lieut.-Col.	Remarks.
BERMINGHAM, William	14 Mar. 1789	..	..	..	..	Resigned 30th March, 1791.
BERNERS, Herbert Johnes	6 June, 1854	13 April, 1855	11 Feb. 1862	..	..	Served in the Indian Mutiny, 1857-8; was present at Jubbulpore and Puttrai (medal); in New Zealand 1864–5. Severely wounded in the action at Te Ranga, mentioned in despatch.
BILLINGHURST, William	26 Dec. 1787	..	..	..	..	Resigned 30th Oct., 1789.
BISHOP, Thomas Handy	25 Dec. 1813	..	..	..	..	From North Gloucester Militia; present at New Orleans. Placed on h.-p. of the Regt., 23rd Oct., 1817; retired 1829.
BLYTH, D'Urban W. Farrer	7 Mar. 1856	24 May, 1858	2 May, 1864	..	..	Served in the suppression of the Indian mutiny from Dec. 1857, to Jan., 1860, including actions at Sahao, Dooleypore, and Puralia; and commanded a detachment of the 43rd Light Infantry at Putowrie; thanked by the Governor-General (medal).
BOLTON, Theophilus	29 June, 1793	12 July, 1794	..	..	..	Died Dec, 1795, of fever in the West Indies.
BONNER, John Edward	30 Jan. 1796	19 Mar. 1796	..	..	..	25th Oct, 1797, to Grenadier Guards; Captain in 64th, 1st May, 1798; out 1804.
BONTIEN, Edward Trant	..	24 Feb, 1803	..	..	..	From 57th Regt., Captain 92nd, 15th Dec., 1804; retired Captain 9th Light Dragoons, Oct, 1811.
BONTIEN, James	..	8 Aug. 1804	..	..	..	From Ensign 9th Foot, 10 Sept., 1803; out 1807.
BOOTH, Henry, K.H.	6 Mar. 1806	11 June, 1807	25 June, 1812	29 Aug. 1822	29 June, 1830	Present at Vimiero, Coruña, the Coa, Busaco, Salamanca, Vittoria, and the attack on the Heights of Vera. Served in the suppression of the revolt in Canada; and conducted the Regt. over the Madawaska Portage; died at Northallerton, 6th May, 1841.
BOOTH, Henry Jackson Parkin	11 June, 1847	9 Aug. 1850	29 July, 1853	3 April, 1857	11 Feb. 1862	Medal for the Kaffir war of 1851-3; died of wounds, Gate Pa, New Zealand, May 1st, 1864.
BOOTHBY, *Sir William, Bart.*	..	..	23 July, 1743	12 May, 1746	..	On first formation of Regt. as Captain-Lieutenant; to Lieutenant-Colonel of Loudon's Foot, 30th March, 1750; Colonel, 11th July, 1760; Major-General, 16th July, 1762; Colonel of 6th Regt, 18th Nov., 1773. Lieutenant-General, 25th May, 1772; General, 19th Feb., 1783; died Feb, 1787.
BOUTTELL, John	6 June, 1795	..	..	..	..	From Essex Militia. Returned to it 31st Aug., 1795.
BOWES, George William	30 Oct. 1804	25 Nov. 1804	..	..	..	To 78th Regt., 25th Nov., 1804. Captain 77th Regt., Aug., 1808; out July, 1809.
BOYS, Thomas	11 April, 1809	2 Aug. 1810	..	.. to West India Rangers, 28th March, 1811; exchanged to h.-p. Waggon Train, 2nd Jan., 1817; died 5th Oct., 1828.	..	From Royal Monmouth and Brecon Militia; appointed
BRADLEY, Stephen	1 Sept. 1804	5 Jan. 1805	..	..	..	Out April, 1806.
BRAMWELL, John	14 July, 1808	28 Sept. 1809	..	..	..	From the Royal Cumberland Militia; present at the Coa, Sabugal, Busaco, and Fuentes d'Onoro; died from wounds received at Ciudad Rodrigo, 1812.
BRETT, Digby Templeton	26 July, 1864	..	..	..	..	Ensign 74th, 8th July, 1862. Served in the New Zealand war in 1865; retired 12th Oct, 1867.
BRETT, Harry Armstrong	8 Sept. 1854	1 May, 1855	29 July, 1862	..	..	Served in the Indian campaign, 1858–9 (medal); in New Zealand war, 1864–5.

43rd Light Infantry.

Name				Notes
BRIGGS, Thomas	..	..	25 Dec. 1813	From Derby Militia. Placed on h.-p. of the Regt., 25th Aug., 1814.
BROAD, Richard	..	..	28 Aug. 1804	From Ensign and Lieutenant 83rd Regt. to 1st Foot, 8th Dec., 1804; died Major 47th Regt., 1813.
BROCK, Saumorey, K.H.	..	6 Aug. 1807	12 Oct. 1815	Ensign 96th, 25th Nov., 1802; to h.-p. 35th, 1803; Lieutenant 48th, 14th April 1804; Captain, 28th March, 1805; placed on h.-p. of 43rd, as Major, 25th March, 1817; appointed to 55th Regt., 29th Aug., 1822; Lieutenant-Colonel in same, 12th June, 1830; exchanged to 48th Regt., 13th May, 1833; placed on h.-p. of that Regt., 30th March, 1835; Colonel, 9th Nov., 1846. Medal and clasps for Vimiero (wounded), Vittoria, Pyrenees, Nivelle, Nive, Orthes; present at New Orleans; died at Guernsey, 22nd April, 1854.
BROCKMAN, Hy. Lynch Drake	14 Jan. 1808	..	..	Present at Vimiero; passage of the Douro and capture of Oporto, and battle of Talavera.
BROMFIELD, James	..	15 Nov. 1864	..	Died at Elvas, of typhus fever, 1809.
BROWN, Sir Geo., G.C.B., K.H.	23 Jan. 1806	18 Sept. 1806	..	To 50th, 21st Nov., 1865.
				To Captain 3rd Garrison Battalion, 20th June, 1811; appointed to 85th, 2nd July, 1812; Major 85th, 26th May, 1814; Brevet-Lieutenant-Colonel, 29th Sept., 1814; placed on h.-p, 17th July, 1823; exchanged to Rifle Brigade, 5th Feb., 1824. Served at the siege and capture of Copenhagen in 1807; in the Peninsula from Aug., 1808, to July, 1811; and again from July, 1813, to May, 1814, including the battle of Vimiero, passage of the Douro, and capture of Oporto, with the previous and subsequent actions; battle of Talavera (severely wounded through both thighs), action of the Light Division at the bridge of Almeida, battle of Busaco, the different actions during the retreat of the French army from Portugal, action at Sabugal, battle of Fuentes d'Onoro, siege of San Sebastian, battles of the Nivelle and Nive, and the investment of Bayonne. Served afterwards in the American war, and was present at the battle of Bladensburg and capture of Washington. Slightly wounded in the head and very severely in the groin at Bladensburg. He received the war medal with seven clasps. Commanded the Light Division throughout the Eastern campaign of 1854-5, including the battles of the Alma (horse shot under him), Balaklava, and Inkerman (severely wounded—shot through the arm), and siege of Sebastopol (medal and four clasps, G.C.B, Grand Cross of the Legion of Honour, 1st class of the Medjidie, Sardinian and Turkish medals); appointed Commander of the Forces in Ireland, March, 1860; in 1863 he became Colonel-in-Chief of the Rifle Brigade; died at Linkwood, 27th Aug., 1865.
BROWN, James	..	..	21 Feb. 1854	From Major 94th Regt.; Colonel, 20th June, 1854; died 6th Nov., 1856.
BROWNE, George	..	2 Sept. 1796	..	To 6th Regt, 1st June, 1797; out 1800.
BROWNE, Hon. Aug. Caulfield Jas.	..	11 May, 1826	..	Ensign 37th Regt, 14th June, 1821; Lieutenant, unattached, 12th May, 1825; exchanged to 75th Regt, 2nd June, 1825; Captain, unattached, 8th April, 1826. Present with the expedition to Portugal in 1826-7; drowned by the upsetting of a boat on Lough Corrib, 6th Aug., 1831.
BROWNE, John	..	27 April, 1756	4 Oct. 1743	Landed with Regt. from Minorca, 5 Oct., 1749; out 1757.
BROWNE, John	..	23 Nov. 1852	..	Out in 1757.
BROWNE, Lord Richard Howe	..	29th May, 1863	..	Lieutenant 7th Fusiliers, 8th Dec, 1854; Captain, 13th July, 1855; Major in 99th, 29th May, 1863. Served at the siege of Sebastopol from 20th March, 1855, including sorties on 22nd March and 9th May, defence of the Quarries, 7th June, and assault on the Redan on the 18th June (severely wounded); also slightly wounded by the bursting of a shell in Sebastopol, 1st Dec, 1855 (medal and clasps, 5th class of the Medjidie, and Turkish medal); retired 29th May, 1863.
BROWNLOW, Frederick	..	15 Jan. 1818	..	From Lieutenant h.-p. 7th Fusiliers.
BRUERE, Albert Sadleir	21 Oct. 1836	21 Aug. 1840	..	Served in the suppression of the Canadian revolt in 1837-8; died at Halifax, Nova Scotia, 27th Dec., 1845.
BRUERE, Frederick Sadleir	11 Sept. 1840	21 July, 1843	9 Aug. 1850	Served in the Kaffir war, 1851-2-3; died at Edinburgh, 29th Jan., 1857.
BRUERE, Henry Sadleir	1 Sept. 1825	19 Feb. 1828	8 April, 1834	11 April, 1848	Served at Gibraltar in expedition to Portugal in 1828; died Oct. 5, 1851.

Names.	Ensign.	Lieutenant.	Captain.	Major.	Lieut.-Col.	Remarks.
Brunton, Richard	10 Nov. 1808	12 Dec. 1809				To Captain 60th Regt, 10th Nov., 1813, was a Deputy-Assistant Quarter-Master-General in Belgium; placed on h.-p. 25th Dec., 1818; appointed to 13th Light Dragoons, April, 1819; Major, 2nd March, 1826; became Lieutenant-Colonel, 31st Dec., 1830; retired 27th June, 1845. Served in the Peninsula from May, 1810, to Feb., 1814, including the action at the Coa, Busaco, Fuentes d'Onoro, Arroys de Molino, Almarez, Vittoria, Maya Pass, Pyrenees, Nivelle, and Nive. Slightly wounded, 30th July; once had his lip shot off, once through the bones of his leg; and also at Waterloo (medal), defending the baggage; died 27th July, 1846.
Buchanan, John	5 June, 1806	5 May, 1808				Served at Copenhagen. Slightly wounded in Spain. Placed on h.-p. 24th Aug., 1814; appointed to 58th, 29th April, 1836; retired 13th May, 1836; medal for Vittoria and the Pyrenees.
Buckle, Wm. Henry	..	25 Dec. 1813				From East Suffolk Militia; placed on h.-p. 25th Aug., 1814.
Budd, John	..	25 June, 1744				Out in 1750.
Bulkeley, James	..	..	21 May, 1778	1777; placed on h.-p. of 43rd, 1784; reappointed to the Regt., 25th Sept., 1787; retired 13th March, 1789.		From Ensign 22nd Regt, Lieutenant 71st, 18th Jan, 1784.
Bunbury, Matthew	4 Sept. 1754	..	..			Out in 1757.
Bunbury, Henry Wm., C.B.	29 June, 1830	..	Captain in 21st, 18th Aug., 1838; exchanged to 33rd, 19th July, 1839. Brevet-Major; 11th Nov., 1851; Major, unattached, 2nd Jan., 1852; to h.-p., 22nd Jan., 1852; to Major 23rd Fusiliers, 17th Mar., 1854; Brevet-Lieutenant-Colonel, 12th Dec., 1854; Lieutenant-Colonel 23rd, 9th Mar., 1855; reduced to h.-p., 10th Nov., 1856. Served with the expedition through the Kohat Pass, in 1850, as A.D.C. to Sir Charles Napier. Served also with the Eastern campaign of 1854-5, including the battle of Inkerman and siege of Sebastopol (medal and clasps); Knight (5th class) of the Legion of Honour, 5th class of the Medjidie; was Assistant-Adjutant-General S.E. district and Shorncliff from June, 1857, to June, 1860; Colonel, 1st July, 1858; retired 8th July, 1862.			To Lieutenant 11th Light Dragoons, 30th Aug., 1833; exchanged to 21st Fusiliers, 4th Oct., 1833;
Burnet, John	..	..	31 Oct., 1792	13 May, 1795		From Captain-Lieutenant 8th Regt., Brevet-Major, 1st March, 1794; to Lieutenant-Colonel 17th, 14th Sept., 1797. Served in the American war in the 8th Regt, and with the 43rd at the siege of Martinique, St. Lucia, and Guadaloupe, at the storm of Fort Fleur d'Epée, and the attack on Point à Petre (wounded in the right arm); Colonel, 30th Oct., 1805; out 31st Oct., 1805.
Burslem, Geo. James	10 Sept. 1825	..	..	17th Nov., 1832; exchanged to 94th, 26th April, 1834; out April, 1838.		Lieutenant 44th Regt, 31st Aug., 1826; Captain 44th, 13th Jan., 1854; is Lieut.-Col. Civil Service Volunteers.
Bury, *Viscount*	..	21 Oct. 1853	..			From Lieutenant 3rd Guards, 14th Dec., 1849; retired 13th Jan., 1854; is Lieut.-Col. Civil Service Volunteers.
Butler, John	10 Oct. 1787	31 May, 1791	..			Died 1st May, 1793, of fever in West Indies.
Byam, Wm. Geo. Munton	7 April, 1825	30 Dec. 1826	h.-p., unattached, 13th March, 1835; appointed to 28th Regt., 8th May, 1835; retired 1835; died 20th Jan., 1852.			With the expedition to Portugal, 1826-7. Exchanged to
Bygrave, Charles	4 Sept. 1795	26 Jan. 1796	..	Foot, 1803; Captain on the Staff, 5th Sept., 1805; died 27th March, 1813.		From the Lancashire Fencibles; exchanged to h.-p. of 10th
Byron, John	31 Mar. 1791	..	..			Superseded 25th May, 1791.
Cairns, William McNeile	22 May, 1863	1 May, 1864	..			From 96th, 17th March, 1863. Served in the New Zealand war of 1864-5.
Calvert, Charles	14 Mar. 1851	29 July, 1853	..			Served in the Kaffir war of 1851-2-3. Retired Sept., 1856.

43rd Light Infantry.

CAMERON, Alexander	..	..	23 Nov. 1796	..	From Lieutenant in the army, 20th Sept, 1795; exchanged to 45th Regt., 7th Oct., 1796; to 8th West India Regt., 1797. Retired Sept, 1799.
CAMERON, Charles	..	30 Nov. 1792	1 Nov. 1793	25 May, 1795	..
CAMERON, Duncan	..	25 Sept. 1759	24 Mar. 1762	17 Aug. 1773	12 Oct. 1787	Adjutant, 6th October, 1762. Served with the 43rd in the West Indies under Monckton, and throughout the American war. Brevet-Major, 19th Feb., 1783, for distinguished conduct; out Dec, 1793.
CAMERON, Ewen	..	16 Mar. 1797	1 Jan. 1798	14 Aug. 1804	..	Was a Volunteer. Served with the expedition to Copenhagen. Killed at the Coa, 24th July, 1810.
CAMERON, Sir John, K.C.B.	..	25 Sept. 1787	30 Sept. 1790	11 July, 1794	9 Oct. 1800	28 May, 1807	Appointed to 9th Foot, 3rd Sept., 1807. Colonel, 4th June, 1814; Major-General, 19th July, 1821; appointed Lieutenant-Governor of Plymouth, 25th Sept., 1823; Colonel of 9th Foot, 31st May, 1833; Lieutenant-General, 10th July, 1837. He served in the West Indies in the 43rd, under Sir Charles Grey, and was present at the siege of Fort Bourbon, the capture of Martinique, St. Lucia, and Guadaloupe, and at the assault made by the enemy on the fortress of Fleur d'Epée; he next served under Brigadier-General C. Graham at Berville Camp in Guadaloupe; and commanded the Regt. engaged in the action of the 30th Sept., 1794, and in the different attacks made by the enemy until the 4th Oct, when he was severely wounded and taken prisoner, in which situation he remained two years. Gold Medal for Vimiero, Corunna, Busaco, Salamanca, Vittoria, St, Sebastian, and Nive. "In consideration of his eminent services, and we can honestly assert that there was not a better soldier in any army; he was nominated a Knight Commander of the Military Order of the Bath, by his Sovereign. The Portuguese Government conferred the Order of the Tower and Sword on Sir John for the able services he rendered to that nation." Died at Guernsey, 23rd Nov., 1844.
CAMPBELL, Archibald	..	19 April, 1742	10 Mar. 1747	..	..	From Ensign 15th Regt, 8th July, 1760.
CAMPBELL, Duncan	..	15 Oct. 1761	..	..	..	
CAMPBELL, Duncan	..	12 Dec. 1809	29 Aug. 1811	..	..	Present with the Regt., at Ciudad Rodrigo (wounded), Badajoz, Salamanca, St. Muños, Vittoria, Pyrenees, Nivelle, Nive, and Toulouse. Killed at New Orleans, 8th Jan., 1815.
CAMPBELL, George Colin	..	13 May, 1812	2 Sept. 1813	..	..	On h.-p. 1815; drowned in Loch Tarbet, 11th Nov., 1830.
CAMPBELL, Sir Neil, C.B.	..	..	..	24 Jan. 1805	..	From Captain in 95th, 4th June, 1801; appointed to 54th, 20th Feb., 1806; Major-General, 27th May, 1825; died at Sierra Leone, 14th August, 1827.
CAMPBELL, Patrick	..	28 Jan. 1740	..	..	..	Adjutant at formation, not in List for 1749.
CAMPBELL, Wm. Frederick	..	21 Feb. 1828	5 April, 1831	..	..	From 58th Regt.; retired 5th June, 1835; Colonel in the Spanish Legion (wounded); died at Ostend, 1846.
CANE, Edward	..	..	..	8 April, 1762	10 July, 1775	From Captain-Lieutenant, 35th; retired, 8th Oct., 1775. Served with the 43rd in the West Indies at the siege and capture of the Havannah; and at the battle of Bunker's Hill. Founder of the house of Cane, army agents, Dublin.
CAPEL, Thomas	..	20 Feb. 1806	11 Dec. 1806	1 July, 1813	..	Present with the Regt, at Vimiero, Corunna, the Coa, Sabugal, Busaco, Fuentes d'Onoro, Ciudad Rodrigo, Badajoz (wounded). Killed at La Petit la Rhune, 10th November, 1813.
CARISBROOKE, John	..	11 Dec. 1800	..	..	..	Retired 24th May, 1804.
CARR, John	..	22 June, 1815	..	..	..	From 48th; h.-p. of 43rd, 25th March, 1817; appointed to 52nd, 7th April, 1825; died 26th July, 1846.
CARRUTHERS, Joseph	..	..	..	1 Oct. 1802	..	Lieutenant 39th, 1st Dec, 1794; Cornet 10th Light Dragoons, 26th June, 1799; Lieutenant, 3rd May, 1800; exchanged to 60th, 26th June, 1801; Captain, 24th June, 1802; appointed Captain-Lieutenant in 43rd from 93rd, 5th Oct., 1802; was on the staff in Guernsey from 1802 to July, 1805, and in the expedition to Copenhagen, 1807; died from the effects of a fall from his horse in the Corunna retreat, 20th Feb. 1809.

NAME.	ENSIGN.	LIEUTENANT.	CAPTAIN.	MAJOR.	LIEUT.-COL.	REMARKS.
CARRUTHERS, Wm.	22 May, 1812	1 Dec. 1813	..	..	..	Placed on h.-p. of the Regt, 25th Dec, 1818; f.-p., July 21st, 1821; placed 2nd time on h.-p., Oct., 25th, 1821. Captain, 7th Jan., 1842; Major, 20th June, 1854; Lieutenant-Colonel, 12th June, 1859; Colonel, 16th July, 1862. Served in the Peninsular campaign of 1813–14; present at the Nivelle, Bayonne, Nive, Tabres, Tournefeuille, and Toulouse; war medal with three clasps.
CARROLI, John	..	12 Jan. 1796	..	..	..	From 11th Regt.; exchanged to h.-p. April, 1801; appointed Paymaster 6th West India Regt.; out Jan., 1806.
CARROLI, Richard	18 Oct. 1809	2 May, 1811	14 Mar. 1816	..	..	Placed on h.-p. 25th May, 1817; appointed Sub-Inspecting Officer of Militia, Ionian Isles, 1st June, 1820; placed h.-p. of Portuguese and Spanish Staff, 1st June, 1821; served with the Regt. in the Peninsula, and was present at the Coa, Castel Nova (wounded), Ciudad Rodrigo, Badajoz, Salamanca, St. Muños, Vittoria, Heights of Vera, Nivelle, Nive, Toulouse; also at New Orleans. Sabugal (wounded),
CARTER, James Colebrooke	26 July, 1864	..	..	..	..	From 77th Regt, 17th Nov., 1863.
CARTER, John	..	25 Jan. 1747	20 June, 1753	..	..	Served at the Capitulation of Montreal, and Expedition to the West Indies; died March, 1762.
CASABON, Isaac	..	26 Mar. 1744	..	..	..	
CASEY, Bartholomew	23 Aug. 1810	21 May, 1812	..	..	..	Died at Gibraltar, 9th April, 1829.
CECIL, Lord Eustace H. B. Gascoine, M.P.	21 Nov. 1851	13 Jan. 1854	..	..	..	To Coldstream Guards, 13th Jan., 1854; Captain and Lieutenant-Colonel, 2nd July, 1861; retired from the service, 28th July, 1863.
CHAMP, Thomas	5 Dec. 1799	18 Nov. 1803	15 Sept. 1808	..	..	Brevet-Major, 27th May, 1825; retired on h.-p., unattached, 19th Sept., 1826, according to the General Order of 25th April, 1826; exchanged to 20th Regt, 6th Sept. 1831; retired 27th Sept. 1831; was at Copenhagen, 1807; medal and clasps for Nivelle, Nive, Toulouse; present at New Orleans; died 22nd Sept., 1851.
CHAPMAN, Joseph	23 Jan. 1800	6 June, 1804	9 Mar. 1809	..	..	Was at Copenhagen, 1807. Appointed to 1st Veteran Battalion, 12th Oct., 1815; retired on f.-p. of it, 24th May, 1816.
CHARLEVILLE, Earl of	15 May, 1840	31 Dec. 1841	..	..	..	Was A.D.C. to the Lord-Lieutenant of Ireland; retired 24th Oct., 1845; died 19th Jan., 1859.
CHICHESTER, Lord S. A.	26 Aug. 1822	..	..	..	..	To Lieutenant 7th Fusileers, 4th Nov., 1824; died at Richmond, 27th May, 1825.
CHOLMONDELEY, the Hon. Thomas Grenville	3 April, 1835	31 Dec. 1839	21 July, 1843	..	..	Served in the suppression of the Canadian revolt, and was one of those who crossed the Portage of the Medawaska. Retired 9th Aug., 1850; appointed Lieutenant-Colonel of 1st Royal Cheshire Militia, 1st Oct., 1852.
CHRISTIAN, Edward	..	15 Aug. 1804	..	..	..	Was at Copenhagen, 1807; died Feb., 1809.
CLARK, John	6 April, 1809	..	..	..	..	Retired 1810.
CLARK, William	11 Feb. 1862	30 April, 1864	..	..	..	Served in the New Zealand war, and was thanked by H.R.H. the Commander-in-Chief for good service at the action at Gate Pa (severely wounded); also served in the expeditions in the province of Taranaki, destroying many Pas and fortified villages.

43rd Light Infantry.

Name				Notes
CLARKE, George	7 July, 1780	..	..	From Sergeant-Major; died Feb., 1783.
CLARKE, John Montague	10 July, 1775	..	..	Resigned 1st Dec., 1779; prisoner in America in 1777.
CLEMENTS, Henry	21 Dec. 1749	10 Dec. 1755	8 Feb. 1775	Captain-Lieutenant of 43rd; Captain, 22nd Sept., 1762; Captain 49th, 28th November, 1769; wounded at Montmorency as Lieutenant of Grenadiers, 31st July, 1759; out in 1763.
CLERK, George	..	..	9 Mar. 1768	From Captain 49th Regt.; resigned 30th July, 1776, and appointed Barrack-Master-General in America.
CLOSE, Arthur R.	13 April, 1855	9 Oct. 1855	29 May, 1863	Served throughout the Indian Campaigns of 1858-9 in Central India and Bundelcund (Medal); killed in New Zealand, 28th July, 1865.
COATES, Henry Wise	18 June, 1812	9 Dec. 1813	..	From East Suffolk Militia; placed on h.-p. of the Regt., 25th March, 1817; died 1827-8.
COCKBURN, Thomas Hugh	..	28 Nov. 1851	..	Ensign in 42nd, 6th March, 1840; Lieutenant, 28th April, 1842; Captain, 18th Sept., 1851; exchanged to 43rd, 28th Nov., 1851; Brevet-Major, 28th June, 1858, for distinguished service in the field; Major, unattached, 3rd April, 1863; sold out, 1st May, 1865. Joined Sir H. Rose's force at Jhansi, as A.D.C.; present at the action of Korneh; the battles in front of Calpee, and capture of Calpee, of the Morar cantonments, and Gwalior; three times especially mentioned in despatches (medal).
CODRINGTON, Sir Wm. John, K.C.B.	24 Oct. 1822	..	..	To Lieutenant Coldstream Guards, 24th April, 1823; Captain, 20th July, 1826; Lieutenant-Colonel, 8th July, 1836; Colonel, 9th Nov., 1846; Major-General, 20th June, 1854; Lieutenant-General, 6th June, 1854; Colonel of 54th, 11th Aug., 1856; Colonel 23rd, 27th Dec., 1860. Was Governor of Gibraltar. Commanded a Brigade of the Light Division, and afterwards a Division throughout the Eastern campaign of 1854-5, including the battles of Alma and Inkerman, siege and fall of Sebastopol (medal and clasps, K.C.B., Commander of the Legion of Honour, Grand Cross of the Military Order of Savoy, 1st Class of the Medjidie, and Turkish Medal). From October, 1855, and until evacuation of the Crimea, he was Commander-in-Chief of the Eastern Army. Was Governor and Commander-in-Chief of Gibraltar from 3rd May, 1859, to 20th Sept., 1865.
COFFIN, Francis	..	3 May, 1782	14 Mar. 1789	Captain-Lieutenant, 14th March, 1789; resigned May, 1792.
COLCLOUGH, Agmond	..	..	27 April,1756	Out in 1757.
COLE, Arthur Lowry, C.B.	22 Aug. 1834	20 Nov. 1838	..	Deputy Assistant Adjutant-General in Canada for three years, 1838-40; was one of those who crossed the Portage of the Madawaska; Captain, 7th Sept., 1841; exchanged to 69th Regt., 24th June, 1842; Brigade-Major, N.E. district, 1844-7; was A.D.C. to the Lord-Lieutenant of Ireland; Major, 14th June, 1850; Lieutenant-Colonel, 17th Regt., 9th March, 1855; commanded the Regt. at the siege of Sebastopol, and at the assault of the Redan, 18th June; mentioned in despatches (medal and clasps, C.B.); to h.-p, 16th Jan., 1861; Colonel, 9th Mar., 1858; retired March, 1861.
COLLINS, Arthur Tooker	..	2 May, 1751	..	Out in 1755.
COLSON, John	1 Sept. 1795	26 Jan. 1796	..	From North York York Militia; resigned 24th Dec., 1796.
COLVILLE, Fiennes Middleton	14 Aug. 1850	23 Nov. 1852	9 Oct. 1855 11 Feb. 1862	Served during the India mutiny campaign of 1857-9; was present at the capture of Kirwee; and commanded three companies of the Regt. during the operations in Bundelcund, under Brigadier Carpenter; mentioned in despatches (medal). Served in the New Zealand war, 1864-5; and was present at Maketa and Te Ranga, and at various operations in Taranaki; very severely wounded on the 22nd Oct., 1865, right thigh-bone fractured; frequently mentioned in despatches, and thanked in General Orders; Brevet-Lieutenant-Colonel and C.B.
COLVILLE, Graham	5 Aug. 1842	11 June, 1847	..	Retired 20th June, 1851.
CONDY, Nicholas	9 May, 1811	24 Feb. 1813	..	From Royal Cornwall Militia; placed on h.-p., 25th Dec., 1818; died 1858.
CONGREVE, Richard Jones	1 July, 1828	..	..	Retired 1st May, 1829.

NAME.	ENSIGN.	LIEUTENANT.	CAPTAIN.	MAJOR.	LIEUT.-COL.	REMARKS.
CONSIDINE, James, K.H.	20 July, 1809	27 Dec. 1810	29 Aug. 1822	11 July, 1826	..	Lieutenant-Colonel, unattached, 1st July, 1828; exchanged to 53rd, 2nd April, 1829; to h.-p. unattached, 6th May, 1836; Colonel, 23rd Nov., 1841; appointed to 10th Foot, 29th March, 1842. Major-General, local rank, 25th May, 1838. Served in the Peninsula from May, 1810, to Feb., 1814; including the combat of the Coa, battle of Busaco; combats of Redinha, Condexia, and Sabugal; sieges and assaults of Ciudad Rodrigo and Badajoz; battle of Salamanca, passage of the Bidassoa, battle of the Nivelle, besides various skirmishes. Served also at the attack on New Orleans, 8th Jan., 1815; severely wounded at the assault of Badajoz, and again at the storming of the locks on La Petite la Rhune; present with the expedition to Portugal, 1826-7; nominated to a special service at Constantinople in 1836. "General Considine was an excellent officer. His system of regimental discipline, and the selection of field movements on parade proved to all military men that he was from the Peninsular school. All his manœuvres were for the practical exhibition of what is most required on service, and to be done in the shortest and most expeditious manner. He was fond of his profession, to which he was an ornament."—*Englishman*. Died at Meerut, 5th Sept., 1845.
CONSIDINE, William	..	22 Feb. 1814	9 Sept. 1819	..	..	Present with the expedition to Portugal, 1826-7; Captain 34th, 25th June, 1829; exchanged to 52nd, 12th Feb., 1830; exchanged h.-p. unattached, 6th March, 1835; appointed to 69th, 22nd Nov., 1836; Military Secretary to the British Legion in Spain, with rank of Colonel, 1835; medal for the action before St. Sebastian, 5th May, 1836, and Order of St. Ferdinand, 2nd class; died at Chester, when Brigade-Major to Sir Charles Napier, 16th May, 1841.
CONYNGHAM, John	..	8 Aug. 1798	24 Mar. 1794	..	..	From Lieutenant 76th; retired May, 1796.
COOKE, Henry	..	..	..	..	..	From Lieutenant h.-p. of 67th, 30th Sept., 1793.
COOKE, John Henry, Sir	15 Mar. 1809	19 April, 1810	31 Dec. 1823	..	..	From Ensign First West York Militia. To h.-p. unattached, 11th May, 1826; Brevet-Major, 28th June, 1838; Captain in the 35th, 27th July, 1838; to h.-p., 15th Dec., 1840; Brevet-Lieutenant-Colonel, 11th Nov., 1851; appointed to the Corps of Gentlemen at Arms, 2nd Oct., 1844; Ensign of the Yeoman of the Guard, Her Majesty's Body Guard, 16th Sept., 1862; Lieutenant, 2nd Feb., 1866. Served with the 43rd Regt. at Walcheren, in 1809. In June, 1811, he joined the Light Division in the Peninsula, and was present at the siege and storming of Ciudad Rodrigo and of Badajoz (wounded at the assault), actions of Castrejon and San Christoval, battle of Salamanca, actions of San Muñoz and San Milan, battle of Vittoria (wounded), actions in the Pyrenees, siege of San Sebastian, the attack on the heights of Vera, battle of the Nivelle, battles of the Nive on the 9th, 10th, 11th, 12th, and 13th Dec., actions at Tarbes and Arcangues, battle of Toulouse, besides various affairs of less importance. On the 8th Jan., 1815, he was present at the attack on the American lines before New Orleans. He served afterwards with the army during the occupation in France; accompanied Lieutenant-Colonel Considine on special service in 1836; was Brigade-Major at Newport in 1839-40; was Honorary Secretary and Military Vice-President for the army recipients of the war medal and clasps. Author of 'Memoirs of the Late War,' &c. He has received the war medal with eight clasps. Knighted by Her Majesty, in consideration of his services, 11th Dec., 1867.
COOKE, Richard	2 Sept. 1762	..	..	..	..	Out in 1764.
COOKE, Robert	11 July, 1794	..	..	..	..	Retired on h.-p., June 6, 1795; died 1805.
COOTE, John Chidley	4 July, 1834	15 Sept. 1837	31 Dec. 1841	..	..	Served in the suppression of the Canadian revolt, and was one of those who crossed the Portage of the Madawaska; retired 11th Dec., 1849.
CUTTERELL, John	15 Mar. 1755	..	..	..	..	Out in 1757.
COTTON, John	24 Dec. 1762	..	..	..	..	Retired 19th July, 1769.
COULSON, Robert Blenkinsop	..	..	20 Feb. 1846	..	..	Ensign and Lieutenant Grenadier Guards, 14th June, 1831; Lieutenant and Captain, 29th July, 1836; retired 9th June, 1846.
COULSON, William	20 June 1783	..	..	..	..	To h.-p. 25th Dec., 1796; died 1822.
CRADOCK, William	3 Mar. 1814	24 Feb. 1820	..	..	..	Died in 1821.
CRAWFORD, John	27 Dec. 1810	25 June, 1812	..	..	..	From Volunteer in 45th. Present with the Regt. at the Nivelle, Nive, and Toulouse; also at New Orleans. Placed on h.-p., 29th April, 1819; appointed to 60th, 18th Oct., 1839; retired same day.

43rd Light Infantry.

Name			Remarks
CREIGHTON, John	16 Oct. 1806	5 Oct. 1808	Was at Copenhagen, Corunna, and the Coa; died of wounds (Sabugal), April, 1811.
CRICHTON, Patrick	6 Oct. 1778	30 May, 1780	To 57th Regt., 23rd Dec., 1783; appointed to an Ind. Co., 1792; out 1808.
CRIGGAN, Charles	28 April, 1793	11 July, 1794	To 8th West India Regt., 25th June, 1798; Major 6th Garrison Battalion, 26th Nov., 1806; out Jan., 1808.
CROFTON, Philip	31 May, 1791	31 May, 1793	From Sergeant-Major of 15th Regt.; Adjutant 14th Mar., 1789; died 6th June, 1793, of wounds, in West Indies.
CROSBIE, Charles	..	..	29 Jan. 1741 At first formation of the Regt.; retired 3rd Feb., 1757.
CROSBIE, Richard Thomas	27 Mar. 1744	19 Mar. 1749	Out in 1757.
CROZIER, Edward	15 June, 1797	..	Died 1798.
CROZIER, Stanley	8 June, 1855	8 Jan. 1856	30 April, 1864 Served in the Indian Mutiny campaign in 1857-8, including the actions of Sahao, Dooleypore, and Purraha (medal); also in the New Zealand war, in 1864-5.
CUFFE, Michael	4 Jan. 1750	..	Out in 1756.
CULLEN, Walter	3 Aug. 1810	..	Died 1811.
CUNNINGHAME, William	13 Feb. 1773	..	
CUPPAGE, Hamlet Wade	18 May, 1861	30 April, 1864	Served in the New Zealand war, 1864-5; was present at the defeat of the Maories, 21st June, 1864, at the Gate Pa, and Te Ranga; suspended 1816.
CURTIS, Samuel	..	24 Nov. 1814	From 39th Regt.
DALLING, *Sir John, Bart.*, K.B.	..	..	27 Feb. 1760 Ensign, 24th Feb., 1747; Captain 4th Regt., 27th Jan., 1753; Major 28th Regt., 2nd Feb., 1757; Lieutenant-Colonel in Army, 27th Feb., 1760. Commanded the Light Infantry of the army during the siege of Quebec and different actions; commanded the 43rd in the expedition to the West Indies, 1760; and at the siege of Havannah. To 36th, 4th Dec., 1767; to 58th Regt., 14th Aug., 1772; Colonel 25th May, 1772; appointed Colonel-Commandant of 60th, 16th Jan., 1776; Major-General, 29th Aug., 1777; Governor of Jamaica, 1st Sept., 1777; Lieutenant-General, 20th May, 1782; was Commander-in-Chief at Madras; created a Baronet for his services; died 16th Jan., 1798.
DALRYMPLE, James	14 Nov. 1770	8 Feb. 1775	To Captain 57th, 31st Dec., 1777, severely wounded at Bunker's Hill when in the 43rd; out Feb., 1784.
DALTON, Blundel	3 June, 1752	27 April, 1756	To Lieutenant 40th, 22nd Oct., 1762; Captain ditto, 1st April, 1767; present at siege of Quebec, and in the West Indies under Monckton; out March, 1771.
DALTON, John	25 Aug. 1794	..	Was a Volunteer. Promoted to Ind. Co., 3rd March, 1795.
DALYELL, Robert	..	26 Aug. 1804	9 Sept. 1819 From Lieutenant 29th Dragoons; Brevet-Major, 12th April, 1814; Lieutenant-Colonel, unattached, 31st Dec., 1822; Major-General, 9th Nov., 1846. Served with the 43rd at the battle of Kioge and surrender of Copenhagen in 1807, also the Corunna campaign of 1808-9; returned to the Peninsula with the Regt. in 1809, where he served until the end of the war in 1814 (except an absence in consequence of a wound), including the action of the Coa, near Almeida, battle of Busaco, retreat to the Lines at Lisbon, advance after Massena, actions of Pombal, Redinha (wounded), Foz d'Aronce, Castel Nova, and Sabugal (severely wounded); battles of Vittoria and Toulouse, for which he received the Brevet rank of Major. Served also in the campaigns of 1815; and was present at the capture of Paris; died at Edinburgh, 24th April, 1848.
DANIEL, John	..	..	Died in West Indies, 1794.

X

Names.	Ensign.	Lieutenant.	Captain.	Major.	Lieut.-Col.	Remarks.
D'Anvers, Henry	4 April, 1816	..	..	..	..	Placed on h.-p., 25th March, 1817; appointed 5th Foot, 18th May, 1826; Lieutenant, unattached, 11th July, 1826; exchanged to 62nd Regt., 24th Feb., 1832; retired 13th March, 1835.
D'Arcey, Edward	18 April, 1809	22 Aug. 1810	..	..	..	From East Suffolk Militia. Served with the Regt. at Vittoria, Pyrenees, assault and capture of St. Sebastian, Nivelle (wounded), and Nive. Had both legs amputated at New Orleans; Captain 60th, 3rd Aug., 1815; appointed Captain of Invalids at Kilmainham Hospital; died 25th Dec., 1848.
Davie, John	..	..	25 Dec. 1813	..	..	From East Suffolk Militia to h.-p., 25th Aug, 1814; died 1822.
Dawes, Wm. Henry	30 Dec. 1826	..	..	..	..	To Lieutenant 22nd Regt, 25th Nov, 1828; out 1834.
Dawson, Henry	28 Jan. 1771	..	..	..	..	Died in America, Sept., 1775.
Delamaine, Thomas L. Henry	1 July, 1802	..	..	..	..	To the Service in India, 18th Feb., 1804.
Delisle, George	1 Sept. 1795	1 Sept. 1795	..	appointed to 1st Foot, 1802	..	From Volunteers; Ensign and Lieutenant in same Gazette; placed on h.-p., 1803; retired 20th June, 1834.
Denham, Augustus	2 Jan. 1823	1 Sept. 1825	..	23rd Fusiliers, 22nd Feb., 1827	..	To Captain, unattached, 31st Oct, 1826; appointed to exchanged to 34th Regt.; retired 30th July, 1836.
Dennis, George	18 Aug. 1778	24 Oct. 1781	24 Sept. 1787	12 Mar. 1794	1 May, 1794	Captain-Lieutenant, 24th Sept., 1787; retired July, 1799.
Dennis, George	1 Sept. 1795	11 Jan. 1796	..	..	..	To 35th Regt.; out 1809; went into holy orders.
Dennis, Henry Parry	21 Aug. 1840	27 Dec. 1842	..	..	..	Retired 29th May, 1849; died 11th June, 1749.
Dennistoun, James Grey	31 May, 1793	11 July, 1794	..	..	..	Died in the West Indies, 11th July, 1794.
Denton, Wellington James	24 May, 1861	..	..	..	..	Retired 22nd May, 1863.
Desbrisay, Jasper	..	5 Mar. 1781	..	..	..	From 70th Regt.; out Oct., 1781.
Deshon, Peter	14 Mar. 1789	1 Sept. 1795	25 June, 1803	16 Aug. 1810	..	Was a Volunteer; exchanged to 85th, 25th Jan., 1813. Served in the expedition to the West Indies under Sir Charles Gray; severely wounded at the Coa. Gold medal for the Nive, silver medal for Busaco, capture and assault of St. Sebastian, Nivelle; retired 22nd May, 1817.
De Younge, Adrian	30 May, 1794	20 July, 1894	1 July, 1802	5th Oct, 1802; appointed to Nova Scotia Fencibles,16th July, 1803.	..	Captain-Lieutenant, 10th July, 1802; placed on h.-p.,
Dick, Charles Crammond	..	2 Feb. 1855	..	..	..	From 25th Regt.; retired 14th Dec., 1856.
Dick, James Abercromby	2 June, 1841	24 Oct. 1845	28 Feb. 1851	..	..	To h.-p. Rifle Brigade, 23rd Nov., 1852. To 52nd, 20th Oct., 1854; died Sept., 1859.
Dickins, Richard	17 Oct. 1728	..	..	..	..	Served in the American war; resigned 4th April, 1782.
Digby, Thomas	5 April, 1809	..	..	..	..	Retired 1810.
Dilkes, Thomas	..	..	14 June, 1765	..	..	Exchanged to 49th, 30th Sept, 1768; Major 49th, 20th Feb, 1773; out July, 1777.

Name			Services
DISBROWE, J. G. Cavendish	..	20 Jan. 1854	Ensign and Lieutenant Grenadier Guards, 2nd Feb., 1844; Captain in 76th, 31st March, 1848; exchanged to 62nd, 1851; Brevet-Major, 20th June, 1859; died Sept., 1860.
DOBSON, George	25 June, 1812	22 Feb. 1814	Placed on h.-p., 19th April, 1815.
DOREHILL, William John	..	29 July, 1853	Ensign 3rd Regt., 16th Jan., 1835; Lieutenant, 10th March, 1838; Captain, 11th Jan., 1850; Brevet-Major, 2nd Feb., 1862; was present with the Buffs in the battle of Punniar (medal), and was severely wounded; retired on h.-p. 23rd July, 1861; appointed Staff-officer of Pensioners at Clonmel, 1st May, 1861.
DORRINGTON, Thomas	22 Nov. 1775	..	To Lieutenant 57th Regt, 1st Dec., 1779; Captain 14th Regt., 13th April, 1781; out Jan., 1784.
DOWDALL, John	19 May, 1759	..	Out 1766.
DOWLING, Oliver	16 Oct. 1775	..	Promoted to 22nd Regt., 26th Oct, 1777; out 31st July, 1797.
DREW, John Godfrey	..	12 April, 1799	From Captain 45th; Brevet-Lieutenant-Colonel, 30th March, 1797; exchanged to 3rd West India Regt., 23rd Jan., 1800; died May, 1801.
DRUMMOND, James	11 Aug. 1778	17 Jan. 1787 2 Dec. 1793 / 31 Dec. 1793	From Ensign 40th Regt., 10th Oct., 1776; Colonel, 29th Jan., 1797; Major-General, 25th Sept., 1803; Colonel of 7th Garrison Battalion, 14th June, 1807; Lieutenant-General, 25th July, 1810; General, 19th July, 1821. Served in America the campaign of 1777, in the Jerseys, and the different actions; the battle of Brandywine and surprising of Wayne's Brigade; battles of Germantown and Monmouth, and the retreat from Philadelphia; with the 43rd at the taking of Washington's dragoons, and the siege of Charleston; and was constantly with the army as Lieutenant of Grenadiers of the 43rd, until the Peace of 1783. In 1793 embarked for the West Indies, and commanded the 43rd at the siege of Martinique, St. Lucia, and Guadaloupe; and was made prisoner on the French retaking the latter place in 1794. In 1795 he made his escape, and returned to England. Returned to the West Indies in command of the Regiment, and on May 29th was appointed Brigadier-General, and sent to command at the Island of St. Lucia, where he remained till 1802. In May, 1803, Brigadier-General in Guernsey; removed to the Portsmouth district 25th Sept., 1803; and on the 16th Mar., 1804, to the Staff at Gibraltar. Died 22nd June, 1831.
DRURY, C. Garling	29 Nov. 1865	..	Transferred to 19th Regt., 29th Dec.
DRURY, Robt. Wm. Henry	25 Dec. 1813	5 Mar. 1818	Placed on h.-p., 25th Dec., 1818; appointed to 28th, 26th Oct., 1820; retired as Captain, 24th July, 1828.
DUFFY, John, C.B., K.C.	..	26 Aug. 1804	17 June, 1813	Lieutenant-Colonel, 22nd Nov., 1813; to 8th Regt., 9th Sept., 1819; h.-p., 20th March, 1828; Colonel, 22nd July, 1830; Major-General, 23rd Nov., 1841; Colonel of 28th, 18th May, 1849; Lieutenant-General, 11th Nov., 1851. Served the campaign of 1796 in the West Indies, under Sir Ralph Abercrombie; on an expedition to the coast of Holland in the winter of 1796; in the East Indies in 1799, and with the force under Sir David Baird, from thence to Egypt in 1801; with the 43rd at the siege and capture of Copenhagen, 1807; the campaign of 1808-9 in Spain, under Sir John Moore; again in the Peninsula from 1810 to the end of 1813, including the battles of Fuentes d'Onoro, action at Sabugal, sieges of Ciudad Rodrigo and Badajoz, battles of Vittoria (wounded), Nivelle and Nive; commanded the assaulting party at the capture of Fort Raynaud, an outwork of Ciudad Rodrigo; gold medal for the assault and capture of Badajoz, on which occasion the command of the Regt. devolved on him, after Colonel McLeod was killed. War medal and seven clasps. Died Oct., 1854.
DU MOULIN, Andrew	10 Aug. 1796	16 Mar. 1797	To h.-p. 9th Regt, 31st July, 1802; was on h.-p. for 56 years; out 1858.
DUNBAR, John	2 Sept. 1772	7 Aug. 1775	Captain-Lieutenant, 22nd Sept., 1762; resigned Oct., 1764.
DUNBAR, Thomas	2 Sept., 1795; Brevet-Lieutenant-Colonel, 1st Jan., 1798; to 3rd West India Regt., 8th Mar., 1801; Colonel, 25th April, 1808; Major-General, 4th June, 1811. Served with the 43rd in the American war; died Dec., 1815.		To Captain 70th, 1st Feb., 1781; Brevet-Major, 1st Mar., 1794; Major 70th, 2nd
DUNBAR, William	19 April, 1742	20 June, 1753	8 April, 1761	Served in the campaign in Canada under Wolfe and Murray; died April, 1762.

Names.	Ensign.	Lieutenant.	Captain.	Major.	Lieut.-Col.	Remarks.
Dundas, George William	..	1 May, 1805	..	..	..	From Ensign 44th. Was with the expedition to Copenhagen; died May, 1808.
Du Verner, William	..	..	20 Sept. 1853	..	..	From Ensign 50th, 22nd Mar., 1844; Lieutenant, 29th Jan., 1846; Captain in 67th, 13th April, 1852; exchanged to 84th, 26th June, 1854; retired 19th Nov., 1858. Served with the 50th in the campaign of the Sutlej (medal); and was present at Buddiwal and Aliwal, slightly wounded, and afterwards severely in the left foot by the bursting of a shell.
Dwen, Edward	23 Jan. 1846	..	..	..	..	From Sergeant-Major, appointed Adjutant of Montgomeryshire Militia, 29th June, 1846; retired from Army, 10th July, 1846.
Eagle, Solomon	3 Sept. 1775	..	..	..	..	Removed to 35th, as he had no pay in the 43rd; not in List, 1778.
East, William	15 Sept. 1779	..	..	..	..	Resigned 23rd Jan., 1782.
Edge, Edward	15 Oct. 1806	4 Oct. 1808	..	..	..	Expedition to Copenhagen and Corunna. Died July, 1810.
Edwards, Benj. Hutchins	14 May, 1812	21 Oct. 1813	..	..	..	Placed on h.-p., 25th Dec., 1818; appointed to 98th, 12th Mar., 1829; exchanged to h.-p. unattached, 1st July, 1836; appointed Adjutant of Glasgow Recruiting District, 7th May, 1847; Liverpool District, 10th Mar., 1848. Captain, 20th Dec., 1864; Major, 20th Feb., 1866. Served in the Peninsula from 1811 to the end of the war in 1814, including the siege and storming of Badajoz (wounded), with the 9th Portuguese Regt. of the Line, and in the 43rd, at the battle of Salamanca, Vera, Nivelle (wounded), Nive, Tabres and Toulouse. Received the war medal with 6 clasps.
Egerton, Wilbraham	4 Nov. 1824	11 July, 1826	1 July, 1828	25 Aug. 1843	..	Was with the expedition to Portugal in 1826-7, and in the suppression of the Canadian revolt, and was one of those who crossed the Portage of the Maiawaska. Died 10th April, 1848, from injuries received by the falling of a stand on a race-course in Ireland.
Elers, Richard Hungerford	..	25 Aug. 1794	10 July, 1802	8 Sept. 1808	..	He was the last Captain-Lieutenant, dated 17th April, 1801. Served with distinction in the West Indies. Expedition to Copenhagen and Corunna. Commanded the 43rd at the battle of Fuentes d'Onoro. Died at Celerico, 1811.
Elliot, John B. Bowes	13 Jan. 1854	8 Dec. 1854	24 July, 1857	..	..	Retired 24th Aug., 1858.
Elliot, Robert	..	27 Jan. 174$\frac{9}{0}$	12 May, 1746	2 Feb. 1757	..	To Lieutenant-Colonel 55th Regt., 23rd Mar., 1761; retired 5th Dec., 1764. Served with the 43rd in Nova Scotia and siege of Quebec. Commanded the Regt. at the battle on the Heights of Abraham.
Elliot, Thomas	24 Jan. 174$\frac{9}{0}$	..	..	..	..	On formation; out in 1749.
Elwes, Thomas	15 June, 1855	30 Jan. 1857	..	..	..	Died of sunstroke in India, 1858.
Enright, Lyons	26 June, 1806	1 Sept. 1808	..	..	..	Expedition to Copenhagen. Retired 10th Sept., 1812.
Erskine, Charles	1 June, 1785	..	..	..	..	To Lieutenant 77th Regt., 25th Dec., 1787; Captain 41st, May 31st, 1791; Major 100th, 10th Feb., 1794; Lieutenant-Colonel 92nd, 1st May, 1795; out, April, 1801.
Essex, *Earl* of	8 Nov. 1821	..	..	..	..	Exchanged to 1st Life Guards, 27th Jan., 1824; to 26th Regt.; placed h.-p., 3rd Mar., 1825.
Estcourt, Sir James B. Bucknall, K.C.B.	7 June, 1821	9 Dec. 1824	5 Nov., 1825	21 Oct. 1836	..	Ensign 44th Regt., 13th July, 1820. Was with the expedition to Portugal, 1826-7. Served in the expedition to the River Euphrates, from Jan., 1835, to June, 1837; as a mark of approbation of his conduct and exertions, he was promoted to Brevet-Lieutenant-Colonel, 29th Mar., 1839; Lieutenant-Colonel, unattached, 25th Aug., 1843; Colonel, 11th Nov., 1851. Served as Adjutant-General throughout the Eastern campaign, 1854, including the battles of the Alma, Balaclava, Inkerman, and siege of Sebastopol; died in the Crimea, 24th June, 1855.

43rd Light Infantry.

FALKLAND, Viscount	..	5 April, 1786	..	To h.-p., 25th Dec. 1787; died 1796.
FARIE, John	..	..	29 Jan. 1741	From Captain in Putney's Regt. Came home with Regt. from Minorca; out June, 1753.
FARMER, Robert	..	1 Sept. 1795	..	Cashiered 1797.
FARNALL, Nathaniel	..	3 Mar. 1764	..	Out 17th May, 1766.
FENTON, James	..	9 Dec. 1778	..	Captain-Lieutenant, 1st Nov., 1793; died 2nd July, 1794, of fever, in the West Indies.
FERGUSON, David	..	..	26 Oct. 1777	From Captain 23rd Regt.; Lieutenant-Colonel in Army, 31st Dec., 1784; Lieutenant-Colonel 68th Regt., 15th June, 1785; out in 1788. Served in all the early wars in Germany, the three last years of which commanding the Grenadier Company of the 23rd; was at the battles of Minden, campaign on the Rhine, Corbach, Warburg, Fellinghausen, Wilhelmstat, and Brucker's Muhl. Served all the War of Independence in America; was at Lexington, Long Island, and Fort Knephausen; commanded the 23rd on the expedition to Pekskill, Danburg, and Brandywine; when Major of the 43rd, at Rhode Island, was appointed to command the flank companies of the 38th, 54th, and Hessian Chasseurs; had the command of the 43rd, and was with Lord Cornwallis on his march through Virginia, &c.
FERGUSON, George	..	18 Dec. 1806	..	Retired 27th March, 1811.
FERGUSON, Robert	..	24 Feb. 1820	..	1823; Captain, unattached, 7th July, 1825; exchanged to 52nd, 13th Feb. 1825; Major, unattached, 31st August, 1830; Lieutenant-Colonel 79th, 13th March, 1835; retired 8th June, 1841.
FERGUSSON, Sir James, G.C.B.	..	7 Aug. 1804	11 Dec. 1806	Entered the army in 1801, as Ensign in the 18th Regt. Served in the campaigns of 1808-9, Vimiera, Corunna, from which he was removed to the 43rd, then training with the 52nd and old 95th under Sir John Moore at Shorncliffe, during which time he was never absent from his Regt., except and subsequently Walcheren; the Peninsular campaigns, from March, 1810, to the end of the war in 1814, having in former assaults received two deep wounds, from wounds; was five times wounded, and "who can sufficiently honour the resolution of Fergusson of the 43rd, who, having in former assaults received two deep wounds,"—*Napier*, was here (Badajoz), 'third siege,' with with his hurts still open, leading the stormers of his regiment; the third time a volunteer, and the third time wounded?"—*Napier*, vol. iv. p. 432, book xvi. Though his promotion was rapid compared with many others, strange to say he had to purchase all his steps. He served with the 43rd Light Infantry during nearly the whole war, till he was appointed Major 79th Regt., Dec., 1812, but was removed to the 85th Regt., up to the investment of Bayonne; was appointed Lieutenant-Colonel, 2nd Battalion, 3rd Regt. (Buffs), May, 1814, and after the close of the war, when the Battalion was reduced, was placed on h.-p., when he went to study at the Military College, Farnham, for some time. In 1819 he was appointed to the command of the 88th, of which gallant Regt. he always spoke in terms of high regard. In 1825, he was removed to the command of 52nd Light Infantry, with which he was so gloriously connected. In 1830 he was appointed Colonel and King's Aide-de-camp. He continued in command of the 52nd Regt. till 1839, when he retired on h.-p.; General Lord Hill, then commanding the army, remarking that, "after commanding Regts. for more than a quarter of a century, he was at liberty to do what he thought proper." He became Major-General in 1841, and Lieutenant-General in 1851, and was appointed to the command of the troops at Malta in 1852, where he was stationed during the early part of the Crimean war, his inability from the diseased state of his lungs, caused by a former wound, alone preventing him from again volunteering his services in the field. He received the thanks of the Duke of Newcastle for the manner in which he provided for the troops in Malta, in which he was so zealously and ably assisted by the Governor, Sir William Reid, and Admiral Sir Houston Stuart. Appointed Colonel of the Governor and Commander-in-Chief at Gibraltar, where he remained until 1859, when his increasing infirmity obliged him to apply to be relieved. Appointed Colonel of the 43rd, 26th March, 1850; he became General on the 21st of Feb., 1860. He received the gold medal for Badajoz as senior surviving Officer of the Light Division storming party; he also received the silver war medal with eight clasps; died at Bath, 4th Sept., 1865.
FERRIAR, Thos. Ilderton	..	20 April, 1815	..	From h.-p. of the 28th Regt.; placed on h.-p. of 43rd, 25th March, 1817.
FIDLOR, David	..	8 May, 1811	..	From Shropshire Militia. Died, 1813, in Spain.
FINLAY, John	..	2 Sept. 1813	25 Sept. 1815	Present at New Orleans; to h.-p., Feb., 1817; reappointed to the Regt., 4th Sept., 1817, h.-p. of Regt., 29th Nov., 1821; appointed 61st Regt., 6th Feb, 1835; retired 13th Feb, 1835.

Names.	Ensign.	Lieutenant.	Captain.	Major.	Lieut.-Col.	Remarks.
FITZGERALD, Thomas	12 Feb. 1807	23 Jan. 1749/1	21 Sept. 1745	..	..	To 5th West India Regt., 20th July, 1809.
FITZPATRICK, James	..	..	..	..	..	Out Sept., 1854.
FITZROY, Lord Charles	..	6 June, 1787	..	..	..	Removed to 3rd Guards, and served in Flanders, 1793-4, at the siege of Valenciennes; Lieutenant-General, 1st May, 1805; General, 1814.
FITZROY, Geo. Henry	27 Aug. 1829	..	..	..	..	To Lieutenant 3rd Guards, 29th June, 1830; Captain, 7th August, 1835; retired 3rd June, 1836.
FLETCHER, Sir Richard John, Bart.	20 Mar. 1823	5 Nov. 1825	..	..	..	Captain, unattached, 30th Dec, 1826; exchanged to 9th Foot, 27th Dec, 1827; retired 1828.
FOLLIET, George	22 Aug. 1810	14 May, 1812	..	..	..	Died of a wound received near St. Sebastian, 31st August, 1813.
FORBES, Thomas	..	15 Nov. 1765	..	..	..	Lieutenant in Army, 25th March, 1763; to h.-p., 11th Dragoons, 19th Dec, 1768; out 1773.
FORD, Johnson	7 Sept. 1826	24 June, 1829	21 Oct. 1836	..	..	Brevet-Major, 9th Nov., 1846; retired 9th August, 1850; died 13th March, 1851.
FORD, Lionel N.	17 Oct. 1809	..	..	..	..	Appointed to 5th Foot, 21st June, 1810; appointed 93rd Regt., 2nd April, 1829; retired 13th August, 1829.
FORLONG, James, K.H.	..	..	8 April, 1825	1 July, 1828	7 May, 1841	From Captain 33rd Regt.; retired 17th Oct., 1851. Served the campaigns of 1813-14, in Germany and Holland, including the actions at Merxem, bombardment of Antwerp, and storming of Bergen-op-Zoom. Served also the campaign of 1815, and was severely wounded at Quatre-Bras,—right collar-bone fractured and ball lodged in the right breast. Died at Toronto.
FORSTER, John	..	25 Aug. 1843	..	..	..	To Lieutenant 7th Fusileers, Sept., 1847; exchanged to 6th Dragoon Guards. Served with that Regt. in the Crimea and India; Brevet-Major for services in the field, promoted to an unattached Majority in May, 1859; was A.D.C. to Lieutenant-Colonel Maunsel, commanding S.E. district, till April 1st, 1861; retired the same year.
FORTESCUE, Chichester	11 Nov. 1813	..	..	..	..	Retired, 1814.
FOWLER, Hans	..	24 Jan. 1749/1	..	..	..	Not in List for 1749.
FOWLER, Richard	22 Feb. 1813	..	..	..	..	Appointed to 95th, 22nd Oct, 1813; Lieutenant in same, (Rifle Brigade) 8th May, 1817; placed on h.-p., 25th Dec., 1818; present with the Rifles at Waterloo (medal); took the additional name of Butler in 1824 (silver medal for Toulouse); retired, 1832; died, 1862.
FRASER, William	..	6 July, 1820	9 Dec. 1824	18 May, 1841	..	Ensign 92nd, 8th April, 1813; Lieutenant in same, 19th Jan., 1814; placed on h.-p. of the Regt., 1814; appointed to 93rd, 4th June, 1815; placed on h.-p. of it, 25th March, 1817; appointed to Rifle Brigade, 1818; placed on h.-p., 25th December, 1818; Brevet-Major, 28th June, 1838; Brevet-Lieutenant-Colonel, 11th Nov., 1851; Colonel, 27th Aug., 1857; retired 20th May, 1858. Served in the Peninsula and South of France with the 92nd, from Oct., 1813, to the end of that war in 1814; has received the war medal with one clasp for the Nive, in which battle he was severely wounded. Served in the suppression of the Canadian rebellion, and was one of those to cross the Portage of the Madawaska.
FREDERICK, Roger	4 Oct. 1808	18 Oct. 1809	..	..	..	Present at Vimiero; lost a leg at the Coa.
FREER, Daniel Gardner	19 Feb. 1824	8 April, 1826	18 May, 1741	..	..	Present with the expedition to Portugal, 1826-7. To 60th, 20th Nov., 1823; exchanged to h.-p. unattached, 5th August, 1842; exchanged to 73rd, 24th May, 1844; exchanged to 75th, 30th May, 1845; Major, 3rd West India legt., 12th Nov., 1847; exchanged to 17th Regt., May, 1848; exchanged to h.-p., unattached, 7th June, 1850.

43rd Light Infantry.

Freer, Edward	4 April, 1809	12 July, 1810	Present at the Coa, Sabugal, Busaco, Fuentes d'Onoro, Ciudad Rodrigo, Badajoz, Salamanca, Vera, Vittoria. Killed at the Nivelle, 10th Nov., 1813.
Freer, William Gardner, K.H.	12 Dec. 1805	5 Feb. 1807	1 Dec. 1813 .. Placed on h.-p. of the Regt., 28th Jan., 1817; replaced again on h.-p. of the Regt., 11th Dec, 1817; Major, unattached, 10th Sept., 1825; appointed to 10th Foot, 8th June, 1826; Lieutenant-Colonel, 24th May, 1833; present with the 43rd at Vimiero (wounded), Corunna, the Coa (wounded); Busaco, Sabugal (slightly wounded); Fuentes d'Onoro, Ciudad Rodrigo, Badajoz (right arm shattered and amputated); Vittoria, Vera, Bidassoa, Nivelle, and Toulouse. Medal with clasps for all the above-named actions. Served 30 years out of a life of 45. "An officer whose military reputation stood deservedly high, and whose zeal for his profession was unbounded. High-minded, noble, and devoted to his military duties, he was the friend of both officer and soldier, and his memory will long be held dear by all who knew him." Died 2nd Aug., 1836. As a mark of esteem for his character, his brother officers of the 10th erected a monument to his memory, on the spot where his remains are interred at Corfu, recording his distinguished military services and their unfeigned regret for the loss of a sincere friend. They have also placed a tablet in his parish church at Oakham recording the above.
French, Alfred Crofton	21 Nov. 1865	..	.. From Ensign 24th, 11th Oct., 1864.
Frome, John Parker	4 June, 1742	..	.. Not in List for 1749.
Gamble, Thomas	..	..	.. 15th, never joined 43rd.
Gardiner, Charles	22 July, 1781	..	.. To Lieutenant 21st Regt., 3rd Feb., 1783.
Gardiner, Charles John	13 May, 1826	14 May, 1829	.. Retired 24th Aug., 1829.
Gardner, Daniel	12 Dec. 1800	4 Mar. 1802	27 Feb. 1804 From Ensign; Lieut. 35th. Killed at Talavera, 28th July, 1809, when Major of Brigade to General Stuart.
Garland, George	6 Feb. 1857	1 April, 1861	29 July, 1865 From Serjeant-Major. Served with the 43rd in the Kaffir war of 1851-3 (medal), and was present in various engagements and operations, as also with the expedition to the Orange River, and battle of Beren. Served as Adjutant of the Regt. in the Indian campaign in 1858, including the surrender of Kirwee, and various operations in Bundelcund (medal); also in the New Zealand war in 1864-5; and was mentioned in despatches of the action at the Gate Pa, for "his gallant endeavours to rally the men under a heavy fire," and was recommended for an unattached Company.
Garland, John Bingley	22 May, 1863	2 May, 1864	.. Served in the New Zealand war, 1864-5, and was thanked by H.R.H. the Commander-in-Chief, on account of good service at the action of the Gate Pa; was also present in the action at Te Ranga.
Gifford, George St. John	..	..	8 Dec. 1804 From Captain 1st Foot; out March, 1808.
Gifford, William	..	..	19 Sept, 1804 Ensign 50th, 9th April, 1789; Lieutenant, 17th Feb., 1794; Captain 26th, 30th Dec, 1795; Major, 26th Dec, 1798; Brevet-Lieutenant-Colonel, 19th July, 1802; Colonel, 4th June, 1811; Major-General, 4th June, 1814. Served with the 50th at Gibraltar for four years, and was at the sieges of St. Fiorenza, Bastia, and Calvi, in Corsica. He subsequently served two years and a half as A.D.C. to the late Lieutenant-General Sir Charles Stuart, and was with that officer in Portugal, and in the expedition against Minorca. He served the campaign in Egypt, and was at the siege of Alexandria; afterwards on the staff of Malta for four years; and in the expedition to Copenhagen. He was for some time Deputy-Adjutant-General at Malta; retired Jan., 1825; died Nov., 1829.
Girardot, John Francis	4 Sept. 1847	..	9 Feb. 1855 From 1st Foot; retired 26th Sept., 1856; Adjutant Royal Sherwood Foresters. Captain Girardot commanded a detachment on board the 'Birkenhead,' when wrecked off Danger Point, Cape of Good Hope, on the night of the 26th Feb., 1852. He served with the 43rd in the Kaffir war of 1852-3 (medal).
Glass, Francis	..	23 Mar. 1802	18 Sept. 1806 From Lieutenant in 95th, 9th Jan., 1802; appointed to 96th Regt., 12th Sept., 1816; to h.-p. 8th Jan., 1818.
Glover, Frederick Guy Eaton	9 Sept. 1854	29 Aug. 1853	30 April, 1864 Died of wounds, 2nd May, 1864, at Tauranga.

NAMES.	ENSIGN.	LIEUTENANT.	CAPTAIN.	MAJOR.	LIEUT.-COL.	REMARKS.
GLOVER, Robert Coke	..	29 July, 1853	30 Jan. 1857	..	..	From Lieutenant 51st. Served with the 51st Regt. throughout the Burmese War of 1852 (medal); on board the East India Company's steam frigate 'Ferooz' during the naval action and destruction of the enemy's stockades on the Rangoon River; during the succeeding three days' operations in the vicinity, and the storm and capture of Rangoon; killed at Tauranga, 30th April, 1864.
GORDON, Thomas	..	16 Dec. 1809	..	..	..	Cornet 2nd Dragoons, 26th Jan., 1809.
GORE, Owen Arthur Ormsby	20 Nov. 1838	16 Feb. 1841	9 June, 1846	..	..	Killed at Cape of Good Hope.
GORE, the Hon. Sir Charles, G.C.B., K.H.	..	4 Jan. 1810	13 Mar. 1815	..	..	From Lieutenant 6th Foot; appointed to 85th, 15th June, 1815; Major (for services in the field), 21st Jan., 1819; Lieutenant-Colonel, 19th Sept., 1822; Colonel, 10th Jan., 1837; Major-General, 9th Nov., 1846; Lieutenant-General, 20th June, 1854; General, 12th Feb, 1863; Colonel, 6th Regt., 8th Mar., 1864; was Quartermaster-General in Canada, 20th April, 1826. Joined the 43rd in the Peninsula in July, 1811, and was present and one of the storming party of Fort San Francisco at the investment of Ciudad Rodrigo; also at the siege and storming of that (9th, 10th, and 11th Dec.), battle of Salamanca, as A.D.C. to Sir Andrew Barnard; and in a similar capacity to Sir James Kempt in the battles of Vittoria, the Nivelle, the Nive fortress and of Badajoz, Orthes, and Toulouse. He was also in the action of San Milan, capture of Madrid, storming of the heights of Vera, bridge of Yanzi, and all the skirmishes of the Light Division from 1812 to the close of the war in 1814; after which he accompanied Sir James Kempt with the troops sent to Canada under his command; returned to Europe in time for the campaign of 1815, and was first and principal A.D.C. to Sir James Kempt, and present at the battles of Quatre Bras (horse shot), and Waterloo (three horses shot), and capture of Paris. He has received the war medal with nine clasps.
GORTON, Harry	1 May, 1855	14 Dec. 1856	..	..	..	Retired 17th May, 1861.
GOSSELIN, George	..	8 April, 1825	..	..	..	From 37th Regt.; Captain, unattached, 8th April, 1826; exchanged to 29th, 10th April, 1826; retired Dec., 1831.
GOULTON, Christopher	29 Jan. 1767	2 April, 1772	..	..	..	Resigned 14th April, 1774.
GRACE, Richard	..	30 June, 1854	..	..	..	From Ensign 88th Regt., 14th April, 1848; died at Madras, 21st Aug., 1855.
GRAHAM, Grenville	1 Dec. 1745	..	..	..	..	Came from Minorca with the Regt, 1794; out in 1752.
GRAHAM, Joseph	31 Oct. 1789	31 July, 1792	..	..	..	To Captain in Lieutenant-General J. F. Campbell's Regt.
GRAHAM, Lumley	13 Aug. 1847	28 Feb. 1851	7 June, 1854	..	..	To Captain in 41st, 7th July, 1854; Brevet-Major, 12th Dec., 1854; placed on h.-p., unattached, 25th March, 1856; appointed Major 19th, 9th March, 1858; Lieutenant-Colonel, 6th June, 1856; Colonel, 4th Dec., 1864; exchanged to 18th Regt, 29th Sept., 1865. Served with the 43rd in the Kaffir war of 1851-2-3 (medal). Served the Eastern campaign, 1854-5, part of the time as A.D.C. to General Eyre, including the battles of Alma and Inkerman and siege of Sebastopol. Severely wounded, right arm amputated, 29th Aug., 1855 (medal and clasps, Knight of the Legion of Honour, 5th class of the Medjidie and Turkish medal).
GRAY, John	..	19 Dec. 1768	..	..	..	Lieutenant, 2nd March, 1868.
GREENE, Dawson Cornelius	3 July, 1840	14 Jan. 1842	11 Dec. 1849	7 Nov. 1856	..	Brevet-Major, 2nd Nov., 1855; exchanged to h.-p., unattached, 24th July, 1857; Major of Depôt Battalion at Canterbury, 24th Aug., 1858; Lieutenant-Colonel, 9th Sept., 1864; to h.-p., 22nd May, 1863. Served with the 43rd in Kaffir war, 1851-2-3 (medal).
GREENE, Francis John	15 July, 1813	..	..	..	..	Cornet 3rd Dragoon Guards, 27th Jan., 1814; Captain, 10th Sept., 1825; retired Nov., 1828.

43rd Light Infantry.

Name			Notes
REY, Hon. Charles	..	18 Aug. 1825	From Captain 17th, 16th June, 1825. Served in the expedition to Portugal in 1826-7; Major, unattached, 19th Feb, 1828; appointed to 60th, 23rd April, 1829; Lieutenant-Colonel, unattached, 12th July, 1831; exchanged to 71st, 30th Aug., 1833; commanded the 71st during the Canadian revolt in 1837-8; on h.-p., unattached, 8th April, 1842; Colonel, 9th Nov., 1846; Major-General, 20th June, 1854; appointed Colonel 3rd Foot, 4th May, 1860; Lieutenant-General, 10th March, 1861; Colonel 71st, 6th July, 1863. Is Equerry to the Queen.
GREY, Hon. Harry Cavendish	5 April, 1831	..	Ensign 90th, 9th Nov., 1830; Lieutenant, unattached, 5th April, 1833; exchanged to 51st, 12th April, 1833; Captain, unattached, 25th Dec, 1835; exchanged to 52nd, 5th Feb, 1836; retired 12th April, 1844; was A.D.C. to the Lord-Lieutenant of Ireland, and to Viscount Falkland, Governor of Nova Scotia.
GRIEVE, G.	..	..	From Ensign 16th Regt.
GRINDLAY, William	16 Mar. 1815	..	To 17th Regt., 20th March, 1823; placed on h.-p. same day; retired Oct., 1823.
GROVES, Thomas	..	..	Lieutenant in 48th, 13th April, 1859.
GRUBBE, Thomas Hunt	25 Mar. 1811	15 Oct. 1812	Served in the Peninsula; present at New Orleans; placed on h.-p., 12th July, 1821; Captain, 8th April, 1826; to 9th Regt, 12th March, 1829; to h.-p., 18th Nov., 1831; died 1843.
GUBBINS, William	22 Feb. 1765	28 Jan. 1771	Resigned 16th Sept., 1776.
GUILLIMAN, George Grieve	..	10 Feb. 1796	From 16th Regt.; out in April, 1801.
GUNNING, John	..	30 Sept. 1768	From 49th; Deputy Adjutant-General in North Britain; Lieutenant-Colonel, 23rd Jan., 1775; Lieutenant-Colonel 82nd Foot, Dec., 1777; Colonel, 15th June, 1781; Major-General, 28th Sept., 1787; Colonel of 65th, 28th Jan., 1788; died Oct., 1797.
HALFORD, Henry	5 Mar. 1818	..	To Lieutenant 33rd Regt., 20th Sept., 1821; h.-p., 8th Aug., 1822; retired June, 1833.
HALLYBURTON, James	..	..	On first formation, from Captain in Putney's Regt.; out 4th Oct., 1743.
HAMMICK, St. Vincent Alex.	12 Mar. 1861	29 May, 1863	Served in the New Zealand war, 1864-5; mentioned in despatch as having "performed his duty as Acting-Adjutant with great coolness and courage under a heavy fire," in the action at Te Ranga; Adjutant, 29th July, 1865.
HAMILTON, Robt. Thos. Francis	..	11 May, 1861	From Captain 97th Regt. Served with the 97th Regt, in Bengal in suppressing the mutiny in 1857-8, and was present in the actions of Nusrutpore (as Orderly Officer to Colonel Ingram, and mentioned in despatches), Chanda, Ummeerpore, and Sultanpore, siege and capture of Lucknow, and storming of the Kaisa Bagh; operations in Bundelkund in 1859, including the pursuit to, night attack and surprise of the rebels on the Kalee Nuddee (medal and clasp). Killed in New Zealand, 30th April, 1865.
HAMILTON, Hans	22 Jan. 1740	21 April, 1756	Out in 1757.
HAMILTON, Henry	30 Sept. 1790	27 Dec. 1797	Retired 17th April, 1801.
HANDS, Benjamin	27 Oct. 1784	..	Resigned 20th March, 1787.
HARPER, William	30 Jan. 1796	..	From Lieutenant in Lieutenant-Colonel Pringle's Regt.; retired 2nd Sept., 1796.
HARRIS, Hon. Arthur Ernest	14 April, 1854	23 July, 1861	From 55th. Served throughout the Indian mutiny campaign of 1857-8, as A.D.C. to Brigadier McDuff. Served in the New Zealand war in 1864-5, and was present at Maketu and Te Ranga (mentioned in despatch); and with the expeditions in the province of Taranaki, and in command of outposts, destroying many Pas and fortified villages.

NAMES.	ENSIGN.	LIEUTENANT.	CAPTAIN.	MAJOR.	LIEUT.-COL.	REMARKS.
HARRIS, John	13 Feb. 1764	11 Mar. 1768	..	..	..	Exchanged to 49th Regt, 19th Dec, 1768; out 1772.
HARRIS, Jonah	16 Dec. 1813	11 Jan. 1816	29 June, 1830	..	..	Served in the Peninsula and the expedition to Portugal, retired 6th April, 1831.
HARRIS, Thomas	11 May 1805	..	..	..	1826–7; from Sergeant-Major;	To h.-p. 1806.
HARRISON, George Foster	30 Jan. 1796	..	..	..	..	To Lieutenant in 44th, 20th Feb, 1800; Captain, 20th Jan., 1804; Captain 39th, 25th Feb, 1804; exchanged to 11th Veteran Battalion, 18th April, 1811; out 1836.
*HARVEST, H.	22 Dec. 1804	9 Dec. 1805	..	..	..	Expedition to Copenhagen; wounded at the Coa; present at Ciudad Rodrigo. Killed at Badajoz, where he led the forlorn hope, 6th April, 1812.
HATCHELL, Christopher Hore	6 July, 1855	5 Sept. 1856	30 April, 1864	..	..	Served in the Indian mutiny campaign in 1857-8; including the action at Dooleypore and Purrah (medal); also in the New Zealand war of 1864–5, and was present at the Gate Pa and Te Ranga.
HATFIELD, John	2 Feb. 1757	7 Mar. 1762	25 Jan. 1771	..	..	Was a Midshipman in the Royal Navy, 1755; Captain-Lieutenant 25th Jan., 1771; Brevet-Major, 19th March, 1783; appointed Captain of Ind. Co. at Plymouth, 13th June, 1787; Lieutenant-Colonel, 1st March, 1794. Served at the reduction of and defence of Quebec, under Wolfe and Murray; capitulation of Montreal; at Martinique, under Monckton; with the Light Infantry at the Grenadas, St. Vincent, and St. Lucia; taking of the Havannah; at Lexington, Bunker's Hill, Brooklyn, Long Island, White Plain, Fort Washington, New York Island, Brandywine, and in all movements of the army during the winter and summer campaigns of 1777-8; with Lord Cornwallis a summer and winter campaign in the Jerseys; under Clinton at the evacuation of Philadelphia, and at the affairs of Monmouth in the Jerseys, at the siege of Charleston, South Carolina; appointed Governor of the Fort at Sullivan's Island, 1780-3. Died at Plymouth, 16th Jan., 1807.
HAVELOCK, Charles Frederick	..	..	23 June, 1843	..	..	Cornet 16th Lancers, 13th Dec, 1821; Lieutenant, 17th May, 1827; Adjutant of the 16th, 6th Oct., 1827; Captain, 12th Dec., 1839; exchanged to 3rd Light Dragoons, 3rd July, 1840; exchanged to 53rd, 5th July, 1844; exchanged to 9th legt., 16th Oct., 1845; Major, 3rd April, 1846; exchanged to 53rd, 6th Aug., 1847; to h.-p., unattached, 27th July, 1849. Served with the 16th Lancers at the siege and capture of Burtpore, in 1825-6, and in that of the Sutlej, including the battle of Sobraon (medal). Served with the Army of the Indus during the campaigns of Affghanistan, in 1829, under Lord Keane, as Brigade-Major to the Cavalry Division, and was present at the siege and capture of Guznee (medal). He acted in the same capacity during the campaign in Affghanistan in 1842, under General Pollock, and was present at the action of Tezeen, and the reacpture of Cabool (medal); he served also as D.A.Q.M. Gen. to the Cavalry division in the campaign in the Sutlej (medal), including the battles of Moodkee, Ferozeshah, and Sobraon, and was most severely wounded in the lungs at Ferozeshah; retired 24th Aug., 1852.
HAVELOCK, Thomas	3 Sept. 1795	26 Jan. 1796	..	..	..	From North York Militia. Appointed Paymaster of the Regt, 24th Jan., 1799.
HAVELOCK, Thomas	27 Sept. 1815	..	..	..	..	Placed h.-p., 25th Mar., 1817; retired 18th Nov., 1831.
HAVELOCK, William, K.H.	12 July, 1810	12 May, 1812	..	..	..	"El chico blanco," Captain 32nd Regt., 19th Feb., 1818; appointed 4th Light Dragoons, 19th July, 1821; Major 4th Light Dragoons, 31st Dec., 1830; Lieutenant-Colonel, 30th April, 1841; killed at Ramnuggur, 22nd Nov., 1848. Served in the Peninsula from July, 1810, to the end of the war in 1814. At Busaco, Sabugal, Salamanca, Vittoria, Bidassoa, Nivelle, Bayonne, Orthes, and Toulouse. Wounded at Quatre Bras. He received the war medal with six clasps.
HAVERFIELD, John	..	..	15 Aug. 1804	..	..	From Ensign 32nd Regt, 27th Feb, 1799; Lieutenant, 10th July, 1800, was Adjutant; appointed to 48th Regt., 6th Aug., 1807; was on the Quarter-Master-General's Staff in the Peninsular war, 1808-9; was A.D.C. to Lord Chatham at Colchester; Major, 6th Sept., 1810; Assistant-Quarter-Master-General at the Horse Guards, 6th Sept., 1810; Brevet-Lieutenant-Colonel, 7th Jan., 1814; appointed same day an Acting Quarter-Master-General; retired 1826.

43rd Light Infantry.

HAVERFIELD, John	.. ..	5 July, 1827	27 Aug. 1829	.. ..	Retired 24th Oct, 1834; to Captain 1st Durham Militia, 1855; Major, 29th Sept., 1860. Served as Inspector under Board of Works, Relief Commission during the famine in Ireland, 1845-6.
HAVERFIELD, William	..	25 July, 1805	3 April, 1806	31 Mar. 1808	Placed h.-p. of the Regt., 25th Mar., 1817; reappointed to it, 17th June, 1819. Wounded at Vimiero and Salamanca; was with the expedition to Copenhagen, 1807, and Walcheren, 1809; commanded the Regt. in the expedition to Portugal in 1826-27; died at Bath, Nov., 1830.
HAWLEY, Vernon	.. ..	..	16 Feb. 1756	11 Aug 1814 / 29 Aug, 1822	Ensign 60th, 1748. Present at siege of Quebec and expedition to the West Indies. Out in 1763.
HAY, Charles Murray	..	20 April, 1820	.. ..	.. ..	To Lieutenant Coldstream Guards, 1st Nov., 1821; Captain, 14th Dec, 1825; Lieutenant-Colonel, 22nd June, 1832; Colonel, 9th Nov., 1846; Major-General, 20th June, 1854; Lieutenant-General, 24th Aug, 1861; Colonel of the 91st, 9th Mar., 1861; died July, 1864.
HAY, John Charles	.. ..	21 Jan. 174$\frac{0}{1}$	30 April, 1742	.. ..	At formation; not in 1749.
HAY, Thomas	.. ..	.. ..	19 Oct. 1815	.. ..	From Captain, 1st West India Regt.; placed h.-p., of 43rd, 25th Mar., 1817; appointed Paymaster 2nd Dragoon Guards, 27th May, 1824.
HAY, William	.. ..	27 April, 1787	14 Mar. 1789	.. ..	To Captain in 83rd Regt., 28th Sept., 1793; Captain in the Army, 25th April, 1793; out May, 1796.
HAYWOOD, Nathaniel	.. ..	..	.. ..	.. ..	Not in List for 1749.
HEAVILAND, Thomas	.. ..	26 Mar. 1744	.. ..	.. ..	From North York Militia.
HEARNE, Daniel James	..	1 Oct. 1795	.. ..	7 Dec. 1797	Wounded at Vimiero; gold medal for Vittoria; retired 1814.
HEBSON, Christopher	..	4 May, 1809	19 May, 1808	25 Mar. 1808	Present at Vimiero and Corunna. Resigned April, 1810.
HENYELL, George	..	22 Oct. 1813	21 May, 1812	14 May, 1812	Appointed to 39th Regt., 24th Nov., 1814; to h.-p., with the 43rd at Salamanca, St. Muños, Vittoria, attack on the Heights of Vera and Nivelle, 25th Feb., 1816. Served as a volunteer in the 94th, at the storming of Badajoz; (wounded), affair before Bayonne; died July, 1831.
HERBERT, Hon. Percy Egerton, C.B., M.P.	..	17 Jan. 1840	7 Sept. 1841	19 June, 1846	27 May, 1853	Brevet-Lieutenant-Colonel for service at the Cape; Lieutenant-Colonel, unattached, 28th May, 1853; Colonel, 28th Nov., 1854; Lieutenant-Colonel, 82nd Regt, 19th Feb, 1858; to h.-p. of 82nd, 16th Nov., 1860; resigned the appointment, 28th April, 1865; A.D.C. to the Queen; was Deputy Quarter-Master-General at Head-quarters. Served with the 43rd, Kaffir war, 1851-3 (medal); expedition to the Orange River, and battle of Berea; commanded two companies of the 43rd at Murray's Krantz, when Colonel Eyre attacked the Hottentots; Brevet-Lieutenant-Colonel for service at the Cape. Served as Assistant Quarter-Master-General to the 2nd Division of the Eastern army, from its formation to Nov., 1855; and subsequently as Quarter-Master-General to the army of the East, until June, 1856; was present at the battle of the Alma (wounded), affair of the 26th Oct., battle of Inkerman, siege and fall of Sebastopol, wounded (medal and clasps); A.D.C. to the Queen, C.B., officer of the Legion of Honour, Commander of 2nd class of St. Maurice and St. Lazarus, 3rd class of the Medjidie, and Turkish medal. Served with the 82nd Regt. in Rondlecund under Lord Clyde in 1858; and was present in various affairs and skirmishes at Bareilly and Shahjehanpore; commanded the districts of Cawnpore and Futtehpore till the spring of 1859, and a force in pursuit of Ferozeshah and a rebel force to the banks of the Jumna (medal).
HERBERT, Hon. Wm. Henry	..	11 June, 1852	.. ..	.. ..	Appointed to Lieutenant in 46th, 25th Aug., 1854; Captain, 16th Nov., 1855; exchanged to 69th, 1st Aug., 1856; exchanged to 84th, 12th Nov., 1858. Served with the 46th in the Crimea from 31st July, 1855, including the siege and fall of Sebastopol; medal with clasps, and Turkish medal.
HERBERT, Isaac	.. ..	..	8 Dec. 1814	.. ..	From Lieutenant 1st Garrison Battalion; placed on h.-p. of 43rd, 25th Mar., 1817; retired on f.-p., 1824.

Names.	Ensign.	Lieutenant.	Captain.	Major.	Lieut.-Col.	Remarks.
Herries, William Robert	6 Mar. 1835	10 May, 1839	27 Dec., 1842	..	..	Served in the suppression of the Canadian revolt, and was one of those who crossed the Portage of the Madawaska. Exchanged to 3rd Light Dragoons, 23rd June, 1843; became Brevet-Major (bronze star for Maharaj Pass); killed at Moodkee, on Lord Hardinge's Staff, 18th Dec., 1845.—"My dear Herries;—you must be prepared for a heavy affliction. Your gallant son has closed his short, but most promising, career at the battle of Moodkee, fought on the 18th instant, about twenty miles from Ferozepoor. Thank God, he suffered no pain. He was buried the day after, in presence of his brother officers, at Moodkee. He was daringly brave, and manly in all his pursuits. He took a sound view of all military questions, and had a mind so well regulated to take a rapid view of what ought to be done, that he would have made a distinguished officer in command. Beloved by his brother officers for the amiability and sincerity of his character, I, in common with all, deplore the loss of one of the most amiable of my society, for whom I entertained a sincere friendship, and who justly deserved my entire confidence from the attachment which mutually subsisted between us. I have had a very severe loss, five aides-de-camp killed, and five wounded. I will take care that our dear friend's sketches shall be carefully preserved and sent home. I wish it were in my power to offer you consolation. In deep distress, your affectionate friend, H. Hardinge. 90 guns are brought in this day. Alas! how his noble spirit would have rejoiced at the sight."—*From Sir Henry Hardinge to Mr. Herries, 26th Dec., 1845.*
Hewett, Rt. Hon. Sir George, Bart., G.C.B.	..	..	..	1 Dec. 1781	32 Oct. 1787	Ensign 70th Regt., 27th April, 1762; Lieutenant 70th, 20th April, 1764; Captain 70th, 2nd June, 1775; Colonel 92nd, 1st Oct, 1794; Colonel 61st Regt., 4th April, 1800; Major-General, 3rd May, 1796; Lieutenant-General, 25th Sept., 1803; General, 4th June, 1813. On Lord Lake's return to England, he succeeded to the chief command in India, and arrived in Calcutta in Oct., 1807; in 1811 he returned home, and was created a Baronet; subsequently received the Grand Cross of the Order of the Bath, and was Commander of the Forces in Ireland, until obliged to relinquish it from ill health; thus terminated the public life of Sir George Hewett. "Having commenced life an almost friendless orphan, without any prospect of advancement, his own steady and upright conduct, diligence, and zeal, carried him up through so many posts of honour and importance, until his name stood nearly at the top of the list of the Army. He went down to the grave full of honours and of years, the 21st March, 1840, only wanting one month of completing his 90th year."
Hewitt, Henry	11 Oct. 1748	..	..	..	..	Out in 1755.
Hill, Edward Rowley	23 Feb. 1813	24 Feb. 1814	..	..	..	Placed h.-p. of the Regt., 25th Mar., 1817. Appointed to 68th, 22nd June, 1820; to h.-p., 1821; appointed to 21st Fusiliers, 10th Oct., 1822; Captain, 26th Sept., 1826; to h.-p., 7th Dec., 1826; to 81st, 16th Dec., 1829; Brevet-Major, 23rd Nov., 1841; Major in 1st West India Regt., 6th May, 1842; Lieutenant-Colonel, 1st Jan., 1847; Colonel, 28th Nov. 1854; Lieutenant-Colonel 63rd, 7th Sept., 1855; appointed to a Depôt Provisional Battalion 21st Sept., 1855; placed on h.-p. of 63rd 10th Sept., 1858; Deputy Adjutant-General at Barbadoes; Major-General, 2nd Feb., 1862. Served in the Peninsula from 1812 to the end of that war in 1814, including the affair of San Muños and retreat from Burgos, as a volunteer; battle of Vittoria, passage of the Bidassoa, battles of Nivelle and Toulouse; also at New Orleans; has the war medal with four clasps.
Hill, Horace Frederick	20 June, 1845	..	..	..	..	To Lieutenant 58th, 2nd March, 1849; to Captain Rifle Brigade, 23rd Mar., 1855; retired 10th May, 1861.
Hill, John Montgommery	16 Mar. 1809	28 June, 1810	31 Dec. 1822	..	..	Retired 1st Sept, 1825; medal for Vittoria, and Pyrenees.
Hill, Lloyd	..	10 Oct. 1778	..	..	..	From the Artillery; exchanged to 1st Foot Guards, as Adjutant, 30th May, 1782; resigned Adjutant, Aug., 1788; out in 1793.
Hill, *Lord* William F. A. M.	8 April, 1834	21 Oct. 1836	..	..	..	Served in the suppression of the Canadian revolt, and was one of those who crossed the Portage of the Madawaska. Appointed to Scots Greys, 10th May, 1839; Captain, 7th April, 1843; was A.D.C. to the Lord-Lieutenant of Ireland; died at Ipswich, in consequence of a fall while hunting, 18th Mar., 1844.
Hinde, Charles	21 July, 1784	..	..	..	..	To Cornet 3rd Dragoons, 9th February, 1785; out in April.
Hobkirk, Samuel	25 April, 1806	7 April, 1808	3 Dec. 1812	..	..	To h.-p., 25th Mar., 1817. Was with the expeditions to Copenhagen and Corunna; at the Coa, Busaco, Fuentes d'Onoro, Ciudad Rodrigo, Badajoz, Salamanca, Vittoria, Nivelle, wounded and taken prisoner before Bayonne, 23rd Nov., 1813; died 1853.

43rd Light Infantry.

HODGSON, Augustus Theodore	25 Aug. 1808	16 Oct. 1809	From the Royal Cumberland Militia. Present at the Coa, Sabugral, Busaco, Fuentes d'Onoro, and Ciudad Rodrigo. Died of wounds at Badajoz, April, 1812.
HOGARTH, Joseph	31 Aug. 1858	17 May, 1861	21 Aug. 1867	Served in the New Zealand war in 1864-5; present at Maketu and Te Ranga.
HOLE, Francis	6 April, 1815	..	..	Ensign 78th. Retired 15th Aug., 1816.
HOLLINGBERRY, John	..	11 Feb. 1767	..	From Lieutenant of Artillery; out April, 1772.
HOLMES, George	27 Aug. 1807	16 Mar. 1809	..	Present at Vimiero and Corunna. Resigned August, 1810.
HOLMES, John	26 June, 1783	27 April, 1787	..	Out of List for 1788.
HOLMES, T. Edmonds	..	..	26 Dec. 1855	From Captain 84th; h.-p. Lieutenant-Colonel without purchase, April 1st, 1866; retired July 20th, 1866. Served in the New Zealand war, 1865.
HOLWELL,	27 Nov. 1793	..	..	Died 29th July, 1794, of fever, in the West Indies.
HOOD, George	21 Feb. 1811	28 May, 1812	..	Appointed Paymaster of the Regt., 25th Oct., 1828. Medal for Toulouse. Died at Glasgow, Jan., 1835.
HOPE, Alexander	23 Dec. 1831	..	..	Present with the Regt. at New Orleans. From 1st Regt, 15th Feb., 1831; Lieutenant, unattached, 30th May, 1834; exchanged to 77th, 13th June, 1834; died Jan., 1835.
HOPKINS, Sir John Paul, K.H.	17 Nov. 1804	19 June, 1805	29 Aug. 1811	From Ensign 61st, 12th Oct., 1804; Major, unattached, 5th Nov., 1825; appointed to 98th Regt., 25th June, 1826; retired 18th Oct., 1831. Present with the Regt. in the Expedition to Copenhagen, 1807. Served in the Peninsula for six years until the Regt. entered France, and was present with it at the Coa (wounded), Busaco, Sabugal (thanked on the field by Sir Sidney Beckwith for his gallant conduct), Fuentes d'Onoro, Redinha, Foz d'Aronce, Castel Nova, Ciudad Rodrigo, Badajoz, Salamanca, Vittoria, attack on the heights of Vera, was an eye-witness to the assault on St. Sebastian. He received the war medal and seven clasps for Busaco, Fuentes d'Onoro, Ciudad Rodrigo, Badajoz. Salamanca, Vittoria, Pyrenees; Military Knight of Windsor, and selected by Her Majesty for the Governor of the Knights. Knighted by Her Majesty, for his military services, 11th Dec., 1867.
HORAN, Thomas	24 Oct. 1804	30 May, 1805	..	Resigned 4th Feb., 1807.
HORAN, Thomas	..	..	10 Mar. 1857	20 July, 1866	Served with the 41st Regt. during the whole of the campaign of 1842 in Affghanistan (medal), and was present in the engagements with the enemy on 28th March and 28th April in the Pisheen Valley; in that of the 29th May near Candahar, 30th Aug. at Goanine, 5th Sept. before Ghuznee, occupation and destruction of that fortress and of Cabool, expedition into Kohistan, storm, capture, and destruction of Istaliff, and in the various minor affairs in and between the Bolan and the Khyber Passes; with the 43rd during the Indian mutiny from Dec., 1857, to 1859, and was present at the surrender of Kirwee and subsequent operations (medal); also served in the New Zealand war in 1864-5.
HOSTE, James William	30 May, 1834	..	..	From Ensign 47th Regt, 27th Dec., 1833; died at Woodstock, New Brunswick, 9th Nov., 1836.
HOULTON, Sir George	20 Nov. 1806	6 Oct. 1808	2 Nov. 1815	Placed on h.-p. of the Regt., 25th March, 1817; appointed Ensign of the Yeomen of the Guard, Her Majesty's Body Guard, 25th Sept., 1835. Served with the Regt. throughout the whole of the retreat to Corunna under Sir John Moore in 1808. Served also in the Walcheren expedition in 1809. Subsequently in the Peninsula, including the retreat to the lines of Torres Vedras in 1810; pursuit of Massena, actions of Pombal, Redinha, Castel Nova, Miranda de Corvo, Foz d'Aronce, Sabugral, Castrejon, San Christoval, San Muños, and San Millan; battles of Salamanca, Vittoria, Fuentes d'Onoro, and Toulouse (severely wounded), Pyrenees, Nivelle, Nive (9th, 10th, 11th, 12th, and 13th Dec., 1813). Siege and storming of Ciudad Rodrigo, and taking of the outwork of that place, Fort Reynard, and siege and storming of Badajoz. He received the war medal with 10 clasps. Served in the storming of the lines at New Orleans, and afterwards with the Army of Occupation in France; died 15th Sept., 1862.
HOUSON, Henry Basil	22 Nov. 1851	6 June, 1854	..	Exchanged to 51st, 13th Oct., 1854; Captain Royal Canadian Rifle Regt., 19th Sept., 1856; retired 17th July, 1864.
HOWARD, William	14 Jan. 1842	..	..	To Lieutenant 3rd Foot, 8th Oct., 1844; exchanged to 63rd, 11th Oct., 1844; retired 6th Nov., 1847.

Names.	Ensign.	Lieutenant.	Captain.	Major.	Lieut.-Col.	Remarks.
Hudson, John	..	..	11 Jan. 1859	..	..	Ensign 63rd, 29th April, 1853; exchanged to 64th; Captain, 25th June, 1858; exchanged to 97th, 11th May, 1861; transferred to Bengal Staff Corps, 17th Nov. 1863; appointed Assistant-Adjutant to General Lehore's Division, 21st Jan, 1862; Brevet-Major, 22nd Mar., 1864. Served as Adjutant 64th Regt, throughout the Persian campaign of 1856–7, including the storm and capture of Reshire, surrender of Bushire, night attack and battle of Kooshab, and bombardment of Mohumrah. Served in Bengal and North-West Provinces in suppressing the mutiny in 1857–8; present with Havelock's column in the actions of Futtehpore, Aoung, Pandoo Nuddee, Cawnpore, Onao, Buseerut Gunge (1st and 2nd), Boorbeake, Chowkee, Bithoor, Alumbagh, and first relief of Lucknow; present in all subsequent operations, including three sorties, until the second relief of Lucknow (thanked by Governor-General in Council); served in defence of Cawnpore and defeat of the Gwalior mutineers, and actions of Kala Nuddee and Kerkeroulie, and capture of Bareilly; acted as Deputy-Adjutant-General with Sir H. Havelock at Mohumrah and at Alumbagh.
Huish, William	..	13 June, 1811	..	..	..	From Lieutenant Carabineers; retired 20th April, 1812.
Hull, Edward	13 Feb. 1764	26 Dec. 1770	..	..	..	Died from wounds at the affair at Lexington, 19th June, 1775.
Hull, Edward	..	31 Dec. 1791	1 Sept. 1795	10 Aug. 1804	8 Sept. 1808	From h.-p. of an Ind. Co.; was Captain-Lieutenant. Expedition to Copenhagen; commanded 2nd Battalion at Vimiero and Corunna; killed at the Coa, 24th July, 1810.
Hull, Edward	..	16 Feb. 1797	..	..	..	From Ensign 35th Regt, 10th June, 1796; out in 1800.
Hull, James Watson	24 July, 1800	24 July, 1802	..	..	..	Was at Copenhagen and Corunna. Severely wounded at the Coa. Retired May, 1812.
Hull, Trevor	21 Sept. 1756	8 April, 1761	22 Feb. 1765	..	..	Captain-Lieutenant, 22nd Feb., 1765; exchanged to 36th, 19th Dec., 1768; Lieutenant-Colonel in Army, 1st Jan., 1798; Lieutenant-Colonel 62nd, 6th Sept., 1798; Colonel, 25th April, 1808; Major-General, 4th June, 1811; died on his passage from Jamaica, July, 1816. Served with the 43rd at Quebec, &c.
Imlack, James	28 Mar. 1800	..	..	..	..	To 3rd West India Regt., 3rd Dec, 1800; out Feb., 1803.
Imlack, James	..	25 Jan. 1813	..	..	..	Ensign 81st, 2nd Feb., 1809; Lieutenant 85th, 23rd July, 1812; present at New Orleans; placed on h.-p. 43rd, 4th Sept., 1817.
Ingram, John	14 Mar. 1794	27 May, 1794	..	..	..	Sold out, 10th May, 1796.
Ingram, William	10 Mar. 1741	..	..	..	..	To Quarter-Master, 26th Nov., 1741.
Innes, Thomas	22 Oct. 1762	22 Feb. 1765	7 May, 1776	..	..	Captain-Lieutenant 22nd Nov., 1775; died 4th March, 1785. Served throughout the American war.
Jackson, Frederick	..	22 Aug. 1834	..	..	..	From Lieutenant 3rd Light Dragoons; placed on h.-p. 29th Aug., 1834; appointed Adjutant of Leicestershire Yeomanry.
Jackson, George	30 April, 1807	15 Mar. 1809	30 Mar. 1820	..	..	Medal for Vimiero and Corunna; retired 1811.
Jackson, John Napper	..	..	..	..	..	Ensign 94th Regt., 1st July, 1805; Lieutenant, 1st Jan., 1806; Captain, 28th Feb., 1812; placed on h.-p. of 43rd, 25th Oct., 1821; appointed to 99th, 25th March, 1824; Major 99th, 11th June, 1829; Lieutenant-Colonel, 23rd Nov. 1841; Colonel, 20th June, 1854; Major-General, 26th Oct., 1858; Colonel 99th, 8th June, 1863 (medal for Fuentes d'Onoro, Ciudad Rodrigo, Badajoz, Salamanca, Vittoria, Nivelle, Orthes, Toulouse); died 25th Jan., 1866.

43rd Light Infantry.

Name					Notes
Jackson, Robert	24 July, 1802	30 June, 1804	..	..	To Cornet 20th Light Dragoons, 12th Aug., 1803; resigned Aug., 1805.
James, Demetrius	..	..	29 Jan. 1741	2 May, 1751 2 Feb. 1757	On first formation of Regt., from Captain h.-p. Served in Minorca; commanded the Regt. in Nova Scotia. During the siege of Quebec, and at the battle of Sillery. Resigned 27th Feb, 1760.
James, William	30 Jan. 1796	10 May, 1796	..	..	From Lieutenant-Colonel Pringle's Regt.; out 1797.
Jekyll, Nathaniel	..	25 Aug. 1794	27 May, 1795	..	Superseded 8th July, 1804.
Jenkinson, Richard C.	2 Feb. 1796	7 Feb. 1797	..	..	From Rutland Fencible Cavalry; died Feb, 1799.
Jenkinson, R.	2 Sept. 1796	..	..	..	From the Rutland Fencibles.
Jenny, Robert	15 Mar. 1754	..	..	..	To Lieutenant in a new Regt., Feb. 12th, 1757.
Johnson, Benjamin	31 July, 1792	..	..	..	Resigned 30th May, 1793.
Johnson, Robert	1 June, 1764	..	..	..	Ensign 20th April, 1761; appointed to 60th, 25th April, 1765; out June, 1771.
Johnston, George	23 Oct. 1804	29 May, 1805	16 Aug. 1810	29 June, 1830	Expedition to Copenhagen, 1807. Medal for Busaco, Fuentes d'Onoro, Ciudad Rodrigo, Badajoz (wounded), Salamanca; retired 23rd Dec, 1831; was at Sabugal and the Coa, and different affairs on Massena's retreat; present at New Orleans; died 1862.
Johnston, Graham	22 Sept. 1745	..	..	..	Landed with the Regt. from Minorca; out in 1754.
Johnston, William	30 April, 1742	..	..	..	Not in List for 1749.
Johnstone, John	..	..	..	..	On first formation of the Regt.; out in 1745.
Johnstone, John	30 Jan. 1796	..	..	29 Jan. 1741	From Ensign in 92nd; superseded 20th Aug., 1796.
Jones, Charles Stanhope	15 Aug. 1816	..	..	..	Placed on h.-p. of the Regt., 25th March, 1817; retired 7th Sept., 1832.
Jones, John Gibson	..	28 Mar. 1811	..	..	Ensign West India Rangers, 25th March, 1808; Lieutenant, 31st Aug., 1809; to h.-p. 1st Garrison Battalion, 8th Dec, 1814; was at the Nivelle, Nive, and Toulouse; died 12th Feb, 1829.
Jones, John Thos. William	16 July, 1830	13 Mar. 1835	..	..	Lieutenant, unattached, 6th March, 1835. Served in the suppression of the Canadian revolt, 1837-8; Captain Canadian Rifles, 23rd July, 1841; retired 14th Nov., 1845.
Jones, Lewis	22 Nov. 1756	..	..	..	Wounded at the battle of Quebec; died 28th Nov., 1759.
Jones, William	26 Sept. 1787	11 May, 1791	20 July, 1794	..	From Provincial h.-p. of the King's Carolina Rangers; was Captain-Lieutenant, 20th July, 1794; to Major 87th, 22nd July, 1795; out Nov., 1797.
Joynt, G. J.	8 Nov. 1804	13 Aug. 1805	..	..	From Sergeant-Major. Served in the expedition to Copenhagen; appointed to 103rd Regt, 14th April, 1808; Captain, 13th June, 1815; to h.-p., 25th March, 1817; died 24th Oct., 1818.
Keating, John Webb	24 April, 1762	..	..	..	Out in 1764.
Kekewick, John	23 Sept. 1800	..	..	..	Retired 24th July, 1801.
Kennedy, Archibald	7 Aug. 1775	..	..	..	Lieutenant in 44th, 23rd May, 1776; out Jan., 1778.

Names.	Ensign.	Lieutenant.	Captain.	Major.	Lieut.-Col.	Remarks.
Kennedy, Francis Charlesworth	..	29 July, 1853	..	..	..	Ensign 51st, 18th Sept., 1849; Lieutenant 51st, 17th Oct., 1851; Captain 25th, 24th Nov., 1857; retired 7th Nov., 1862. Served with the 51st throughout the Burmese war of 1852; was on board the East India Company's steam sloop 'Sesostris' during the naval action and destruction of the enemy's stockades on the Rangoon river. Served during the succeeding three days' operations in the vicinity (including the storming of the White House redoubt), and at the storm and capture of Rangoon; also at the assault and capture of Bassein (medal).
Kennedy, *Hon.* John	..	25 Jan. 1839	3 Aug. 1841	..	..	Retired Jan., 1842. Died 3rd Sept., 1846.
Kennedy, James	..	9 May, 1815	..	..	..	From 45th Regt.; Lieutenant 63rd Regt., 5th Nov., 1847, placed on h.-p. of the legt. same day; appointed to 36th, 26th Nov., 1847; appointed A.D.C. to General Thorne, Jan., 1848; retired July 23rd, 1852.
Kennedy, John Shaw						
Kennedy, *Sir* J. Shaw, K.C.B.	18 April, 1805	23 Jan. 1806	16 July, 1812	..	..	Placed on h.-p. of the Regt., 25th March, 1817; Brevet-Major, 18th June, 1815; Brevet-Lieutenant-Colonel, 21st Jan., 1819; Major, unattached, 16th July, 1830; Colonel, 10th Jan., 1827; Major-General, 9th Nov., 1846; Lieutenant-General, 20th June, 1854; Colonel, 47th Foot, 27th Aug., 1854. Served with the 43rd Light Infantry at the siege of Copenhagen and battle of Kioge in 1807. In 1808 with the corps of Sir David Baird from Corunna to Sahagun, and in the retreat under Sir John Moore. In 1809 with the Light Division in the march from Lisbon to Talavera, where he became Adjutant of the 43rd. Served as A.D.C. to General Robert Craufurd during 1809 and 1810, and was present in the numerous affairs that took place between the Coa and Aqueda, and severely wounded at the action of Almeida. Served at the siege of Ciudad Rodrigo, and at the assault of the fort and of the place. Stood with General Craufurd when, in the assault, he placed himself on the crest of the glacis, where he fell mortally wounded. Was the bearer of the Duke of Wellington's summons to the Governor demanding the surrender of the place. Served with the 43rd at the siege and storming of Badajoz, during the investment of the forts of Salamanca, the advance and retreat from that place to the Douro, the action of Salamanca, and the investment of the Retiro and occupation of Madrid. Served as A.D.C. to General Baron Alten on the retreat from Madrid to Salamanca, and in the affairs that took place between Salamanca and Rodrigo. Served as the only officer of the Quarter-Master-General's Department to the 3rd Division of the Army, in the actions of Quatre Bras and Waterloo. Reconnoitered for the line of march of the Division on the 17th of June from Piermond and the Ligny Road, crossing the Dyle at Weys, a line of march separate from the rest of the Army, and a movement of great delicacy, being performed in open day in presence of Napoleon's advance. On the 18th of June was allowed, in presence of the Duke of Wellington, to form the Division in an order of battle new and unusual, that of oblongs in exchequer, to meet the formidable masses of cavalry seen forming in its front, and in this formation the Division resisted repeatedly, with perfect success, attacks of cavalry and artillery probably as formidable as any known in military history. On the 18th was struck on the side and disabled for some time; and had one horse killed and one wounded. Commanded at Calais, during the three years of the Army of Occupation, the establishment formed there to keep up the communication between the Army and England. Served nine years as Assistant-Adjutant-General at Manchester, during periods of disturbance, and generally in command. Organised the Constabulary Force of Ireland. After attaining the rank of Major-General, was named by the Duke of Wellington to several very important commands. He received the war medal with three clasps; died 30th May, 1865.
Keppel, E. G. Walpole	4 June, 1818	29 Aug. 1822	1 Sept. 1825	23 Dec. 1831 to h.-p., unattached, 14th Oct., 1836; Brevet Lieutenant-Colonel, 20th June, 1854; died Oct., 1858.		Was with the expedition to Portugal, 1826-7; exchanged to h.-p., unattached, 14th Oct., 1836; Brevet Lieutenant-Colonel, 9th Nov., 1846; died Oct., 1858.
Kerr, Alexander	..	15 June, 1804	11 Mar. 1806	..	..	From Ensign 69th; was A.D.C. to General Craig; died in Portugal, 1809.
Kerr, Charles	17 Aug. 1773	22 Nov. 1775	1 June, 1783	..	..	Served in the American war; resigned 27th April, 1787.
Kershaw, William	25 Dec. 1813	..	..	..	..	From Derby Militia.
Kersteman, Thomas	..	..	8 Nov. 1821	..	..	From Captain 6th Dragoons; retired 12th May, 1824.

43d Light Infantry.

Name				Notes
KING, Hon. Sir Henry, K.C.B.	..	..	16 July, 1802	From 1st Guards; appointed Major of 5th, 24th Aug., 1804; Lieutenant-Colonel, 28th Jan., 1808; Colonel, 4th June, 1814; Major-General, 27th May, 1825; appointed Colonel of 1st West India Regt.; Lieutenant-General, 28th June, 1838; died at Grove Lodge, Windsor, 25th Nov., 1839 (gold medal for Busaco and Salamanca).
KING, William	..	3 July, 1800	..	Retired 12th Dec, 1800.
KIPLING, Robert	..	3 Feb. 1797	16 Sept. 1797	13 Aug. 1804	Retired 1807; died 2nd Dec, 1830. Enlisted in 1772, and served in upwards of thirty-five years, in the different ranks of Private, Corporal, Sergeant, Sergeant-Major, Adjutant, Ensign, Lieutenant, and Captain. He was with the regiment at the battle of Bunker's Hill, and through the whole of the ten years' American war, in the Light Brigade. On retiring from the service, his brother officers presented him a valuable sword, with the following inscription on the blade, and on the scabbard—"To Capt. Robert Kipling, this sword is presented by his brother officers as a small token of their sincere regard, and of the high sense they entertain of his meritorious services during a period of thirty-five years in the different ranks of Private, Corporal, Sergeant, Sergeant-Major, Adjutant, Ensign, Lieutenant, and Captain, in His Majesty's 43rd Light Infantry Regiment."
KIRWAN, John	..	20 July, 1794	6 June, 1795	..	Died of fever, in West Indies, same year.
KNIGHT, Christopher	..	..	12 Mar. 1754	7 Mar. 1762	Ensign, 14th Sept., 1749; Adjutant from 8th Aug., 1757, to 6th Oct., 1862; Captain-Lieutenant, 8th April, 1861. Served at the siege of Quebec, and in the expedition to the West Indies under Monckton; out Feb., 1765.
KNIGHT, Henry	..	25 Dec. 1758	17 Mar. 1762	3 Sept. 1772	Major in Army, 21st May, 1778; Major 45th Regt., 20th Sept., 1778; Lieutenant-Colonel, 19th Feb., 1783; exchanged to Major 21st, 31st Dec, 1784; out May 4th, 1789; A.D.C. to Sir Wm. Howe. Served at the siege of Quebec, and expedition to the West Indies under Monckton; wounded at the Havannah, 1762.
KNOTT, Thomas	..	30 May, 1780	21 April, 1784	..	Resigned July, 1792.
KNOX, Hon. John	..	22 May, 1749	4 Sept., 1754	..	To Captain, 8th Jan., 1761; appointed Captain of an Ind. Co. at Berwick, 16th Feb., 1775; to 67th Regt., 5th Feb, 1778; Major 36th Regt., 23rd Nov., 1780; Lieutenant-Colonel, Aug., 1795; Colonel, 21st Aug., 1795; Major-General, 18th June, 1798. Served with the 43d at siege of Quebec and different actions, at the capitulation of Montreal; also in India in the campaign against Tippoo Sahib, and siege of Seringapatam. His services in the expedition to Holland are mentioned in the despatches of the Duke of York, dated "Head-quarters, Alkmaar, 6th Oct., 1799," and he was selected by his Royal Highness to conclude the armistice between the combined English and Russian, and French armies, to which he signed his name, 18th Oct., 1799, at Alkmaar with citizen Rostollan, General of Brigade, deputed by Brune, Commander-in-Chief of the French and Batavian army; Author of 'Campaigns in North America;' appointed Governor of Jamaica; lost on the passage out, 1801.
LALOR, Thomas	..	..	17 Oct. 1809	..	From 9th Light Dragoons; was at Corunna and most of the actions in the Peninsula and at New Orleans; placed h.-p., 22nd July, 1819; retired May, 1829; died Mar. 9th, 1837.
LAMBERT, Robert	..	1 May, 1835	15 May, 1840	25 Aug. 1843	Served in the suppression of the Canadian revolt in 1837-8; retired 16th Oct., 1851.
LAMBRECHT, Rich. William	..	21 April, 1814	..	..	3rd Garrison Battalion, 7th Oct., 1815; Lieutenant Ceylon Rifles, 8th Sept., 1825; retired 23rd May, 1829.
LANGLANDS, C. John	..	19 May, 1861	..	..	Killed at Gate Pa, 1864.
LANGLANDS, John S.	..	27 July, 1866	..	..	From Ensign 97th, 8th May, 1866.
LAURIE, Walter Sloane	..	..	21 Dec. 1770	..	From Lieutenant 36th, 14th Jan., 1769; present at the affair at Lexington; resigned 18th Dec, 1775.
LAWRENCE, Frederick	..	..	..	25 Dec. 1813	From Derby Militia; placed h.-p., 26th Sept., 1814; died at Karlsbad, 20th Sept., 1840.
LEAR, George	..	1 Nov. 1793	..	..	To Lieutenant in a Regt. raised by Lieutenant-Colonel Hewett, 31st Dec, 1793.

Names.	Ensign.	Lieutenant.	Captain.	Major.	Lieut.-Col.	Remarks.
LE BLANC, Francis			17 Dec. 1818	31 Dec. 1822		Ensign 4th, 30th May, 1807; Lieutenant, 16th March, 1809; Captain 4th Garrison Battalion, 28th Sept., 1813; to Rifle Brigade, 1st Dec, 1814; Lieutenant-Colonel, unattached, 11th July, 1826; appointed to 53rd, 9th Aug., 1827; to h.-p., 28th Feb., 1828; Colonel, 23rd Nov., 1841; exchanged to 46th, 16th May, 1846; retired the same day. He was with the 1st Battalion of the 4th on Sir John Moore's retreat, and at the battle of Corunna; with the 2nd Battalion at Gibraltar and Ceuta, was removed to the 1st, and was with them at Fuentes d'Onoro, Badajoz, Salamanca, Vittoria, and St. Sebastian; he commanded the storming party at the second assault of the latter place the day of its capture, when he was severely wounded, and for this he was promoted to a company in the 4th Garrison Battalion. He received the war medal with six clasps for Corunna, Fuentes d'Onoro, Badajoz, Salamanca, Vittoria, and St. Sebastian, also a medal for Waterloo.
LECKY, Averell		19 April, 1815				
LEE, John	3 Feb. 1803	7 June, 1804	7 Mar. 1805			Ensign 45th Regt.; Lieutenant 17th June, 1813; placed h.-p. of 43rd, 25th Mar., 1817; appointed to 67th, 9th July, 1818; died 23rd April, 1829.
LEES, Edward Smith	15 May, 1793			23rd Nov., 1815; placed h.-p., 25th Mar., 1816.		Appointed to 1st Regt., 14th March, 1805; Major, Was on the staff at Constantinople and Gibraltar; died 1817.
LEGARD, Sir Charles, Bart.	6 Feb. 1866					To an Inl. Co., 30th July, 1793.
LEHUNTE, Francis	2 Mar. 1757	8 April, 1762				Retired 26th July.
						Present with the Regt. during the siege of Quebec, and the different actions; also in the expedition to the West Indies, under Monckton; died March, 1762.
LEITRIM, Earl of	9 Dec. 1824	31 Oct. 1826	5 April, 1831			Served at Gibraltar, and with the expedition to Portugal in 1835; was A.D.C. to the Lord-Lieut. of Ireland; Colonel of Leitrim Militia, 2nd Feb, 1843.
LENNOX, Lord Fitzroy, G.C.G.	15 Sept. 1837	11 Sept. 1840		1826-27. To h.-p., 20th March, the "President" steamer, on passage from New York, Mar., 1841.		To f.-p. of the 51st, 20th June, 1854; retired same day. Appointed to 10th Hussars, 16th Feb, 1841. Lost in
LEVINGE, Sir Rich. Geo. Aug., Bart.	25 Nov. 1828	8 April, 1834		revolt in 1837-8; Captain, unattached, 15th May, 1840; appointed to 5th Dragoon Guards, 27th Jan., 1843, retired same day; Lieut.-Col. Westmeath Militia, 3rd Jan., 1846.		Served at Gibraltar, and in the suppression of the Canadian
LINDSAY, Hon. Charles Hugh, M.P.	5 June, 1835	3 July, 1840	9 May, 1845			Served in the suppression of the Canadian revolt, 1837-8; exchanged to 1st Guards, 20th Feb, 1846; Captain and Lieutenant-Colonel, 14th July, 1854. Present at Inkerman and siege of Sebastopol (medal and clasps); retired 31st Aug., 1855; is Lieutenant-Colonel of the St. George's Rifle Volunteers.
LINDSAY, George	29 Sept. 1743					Not in List for 1749.
LIVSEY, William	26 Oct. 1855	3 April, 1857	30 April, 1864			Served in the suppression of the Indian mutiny from Dec., 1857, to Jan., 1860, including actions at Sahao and Puttrai (medal); also served in the New Zealand war in 1864-5, including the expeditions in the province of Taranaki, and in command of outposts, destroying many Pas and fortified villages.

43rd Light Infantry.

LLOYD, John	..	..	..	29 Jan. 1741	..	..	Not in List, 1749.
LLOYD, Thomas	..	..	..	..	10 Aug. 1804	Ensign, 1st Aug., 1797; Lieutenant, 6th May, 1799; Captain 6th Battalion of Rifles, 8th Oct., 1803; Major 94th Regt., 4th Oct., 1810; Brevet-Lieutenant-Colonel, 17th Aug., 1812; killed at the passage of the Nivelle, 10th Nov., 1813. Present with the 43rd in the expedition to Copenhagen, 1807, and at the Corunna retreat; the Coa (severely wounded), Sabugal, Busaco (gold medal for Salamanca, Vittoria). "This Lloyd, a Captain of the 43rd, was known throughout the army for his genius, wit, and bravery, his happy temper, and magnificent person; he fell gloriously at the battle of the Nivelle in 1813."
LOCKYER, Hen. Fred., C.B., K.H.			23 May, 1816	..	..	Ensign 71st, 25th Mar., 1813; Lieutenant, 19th Jan., 1814; placed h.-p. of 43rd, 25th Mar., 1817; appointed 3rd Regt., 10th Aug., 1820; Captain, 20th June, 1822; Major, 12th June, 1835; exchanged to 97th, 26th June, 1835; Lieutenant-Colonel, 26th Oct., 1841; Colonel, 11th Nov., 1851; Major-General, 26th Oct., 1858. Served in the Peninsula with the 71st, from Aug., 1813, to the end of the war, including the battles of Nivelle, Nive, Orthes, Aire (severely wounded), and Toulouse. Commanded the 2nd Brigade, 2nd Division, in the Crimea; appointed to the command of the forces in Ceylon, in Aug., 1855. He received the war medal with three clasps, and the Crimean medal with clasp for Sebastopol, C.B., Officer of the Legion of Honour, and 3rd class of the Medjidie (medal for Nive, Orthes, Toulouse).
LONGLEY, Arthur	..	..	16 Jan. 1863	30 April, 1864	..	Ensign 83rd, 19th Dec., 1862. Served in the New Zealand war, 1864-65, and was present at Maketu and Te Ranga. Served with the expeditions in the province of Taranaki, destroying many Pas and fortified villages.
LORD, Samuel Hall	..	..	18 Feb. 1804	30 April, 1789	..	From Lieutenant h.-p. 60th to h.-p. 13th March, 1789; resigned 30th May, 1790.
LOSAC, Henry	..	..	..	..	..	
LOSAC, James	..	..	26 June, 1770	17 Aug. 1773	27 April, 1787	Became Captain-Lieutenant in the Regt., 25th Oct., 1781; Brevet-Major, 1st Mar., 1794; promoted to Major 82nd Regt., 10th May, 1796; Lieutenant-Colonel of 23rd, 14th Nov., 1804; out 1808; was Major of Brigade to General Grenville during the American war.
LCNN, John Campbell	..	..	9 June, 1808	17 Aug. 1809	..	Present at New Orleans; exchanged to h.-p., 25th April, 1816; retired Oct., 1825.
LYTTON, William	..	..	2 May, 1760	..	..	Ensign 24th Sept., 1759; resigned 4th Oct., 1761.
LURGAN, Lord, K.P.	..	..	5 Nov. 1847	..	..	Appointed to 76th Regt., 11th Dec., 1849; appointed to 16th, 8th Mar., 1850; to 26th, 15th March, 1850; retired 22nd Jan., 1852.
LUSHINGTON, Matthew	..	..	11 Mar. 1824	13 May, 1826	..	Retired 15th July, 1827.
LYONS, Rob. Colville Jones	..	26 July, 1864	..	..	Served in the New Zealand war, 1865, including the expeditions in the province of Taranaki, destroying many Pas and fortified villages.
LYSAGHT, Nicholas	..	..	9 April, 1756	25 Dec. 1758	22 Feb. 1765	Captain-Lieutenant, 5th October, 1764; out June, 1765. Served in siege of Quebec, and different actions; also in expedition to the West Indies under Monckton; appointed Governor of the city of Cork, 14th Feb, 1778.
LYTTLETON, Sands	..	..	17 Feb. 1745/6	..	..	Not in 1749; probably never joined.
MACDOWALL, John Alexander	..	..	..	..	Ensign 85th, 13th March, 1782; Lieutenant, 20th March, 1783; died 27th June, 1794, of fever, in West Indies.
MACRASCAL, William	..	..	6 Oct. 1787	25 Dec. 1787	..	From Lieutenant h.-p. of 71st, 25th Sept., 1785; to a company of Invalids, 29th Sept., 1790; not in List for 1791.
M'CARTHY, Arthur	..	..	8 Jan. 1795	..	..	
M'DONALD, James	..	..	..	..	2 Feb. 1797	Lieutenant 7th, 39th Oct., 1793; Captain 7th, 29th July, 1795; died Oct., 1798.

Names.	Ensign.	Lieutenant.	Captain.	Major.	Lieut.-Col.	Remarks.
M'Donald, Sir John, G.C.B.	.. ..	.. ..	.. ..	20 Feb. 1806	.. ..	Ensign, 15th April, 1795; Lieutenant 89th, 2nd Feb., 1796; Captain, 22nd Oct., 1802; Major h.-p. 10th West Ind. Regt., 28th Feb., 1805; Lieutenant-Colonel, 17th March, 1808; exchanged to h.-p. 1st Garrison Battalion; Colonel, 4th June, 1814; appointed Deputy Adjutant-General, 14th Aug., 1818; Major-General, 27th May, 1825; Adjutant-General, 27th July, 1830; Lieutenant-General, 28th June, 1838; Colonel of 42nd Regt., 15th Jan., 1844. Served with the 89th in Ireland during the rebellion of 1798, and was present at the battles of Ross, Vinegar Hill, and other principal actions. In 1799-1800 he was at the siege of La Valetta and capture of Malta. He served in Egypt the three following years, and was present in the action on landing on the 8th March, also in the two other general actions fought on the 13th and 21st March, 1801. In 1807 he was employed as military secretary to Lord Cathcart, when his lordship commanded the King's German Legion as a distinct army in Swedish Pomerania, as well as during the subsequent attack upon and capture of Copenhagen and the Danish fleet. In 1809 he served in the Walcheren expedition, and had charge of the Adjutant-General's department of the reserve, commanded by Sir John Hope. The following year he was employed as Deputy-Adjutant-General to the force attached to the defence of Cadiz, under General Graham, and was present at the battle of Barossa. In 1813-14 he was employed in charge of the left wing of the Peninsular army, and in that capacity was present in the actions of the 9th, 10th, 11th, and 12th Dec., 1813, upon the Nive, and in the affairs which attended the closing of the blockade of Bayonne, and at the action brought on by the general sortie from that fortress. Sir John had received a medal for service in Egypt, and the gold medal and one clasp for Barossa and the Nive. He died 28th March, 1850.
M'Dowall, Frederick	17 May, 1766	.. ..	.. ..	.. ..	.. ..	From Ensign 8th Regt., 20th May, 1761; out 26th April, 1767.
M'Dowall, John Alexander ..	.. ..	25 Dec. 1787	.. ..	.. ..	.. ..	Ensign 85th, 13th March, 1782; Lieutenant, 20th March, 1783. Served in the expedition under Sir Charles Grey; died 27th June, of fever, in West Indies.
M'Dermid, John	.. ..	26 June, 1806	.. ..	.. ..	.. ..	Wounded at the Coa; killed at Sabugal, 3rd April, 1811.
M'Goun, Thomas	26 Sept. 1856	22 April, 1859	.. ..	.. ..	.. ..	From Ensign 51st Regt.; retired 17th Nov., 1863. Served in the suppression of the Indian mutiny from Dec., 1857, to Jan., 1860; including the actions at Girwasa, Dooleypore, Puraha, Putowrie, and Raichoro (medal).
M'Kenzie, Robert	22 Feb. 1775	22 Oct. 1775	.. ..	.. ..	.. ..	
M'Kenzie, Thomas	8 June, 1804	14 Aug. 1804	27 Sept. 1809	.. ..	.. ..	From h.-p. of 77th; was Adjutant 28th Sept., 1804; present at Copenhagen, the Coa, Sabugal, and Busaco; died 3rd Dec., 1812.
M'Lachlan, Robert	.. ..	Lieutenant 77th, 3rd July, 1799.	4 April, 1805	.. ..	.. ..	Ensign 48th, 21st Sept., 1796; Lieutenant, 11th Dec., 1797; Lieutenant 79th, 27th Sept., 1798; Lieutenant 77th, 3rd July, 1799. Served with the 43rd at Vimiero, Corunna retreat, and battle of Corunna; died in Portugal, Aug. 15th, 1809.
M'Lean, Charles	25 Feb. 1762	15 Feb. 1764	10 July, 1775	.. ..	.. ..	Captain-Lieutenant, 10th July, 1775; Brevet-Major, 19th March, 1803, for distinguished service; retired 31st May, 1785. Served during the War of Independence.
M'Lean, John	2 May, 1811	10 Dec. 1812	.. ..	.. ..	.. ..	Captain 20th Regt., 25th Dec., 1830; Major, 18th April, 1839; to h.-p, 17th April, 1840; retired 7th Sept., 1841; Major 46th; Lieutenant-Colonel, unattached, 7th Oct., 1851; out 1855. Served with the 43rd in the Peninsula from June, 1812, to the end of the war in 1814, including the action of the 14th Nov., 1812; on retreat from Salamanca, battles of Vittoria, the Nivelle (wounded), Nive, and Toulouse; present also in the action before New Orleans, 8th Jan., 1815, and at the surrender of Paris; war medal and five clasps.
M'Lean, John Leyburn ..	23 Mar. 1810	27 Mar. 1811	7 April, 1825	.. ..	.. ..	Placed h.-p., 18th Aug., 1825; exchanged to 50th, 30th Jan., 1833. Retired from service 27th Jan., 1837; is a Military Knight of Windsor. Served with the 43rd in the Peninsula from 1812 to the end of the war, including the battles of Vittoria, passage of the Bidassoa, Nivelle, Nive, and Toulouse; was also at New Orleans; he has received the war medal with five clasps.

43rd Light Infantry.

McLeod, Charles .. .. | 26 Nov. 1806 | 16 Aug. 1810 | Lieutenant in 62nd Regt., 21st March, 1800; Captain 3rd West India Regt., 22nd April, 1802. Served with the 43rd; expedition to Copenhagen in 1807; in the Peninsula, at the Coa, when he succeeded to the Command of the Regt.; at Busaco; storming of Ciudad Rodrigo. "As the rear-guard approached the Coa, we perceived that a part only of our cavalry, infantry, and artillery had yet crossed the bridge; it became, therefore, indispensably requisite for us to keep possession of a small hill looking down on and perfectly commanding the bridge until everything had passed over, cost what it might. I trust I shall be pardoned for saying that the soldiers of the old and gallant 43rd, and that part of our own Battalion whose lot it was to defend this important hill, against a vast superiority of numbers, proved themselves worthy of the trust. If any are now living of those who defended the little hill above the bridge, they cannot fail to remember the gallantry displayed by Major M'Leod of the 43rd, who was the senior officer on the spot. How he or his horse escaped being blown to atoms, when in the most daring manner he charged on horseback at the head of a hundred or two skirmishers of the 43rd and of our Regt. mixed together, and headed them in making a dash at a wall lined with French infantry, which we soon dislodged, I am at a loss to imagine. This gallant officer was killed afterwards, whilst heading his Regt, at the storming of Badajoz, and was sincerely regretted by all who knew him." —*Leach's Rough Sketches.*

M'Leod, Coll. .. .. | 29 Mar. 1861 | 30 June, 1863 | .. | Died in New Zealand, 26th July, 1864.

M'Leod, Henry George, K.H. .. .. | .. | 29 Mar. 1820 | .. | Lieutenant in Royal Artillery, 15th Jan., 1808; Captain, 29th Sept., 1813; Captain 35th, 10th Dec, 1813; to h.-p., 25th June, 1817; Captain 52nd, 3rd Jan., 1822; Brevet-Major, 21st June, 1817; placed on h.-p. 4th May, 1826; Lieutenant-Colonel, and Deputy-Adjutant-General at Jamaica, 18th Aug., 1825. Medal for Waterloo. Not in List for 1839.

M'Neill, John .. .. | 17 Sept. 1858 | .. | .. | Retired 12th March, 1861.

M'Pherson, ... | 17 Oct. 1762 | .. | .. | To Lieutenant in 40th Regt., 27th Oct., 1762.

Mackenzie, Patrick .. .. .. | .. | .. | 23 Jan. 1800 | Lieutenant in 77th Regt., 26th May, 1781; Lieutenant in 1st, 6th Aug., 1788; Captain 1st Regt., 2nd Jan., 1794; Lieutenant-Colonel 81st, 28th Aug., 1804; Colonel, 4th June, 1813; out Aug., 1819.

Mackenzie, Robert .. .. | .. | 22 Oct. 1762 | 10 July, 1775 | Captain-Lieutenant, 8th Feb., 1775; Military Secretary to Sir Wm. Howe; resigned 28th March, 1778; wounded severely at Bunker's Hill.

Mackey, George .. .. | 26 April, 1786 | .. | .. | From h.-p. of the Royals; exchanged to 36th, 30th Sept., 1786.

Mackinnos, Henry .. .. | 31 May, 1790 | 30 Nov. 1792 | .. | Captain of Ind. Com., 11th April, 1793; to Coldstream Guards, 9th Oct., 1793; Lieutenant-Colonel, 18th Oct., 1799; Colonel, 25th Oct., 1809; Major-General, 1st January, 1812; killed at Ciudad Rodrigo, 19th Jan., 1812.

Macintosh, William .. .. | 3 May, 1760 | .. | .. | Lieutenant 27th Regt, 25th Dec, 1762; not in List for next year.

Mackrill, William .. .. | .. | 24 Oct. 1781 | .. | From Ensign 64th Regt.; placed on h.-p. 4th April, 1786.

Macpherson, Philip, C.B. .. .. | .. | 2 Nov. 1809 | 13 June, 1811 | Placed on h.-p. of 28th, 1815; exchanged to 30th Regt., 25th April, 1816; placed on h.-p. 25th March, 1817; appointed to 46th Regt., 19th May, 1825; appointed to 35th Regt., 12th Oct., 1826; Captain, unattached, 13th Mar., 1827; appointed to 17th Foot, 26th Nov., 1841; Brevet-Lieutenant-Colonel, 4th July, 1843; Major 17th Foot, 1st Aug., 1844; Colonel of 13th Light Infantry, 15th Aug., 1863. Embarked for the Peninsula in May, 1809, as a volunteer in the 52nd, and served as such in the advance up to Talavera, and the retreat from thence, to 2nd Nov, 1809, when he was promoted to an Ensigncy in the 43rd, from which time he served with the Light Division until the end of the war in 1814, including the following battles, sieges, &c., viz.:—Coa, Mortiagoa, skirmish near and battle of Busaco, Coimbra, Alengner, Pombal, Redinha, Miranda de Corvo, Foz d'Aronce, Sabugal, Fuentes d'Onoro, Espigo, Soiba, siege and storm of Ciudad Rodrigo, siege and storm of Badajoz, March and April, 1812; Carvellejo, Peteugua, Salamanca, capture of Madrid and the Retiro, San Muños, affairs in the Pyrenees, Nivelle, Bayonne, Nive, Tabres, Tournefeuille, and Toulouse; contused on the head in the trenches of Badajoz by the bursting of a shell. He received the war medal with eight clasps for Busaco, Fuentes d'Onoro, Ciudad Rodrigo, Badajoz, Salamanca, Nivelle, Nive, and Toulouse. Served as A.D.C. to Sir Charles Napier throughout the operations in Scinde, including the battles of Meeanee and Hydrabad (medal and C.B., and twice mentioned in despatches). He also served in the Crimea in the Command of the 1st Brigade of the 4th Division, on the heights and siege before Sebastopol, from 18th Dec., 1854, to 15th June, 1855; when he was obliged to leave from ill-health, brought on by over-fatigue in the trenches. Was General of the day in the trenches in command of the left attack on the occasion of several sorties by the enemy, and on one particular occasion on the night of the 11th May, 1855, when the enemy was repulsed with considerable loss, was thanked personally by Lord Raglan. Medal and clasps; Knight of the Legion of Honour, 4th class of the Medjidie, and Turkish Medal. Died 2nd Feb., 1864.

NAMES.	ENSIGN.	LIEUTENANT.	CAPTAIN.	MAJOR.	LIEUT.-COL.	REMARKS.
MACQUEEN, Donald R.	11 Aug. 1863	..	..	..	..	Ensign 18th, 11th Aug., 1863; served in the New Zealand war, 1864–5, with the 43rd, including expeditions in the province of Taranki, destroying many Pas and fortified villages; Lieutenant 75th, 26th June, 1867.
MADDEN, John	5 May, 1784	24 Sept. 1787	..	..	..	Died 23rd Aug., 1791.
MADDEN, Molesworth Monson, K.H.	30 Nov. 1806	..	..	..	..	Lieut., 18th Oct., 1798; present at Vimiero (wounded) and Corunna; Captain 102nd, 19th April, 1809 (afterwards altered to 100th Regt.); disbanded; placed on h.-p. of it, 25th May, 1818; appointed to 92nd, 7th June, 1821; exchanged to h.-p., 7th June, 1821; appointed to 50th, 13th Aug., 1830; exchanged h.-p., unattached, 13th Sept., 1833; Brevet-Major, 22nd July, 1830; died at Edinburgh, 30th May, 1839.
MADDEN, Wyndham Carlyon	18 Feb. 1808	3 May, 1809	..	..	..	Captain 92nd Regt., 10th Feb., 1820; exchanged to h.-p. of 100th, 7th June, 1821; retired 1825; went into holy orders. Served with the 43rd in the Peninsular war; was wounded at Vimiero, Badajoz, and the Nivelle (war medal and five clasps for Vimiero, Ciudad Rodrigo, Badajoz, Nivelle, and Toulouse); served also at New Orleans; died Rector of Burgampton, in Norfolk; died 13th May, 1864, aged 70.
MAGOUGH, John	..	14 May, 1744	..	..	..	Exchanged to Graham's Regt., 22nd June, 1747.
MAGUIRE, Thomas Collings	25 Aug. 1854	10 Aug. 1855	..	..	..	Served in the suppression of the Indian mutiny, from Dec., 1857, to Jan., 1860, including the actions of Sahao, Tola, Burgowra, and surrender of Kirwee (medal); died at sea, 31st March, 1861.
MAHONY, Con.	1 Nov. 1797	..	..	..	..	Out Dec. 11, 1800.
Mair, Alexander	23 Nov. 1773	23 June, 1782	..	..	..	Captain 40th, 10th Aug., 1778; Major 88th, 12th Oct., 1779; h.-p., 25th June, 1783. Accompanied the Regt. to Boston in 1774, and served with the Light Infantry till Oct., 1778; was present at the various actions and active services in which his company was engaged during that period, and was repeatedly and most severely wounded. In Nov., 1788, he embarked at New York for the West Indies, was present at the reduction of St. Lucia, and in the sea action off Grenada, on the 6th July, 1799. He continued to serve in the different Caribbean Islands until his Regt. was ordered home at the peace, when he was placed upon h.-p., though nearly the senior Major in the Army, and having purchased all his commissions. After remaining ten years upon h.-p., he accepted a company of invalids, in 1790, and the command of the corps at Portsmouth. In 1794 he obtained the brevet of Lieutenant-Colonel, and on 21st Aug., 1795, that of Colonel, when he was appointed commander of troops at Hilsea. He subsequently was nominated to the Lieutenant-Governorship of Landguard Fort, whence, at his own request, he was removed to the Deputy-Governorship of Fort George, and appointed Colonel of the 7th R.V.B. He died on the 26th Jan., 1837, aged 81 years.
MAITLAND, Hon. Charles	..	24 Jan. 174⁹⁄₅₀	2 Mar. 1746	..	..	Out in 1751.
MAITLAND, David	..	1 June, 1750	2 Feb. 1757	..	..	From Lieutenant 5th Regt.; present with the Regt., at the siege of Quebec, and the different actions; taken prisoner at Sillery; died 26th Sept., 1764.
MAITLAND, Hon. Richard	..	..	4 Sept. 1754	..	..	2nd Lieutenant, 30th Sept., 1743; Lieutenant, 8th June, 1749; Captain-Lieutenant, 29th Jan., 1752; Lieutenant-Colonel, 22nd Aug., 1760. Served with the 43rd during the siege of Quebec, and the different actions; appointed Deputy-Adjutant-General at Quebec, 30th May, 1764; died Jan., 1771.
MALCOLM, Allan	..	6 Feb. 1777	..	..	..	Ensign 71st, 30th Nov., 1775.
MALLIET, Antony	26 Jan. 174⁹⁄₅₀	..	..	..	..	At formation; out in 1754.
MAPLETOFT, Harold K.	30 June, 1792	..	..	..	..	To Lieutenant 12th Regt.; Captain 107th Regt., 30th April, 1794.

43rd Light Infantry.

Name				Service
MARLAND, John	..	..	..	From Ensign 40th Regt.
MARSH, James	..	..	28 Aug. 1776	Adjutant 46th, 22nd Jan., 1755; Captain 46th, 2nd Feb., 1757; Brevet-Major 46th Regt., 23rd July, 1772; Major, 20th Feb., 1773; commanded the 43rd at siege of Rhode Island; Colonel in Army, 20th Nov., 1782; Colonel 77th Regt., 12th Oct., 1787; Major-General, 12th Oct., 1793; Lieutenant-General, 2nd Jan., 1798; General, 25th Sept., 1803; died 1804.
MATTHEWS, John Elchin	16 April, 1812	22 April, 1813	..	Present at the Nivelle, Nive, Toulouse, and New Orleans; placed on h.-p. of Regt., 25th Dec., 1818; reappointed to the Regt., 29th April, 1819; out July, 1820.
MAW, Thos. Arthur Crank	22 Nov. 1756	..	..	Served at siege of Quebec (wounded), and expedition to West Indies under Monckton; not in List, 1763.
MAY, Charles	..	31 Dec. 1777	..	From Ensign 57th Regt., 27th Nov., 1775; prisoner on parole in England, Jan., 1780; out 1783.
MAYNE, Charles	25 Nov. 1808	13 Dec. 1809	..	From R. M. College. Slightly wounded in Spain. Died 1813.
MEADE, John	5 May, 1829	29 Aug. 1834	11 Sept. 1840	From Lieutenant 7th Fusiliers, 22nd Aug., 1824; served in the suppression of the Canadian revolt, and was one of those who crossed the Portage of the Madawaska; retired 19th June, 1846.
MEARA, Malachi	26 Jan. 1796	..	..	Ensign 92nd, 12th Nov., 1794; out next List.
MELVILLE, Daniel	27 Jan. 1741	..	..	On first formation; not in List, 1750.
MEDHURST, Frederick Edward	..	29 July, 1853	..	From Ensign 51st Regt.; promoted to unattached Company, 16th Jan., 1863; Captain in 28th Regt., 23rd June, 1864. Served with the 51st Regt. throughout the Burmese war of 1852 (medal); on board the East India Company's steam-sloop 'Sesostris' during the naval action and destruction of the enemy's stockades on the Rangoon River; served during the succeeding three days' operations in the vicinity (including the storming of the White House Redoubt) and at the storm and capture of Rangoon; also at the assault and capture of Bassein, 19th May. Employed in the suppression of the Indian mutiny during 1857-9, present at the surrender of Kirwee, and action at Sahao (medal).
MEIN, Nicholas Alexander	..	..	..	Ensign 52nd, 13th May, 1797; to 74th, 18th Jan., 1798; Lieutenant 12th Regt., 17th Feb., 1799; Captain 85th, 4th June, 1801; placed on h.-p.; reappointed, 25th May, 1803; Major 85th, 21st Sept., 1809; present at New Orleans; Brevet-Lieutenant-Colonel, 4th June, 1814; retired 9th Sept., 1819.
MERCER, Monsieur	22 Feb. 1857	..	..	Out in 1763. Served at the siege of Quebec, and in the expedition to West Indies under Monckton.
MEYRICKE, John	4 May, 1809	23 Aug. 1810	..	From the Shropshire Militia. Present at Vittoria, Vera, Nivelle, Nive, and Toulouse. Killed at New Orleans, Jan., 1814.
MICHELL, Christopher	20 Sept. 1793	..	..	Died 30th Dec., 1793, of fever, in West Indies.
MILES, John Marshall	10 Dec. 1812	23 Feb. 1814	..	Was a Volunteer. Placed on h.-p. of Regt., 25th March, 1817 (wounded at Nivelle); died 2nd July, 1848.
MILLER, Taverner Charles	1 May, 1864	6 Feb. 1866	..	From Ensign 59th, 16th May, 1862. Served in the New Zealand war of 1865, including expeditions in the province of Taranaki, destroying many Pas and fortified villages.
MILLER, William	11 Mar. 1768	13 Feb. 1773	19 Dec. 1775	Adjutant, 17th Aug., 1773; Captain by purchase, vice Laurie; Brevet-Major, 19th March, 1783; died 12th Aug., 1789. Served in the American War of Independence.
MILLES, the Hon. Lewis Watson	28 April, 1848	20 June, 1851	10 April, 1855	To Rifle Brigade, 9th Oct., 1855; Major, 20th July, 1858; retired 1861. Served with the 43rd Light Infantry in the Kafir war, 1851-2 (medal). Served in India during the rebellion of 1857-8, and was severely wounded at Cawnpore on the 28th Nov., 1857.

Names.	Ensign.	Lieutenant.	Captain.	Major.	Lieut.-Col.	Remarks.
Millington, George	6 Nov. 1779	..	..	..	..	Resigned 29th Oct., 1784.
Milnes, William	6 June, 1845	25 April, 1848	7 April, 1852	..	..	To h.-p., 10th April, 1857.
Mitford, Percy	27 May, 1853	..	..	..	..	Ensign 51st, 26th Aug., 1853; Lieutenant, 1st Dec., 1854; exchanged to Scots Fusilier Guards, 9th Aug., 1855; retired, 30th Nov.
Molesworth, Robert	10 Dec. 1755	2 Feb. 1757	5 Oct. 1764	..	..	Exchanged to 38th, 28th Nov., 1767; out April, 1771. Served with the 43rd at siege and capture of Quebec; also in the expedition to the West Indies under Monckton.
Molyneux, Charles Berkeley	8 Oct. 1844	..	..	..	..	To Cornet 4th Light Dragoons, 20th June, 1845; Lieutenant, 1st April, 1847; Captain, 15th March, 1850; retired 31st Aug., 1855.
Monck, Charles J. Kelly, *Viscount*	12 Sept. 1811	25 Feb. 1813	..	..	..	Placed on h.-p. of the Regt., 25th Sept., 1816; retired Jan., 1831. Served in the Peninsula from 1813 to end of the war, including the battles of Vittoria, Pyrenees, Nivelle, Nive, and Toulouse (medal with five clasps); present at New Orleans; died 20th April, 1849.
Monck, *Hon.* Richard	2 Mar. 1849	17 Oct. 1851	..	..	..	To Captain Rifle Brigade, 23rd March, 1855; Coldstream Guards; served with 43rd in the Kaffir war, 1853 (medal); Captain and Lieutenant-Colonel, 17th Nov., 1863; Military Secretary to Governor-General of Canada.
Money, Arthur Campbell	17 May, 1861	17 Nov. 1863	..	..	..	Served in the New Zealand war, 1864-5; present at the actions of Maketu and Te Ranga.
Money, William	24 Mar. 1764	26 June, 1770	..	..	..	Ensign, 14th March, 1762; out 1772.
Monins, John	..	24 May, 1765	..	..	..	Lieutenant, 25th Aug., 1762; sold out 15th May, 1770.
Montague, Geo. Wroughton	3 April, 1806	..	..	..	..	Lieutenant 7th Fusiliers, 30th April, 1807; Captain 82nd Regt., 28th June, 1810; Major, 10th Dec, 1818; appointed to 56th Regt., 12th April, 1821; Lieutenant-Colonel, unattached, 19th May, 1825; placed on h.-p.; out 1827.
Montgomery, Alexander	..	..	21 Sept. 1756	..	..	Captain in Army, 17th Aug., 1747. Served at the siege of Quebec, and expedition to West Indies under Monckton; out Feb., 1764.
Montgomery, Archibald	28 Sept. 1743	..	..	..	..	Not in List, 1749.
Montgomery, William	..	..	..	..	29 July, 1799	Ensign in Army, 17th Jan., 1781; in 98th, 25th Dec., 1781; Lieutenant in the Army, 21st Feb., 1784; Lieutenant 4th Regt., 1st Oct., 1794; Captain, 1st Oct., 1794; Major 78th Regt., 15th July, 1795; appointed to 3rd West India Regt., 4th Oct., 1797; Lieutenant-Colonel, 25th July, 1799; died 25th Oct., 1800.
Moore, John	25 Jan. 1740/1	1 Dec. 1743	..	..	..	Not in List, 1749.
Moore, Richard	1 Nov. 1804	..	..	..	..	Appointed to 3rd Regt., Garrison Battalion, 21st March, 1805; Lieutenant in 28th, 13th Nov, 1805; out March, 1808.

43rd Light Infantry.

Name			Notes
MOORE, Sir Lorenzo, C.B., K.C.H.	..	30 Sept. 1791	Placed on h.-p. of 43rd, 30th Dec., 1791; Lieutenant 5th Dragoons, 9th May, 1794; Captain 58th, 4th Sept., 1795; Captain 6th Dragoons, 6th Dec., 1794; Captain 56th, and Captain-Lieutenant, 17th April, 1796; Captain 34th, 26th Jan., 1797; Major 35th, 1st May, 1805; Lieutenant-Colonel 35th, 14th Sept. 1809; Colonel, 12th Aug., 1819; Major-General, 22nd July, 1830; died at Dresden, March, 1837.
MOREL, Charles Carew de	24 Oct. 1845	29 May, 1849 | 23 Nov. 1852	Captain 67th, 20th Sept., 1853; Major, 12th Dec., 1854; to h.-p., 21st Sept., 1855; to Major Depôt Battalion, 1st Oct., 1856; Lieutenant-Colonel, 16th Oct., 1860; to h.-p., 15th Feb, 1862; sold out, Aug., 1862. Served in the Eastern campaign of 1854–5 as A.D.C. to General Estcourt, including the battles of Alma, Balaklava, and Inkerman, and siege of Sebastopol (medal and clasps, Brevet-Major, Knight of the Legion of Honour, and 5th class of the Medjidie); retired Aug., 1862.
MORLAND, John	..	23 Mar. 1782	Ensign 40th, 14th Oct., 1778; placed on h.-p. of Regt., 25th June, 1783; died 1820.
MORLEY, Arthur Geo. Evelyn	..	29 July, 1853	Ensign 51st Regt., 1st Oct., 1850; appointed to unattached Company, 16th April, 1861; Captain, unattached, 16th April, 1861; Captain 9th Regt., 4th Feb, 1862. Served with the 51st Regt., throughout the Burmese war of 1852 (medal); on board the East India Company's frigate 'Ferooz,' during the naval action and destruction of the enemy's stockades on the Rangoon River; served during the India succeeding three days' operation in the vicinity (including the storming of the White House Redoubt), and at the storm and capture of Rangoon; with the 43rd during the India mutiny campaign, including the surrender of Kirwee (medal).
MORLEY, John Evelyn K.	..	24 Feb. 1857	Ensign Rifle Brigade, 14th Mar., 1856. To 15th Hussars, 24th Jan., 1860; retired, 30th Nov., 1860.
MORRIS, Benjamin	..	7 April, 1825	From Lieutenant 25th Regt.; Captain, unattached, 13th May, 1826; appointed to 25th llegt., 19th Sept., 1826; retired 10th Oct., 1863.
MORRIS, William	..	13 April, 1767	2 Sept. 1772	30 May, 1780	Captain-Lieutenant, 30th May, 1780; placed h.-p. of the Regt., 1784. Served with the Regt. in the American war.
MORRIS, Witherington	..	..	30 Jan. 1740	Out in 1756.
MORRISON, William	..	25 Oct. 1804	17 June, 1805	27 Dec. 1810	Expedition to Copenhagen and to New Orleans. Served exchanged to h.-p. of the Regt., 11th Dec., 1817; died 9th July, 1830. Detained prisoner in France for a short time.
MUNBEE, Valentine	..	..	..	10 May, 1798	From Captain Londonderry Regt., 31st Dec, 1794; Captain-Lieutenant 43rd, 10th May, 1796; retired Feb., 1804.
MUNDY, Godfrey Charles	..	..	..	6 Sept. 1831	Ensign 54th, 25th Nov., 1821; appointed to 2nd Foot, 6th Dec., 1821; Lieutenant, 28th Aug., 1823; Captain, 13th May, 1826; served in the suppression of the Canadian revolt, and was one of those who crossed the Portage the Madawaska; Major, unattached, 31st Dec., 1839; Brevet-Lieutenant-Colonel, 28th Nov., 1845; appointed Deputy-Adjutant-General in New South Wales; Adjutant-General, Kilkenny, 1852 to 1854; Brevet-Colonel, 20th June, 1854; appointed Under-Secretary for War, 1854; Major-General, 24th April, 1860; Author of 'Pen and Pencil Sketches in India,' 'Our Antipodes,' &c.; died July, 1860, Lieutenant-Governor of Jersey.
MURCHISON, Robt. P.	..	5 June, 1804	8 Mar. 1809	Ensign 57th Regt., 23rd July, 1803; Adjutant, 4th Dec, 1806. Served in expedition to Copenhagen; present at Vittoria and Vera. Died of wounds at the Nivelle.
MURE, Charles Reginald	..	16 Aug. 1850	29 July, 1853	8 Jan. 1856	Served the Kaffir war of 1851-3 (medal); also in the Crimea as A.D.C. to Major-General Markham from 29th July to Sept. 20th, 1855 (medal and clasp for Sebastopol, 5th class of Medjidie, and Turkish medal); Captain 7th, 8th Jan., 1856; placed h.-p., 10th Nov.; killed at the Gate Pa, 30th April, 1864.
MURPHY, Bernard	..	..	31 Dec. 1807	2 Dec. 1813	Adjutant, 31st Dec., 1807; exchanged to 1st West India Regt., 19th Oct., 1815; to h.-p. 7th West India Regt, 29th Aug., 1816.
MURPHY, William	..	30 Aug. 1810	4 June, 1812	..	Died 1814.

Names.	Ensign.	Lieutenant.	Captain.	Major.	Lieut.-Col.	Remarks.
Murray, John James	26 Feb. 1774	10 Mar. 1777	..	..	..	Resigned 17th Oct, 1778.
Murray, Somerville	25 Feb. 1774	..	..	..	..	
Nairn, James	..	22 Jan. 1747	..	..	..	Out 1750.
Napier, Sir Wm., F.P., K.C.B.	..	..	11 Aug. 1804	14 May, 1812	..	Ensign Royal Irish Artillery, 14th June, 1800; Lieutenant 62nd Regt, 18th April, 1801; placed h.-p. of it, 1802; appointed Cornet in the Blues, 23rd Aug., 1803; appointed 52nd, 24th Dec, 1803; 2nd June, 1804, to a Battalion of the Regt.; Brevet-Major, 30th May, 1811; Brevet-Lieutenant-Colonel, 22nd Nov., 1813; placed h.-p. of the Regt, 17th June, 1819; Colonel, 22nd July, 1830; Major-General, 23rd Nov., 1841; Colonel of 27th Regt, 5th July, 1848; Lieutenant-General, 11th Nov, 1851; General, 17th Oct., 1859. He served at the siege of Copenhagen, and battle of Kioge in 1807; Sir John Moore's campaign of 1808-9; the subsequent Peninsular campaigns from 1809 to the end of the war in 1814, including the combat of the Coa (wounded), battle of Busaco, combats of Pombal, Redinha, Castel Nova (severely wounded at the head of six companies of the 43rd, supporting the 52nd), Foz d'Aronce, battle of Salamanca, passage of the Huebra, combat of Vera, when Soult attempted to relieve St. Sebastian, and again when the allies passed the Bidassoa, battles of the Nivelle, Nive (wounded defending the churchyard of Archanges), and Orthes (gold medal for Salamanca, Nivelle, Nive; silver for Busaco, Fuentes d'Onoro, Orthes). He was Lieutenant-Governor of Jersey; Author of 'The History of the Peninsular War;' died 12th Feb., 1860.
Nason, John	5 Oct. 1808	19 Oct. 1809	..	..	..	Killed at the Coa, near Almeida, 24th July, 1810.
Neale, Richard Henry	20 Mar. 1806	14 Jan. 1808	..	..	..	Appointed to 15th Light Dragoons, 3rd May, 1810; retired 1813; was Curate of Alburton, Hewelsfield, Lidney, Gloucestershire, in 1848. Medal for Vimiero and Corunna; was also with the expedition to Copenhagen.
Nicholl, Spencer P. Talbot	16 Aug. 1861	30 April, 1864	..	..	..	Served in the New Zealand war, 1864-5; thanked by H.R.H. the Commander-in-Chief on account of good service in the action of the Gate Pa (wounded in the head); appointed Inspector of Musketry, 1st May, 1864.
Northall, Edward	..	..	3 Jan. 174⁹⁄₈	..	..	From General Howard's Regt., on first formation; out 23rd July, 1743;
Nott, Charles Sergison	..	29 July, 1853	..	..	..	Ensign 31st, 25th Nov., 1845; to 51st, 17th Sept., 1847. Lieutenant, 9th Jan., 1852; retired 8th Dec., 1854.
Nugent, Charles Edmund	30 July, 1829	24 Oct. 1834	..	..	..	Exchanged to h.-p. unattached, 2nd May, 1835; appointed to 82nd Regt, 23rd Mar., 1837; retired 24th Mar., 1837.
Nugent, Walter E.	27 April, 1756	13 Mar. 1760	..	..	..	Resigned Dec, 1762. Served at siege at Quebec; wounded at the Havannah, 1762.
O'Brien, James Thomas	10 July, 1863	29 July, 1865	..	..	..	Served in the New Zealand war, 1864-5, including the expeditions in the province of Taranaki, destroying many Pas and fortified villages.
O'Bryan, John	30 Jan, 1796	..	..	..	..	From 92nd Regt., never joined; superseded, absent without leave, 26th Aug., 1796.
O'Connell, John	9 Mar. 1809	14 Dec. 1809	..	..	..	Served in the Peninsula; volunteered for the storming party at Ciudad Rodrigo; wounded at Badajoz. Volunteered also for the storming party at St, Sebastian, where he was killed, 31st Aug., 1813.

43rd Light Infantry.

O'CONNELL, Richard	.. ..	12 May, 1812	15 July, 1813	.. ..	.. ..	Exchanged to h.-p. of 71st, 22nd May, 1816; appointed to 65th, 21st Aug., 1828; Captain, 16th July, 1841, 65th Regt. Served with the 43rd in the Peninsula (medal for Badajoz, Salamanca, Vittoria).
O'DONNEL, James	.. ..	30 Mar. 1797	1 July, 1802	.. ..	.. ..	From Volunteer; out 11th June, 1807; superseded 3rd Dec., 1807.
O'FLAHERTY, George	.. ..	16 Dec. 1797	25 June, 1803	29 May, 1805	3 Dec. 1807	Served in the expedition to Copenhagen, at Vimiero and Corunna. Present at the Coa, Busaco, Sabugal (wounded). Appointed to 8th Veteran Battalion, 29th Aug., 1811; Battalion reduced; placed h.-p. of it, 1814; appointed 1st Veteran Battalion, 7th July, 1815; Battalion reduced, 24th May, 1816; retired on f.-p. of 8th Veteran Battalion; died at Bruges, 15th Sept., 1833.
OGILVIE, John	.. ..	.. ..	8 Dec. 1804	.. ..	.. ..	Ensign 16th Jan., 1804, in 26th Regt. Served in expedition to Copenhagen; killed in a duel, 1808.
OGLANDER, Henry, C.B.	.. ..	28 Aug. 1806	8 Sept. 1808	.. ..	.. ..	Captain 47th, 2nd April, 1812; Brevet-Major, 14th Oct., 1813; Major, 27th Oct., 1814, 1st Garrison Battalion; placed h.-p. of it, 1814; appointed to 40th Regt., 30th Mar., 1815; Lieutenant-Colonel, 14th Dec., 1815, Watteville's Regt.; placed h.-p. of the Regt, 25th July, 1816; appointed to 26th Regt., 23rd Oct., 1817; Colonel, 10th Jan., 1837. Expedition to Copenhagen in 1807; Corunna campaign; Peninsula from Aug. 1810, including battles of the Coa, Almeida, Busaco, Redinha, Foz d'Aronce, Sabugal, Fuentes d'Onoro, siege and capture of Ciudad Rodrigo, siege and capture of Badajoz, and battle of Vittoria, siege and capture of San Sebastian, and blockade of Bayonne; lost left arm at the assault of Badajoz, also wounded in the arm, thigh, and body, with first finger of right hand, and wounded in the body, siege of St. Sebastian (gold medal for St. Sebastian); died on board the 'Bohamany,' coast of China, 23rd June, 1840.
O'MEARA, Matthew	.. ..	30 Jan. 1796	21 Dec. 1796	.. ..	.. ..	From 92nd Regt.; retired 1797.
ONSLOW, Arthur Brett	.. ..	29 Jan. 1860	11 Feb. 1862	.. ..	.. ..	From Ensign 98th, 30th Dec., 1859; served in the New Zealand war, 1864-5.
OSBORNE, Herbert Boyles	..	31 May, 1859	.. ..	.. ..	.. ..	Exchanged to Ensign 53rd, 2nd Dec, 1859; Lieutenant, 22nd Dec., 1862.
OXENDEN, William Dixwell	..	6 April, 1831	3 April, 1835	.. ..	.. ..	Served in the suppression of the Canadian revolt, and was one of those who carried the Portage of the Madawaska; appointed to 58th Regt, 26th Jan., 1839; retired 2nd Oct., 1840; died 25th May, 1859.
PAGET, Henry William	.. ..	5 April, 1833	2 May, 1835	.. ..	.. ..	Adjutant 43rd; Ensign 95th, 14th Dec., 1832, to 8th March, 1839; served in the suppression of the Canadian revolt, and was one of those who crossed the Portage of the Madawaska; Lieutenant, unattached, 1st May, 1835; Captain, unattached, 3rd July, 1840; exchanged to 56th Regt., 9th April, 1841; Major, unattached, 3rd April, 1846; was A.D.C. to his uncle, the Marquis of Anglesea, when Master-General of the Ordnance; was Assistant Quartermaster-General at Cork; died at St. Leonards-on-Sea, 11th Jan., 1853.
PAINE, Samuel	.. .. ..	25 Dec. 1762	.. ..	.. ..	.. ..	Out in 1764.
PAKENHAM, Robert Maxwell	..	6 July, 1852	8 Sept. 1854	.. ..	.. ..	From Royal Military College, appointed Adjutant, 9th Oct., 1855; exchanged to 84th, 10th March, 1857; killed in India, 1857.
PARRY, Love Albert	.. ..	13 June, 1787	31 May, 1790	.. ..	.. ..	To Captain 39th, 23rd Oct., 1793; Captain in Army, 19th April, 1793; Major 81st, 27th Feb., 1796; Lieutenant-Colonel 81st, 13th Dec. 1797; out July, 1803.
PATRICK, Robert	.. ..	.. ..	.. ..	16 Nov. 1794	.. ..	Lieutenant in the Army, 17th Aug., 1781; Lieutenant 6th Regt., 10th Sept., 1783; was Captain-Lieutenant; retired 7th Dec., 1797.

NAMES.	ENSIGN.	LIEUTENANT.	CAPTAIN.	MAJOR.	LIEUT.-COL.	REMARKS.
PATRICKSON, Christopher, C.B.	..	..	25 May, 1803	28 Sept. 1809	17 June, 1813	Ensign 31st Regt, 31st Aug., 1793; Lieutenant, 25th March, 1794; appointed to 9th Dragoons, 14th June, 1794; Captain 23rd Light Dragoons, 25th March, 1800; appointed to 40th Regt., 28th Aug., 1801; placed on h.-p. of the Regt., 1802; Brevet-Lieutenant-Colonel, 30th May, 1811; Colonel, 19th July, 1821; retired 1826. Served in Ireland with the 9th Dragoons during the rebellion in 1798; with the 43rd at Copenhagen and in Spain, under Sir John Moore, in 1808–9. Served afterwards in the Peninsula (a great part of the time in command of the Regt.), from Sept., 1809, to the end of that war in 1814 (except during two short intervals, when he was ordered to England to command the 2nd Battalion), including the action of Coa, battle of Busaco, lines of Torres Vedras, actions of Redinha, Foz d'Aronce, Condexia, and Sabugal; battles of Fuentes d'Onoro, Vittoria, and Toulouse; commanded the 43rd at the attack on New Orleans (gold medal for Toulouse, silver for Busaco, Fuentes d'Onoro, and Vittoria). Joined the army in Flanders, on the 16th June, 1815, and was present at the capture of Paris; died 25th Sept., 1856.
PATTENSON, Cooke Tylden ..	19 Feb. 1807	9 Mar. 1809	18 Aug. 1814	..	..	Placed on h.-p. of the Regt., Feb., 1817; exchanged to 95th, 19th June, 1817; placed on h.-p. of the Regt., 25th Dec., 1818 (medal for Ciudad Rodrigo (wounded), Badajoz, Salamanca, Vittoria, Pyrenees, and Toulouse).
PAUL, Walter John	16 Feb. 1841	25 Aug. 1843	..	..	..	Retired 9th Aug., 1850.
PEACHY, James	..	..	2 Feb. 1797	..	..	From Lieutenant 7th, 31st Oct., 1793; Captain 7th, 30th July, 1795; died 1797.
PEARSON, Thomas Alymer ..	10 Sept. 1828	23 Dec. 1831	21 Aug. 1840	..	..	From Ensign 90th. Served in the suppression of the Canadian revolt, and was one of those who crossed the Portage of the Madawaska. Appointed A.D.C. to his father, in command of Northern District, Ireland; retired 31st Dec, 1841.
PEARSON, *Sir* Thos., C.B., K.C.H.	..	..	..	..	16 Nov. 1815	2nd Lieutenant, 2nd Oct., 1796; Lieutenant, 25th April, 1799; Captain, 7th Aug., 1800; Major, 8th Dec, 1804; Brevet-Lieutenant-Colonel, 4th June, 1811; appointed Inspecting Field Officer of Militia in Canada, 28th Feb., 1812; placed on h.-p. of 43rd, Feb., 1817; exchanged to 23rd, 24th July, 1817; Colonel, 19th July, 1821; Major-General, 22nd July, 1830; Lieutenant-General, 23rd Nov., 1841. Served at the Helder in 1799, including the actions of the 27th Aug., 2nd and 6th Oct., with the expedition to the Ferrol in 1800; the Egyptian campaign of 1801, including the storming of the heights of Aboukir (severely wounded in the thigh), and actions of the 13th and 21st March; siege and capture of Copenhagen in 1807; capture of Martinque in 1809; Peninsular campaign during the latter part of 1810 and 1811, including the occupation of Torres Vedras, first siege of Badajoz, battle of Albuera, succeeded to the command of the Fusilier Brigade; action at Fuentes Guinaldo, at which he received a severe wound which shattered the thigh bone. Served afterwards throughout the American war, including the action at Chrystler's Farm (horse shot under him); attack and capture of Oswego, actions at Chippewa and Lundy's Lane (wounded in the arm); siege of Fort Erie, where he was dangerously wounded by a rifle ball in the head in an attack made by the Americans on the British position; this was the last action in Canada, "where no one distinguished himself more than Colonel Pearson," Commanded the Northern District of Ireland; Colonel of 85th, 21st Nov., 1843. Medal and a clasp for the battles of Albuera and Chrystler's Farm; died at Bath, 20th May, 1847.
PEARSON, Thomas Horner ..	28 April, 1863	26 July, 1864	..	..	..	Served in the New Zealand war of 1864-5; and was present at the Gate Pa and Te Ranga, and with the expeditions in the province of Taranaki, destroying many Pas and fortified villages.
PEASE, Charles Clifford ..	29 Dec. 1865	..	..	..	..	
PELLEW, *Hon.* R. Reynolds ..	15 Aug. 1850	27 May, 1853	..	..	..	Ensign 90th Regt., 28th Feb., 1828; exchanged to Rifle Brigade, 24th June, 1853. Served with the 43rd in the Kaffir war of 1851–2 (medal); with the Rifles at the siege of Sebastopol, and was wounded at the attack on the Redan on 8th Sept. (medal and clasps), 5th class of the Medjidie; Brevet-Major, 20th July, 1858; was A.D.C. to General Van Straubenzie; was at the storming of Canton, and capture of Lucknow, where he died of dysentery, 6th Dec, 1858.
PERCIVAL, William	23 May, 1746	..	..	..	..	Not in List for 1754.

43rd Light Infantry.

Name				Notes
PEYTON, John	18 Sept. 1806	3 Oct. 1808	..	Expedition to Copenhagen; cashiered, May, 1809.
PEYTON, Charles Yates ..	29 July, 1862	..	..	From Royal Military College; retired 22nd May, 1863.
PHILLIPS, Robert Newton	..	5 July, 1844	17 Oct. 1851	29 July, 1853	Ensign 53rd, 27th May, 1836; Lieutenant, 2nd Oct., 1840; Captain, 12th Jan., 1844; Lieutenant-Colonel in Army, 28th May, 1853; exchanged to 94th, 21st Feb., 1854; appointed to a Provisional Battalion; Colonel, 28th Nov., 1854; placed h.-p. of Depôt Battalion, 6th Feb., 1863. Served with the 43rd in the Kaffir war, 1851-3 (medal); commanded the 43rd at Berea beyond the Orange River, and in several skirmishes. Was promoted to Lieutenant-Colonel for distinguished service in the field; Major-General, 8th Dec. 1867.
PHILPOT, Bryan	..	23 Sept. 1794	..	..	Ensign 2nd, 15th Feb., 1782; Lieutenant 2nd Regt., 21st July, 1789; Captain, 29th March, 1793; Major 59th, 28th Aug., 1801; Lieutenant-Colonel, 1st Oct., 1803; appointed to 77th Regt, 31st March, 1804; appointed to 65th, 21st Nov., 1806; out May, 1807.
PIJOLAS, Antony ..	..	27 April, 1756	..	From Ensign 17th Regt, 3rd June, 1752; out 1757.
PIGOU, Peter	..	12 May, 1746	19 Mar. 1749	Killed in Nova Scotia, 1758.
PITTS, John	8 Nov. 1804	22 May, 1805	10 Oct. 1811	Served in the Peninsula. To Lieutenant 81st, 10th Sept., 1807; returned to the Regt.; Adjutant, 11th Dec., 1806; exchanged to h.-p. of 94th, 30th March, 1820; died 25th Oct., 1829.
POLLOCK, James ..	10 April, 1806	18 Feb. 1808	..	Resigned, Oct., 1809.
POLLOCK, John	25 Nov. 1813	2 Nov. 1815	..	Present at New Orleans; placed on h.-p. of the Regt., 25th March, 1817; appointed to 5th Foot, 26th Nov., 1818; Captain, 12th Dec., 1822; retired 23rd Sept., 1824.
POLLOCK, Samuel ..	30 May, 1805	21 May, 1806	18 Feb. 1813	Placed on h.-p. of the Regt., 25th March, 1817; appointed to Rifle Brigade, 15th April, 1842; retired same day. Served in the Peninsula from the beginning of the war until severely wounded at Badajoz, including the combat of the Coa, the affairs on Massena's retreat, and Sabugal (medal for Corunna, Busaco, Fuentes d'Onoro, Ciudad Rodrigo, Badajoz); died at Strathallan House, Isle of Man, 26th March, 1865.
PONSONBY, A. E. Valette	10 July, 1846	9 Aug. 1850	..	In the Crimea as A.D.C. to Sir George Brown; and in the expedition to Kertch, attack of 18th June, and as A.D.C. to Sir William Codrington on the 8th Sept., and fall of Sebastopol (medal and clasp, Sardinian and Turkish medals, and 5th class of the Medjidie); to Captain, unattached, 29th July, 1853; Captain 62nd, 20th Jan., 1854; Captain and Lieutenant-Colonel Grenadier Guards, 12th March, 1861; exchanged to 12th, 21st April, 1863.
POWELL, William ..	24 April, 1814	..	..	Exchanged to h.-p. of 27th Regt., 4th March, 1818; retired May, 1832.
PRATT, Lord Charles Robert ..	20 Aug. 1867	..	..	To 52nd Regt.
PRESTON, James ..	23 Jan. 1741	..	..	On formation; not in 1749.
PRICE, Barrington ..	..	3 July, 1806	..	Present at Vimiero and Corunna. Captain 102nd Regt, 3rd Oct., 1811; placed on h.-p. of 50th, 1815.
PRICE, John	15 Aug. 1775	..	..	Out 1781.
PRITCHARD, William ..	..	..	29 Jan. 1741	First formation of Regt., from Captain h.-p.; died Sept., 1745.
PRIESTLEY, George ..	9 Dec. 1831	4 April, 1835	..	Appointed Ensign 84th Regt., from Sergeant-Major of 43rd; was Adjutant; retired 15th Sept., 1835. Served with great credit to himself when in the 43rd. Became a settler in New Brunswick, and Major of Militia. During the Canadian revolt he organised twenty Battalions of the Provincial Militia, and was thanked by the Governor for his services. Is Barrack Master at Fredericton.

NAMES.	ENSIGN.	LIEUTENANT.	CAPTAIN.	MAJOR.	LIEUT.-COL.	REMARKS.
PRIMROSE, *Sir* James Maurice, C.S.I.	6 Jan. 1837	7 May, 1841	11 April, 1848	9 Feb. 1855	20 Mar. 1857	Adjutant, 7th June, 1841; Colonel, 20th March, 1862. Served in the Kaffir war of 1851-3 (medal), and was for some time D.A.Q.M.Gen. of 2nd Division; accompanied the expedition to the Orange River Sovereignty, and was present at the action of the Berea; commanded the Regt. on its march from Bangalore through Central India to Calpee, 1858 (a distance of 1300 miles, during the hottest season of the year), and through the various operations in Bundelcund, and towards the conclusion of the rebellion he commanded one of the seven columns under Brigadier Wheeler, especially ordered to clear a large district infested by numerous bands under rebel Chiefs (medal); is Deputy-Adjutant-General at Madras.
PROBY, *Lord*, M.P.	8 Feb. 1842	19 June, 1846	..	..	..	Appointed to 74th Regt., 11th June, 1847; Captain, 14th March, 1851; exchanged to 14th Regt., 11th Nov., 1853; retired 16th Dec., 1863.
PROCTOR, Henry	5 April, 1781	20 Dec. 1781	30 Nov. 1792	13 Feb. 1795	..	Captain-Lieutenant; appointed to Lieutenant-Colonel, 41st Regt., 9th Oct., 1800; Lieutenant-Colonel in Army, 1st Jan., 1800; Colonel in Army, 25th July, 1810; Major-General, 4th June, 1813. Served on the Staff in North America; Commanded the Army in the action at Rivière au Rasin, 22nd Jan., 1813; died Oct., 1822.
PROCTOR, John	3 Dec. 1803	8 June, 1804	4 May, 1809	..	..	Placed on h.-p. of the Regt., 25th March, 1817; appointed to 30th Regt., 8th June, 1826; Brevet-Major, 22nd July, 1830; Major, 5th Aug., 1842; Brevet-Lieutenant-Colonel, 9th Nov., 1846; retired 30th July, 1847. Was at Copenhagen, 1807 (medal for Vittoria).
PROCTOR, Thomas	..	2 Sept. 1795	20 Feb. 1796	4 June, 1807	..	From h.-p. of 101st Regt.; died at Campo Mayor, 1809.
PROCTOR, Thomas	7 Oct. 1815	..	..	..	..	Placed on h.-p. of 14th Regt., 25th Mar., 1817; retired 1825.
PROCTOR, William	10 Aug. 1796	9 Nov. 1796	..	..	..	Was a Volunteer; placed on h.-p. of 9th Foot, 1802; appointed to New Brunswick Fencibles, 30th June, 1804; afterwards changed to 104th.
PURCELL, Toby	12 May, 1754	9 April, 1756	..	..	..	Died 13th March, 1760. Served during the siege of Quebec and different actions.
PYNE, William	..	..	12 Nov. 1794	..	..	Lieutenant 103rd, disbanded 1783-4; Lieutenant 58th Regt., 25th June, 1789; died April, 1798.
QUARRELL, Richard	14 Feb. 1787	19 Oct. 1787	18 Aug. 1808	..	Sept., 1795; Lieutenant-Colonel, 14th Sept., 1799; out Aug., 1804.	To Captain 10th Regt., 25th Jan., 1791; Major, 26th
RAGLAN, *Lord*, G.C.B.	..	..	..	..	..	Cornet 4th Dragoons, 9th June, 1804; Lieutenant, 30th May, 1805; Captain, 5th May, 1808; Major, 9th June, 1811; Lieutenant-Colonel, 27th April, 1812; exchanged to 1st Guards, 25th July, 1814; Colonel, 28th Aug., 1815; Major-General, 27th May, 1825; Lieutenant-General, 28th June, 1828; Colonel of 53rd, 19th Nov., 1830; General, 20th June, 1854; Colonel of the Blues, 8th May, 1854; Master-General of the Ordnance; Field-Marshal, 5th Nov., 1854; Commander-in-Chief of the Eastern Army, at the Alma, Inkerman, Balaklava, and siege of Sebastopol; died in the Crimea, 29th June, 1855. Was A.D.C. and Military Secretary to the Duke of Wellington during the campaigns in Spain, Portugal, France, and Flanders, and was present at Roleia, Vimiero, Talavera, and Busaco (wounded), the attack and capture of Oporto, the pursuit of Soult, retreat to the Lines of Torres Vedras (occupation of them), pursuit of Massena, battles of Fuentes d'Onoro, 1st siege of Badajoz, 1st siege and capture of Ciudad Rodrigo and Badajoz; battle of Salamanca, capture of Madrid and the Retiro; siege of the Castle of Burgos, the retreat of Burgos; battles of Vittoria, and the Pyrenees and action of Irun, passage of the Bidassoa, Nivelle, Nive, battles of Orthes and Toulouse, and in every affair which took place; also at Quatre Bras and Waterloo (severely wounded, right arm amputated). He received the gold cross and five clasps for Fuentes d'Onoro, Badajoz, Salamanca, Vittoria, Pyrenees, Nivelle, Nive, Orthes and Toulouse; silver war medal and five clasps for Roleia, Vimiero, Talavera, Busaco, and Ciudad Rodrigo. For a memoir of Lord Raglan's services, see *United Service Journal*.

43rd Light Infantry.

REMMINGTON, Gervas	..	..	..	4 Dec. 1767	Captain 36th, 11th April, 1745; Major 36th, 18th Jan., 1757; retired 8th Feb., 1775.
RICH, Evelyn Arthur	4 Jan. 1861	29 July, 1862	..	..	Retired June, 1863.
RICH, Thomas	23 April, 1748	..	..	..	Not in List for 1750.
RICHARDS, Moses	16 May, 1805	10 April, 1806	..	..	Was at Corunna. Died in Spain, 1809.
RICHARDSON, William	..	..	24 April, 1779	..	Joined as Captain-Lieutenant, from Lieutenant 26th Regt., 31st Oct., 1770, to Captain in 2nd Battalion 60th, 30th May, 1780; out in 1784.
RICHARDSON, Wm. Stewart	26 Aug. 1853	9 Feb. 1855	24 Aug. 1858	..	From Ensign in 51st, 23rd Nov., 1852; exchanged to Captain 46th, 9th Nov., 1859.
RIDOUT, George	22 Aug. 1805	2 July, 1806	..	..	Served in the Peninsula, at Vimiero, Corunna, the Coa, Sabugal, Busaco, Fuentes d'Onoro, Ciudad Rodrigo, Badajoz (wounded severely), Salamanca (wounded); died 23rd Nov., 1812, of wounds received at the affair on the Huebra, on the retreat from Burgos.
RIVERS, James	29 June, 1775	29 Feb. 1776	..	..	To Captain 60th Regt., 10th Oct., 1778; 3rd Battalion reduced.
RIVINGTON, John	7 Nov. 1782	..	..	..	Placed h.-p., 25th May, 1786.
ROBERTS, David	..	11 Aug. 1778	..	..	From Ensign 38th, 24th Nov., 1775; Captain 57th, 31st Dec., 1781; out 29th June, 1785.
ROBERTSON, Alexander	..	25 Dec. 1770	..	..	From Lieutenant h.-p. late 108th Regt.; Lieutenant in Army, 1st Nov., 1761; Captain-Lieutenant 35th Regt., 6th Feb., 1777; Assistant Quartermaster-General in North America during the War of Independence; Captain in Army 6th Feb., 1777; in 15th Regt., 3rd Mar., 1779; out May, 1785.
ROBERTSON, James	16 Sept. 1761	14 Sept. 1763	..	14 Sept. 1797	Exchanged to h.-p., Nov., 1766.
ROBINS, William	..	..	12 May, 1794	..	From Lieutenant 60th, 5th Dec., 1787; died April, 1799.
ROBINSON, Edward	19 Oct. 1787	..	..	..	Promoted to a Lieutenancy in an Ind. Com., 10th May, 1791.
ROBINSON, Hugh	14 Dec. 1849	6 July, 1852	7 Nov. 1856	..	Exchanged to 15th Regt., 11th Jan., 1859. Served in the Kaffir war, 1851-3 (medal); retired 20th Dec., 1859.
ROBINSON, John Neville	7 Nov. 1811	18 Mar. 1813	..	..	Died in England, Mar., 1818.
ROCHE, Winthrope C.	23 Nov. 1775	17 Oct. 1778	28 April, 1787	..	Retired 29th April, 1792. Served in the War of Independence; wounded at defence of Rhode Island.
ROCKE, H. B. H.	..	..	1 May, 1855	..	Ensign 10th, 10th Dec., 1847; to 78th, 23rd May, 1848; Lieutenant, 26th March, 1850; Captain 96th, 17th, Aug., 1852; to Captain 1st Royals 9th April, 1861; retired 21st Nov., 1862.
ROGERS, Thomas	17 Oct. 1799	..	..	..	Cornet 26th Dragoons, 23rd Jan., 1800; to Ensign 40th, July, 1802; h.-p. of 40th, Feb., 1802.
ROWAN, Frederick Charles	5 May, 1863	..	..	..	From Ensign 59th Regt., 5th May, 1863; retired July 10th, 1866.

Names.	Ensign.	Lieutenant.	Captain.	Major.	Lieut.-Col.	Remarks.
Russell, Charles	25 April, 1765	..	..	..	..	Ensign 1st Feb, 1765; out in 1767.
Rylance, Thomas	6 Feb. 1805	10 Dec. 1805	14 May, 1812	..	..	Served in the expedition to Copenhagen, and in the Peninsula, at the Coa and Busaco, until severely wounded at Sabugal; lost at sea on passage from Gibraltar to England, Dec., 1823.
Salmon, Charles	..	..	..	..	..	Ensign 53rd, 28th Oct., 1858.
Sanders, Frederick Parris	19 Feb. 1828	16 July, 1830	31 Dec. 1839	..	..	Served at Gibraltar and in N. America; retired 11th Sept., 1840; Adjutant Radnor Militia, Feb. 3rd, 1846.
Sandford, Henry Ayshford	7 Aug. 1840	5 Aug. 1842	9 Aug. 1850	..	..	Retired 28th Feb., 1851.
Sansom, William	..	28 Jan. 1749	..	..	..	Not in 1749.
Sargeant, Samuel Tomyns	..	29 July 1853	18 May, 1849	..	..	Ensign 51st, 18th May, 1849; Lieutenant, 9th July, 1852; appointed Instructor of Musketry, 13th Oct., 1858, to 10th June, 1860. Served with the 51st Regt. throughout the Burmese war of 1852 (medal); on board the East India Company's steam frigate 'Ferooz' during the naval action and destruction of the enemy's stockades on the Rangoon River; during the succeeding three days' operations in the vicinity, and at the storm and capture of Rangoon; retired 18th April, 1865.
Satterthwaite, William	..	..	5 Sept. 1799	..	..	Lieutenant 49th Regt., 29th June, 1797; died July, 1802.
Scaffe, John	..	9 July, 1802	30 May, 1805	..	..	Ensign 9th, 1799; Lieutenant in 9th, 14th Feb, 1800; retired Dec., 1807.
Scotland, Thomas	..	31 Dec. 1781	..	..	..	From Ensign 40th, 16th Sept., 1780; not in List for 1783.
Sergesson, Francis	4 July, 1794	23 Dec. 1795	..	Oct., 1800; placed h.-p. of Regt., 1802; Lieutenant-Colonel, 1808; out in 1813.		Captain 62nd Regt., 13th July, 1797; Major 62nd, 13th
Seymour, Albert Charles	26 June, 1867	..	..	..	..	
Seymour, Frederick	..	..	28 Mar. 1834	..	..	Cornet 7th Hussars, 28th Sept., 1815; Lieutenant 25th Light Dragoons, 14th May, 1818; exchanged to 7th Hussars, 16th July, 1818; Captain 41st, 9th Aug, 1821; exchanged to h.-p. of 15th Hussars, 3rd Jan., 1822; appointed to 65th, 1824; exchanged to h.-p. of 5th Dragoon Guards, 15th Sept., 1825; retired 8th April, 1834; appointed Major Antrim Militia, 27th Dec, 1845.
Sharpe, William	2 June, 1814	..	..	..	..	Placed h.-p. of 1st Veteran Battalion, 7th June, 1821.
Shaw, Abraham	1 Dec. 1804	14 Aug. 1805	..	..	..	Appointed to 52nd, 20th Nov., 1806; Captain West India Regt., 13th May, 1813; placed h.-p. of 5th West India Regt., 2nd July, 1818; died 1830.
Shaw, Richard James	25 Feb. 1813	16 Mar. 1815	..	..	..	Present at New Orleans; placed h.-p. of the Regt, 25th Mar., 1817; not in List of 1825.
Shaw, Robert	20 June, 1753	21 Sept. 1756	13 Feb. 1764	1772. Siege of Quebec and different actions, also in the expedition to the West Indies under Monckton, and siege of Havannah.		Captain-Lieutenant 43rd, 15th Sept., 1763; out May,
Shaw, William	9 Nov. 1779	..	..	..	..	Promoted to Lieutenant 82nd Regt., 5th May, 1782; h.-p., as the Regt, was disbanded, 1783; Lieutenant 19th, 8th July, 1794; out Sept., 1795.

43rd Light Infantry.

SHELBROOKE, Henry Neville E.	18 April, 1865	..	..	..
SHERLOCK, William	10 Mar. 1777	15 Sept. 1779	..	Retired 28th Feb, 1784. Was a prisoner in America.
SHERRAN, William	..	6 Aug. 1803	8 Sept. 1808	Ensign 9th Foot, 22nd Aug, 1799; Lieut., 10th July, 1801; placed h.-p. of 43rd, 25th Sept., 1816; present at Copenhagen (medal for Ciudad Rodrigo, Badajoz, Salamanca); present at New Orleans; died at Folkestone, 13th Oct., 1847.
SIDNEY, Philip	28 June, 1810	..	..	Died in Portugal, 1812.
SIMMES, John	29 Jan. 174¾	..	..	Out in 1789.
SIMPSON, Robert, K.H. ..	..	9 June, 1804	17 Aug, 1809	Ensign 81st, 8th Dec, 1803; appointed to 6th Veteran Battalion, 24th Feb., 1820; exchanged h.-p. of 18th Foot, 11th Jan., 1821; Brevet-Major, 8th Jan., 1815. Joined the 43rd while under the instruction of Sir J. Moore, his relative and patron. He served in the expedition to Copenhagen, and subsequently in the Corunna retreat, and through part of the Peninsular war; he was present at Vittoria, the affairs at Archanges and Toulouse. At the attack on New Orleans, leading the storming party against the principal redoubt of the enemy's position, was thrown into the trenches by a round shot, causing a severe wound, which resulted in the amputation of his left leg and thigh, and rendered him unfit for further active duties; retired with the rank of Major, but afterwards received that of Lieutenant-Colonel, with the Hanoverian Guelphic Order. He continued as Town Major for Hull for nearly twenty years, and died there on the 12th April, 1844, in the 61st year of his age, greatly regretted; at the funeral "nearly all the shops were wholly or partially closed."
SINGLETON, William ..	..	..	29 Jan. 1741	On first formation, from Captain h.-p.; out Feb. 24th, 1843-4.
SKENE, Andrew Philip ..	15 April, 1774	..	..	Lieutenant, 30th Oct., 1762; Captain by Brevet, 19th Dragoons, 31st July, 1788; out 1792; was for some time Brigade-Major, and served in the American war.
SKEY, Roughey.. ..	..	2 May, 1751	..	2nd Lieutenant, 11th June, 1746; Lieutenant-Colonel 49th, 9th Mar., 1761; out Nov., 1769. Served during the siege of Quebec, and expedition to West Indies under Monckton.
SKIPP, Geo. Wm. Shaw ..	4 April, 1805	17 Dec. 1805	..	From 117th Regt.; cashiered 1797.
SKIPTON, John	23 Dec. 1795	20 Feb. 1796	..	
SKIPWITH, Henry ..	24 Oct. 1834	25 Jan. 1839	5 Aug. 1842	Was one of those who crossed the Portage of the Madawaska; Colonel, 28th Nov., 1854. Commanded the Regt. in the Kaffir war of 1851-3 (medal); retired 7th Nov., 1856.
		28 Feb. 1851	17 Oct. 1851	
SLADE, Hercules Henry ..	17 Mar. 1815	..	..	Placed h.-p. of the Regt, Mar., 1817; exchanged to f-p. of it, 23rd Oct., 1817; placed h.-p. of it, 25th Oct., 1821; retired 1831.
SMITH, Fredk. Augustus, V.C.	..	..	9 April,1861	Ensign 1st Foot, 1st Jan., 1849; Lieutenant, 30th April, 1852; Captain, 30th March, 1855; Brevet-Major, 21st March, 1865. Served with the Royals in the Eastern campaign of 1854, and up to 2nd July, 1855, including the battles of Alma and Inkerman, and siege of Sebastopol (medal and three clasps, and Turkish medal). Served with the 43rd in the New Zealand war in 1864, and was present in the action of Maketu and assault of Te Ranga (wounded), mentioned in despatches; Victoria cross and Brevet of Major.
SMITH, James Galloway ..	22 Aug. 1816	..	..	Placed h.-p. of Regt., 25th Mar., 1817; retired Oct., 1825.
SMITH, James Webber, C.B.	11 July, 1826	..	..	Was with the expedition to Portugal in 1826-7; to h.-p., unattached, 20th Sept., 1828; appointed to 48th, 21st May, 1829; Lieutenant, 25th Dec., 1835; Captain, 7th Sept, 1838; Major, 11th Dec, 1849; Lieutenant-Colonel 95th, 24th Dec., 1852. Served in the campaign of April, 1834, against the Rajah of Coorg. Severely wounded at the Alma, when in command of the 95th; Colonel, 28th Nov., 1854; Major-General, 20th April, 1866.

Names.	Ensign.	Lieutenant.	Captain.	Major.	Lieut.-Col.	Remarks.
Smith, John Spencer	..	3 April, 1801	..	..	..	From h.-p. of the 8th Regt., 7th July, 1790; Lieutenant 1st Foot Guards, 18th Jan., 1792; placed h.-p. of 85th, 1803. Not in List for 1829.
Sorell, William	..	..	..	11 Aug, 1804	..	Ensign, 18th Aug., 1790, 31st Regt.; Lieutenant, 31st Aug., 1793; Captain, 1st Sept., 1795; appointed to 4th Foot, 14th Aug., 1800; appointed to 18th Foot, 24th May, 1803; Brevet-Lieutenant-Colonel, 17th April, 1807; appointed to 4th Garrison Battalion, 28th May, 1807; placed h.-p. of Homperch's Mounted Riflemen, 1808; appointed 46th Regt., 12th Nov., 1812; retired 1813. Served in the West Indies with the 2nd Grenadier Battalion in 1793; and in that, and subsequent years, served in the Army under Sir Ralph Abercrombie, at the capture of Martinique, Guadaloupe, and St. Lucia; the siege of Fort Bourbon, night attack on the Vigie, and assault of Morne Fortunée, where he was severely wounded. In 1797 he was A.D.C. to Lieutenant-General Sir James Pulteney; served the expedition to North Holland in 1799; and was present at the action of the 27th Aug., on the landing near the Helder; as also of those of the 10th Sept., 2nd and 6th Oct. of the same year. As military secretary he accompanied the Army to Ferrol and the coast of Spain in 1800. Returned to England and continued to serve with the Army on the south coast until promoted in the 43rd; the 2nd Battalion of which he commanded during the organisation and training of the Light Brigade, under Sir John Moore. On the 17th April, 1807, he was promoted to Lieutenant-Colonel, and appointed Deputy Adjutant-General at the Cape of Good Hope. In 1816 proceeded to Van Diemen's Land as governor, and during the period of eight years, in which he conducted the affairs of that rising Colony, he secured the full approbation of the Government at home. The following extracts from Mr. Montgomery Martin's work, 'Van Diemen's Land, Moral, Physical, and Political,' will shew how highly his character was appreciated in his public capacity by the colonists themselves:— "Courteous and affable, he won 'golden opinions' from all sorts of people; secured the universal affection and esteem; whilst his readiness to correct abuse or error—which his clear and comprehensive mind easily traced to its source—rendered his popularity as unbounded as it was merited. Prior to his embarkation for England, an address expressive of the most affectionate attachment, and recapitulating the numerous benefits he had secured for the land he had for several years ruled, was presented, to which a suitable and earnest reply was returned. Each colonist seemed as if he were losing a cherished personal friend. The people followed him *en masse* to the shore, all eager to manifest their regard." Died 4th June, 1848.
Spencer, *Hon. Sir Augustus Almeric*, K.C.B.	8 April, 1825	5 July, 1827	6 April, 1831	..	..	Served in the expedition to Portugal, 1826-7. Promoted to a Majority in the 44th Regt., 21st July, 1843; Lieutenant-Colonel, 17th May, 1845; Colonel, 20th June, 1854; Major-General, 13th Feb., 1860. Served in the Eastern campaign of 1854-5, and commanded the 44th Regt. in the battles of Alma and Inkerman, siege of Sebastopol, and attack and occupation of the Cemetery on the 18th June (wounded). Appointed Brigadier-General, and commanded the 1st Brigade, 4th Division, in support in the right attack on the assault of the Redan, and fall of Sebastopol on 8th Sept., and subsequently commanded the British land forces in the expedition to Kinburn, resulting in the capture of those forts and the garrison of 1200 men (medal and clasps, C.B., Officer of the Legion of Honour, Sardinian and Turkish medals, and 3rd class of the Medjidie); commanded Mysore Division in East Indies, 1860-5; appointed to command the Western district, 1st April, 1866; Colonel of the 96th, 28th Oct., 1866.
Spencer, Henry	17 Oct. 1787	30 April, 1792	..	..	..	Died in West Indies, 1794.
Spendelove, Roger	..	14 May, 1744	9 April, 1756	8 Feb. 1775	..	Cornet or Ensign, 4th Oct., 1740; Captain-Lieutenant, 4th Sept., 1754; appointed to the Regt. on its formation. Served with the Regt. during the siege of Quebec and the different actions; twice wounded in West Indies, 1762; was present at Lexington; died from wounds received at the battle of Bunker's Hill.
Splatt, Hawtrey Collins	30 April, 1864	21 Aug. 1867	..	..	..	From Ensign 14th Foot, 22nd Sept., 1862. Served in the New Zealand war, 1863-5, and was present in the action at Koheroa.
Spread, William	9 April, 1756	25 Feb. 1757	..	..	..	Served with the Regt. at the siege of Quebec and different actions; out in 1763.
Stanton, Samuel	1 Oct. 1795	26 Jan. 1796	..	..	..	From Durham Militia; retired 16th Dec., 1797.
Stanton, Samuel	..	21 Nov. 1766	..	..	..	From h.-p.; 2nd Lieutenant, 24th Dec., 1760; resigned March, 1768.

43rd Light Infantry.

STAPLETON, Francis George	30 Nov. 1849	12, Mar. 1852	10 Aug. 1855	Ensign 32nd Regt., 30th Nov., 1829; appointed to Grenadier Guards, 9th Oct., 1855; A.D.C. to Earl of Mulgrave at Halifax; present with the 43rd in the Kaffir war of 1851-3; battle of Berea, mentioned in despatches (medal); exchanged to 33rd Regt, 22nd April, 1862; retired 9th March, 1866.
STEEL, Alexander	14 Dec. 1809	7 Nov. 1811	..	Adjutant, 3rd Aug., 1815. To 29th, 3rd Jan., 1822; placed on h.-p. of 29th Regt., 20th June, 1822; retired 1829; appointed Barrack Master at Belfast, where he died, Jan., 1830. Served in the Peninsula in the 43rd, at Ciudad Rodrigo, on the storming party at Badajoz, Salamanca, Vittoria, Heights of Vera, Nivelle. "The first man into the Rocks at La Petite la Rhune" (wounded). Severely wounded before Bayonne, 23rd Nov., 1813; one of the storming party of the Crescent Battery at New Orleans.
STEEL, Lawrence	..	21 Nov. 1811	21 April, 1813	Present at Vimiero and Corunna, at Salamanca, Vittoria, Nivelle, Nive, and Toulouse; also at New Orleans. Adjutant from Sergeant-Major. Exchanged to h.-p. of 7th Fusiliers, 15th Jan., 1818; died 16th Jan., 1835.
STEGGALL, William Charles	..	..	25 Dec. 1813	From East Suffolk Militia; placed on h.-p. of the Regt., 25th Aug., 1814; died 1851.
STEPHENSON, John	26 May, 1808	25 May, 1809	..	Wounded at the Coa; appointed to 6th Dragoon Guards, 29th Feb, 1812; Captain, 27th July, 1815; Major, 29th Jan., 1824; retired 14th April, 1837; died at Twickenham, 27th July, 1850 (medal for Vimiero and Corunna).
STERLING, John	..	..	3 Jan. 174$\frac{0}{1}$	On formation of the Regt.; resigned May, 1746
STEVENS, William	..	13 Aug. 1804	..	Out 1806.
STEWART, James	..	..	4 Dec. 1767	Captain in Army, 19th Oct., 1761; Captain 28th Regt., 13th Feb., 1765; exchanged to 8th Dragoons, 28th March, 1770; Major 8th Dragoons, 6th Nov., 1772; Lieutenant-Colonel 5th Dragoons, 7th Jan., 1778; out Feb., 1798.
STEWART, William	..	..	4 May, 1770	Lieutenant, 11th April, 1762; Lieutenant 46th, 21st June, 1765; exchanged with Jas. Stewart, 4th May, 1770; out Dec., 1770.
STOKES, John	..	8 May, 1798	..	Ensign 2nd West India Regt., 3rd July, 1797; exchanged to 67th, 14th Aug., 1798.
STREFTEL, W. C.	..	25 Feb. 1757	..	From Lieutenant East Suffolk Militia.
STRODE, Thomas Lear	..	1 Dec. 1804	25 Dec. 1807	From Ensign 96th. Served in the expedition to Copenhagen and Walcheren, and in the Peninsula, present at Vimiero, Corunna, and Ciudad Rodrigo; retired 25th June, 1812.
STUART, Hon. Charles W., K.B.	..	..	..	8 Oct. 1775 | From Captain 35th Regt., 12th March, 1773; Lieutenant-Colonel 26th Regt., 26th Oct., 1777; Colonel, 20th Nov., 1782; Major-General, 12th Oct., 1793; Lieutenant-General, 1st Jan., 1798; appointed Colonel of 26th, 25th March, 1795.
STUART, John Patrick	..	..	7 July, 1854	1840; to h.-p. the same day; Captain, 4th March, 1853; to h.-p, 10th April, 1855; appointed Staff Officer of Pensioners at Inverness, 1st Jan., 1855; Brevet-Major, 10th Feb, 1865. | Ensign 21st, 30th Dec, 1838; Lieutenant, 3rd Oct.
STUART, Richard	..	..	..	5 Nov. 1800 | Ensign in 51st, 6th Dec, 1751; Lieutenant 51st, 23rd Dec., 1778; Captain, 29th Oct., 1793; Brevet-Major, 12th Sept., 1794; Brevet-Lieutenant-Colonel, 30th Nov., 1796; Major 72nd Regt., 11th Oct., 1798; Colonel, 25th Sept., 1803; died in Lisbon, 1810, in consequence of a fall from a balcony.

NAMES.	ENSIGN.	LIEUTENANT.	CAPTAIN.	MAJOR.	LIEUT.-COL.	REMARKS.
SWINBURN, *Sir John, Bart.*	28 Aug. 1804	16 May, 1805	15 Aug. 1810	..	..	Exchanged to h.-p. 73rd, 1st Oct., 1818; appointed to 32nd, 8th June, 1826; Brevet-Major, 22nd July, 1830; Brevet-Lieutenant-Colonel, unattached, 9th Nov., 1846; Colonel, 20th June, 1854; served with the 43rd at the siege of Copenhagen in 1807; the campaign of 1808 in Portugal; wounded in the head at the retreat to Vigo; subsequently, campaign in the Peninsula until 1812, including the action at the Coa, battle of Fuentes d'Onoro, action of Sabugal, battle of Busaco (wounded in the hip); joined the army at Toulouse (medal for Busaco, Fuentes d'Onoro); present at New Orleans; present at the capture of Paris; retired 25th June, 1812.
SYNGE, Francis Hutchinson	..	7 Sept. 1841	9 June, 1846	17 Oct. 1851	24 July, 1857	1 May, 1864	Served as Brigade-Major with the Osmanli Irregular Cavalry in Asia Minor, and marched with them across the Balkans to Shumla; with the 43rd in Bundelcund, during the Indian mutiny; commanded three companies in the action of Girwasa, and four companies in the actions of Oudpore and Doolypore (three times mentioned in despatches). medal. Served in the New Zealand war in 1864-5, and commanded the line of skirmishers in the action of Te Ranga (horse shot in two places), mentioned in despatches.
TAFFE, John	19 July, 1769	..	..	..	..	Out Aug., 1773.
TAGGART, Charles	19 June, 1805	22 May, 1806	..	..	..	Present at the Coa; retreat to and occupation of the lines of Torres Vedras; subsequent advance in pursuit of Massena, and actions of Pombal and Redinha; Sabugal, Fuentes d'Onoro, Busaco, and Ciudad Rodrigo; killed at Badajoz, April, 1812.
TAIT, John	17 Jan. 1787	..	..	..	..	Out in next List, unless the same person spelt with a final e; Ensign in 1767.
TALBOT, George	8 April, 1826	9 Sept. 1828	3 April, 1835	29 July, 1853	7 Nov. 1856	Ensign 33rd, 2nd Feb, 1826. Served at Gibraltar; and with the expedition to Portugal in 1808; A.D.C. to Governor-General of Canada, 1842; at the death of Sir C. Bagot was appointed A.D.C. to Sir Richard Jackson, afterwards his military secretary, and continued in that office with his successor, Lord Cathcart; on his departure from Canada, again resumed the office of A.D.C. to Sir B. D'Urban; at his death, reassumed the military secretaryship to the present General Sir W. Rowan. In June, 1851, proceeded to Madras as military secretary to Sir Richard Armstrong, Commander-in-Chief, and remained with him as such during his command; after which appointed military secretary to his successor, General Stavely, continued such till his death, then with his successor, General Sewell; after which rejoined and commanded the 43rd Regt., until appointed Deputy Major-General of Her Majesty's forces Madras, which he retained until the early part of the year 1861; Brevet-Major, 9th Nov., 1846; Brevet-Lieut.-Colonel, 20th June, 1854; Colonel, 18th Feb., 1858; retired 11th Feb., 1862.
TALBOT, Henry Charles	5 Sept. 1856	24 Aug. 1858	18 April, 1865	..	..	Served in the campaigns in Central India, 1858-9, with the Saugor field force (medal), including the actions of Sahao, Girwasa, Doolypore, Purrah, and Puttrai; also in the New Zealand war in 1864-5; and was present in the actions of Maketu and Te Ranga; retired 21st Aug., 1867.
TALBOT, James	19 April, 1742	4 Jan. 1749	2 Feb. 1757	..	..	Died April, 1762; present with the Regt. in Nova Scotia, siege of Quebec, and the different actions.
TAYLOR, Charles	4 April, 1782	..	..	..	..	Resigned 19th March, 1784.
TEMPLETOWN, Geo. Frederick, *Viscount*, C.B.	24 April, 1823	29 Oct. 1825	..	..	..	Exchanged to 34th, 24th Nov., 1825; Captain, unattached, 12th Dec., 1826; appointed to 60th Regt., 13th Feb., 1827; exchanged to 62nd, 8th June, 1830; Major in same, 16th June, 1837; Lieutenant-Colonel, 16th April, 1841; exchanged to Coldstream Guards, 7th Jan., 1842; Colonel, 11th Nov., 1851; Major-General, 26th Oct., 1858; Lieutenant-General, 9th March, 1865; Colonel-Commandant of 60th Rifles, 24th Oct., 1862. Served with 1st Battalion of Coldstream Guards throughout the Eastern campaign of 1854, including the battles of the Alma, Balaklava, and Inkerman (wounded and horse killed), and siege of Sebastopol (medal and clasps, C.B., Officer of the Legion of Honour, 3rd class of the Medjidie, and Turkish medal).

43rd Light Infantry.

REY, *Hon.* Charles	..	..	18 Aug. 1825	From Captain 17th, 16th June, 1825. Served in the expedition to Portugal in 1826-7; Major, unattached, 19th Feb, 1828; appointed to 60th, 23rd April, 1829; Lieutenant-Colonel, unattached, 12th July, 1831; exchanged to 71st, 30th Aug., 1833; commanded the 71st during the Canadian revolt in 1837-8; on h.-p., unattached, 8th April, 1842; Colonel, 9th Nov., 1846; Major-General, 20th June, 1854; appointed Colonel 3rd Foot, 4th May, 1860; Lieutenant-General, 10th March, 1861; Colonel 71st, 6th July, 1863. Is Equerry to the Queen.
GREY, *Hon.* Harry Cavendish	5 April, 1831	..	..	Ensign 90th, 9th Nov., 1830; Lieutenant, unattached, 5th April, 1833; exchanged to 51st, 12th April, 1833; Captain, unattached, 25th Dec, 1835; exchanged to 52nd, 5th Feb., 1836; retired 12th April, 1844; was A.D.C. to the Lord-Lieutenant of Ireland, and to Viscount Falkland, Governor of Nova Scotia.
GRIEVE, G.	16 Mar. 1815	..	..	From Ensign 16th Regt.
GRINDLAY, William	..	..	..	To 17th Regt, 20th March, 1823; placed on h.-p. same day; retired Oct., 1823.
GROVES, Thomas	..	..	..	Lieutenant in 48th, 13th April, 1859.
GRUBBE, Thomas Hunt	25 Mar. 1811	15 Oct. 1812	..	Served in the Peninsula; present at New Orleans; placed on h.-p., 12th July, 1821; Captain, 8th April, 1826; to 9th Regt., 12th March, 1829; to h.-P., 18th Nov., 1831; died 1843.
GUBBINS, William	22 Feb. 1765	28 Jan. 1771	..	Resigned 16th Sept., 1776.
GULLIMAN, George Grieve	..	10 Feb. 1796	..	From 16th Regt.; out in April, 1801.
GUNNING, John	..	..	30 Sept. 1768	From 49th; Deputy Adjutant-General in North Britain; Lieutenant-Colonel, 23rd Jan., 1775; Lieutenant-Colonel 82nd Foot, Dec., 1777; Colonel, 15th June, 1781; Major-General, 28th Sept., 1787; Colonel of 65th, 28th Jan., 1788; died Oct., 1797.
HALFORD, Henry	5 Mar. 1818	..	..	To Lieutenant 33rd Regt, 20th Sept., 1821; h.-p., 8th Aug., 1822; retired June, 1833.
HALLYBURTON, James	..	..	29 Jan. 1741	On first formation, from Captain in Putney's Regt.; out 4th Oct., 1743.
HAMMICK, St. Vincent Alex.	12 Mar. 1861	29 May, 1863	..	Served in the New Zealand war, 1864-5; mentioned in despatch as having "performed his duty as Acting-Adjutant with great coolness and courage under a heavy fire," in the action at Te Ranga; Adjutant, 29th July, 1865.
HAMILTON, Robt. Thos. Francis	..	..	11 May, 1861	From Captain 97th Regt. Served with the 97th Regt. in Bengal in suppressing the mutiny in 1857-8, and was present in the actions of Nusrutpore (as Orderly Officer to Colonel Ingram, and mentioned in despatches), Chanda, Ummeerpore, and Sultanpore, siege and capture of Lucknow, and storming of the Kaisa Bagh; operations in Bundelkund in 1859, including the pursuit to, night attack and surprise of the rebels on the Kalee Nuddee (medal and clasp). Killed in New Zealand, 30th April, 1865.
HAMILTON, Hans	22 Jan. 1749	21 Sept. 1745	27 April, 1756	Out in 1757.
HAMILTON, Henry	30 Sept. 1790	15 May, 1793	27 Dec. 1797	Retired 17th April, 1801.
HANDS, Benjamin	27 Oct. 1784	..	..	Resigned 20th March, 1787.
HARPER, William	30 Jan. 1796	..	..	From Lieutenant in Lieutenant-Colonel Pringle's Regt.; retired 2nd Sept., 1795.
HARRIS, *Hon.* Arthur Ernest	14 April, 1854	28 Mar. 1855	23 July, 1861	From 55th. Served throughout the Indian mutiny campaign of 1857-8, as A.D.C. to Brigadier McDuff. Served in the New Zealand war in 1864-5, and was present at Maketu and Te Ranga (mentioned in despatch); and with the expeditions in the province of Taranaki, and in command of outposts, destroying many Pas and fortified villages.

NAMES.	ENSIGN.	LIEUTENANT.	CAPTAIN.	MAJOR.	LIEUT.-COL.	REMARKS.
HARRIS, John	13 Feb. 1764	11 Mar. 1768	..	..	..	Exchanged to 49th Regt, 19th Dec., 1768; out 1772.
HARRIS, Jonah	16 Dec. 1813	11 Jan. 1816	29 June, 1830	..	..	Served in the Peninsula and the expedition to Portugal, 1826-7; from Sergeant-Major; retired 6th April, 1831.
HARRIS, Thomas	11 May 1805	..	..	..	..	To h.-p. 1806.
HARRISON, George Foster	30 Jan. 1796	Jan., 1804; Captain 39th, 25th Feb, 1804; exchanged to 11th Veteran Battalion, 18th April, 1811; out 1836.				To Lieutenant in 44th, 20th Feb, 1800; Captain, 20th
*HARVEST, H.	22 Dec. 1804	9 Dec. 1805	..	..	..	Expedition to Copenhagen; wounded at the Coa; present at Ciudad Rodrigo. Killed at Badajoz, where he led the forlorn hope, 5th April, 1812.
HATCHELL, Christopher Hore	6 July, 1855	5 Sept. 1856	30 April, 1864	..	..	Served in the Indian mutiny campaign in 1857-8; including the action at Dooleypore and Purrah (medal); also in the New Zealand war of 1864-5, and was present at the Gate Pa and Te Ranga.
HATFIELD, John	2 Feb. 1757	7 Mar. 1762	25 Jan. 1771			Was a Midshipman in the Royal Navy, 1755; Captain-Lieutenant 25th Jan., 1771; Brevet-Major, 19th March, 1783; appointed Captain of Ind. Co. at Plymouth, 13th June, 1787; Lieutenant-Colonel, 1st March, 1794. Served at the reduction and defence of Quebec, under Wolfe and Murray; capitulation of Montreal; at Martinique, under Monckton; with the Light Infantry at the Grenadas, St. Vincent, and St. Lucia; taking of the Havannah; at Lexington, Bunker's Hill, Brooklyn, Long Island, White Plain, Fort Washington, New York Island, Brandywine, and in all movements of the army during the winter and summer campaigns of 1777-8; with Lord Cornwallis in summer and winter campaign in the Jerseys; under Clinton at the evacuation of Philadelphia, and at the affairs of Monmouth in the Jerseys, at the siege of Charleston, South Carolina; appointed Governor of the Fort at Sullivan's Island, 1780-3. Died at Plymouth, 16th Jan., 1807.
HAVELOCK, Charles Frederick	..	..	23 June, 1843			Cornet 16th Lancers, 13th Dec., 1821; Lieutenant, 17th May, 1827; Adjutant of the 16th, 6th Oct., 1827; Captain, 12th Dec., 1839; exchanged to 3rd Light Dragoons, 3rd July, 1840; exchanged to 53rd, 5th July, 1844; exchanged to 9th Regt, 16th Oct., 1845; Major, 3rd April, 1846; exchanged to 53rd, 6th Aug., 1847; to h.-p., unattached, 27th July, 1849. Served with the 16th Lancers at the siege and capture of Burtpore, in 1825-6, and in that of the Sutlej, including the battle of Sobraon (medal). Served with the Army of the Indus during the campaigns of Afghanistan, in 1829, under Lord Keane, as Brigade-Major to the Cavalry Division, and was present at the siege and capture of Guznee (medal). He acted in the same capacity during the campaign in Afghanistan in 1842, under General Pollock, and was present at the action of Tezeen, and the recapture of Cabool (medal); he served also as D.A.Q.M. Gen. to the Cavalry division in the campaign in the Sutlej (medal), including the battles of Moodkee, Ferozeshah, and Sobraon, and was most severely wounded in the lungs at Ferozeshah; retired 24th Aug., 1852.
HAVELOCK, Thomas	..	3 Sept. 1795	26 Jan. 1796	..	..	From North York Militia. Appointed Paymaster of the Regt, 24th Jan., 1799.
HAVELOCK, Thomas	27 Sept. 1815	..	..	..	..	Placed h.-p., 25th Mar, 1817; retired 18th Nov., 1831.
HAVELOCK, William, K.H.	12 July, 1810	12 May, 1812	..	..	..	"*El chico blanco*," Captain 32nd Regt., 19th Feb., 1818; appointed 4th Light Dragoons, 19th July, 1821; Major 4th Light Dragoons, 30th April, 1841; killed at Ramnuggur, 22nd Nov., 1848. Served in the Peninsula from July, 1810, to the end of the war in 1814. At Busaco, Sabugal, Salamanca, Vittoria, Bidassoa, Nivelle, Bayonne, Orthes, and Toulouse. Wounded at Quatre Bras. He received the war medal with six clasps.
HAVERFIELD, John	..	..	15 Aug. 1804			From Ensign 32nd Regt., 27th Feb., 1799; Lieutenant, 10th July, 1800, was Adjutant; appointed to 48th Regt., 6th Aug., 1807; was on the Quarter-Master-General's Staff in the Peninsular war, 1808-9; was A.D.C. to Lord Chatham at Colchester; Major, 6th Sept., 1810; Assistant-Quarter-Master-General at the Horse Guards, 6th Sept., 1810; Brevet-Lieutenant-Colonel, 7th Jan., 1814; appointed same day an Acting Quarter-Master-General; retired 1826.

43rd Light Infantry.

Name				Notes
TEMPLE, Richard	..	21 Jan. 174⁹⁄₀	..	Appointed to Regt. at formation; out Sept, 1756.
THELKELD, Thomas	..	26 Nov. 1741	..	From Quarter-Master.
THOMAS, James	..	9 April, 1825	..	Ensign 37th Regt, 5th Dec, 1815; h.-p., 25th May, 1817; appointed to 64th, 10th March, 1821; appointed Adjutant to 43rd, 16th July, 1830. Served in the suppression of the Canadian revolt, and was one of those who crossed the Portage of the Madawaska; to Captain 52nd, 7th Aug., 1840; to 60th, 3rd March, 1843; retired 25th June, 1844; went into holy orders.
THOMPSON, George	..	..	25 Dec. 1770	To 60th as Major, 24th Oct., 1781; h.-p. in late 119th; Brevet-Major, 29th Aug., 1777; Brevet-Lieut.-Colonel, 19th Feb., 1783; out Oct., 1784.
THORNE, William	25 Dec. 1764	14 Nov. 1770	10 Mar. 1777	Captain-Lieutenant, 10th March, 1777; resigned 16th July, 1787. Served in the American war.
THORNLEY, Thomas	21 Oct. 1813	28 Sept. 1815	..	Present at New Orleans; placed on h.-p. of the Regt., 3rd April, 1817; died 30th April, 1850.
TIDY, Clement	31 May, 1793	..	..	
TIDY, Francis Shelly, C.B.	31 Dec. 1792	24 May, 1794	..	Promoted to a Captain in 1st West India Regt. Served in the expedition under Sir Charles Grey, on the reduction of all the French islands, was stationed at Point à Petre, Guadaloupe, where a mortality of from ten to thirteen men a day, reduced the Regt. to ninety-six rank and file; and Guadaloupe being disputed inch by inch, the 43rd, at the time of its capture at Berville, did not contain more than two officers and twenty men fit for duty. He was confined for fifteen months on board a hulk, subject to the tyranny and cruelty of Victor Hughes, thence sent to France, and afterwards obtained permission to go to England on parole, on arrival was appointed Adjutant of the 43rd. He embarked as a private individual, being still a prisoner, with the 43rd, a second time for the West Indies, in order that the moment his exchange was completed, he might resume his duties as Adjutant. In Dec., 1798, he was promoted to a company in the 1st West India Regt.; in 1799 to the Royals; was A.Q.M.Gen. in North Britain; May, 1803, embarked a third time for the West Indies; after the capture of St. Lucia, was appointed Secretary to the Colony; was afterwards Brigade Major to Sir William Myers, and subsequently A.D.C. to Sir G. Beckwith; promoted to a Majority in the 8th West India Regt., and removed to the 14th Foot, 10th Sept., 1807; in 1808 he served as an Assistant-Adjutant-General in the expedition to Spain under Sir David Baird; and in 1809 in the Walcheren expedition; Brevet of Lieutenant-Colonel, 4th June, 1813; Lieutenant-Colonel 44th Regt., 11th Nov., 1825; appointed Inspecting Field Officer of a Recruiting District, 25th Aug., 1829; Colonel, 22nd July, 1830; was at the battle of Waterloo; died at Kingston, Upper Canada, Sept., 1836.
TONN, William	9 June, 1773	3 Sept. 1775	20 Mar. 1778	Died 26th July, 1792. Served throughout the War of Independence.
TOP, Robert Mercer	7 Sept. 1858	23 July, 1861	..	Served in the New Zealand war, 1864-5; present at the Gate Pa and Te Ranga, and with expeditions in the province of Taranaki, destroying many Pas and fortified villages.
TORRIANO, George	..	..	21 Sept. 1789	Ensign 64th, 14th March, 1775; Lieutenant 64th, 28th Nov., 1776; to h.-p. of 86th as Captain, 30th March, 1791; appointed Assistant-Inspector-General of Barracks at Portsmouth, 1813; out 1828.
TOWNSHEND, Charles	..	12 May, 1778	..	Ensign in 4th, 24th Jan., 1777; Captain 45th, 11th Aug., 1778; out Jan., 1783.
TRAFFORD, Henry Trafford	..	13 Oct. 1854	3 April, 1857	Ensign 51st, 31st Mar., 1849. Retired 29th July, 1862. Served with the 51st Regt, in Burmah from Sept., 1852, to the end of the war; and was present with Captain Irby's detachment of four companies with Brigadier-General Cheape's force during the whole of the succeeding operations in the Donabew district, ending in the assault and capture on the 19th March, 1853, of the stronghold of the Burmese chief (Myattoon medal).

Names.	Ensign.	Lieutenant.	Captain.	Major.	Lieut.-Col.	Remarks.
Trant, William	23 April, 1807	25 May, 1808	..	..	..	Appointed to 84th, 7th July, 1808; placed on h.-p. of the Regt., 11th Dec, 1817.
Treby, John	..	..	15 Aug. 1775	..	..	Lieutenant 44th, 10th March, 1753; Captain 44th, 15th Sept., 1758; Brevet-Major, 30th Jan., 1776. Retired May, 1776.
Trevylian, Wm. Pitt	15 Mar. 1784	26 Sept. 1787	..	..	..	Out Oct., 1788.
Trydell, John Frederick	..	29 July, 1853	..	..	..	Ensign, 23rd March, 1847; Ensign in 51st, 20th July, 1847; Lieutenant 51st, 23rd June, 1852; Captain in 22nd, 23rd July, 1858; Captain Ceylon Rifles, 12th June, 1860; to Captain 51st, 4th Sept., 1867. Served with the 43rd in India during the mutiny, and was present at the surrender of Kirwee (medal).
Tryon, Samuel	28 Jan. 1823	10 Sept. 1825	19 Feb. 1828	..	..	Served at Gibraltar; expedition to Portugal, 1826-7; was one of those to cross the Portage of the Madawaska; returned to Fredericton on the staff, A.D.C. of the Lieutenant-Governor, Major-General Sir John Harvey, K.C.B., 1841; appointed Major of Brigade at Halifax, Nova Scotia, by the then Commander-in-Chief, Lord Hill, in acknowledgment of services rendered during the threatened invasion of New Brunswick by the State of Maine; served on the staff in Nova Scotia until 1853, when the office of Major of Brigade was abolished. Brevet-Major, 23rd Nov., 1841; Major, unattached, 27th Dec., 1842; Lieutenant-Colonel, 11th Nov., 1851; Major-General, 28th Nov., 1854.
Tudor, Edward	..	7 Mar. 1762	..	..	..	Out in 1764.
Tufton, Henry	..	2 Nov. 1826	..	..	..	Retired 30th July, 1829.
Tylden, Sir John Maxwell	..	23 Nov. 1804	28 Sept. 1809	..	..	Major, 19th Dec., 1811; placed h.-p. of 3rd Regt, 25th Feb., 1816; to 52nd, 19th July, 1818. Served as Brigade-Major in South America, and was present at the capture of Monte Video and unsuccessful attack on Buenos Ayres. Served with the 43rd in Sir John Moore's Peninsular campaign in 1808, and again with the Regt. in the Peninsula in 1809. Served in Java in 1816, with the 43rd at the Nive, and with the 52nd at Orthes and Toulouse; and was Assistant-Adjutant-General during the operations against New Orleans. Silver medal for Java, Nive, Orthes, Toulouse; retired 12th Aug., 1819; died 18th May, 1866.
Underwood, Sidney E.	..	..	..	..	..	Appointment cancelled 2nd Nov., 1866.
Unett, William	18 Jan. 1816	..	..	..	..	Placed h.-p. of Regt, 25th Mar., 1817; Captain in Herefordshire Militia, 10th May, 1832; retired from the Army, Jan., 1833.
Upton, Clarges	..	..	..	..	..	
Utterton, Edwin	..	..	23 Sept. 1862	1855. 8th Sept. (medal and clasps).	..	Ensign 23rd, 30th April, 1855; Lieutenant, 10th Sept., 1855. Served at the siege and fall of Sebastopol, 1855, including the assault on the Redan, Killed at Gate Pa, April 29th, 1864.
Venner, John Henry	..	12 Jan. 1805	..	..	..	Ensign 8th Oct., 1803, 10th Battalion of Reserve; appointed to 40th Regt., 6th Aug., 1804; out 1806.
Vesey, George Francis	..	..	8 May 1866	..	..	Ensign 19th, 14 April, 1858; Lieutenant 19th, 24th Dec, 1858. Served as a Midshipman in the Baltic Fleet in 1854 (medal).
Vignoles,	14 April, 1795	..	..	..	..	On h.-p. of Ind. Co, Sept. 8th, 1795.

43rd Light Infantry.

VIGNOLES, Charles Henry	24 Nov. 1775	30 May, 1780	24 Sept. 1787	..	Adjutant, 25th Feb, 1785; died 10th June, 1793, in West Indies, of fever.
VILLERS, Ernest	24 July, 1857	1 April, 1861	..	..	Appointed A.D.C. to Lord Strathnairn, 1866.
WALDY, William Thomas	..	..	9 Nov. 1859	..	1854; Captain, 17th July, 1857; exchanged to 23rd, 23rd Sept., 1862. Served with the 46th Regt. at the siege of Sebastopol in 1854-5 (medal and clasp, and Turkish medal); retired 20th Feb, 1863.
WALKER, Geo. Fred. Arthur	21 July, 1843	..	..	..	Ensign 46th, 22nd April, 1853; Lieutenant, 6th June, Ensign 9th Foot, 27th Jan, 1843; died 24th May, 1845.
WALKER, George Henry W.	..	24 June, 1853	..	..	2nd Lieutenant Rifle Brigade, 31st Dec, 1845; Lieutenant, 22nd Dec, 1848; retired 1854.
WARD, Hunter	9 Sept. 1819	31 Dec. 1822	10 Sept. 1825	..	Exchanged to h.-p. of 5th Dragoon Guards, 28th Mar, 7th April, 1837; Brevet-Major, 28th June, 1838; Major in 48th, 31st Dec., 1847; Brevet-Lieutenant-Colonel, 19th Oct., 1849; died Dec., 1852.
WARD, Walter Alex.	29 Oct. 1825	..	..	..	Served with the expedition to Portugal, 1826-7; to h.-p. of 18th Foot, 21st Feb., 1828; appointed to 3rd Foot, 16th Mar., 1830; retired 6th Sept., 1833.
WARD, Hon. Henry William Crosbie	19 June, 1846	9 Aug. 1850	27 May, 1853	..	Served in the Kaffir war, 1851-2-3 (medal); retired July, 1855.
WARDROBE, Ed.	25 April, 1797	4 April, 1798	..	..	Out in 1800.
WARNER, Charles Wm. Pole	5 Sept. 1860	..	..	..	Appointed to 42nd, 28th Dec., 1860; retired 16th April, 1861.
WARNER, Henry Smith	12 Oct. 1804	17 April, 1801	..	..	To Ensign 40th, 25rd Oct., 1804.
WARNER, Thomas Francis	21 Dec. 1797	2 Dec. 1813	..	..	Captain 40th Regt., 14th Sept., 1804; retired 1811.
WARREN, Massey Hutchinson	4 June, 1812	..	..	..	Placed h.-p. of the Regt., 25th Mar., 1817; appointed to 65th, 26th Aug., 1836. Medal for Nivelle, Nive, Toulouse; retired 2nd Sept., 1836.
WARSFOLD, William	23 May, 1776	..	..	..	Resigned 1st Dec, 1779.
WASP, James	7 Sept. 1841	8 June, 1846	..	..	From Serjeant-Major of 43rd; appointed Ensign 1st Foot, 27th Aug., 1841; retired 13th Aug., 1847.
WATKINS, Matthew	..	..	24 Feb. 1744¾	30 Mar. 1750	Died April, 1751.
WATSON, Atherton	31 May, 1791	..	..	..	
WATSON, Robert	17 April, 1805	17 Dec. 1805	..	..	Out Feb., 1806.
WEBB, Richard Ponsonby	20 April, 1814	..	..	..	Exchanged to h.-p. of 88th Regt., 24th Oct., 1822; retired July, 1831.
WEIR, John	21 Mar. 1775	19 Sept. 1775	..	..	Captain 41st, 10th May, 1779; served all through the War of Independence; wounded at the battle of Brooklyn, and at German Town; out in 1788.
WELLS, John	25 July, 1801	18 Feb. 1804	..	..	Appointed Paymaster of the 2nd Battalion, 23rd Nov., 1804; *Vide Paymasters.*

NAMES.	ENSIGN.	LIEUTENANT.	CAPTAIN.	MAJOR.	LIEUT.-COL.	REMARKS.
WELLS, Joseph	..	10 May, 1798	18 Feb. 1804	10 Oct. 1811	4 Aug. 1814	Commenced as a Lieutenant in the Sheffield Volunteers, the light company of which presented him with a sword on his quitting that corps to be Ensign in the then Scotch Brigade, 3rd of Jan., 1798 (this corps he never joined). He joined at the Island of Martinique in March, 1799; Adjutant in July, 1800. Served in the expedition to Copenhagen in 1807; in the Peninsula, under Sir David Baird, in the autumn of 1808; to reinforce the Army of Sir John Moore, and finally in the retreat of Dec. and Jan., 1809; joined the Regt. a second time in the Peninsula, May, 1810; and excepting once, when he was employed on detachment, which was the period when Massena broke up from Santarez in March, 1811, he constantly was present with his corps until invalided to England for the recovery of a severe wound received at the storming of Badajoz; present at the Coa, 24th July, 1810; the battle of Busaco, 27th Sept., 1811; and the sieges and assaults of both Ciudad Rodrigo and Badajoz in Jan., March, and April, 1812; and was the senior surviving officer of the 43rd upon the fall of Lieutenant-Colonel M'Leod at Badajoz, but being himself severely wounded the same night, he was prevented from continuing in the command that had thus devolved upon him; joined the 2nd Battalion in the autumn of 1813; he continued in the command thereof until appointed Inspecting Field Officer in Canada, the 16th Nov., 1815. Upon quitting the 43rd, in which he had served nearly eighteen years, he had the gratification of being presented with a silver tureen and tankard, as mementoes of regret at his departure; the former from the officers, the latter from the non-commissioned officers of the 2nd Battalion of the corps. Retired 20th Mar., 1827 (gold medal for Badajoz, silver for Busaco, Ciudad Rodrigo, and Badajoz); died 4th Feb., 1853.
WEST, Lord, C.B.	..	13 Aug. 1833	5 June, 1835	..	..	Served in the suppression of the revolt in Canada, 1837-8; appointed to 15th, 20th Nov., 1838; Captain, unattached, 15th April, 1842; exchanged to 21st, 6th May, 1842; Brevet-Major, 3rd April, 1846; Brevet-Lieutenant-Colonel, 2nd Aug., 1850; Major in 21st, 23rd April, 1852; 2nd Lieutenant-Colonel, 21st Feb., 1855; Colonel for distinguished services, July, 1855 (antedated to 28th Nov., 1854); commanded a Brigade with the temporary rank of Major-General, Aug., 1856, to Sept., 1858, at Shorncliffe; Major-General, 29th Oct., 1864. Served on Sir Hugh Gough's staff throughout the Sutlej campaign of 1845-6, as A.D.C. in the battles of Moodkee and Ferozeshah, and as officiating Military Secretary during the remainder of the campaign, in the battle of Sobraon (medal and clasps). Landed with the 21st Fusiliers in the Crimea, and was present at the battles fought there; commanded a detached wing at Inkerman, and subsequently the Regt. during the siege from 17th Nov., 1854, to 6th Aug., 1855, including a special command of two Regiments in support of the storming party of the left column against the Redan on the 18th June; commanded the Regt. again on the 8th Sept., and during the assault; he commanded a Brigade in the expedition to Kinburn (medal and clasps, C.B., Officer of the Legion of Honour, Sardinian and Turkish medals, and 3rd class of the Medjidie).
WEST, Hon. Frederick	20 Sept. 1786	17 Oct. 1787	..	..	..	Ensign in 36th, 28th June, 1786; out Mar., 1789.
WEST ..	30 April, 1789	..	..	..	..	From Ensign 68th.
WESTMACOTT, William	Feb. 1783	..	..	..	..	Died 24th June, 1783.
WEYLAND, Richard	3 Aug. 1841	28 Dec. 1845	..	..	..	Retired 6th June, 1854.
WHALLEY, Richard	19 April, 1810	16 April, 1812	28 Feb. 1851	..	..	Died 1813.
WHICHCOTE, Benjamin	31 Jan. 1811	16 July, 1812	9 Dec. 1819	..	..	Present at New Orleans; exchanged to 6th Dragoons, 8th Nov., 1821; Major 6th Dragoons, 31st Dec., 1825; retired 24th April, 1828.
WHITE, Francis Samuel	8 Sept. 1854	..	..	..	..	Appointment cancelled 15th Sept.
WILKINSON, Fred. Greene	27 Dec. 1842	18 Aug. 1847	17 Oct. 1851	..	..	Adjutant, 25th April, 1848; exchanged to 42nd, 28th Nov., 1851; Major, 9th Oct., 1855; Lieutenant-Colonel, 16th March, 1858; to a Depôt Battalion, 27th Sept. 1861; Colonel, 16th March, 1863; placed on h.-p., 1st March, 1864. Served with the 42nd Highlanders in the Crimea up to Oct., 1854, including the battle of Alma and siege of Sebastopol (medal and clasp, 5th class of the Medjidie, and Turkish medal). Served the campaign of 1857-8 against the mutineers in India, including the action of Kudgegunge, siege and fall of Lucknow, attack on the port of Rooyah, action at Allygunge, and capture of Bareilly (medal and clasp).
WILKINSON, John	..	..	1 Feb. 1781	..	..	Ensign 54th, 7th Feb, 1770; Lieutenant, 1779; Captain 64th, 30th Sept., 1781; out in 1783.

43rd Light Infantry.

Name	Date	Remarks
WILKINSON, Thomas	18 Jan. 1810	Ensign 4th Garrison Battalion, 1st Sept., 1808; exchanged to 85th, 25th June, 1813; Captain 85th, 26th May, 1814. Served with the 43rd in the Peninsula, was present at Ciudad Rodrigo and Badajoz (wounded); killed at New Orleans, Jan., 1815.
WILKINSON, Thomas	2 April, 1772	Resigned 7th Aug., 1775.
WILLIAMS, Jeffreys	14 Sept. 1804	Resigned Jan., 1805.
WILLIAMS, John Maxwell	22 April, 1813	Present at New Orleans; appointed 2nd Foot, 2nd May, 1816; exchanged h.-p. of 58th, 14th Oct., 1819; died 1827.
WILLIAMS, William	2 Aug. 1810	Resigned March, 1814.
WILLIAMSON, Ralph B. R.	13 Oct. 1867	
WILMOT, Alfred	15 Dec. 1804	Retired 1806.
WILMOT, Henry, V.C.	29 May, 1849	1 May, 1858. Appointed to Rifle Brigade, 10th Aug., 1855; Brevet-Major, 20th July, 1858. Served with the 2nd Batalion during the Indian Mutiny until Nov., 1858; subsequently on the staff of Sir Hope Grant; was present at the capture of Lucknow (Victoria Cross, Brevet of Major, medal and clasp), Retired 3rd February, 1862.
WILMOT, Robert	22 April, 1755	Wounded at Vimiero.
WILSON,		No one of this name—(error in 'London Gazette').
WOOD, Charles W. A. Harcourt	12 April 1839	Retired 7th Sept., 1841.
WOODFORD, Alex. George	31 Dec. 1841	Appointment cancelled 8th Feb., 1842; appointed to 56th, 2nd June, 1843; Lieutenant in same, 3rd April, 1846.
WORSFOLD, William	23 May, 1776	Resigned 1st Dec., 1779.
WORTHINGTON, G. Talbot	2 April, 1762	Exchanged 15th Nov., 1765.
WRIGHT, Charles Ravenhill	3 Jan. 1822	11 July, 1826. Ensign 29th Regt., 25th Dec., 1813; Lieut., 26th July, 1821; served in the expedition to Portugal in 1826-7, and in the suppression of the Canadian revolt in 1837-8, and was one of those who crossed the Portage of the Madawaska; retired on f.-p. as Major, 9th May, 1845; died June, 1854.
WRIGHT, George	2 Sept. 1796	From Captain North York Militia; superseded 21st Mar, 1797, absent without leave.
WROTTESLEY, the Hon. Charles Alex.	7 Feb. 1797	19 Sept. 1826. Cornet 16th Lancers, 21st Dec., 1815; Lieutenant, 5th July, 1821; Captain, unattached, 10th June, 1825; Major, unattached, 5th April, 1831; exchanged to 95th Regt., 25th July, 1834; exchanged to 29th Regt., 7th Sept., 1838; Lieutenant-Colonel, 3rd July, 1839; exchanged to h.-p., unattached, 8th April, 1842; exchanged to 7th Hussars, 16th April, 1847; retired same day; died 24th Feb, 1861. Served with 16th Lancers at siege of Burtpore, 1825-6.
WROTTESLEY, Hon. Henry	9 June, 1846	11 Dec. 1849. Appointed to 25th, 9th June, 1846; appointed to 43rd same day; killed at the Cape of Good Hope, 11th March, 1852.
WYKE, George	13 July, 1794	Was a Volunteer; Lieutenant in 35th, 16th Nov., 1794; Captain 35th, 9th Aug., 1799; promoted to Captain for his gallantry in commanding two forlorn hopes at the storming of forts Bourbon and Point à Petre; was A.D.C. to General Lee. Served through the whole of the campaigns in Holland in 1799, during which Captain Robinson and himself, commanding flank companies of the 35th, were transferred to the Grenadier Guards in consequence of their services. Saved the Duke of Gloucester, who had gallantly pushed too far forward and got into great danger. Appointed to Grenadier Guards, 26th Nov., 1799; Captain 9th Regt., 27th April, 1803; exchanged to Captain of Ind. Co., Jan, 1806; retired on h.-p. 1827; was Commissioner of Her Majesty's Customs; died in London, 5th March, 1846.
YOUNG, Gerald Henry Baird	3 April, 1751	

CHAPLAINS.

Names.	Date of Appointment.	Remarks.
Bourne, John	3 Jan. 1740/9	Retired 11th Nov., 1761.
Derby, John	11 Nov. 1761	Retired 2nd Oct., 1775.
Pomeroy, John	18 Mar. 1794	
Poole, Harry	31 May, 1790	Retired 17th Mar., 1794.
Taylor, Christopher	2 Oct. 1775	Retired 30th May, 1790.
Watkins, George	31 Jan. 1756	

PAYMASTERS.

Name.	Date of Appointment.	Remarks.
Amos, John Green	6 Sept. 1827	Appointed Lieutenant in the Bedfordshire Militia, 26th July, 1803; Captain, 24th Oct., 1807; volunteered to the army, and appointed Captain in the 40th Regt., with temporary rank, 25th Dec., 1813; placed h.-p. of the Regiment, 1814; reverted to his former h.-p., 25th Oct., 1828; died at Bedford, 22nd Mar., 1848.
Denton, Joseph	27 May, 1856	From Quarter-Master; died 17th Sept, 1858.
Fraser, David	11 Oct. 1810	From Quarter-Master of the Regt., 22nd Aug., 1805; placed h.-p. of the Regt., Mar., 1817; struck off h.-p. list, 1817.
Havelock, Thomas	24 Jan. 1799	Ensign, 3rd Sept, 1795; Lieutenant, 26th Jan., 1796; was with the expedition to Copenhagen; resigned, 11th Oct., 1810.
Hood, George	25 Oct. 1828	Ensign, 21st Feb, 1811; Lieutenant, 28th May, 1812; Paymaster of Glasgow recruiting district, 1st Sept, 1848. Medal for Toulouse; present at New Orleans; crossed the Portage of the Madawaska; died at Glasgow.
Lennox, Charles Edwards	8 May, 187	2nd Lieut, 12th June, 1852; Lieut., 3rd Sept, 1854; Captain, 1st Jan, 1862. Served in the Burmese war of 1852-3 (medal).
Mackinnon, Daniel Henry	27 Oct. 1848	Cornet 16th Lancers, 1st July, 1836; Lieutenant, 23rd Mar., 1838; Captain, 15th Oct., 1847; exchanged to 6th Dragoon Guards, 12th Nov., 1847; to h.-p. 6th June, 1851. Appointed Staff Officer of Pensioners, 11th Feb., 1854; Brevet-Major, 13th Dec., 1858. Served with the 16th Lancers in the campaign in Affganistan under Lord Keane: was present at the siege and capture of Ghuznee (medal). Served also throughout the Sutlej campaign of 1845-6, and was present at the affair of Buddiwal (charger killed under him by a cannon shot), and battles of Aliwal and Sobraon (medal and clasp).
McCrea, Herbert Taylor	6 June, 1851	Lieutenant from 94th Regt, 12th Dec., 1846; retired upon h.-p., 27th May, 1856.
Morgan, Horatio	17 Sept. 1858	From Captain in Turkish Contingent; Hon. Captain, 17th Sept., 1863.
Richards, John	13 July, 1809	Died in Portugal, 1812.
Tierney, Thomas	23 July, 1812	Was at New Orleans; placed h.-p. of the Regt., 6th Sept., 1827; died in Dublin, 25th May, 1845.
Wells, John	23 Nov. 1804	Present at Vimiero; from Lieutenant in the Regt.; resigned July, 1809.

MEDICAL STAFF.

NAMES.	ASSISTANT SURGEON.	SURGEON.	REMARKS.
ACHESON, Hamilton	..	28 Feb. 1792	Died in West Indies, 22nd Jan., 1793.
AGAR, Rowland	19 April, 1844	..	Appointed to the Staff, 31st Dec., 1847.
BARCLAY, Alexander, M.D.	..	13 April, 1852	Surgeon 91st Regt., 22nd Dec., 1843; Surgeon-Major, 22nd Dec., 1863. Served in the Kaffir war of 1846-7, and with the 43rd in that of 1851-2-3; for the most part in medical charge of the R, B, 91st, or of the 43rd; was present at the various attacks on the Amatola and Waterkloof fortresses; accompanied the expedition across the Orange River against the Baxutos, in 1852; and was present in charge of Headquarter Column at the action of Berea (medal); accompanied the 43rd on the march from Bangalore to Calpee in 1857-8, and was senior medical officer of the 2nd Brigade, Saugor field division, during the hot weather campaign in Central India, and the subsequent operations (medal).
BIDDLE, John Matthew	..	5 Aug. 1853	From Assistant-Surgeon 94th, 3rd June, 1853; appointed to 60th, 31st Aug., 1855; Captain in 100th Regt., 26th July, 1861. Served with the 60th Rifles in the Indian campaign of 1857, and was present at the actions on the Hindun, battle of Budlee ke Serai, and forcing the heights before Delhi, throughout the siege operations, including the action of the 19th June, attack on the Subjee Mundee, final attack and assault of Delhi. Served with the 8th Hussars in 1858-9, and was present at the battle of Siudwaho, and actions of Koorwye and Nabarghur (medal and two clasps).
BROWN, Andrew	..	..	Served with the expedition to Portugal, 1826-7; appointed to 18th Regt., 25th Feb., 1831; to Grenadier Guards, 20th Jan., 1832; Surgeon, 26th June, 1840; Surgeon-Major, 29th Dec., 1854; retired on h.-p. 24th Jan., 1858.
BROWN, George	12 Jan. 1826	..	
BROWNE, Robert	30 Sept. 1851	..	From Assistant-Surgeon 38th Regt., 1st March, 1844; Surgeon 83rd, 14th July, 1856; exchanged to 25th Regt., 21st Mar., 1863; Surgeon-Major, 1st Mar., 1864. Died in Ireland, 9th May, 1864.
CARTER, W. Barwell	23 Mar. 1809	..	Appointed to 8th Light Dragoons, 22nd Feb., 1810; died 1823.
CATHCART, Samuel	9 June, 1796	..	From Hospital Mate.
COOKE, Thomas	25 June, 1797	..	From Assistant-Surgeon 98th; resigned 6th Jan., 1857.
CROKER, Arthur	26 Sept. 1856	..	
CUMIN, William, M.D.	7 May, 1807	..	Surgeon 88th Regt., 15th Oct., 1812. Medal for Vimiero, Busaco, Fuentes d'Onoro, Badajoz, Salamanca, Vittoria, and Pyrenees. Retired 30th Nov., 1815.
CUNNINGHAM, George A.	..	25 June, 1744	Not in List, 1754.
DALTON, Thomas	24 Sept. 1803	..	From Assistant-Surgeon 47th.

Names.	Assistant Surgeon.	Surgeon.	Remarks.
Davidson, Patrick, M.D.	..	27 Oct. 1846	Killed at the Cape of Good Hope.
Duffin, John	6 Jan. 1857	..	From the Staff, 28th July, 1854. Died Aug., 1857.
Edwards, Henry	15 Oct. 1812	..	Placed h.-p. of the Regt., 25th Dec., 1818; retired. Medal for Badajoz, Pyrenees, St. Sebastian, Nivelle, Nive, and Toulouse; was at New Orleans.
Everall, John	..	18 Oct. 1762	
Foaker, George Norton	17 Feb. 1837	..	Appointed to Staff, 1st May, 1835; Surgeon, 15th Dec., 1845; appointed to Surgeon 7th Dragoon Guards, 2nd Oct., 1846; exchanged to 8th Hussars, 9th July, 1850; to 12th Lancers, 16th Dec., 1853. Died, 10th Nov., 1854.
Franklin, Wm.	1788	..	Promoted to 15th Regt, 30th May, 1790.
Galeani, Michael, M.D.	16 June, 1825	..	Surgeon 28th Regt., 7th Nov., 1834; appointed to 46th, 19th June, 1835; retired h.-p. of the Regt., 17th Feb., 1843.
Garnet, J. Armstrong	31 May, 1790	..	
Gilkrest, James, M.D.	..	15 Dec. 1804	Assistant Surgeon 53rd Regt., 19th Aug., 1801; appointed a Deputy Inspector, 5th Nov., 1829; appointed an Inspector General, 16th Dec., 1845. Was present with the expedition to the West Indies in 1801, under Sir Thomas Trigge, including the capture of the Islands of St. Martin, St. John, St. Bartholomew, St. Thomas, and Santa Cruz. Served as Surgeon of the 43rd throughout the wars in the Peninsula, including the battle of Vimiero, retreat to and battle of Corunna, retreat from Burgos, actions of the Coa (near Almeida), Busaco, Sabugal, Fuentes d'Onoro, Salamanca, Vittoria, the Pyrenees, Nivelle, Nive, and Toulouse, and the sieges of Cuidad Rodrigo and San Sebastian, at which latter he accompanied the storming party; served also at New Orleans, and with the expedition to Portugal, 1826-7. He received the war medal and twelve clasps for Vimiero, Corunna, Busaco, Fuentes d'Onoro, Cuidad Rodrigo, Salamanca, Vittoria, Pyrenees, St. Sebastian, Nivelle, Nive, Toulouse.
Goode, James	3 Oct. 1857	..	From the Staff, 3rd Oct., 1857; to Staff Assistant-Surgeon, Jan. 19th, 1864. Served with the 43rd in the Indian Mutiny Campaign, and was present at the surrender of Kirwee. Towards the end of 1859 he had charge of No. 4 Column, Saugor Field Division; and was present at the affair at Raichore (medal).
Grant, Rob. Alexander Peter	26 Oct. 1860	..	From Assistant-Surgeon, 13th June, 1859. Served in the New Zealand war, 1863-6, and was mentioned in despatches for zealous and efficient services rendered to the wounded under a heavy fire.
Hair, Archibald, M.D.	12 Nov. 1812	..	From Forfar Militia; Surgeon Royal Horse Guards, 12th Jan., 1826; retired on h.-p. of the Regt., 2nd June, 1843. Peninsular campaign from Nov., 1812, to the end of the war in 1814, including the battle of Vittoria, siege of San Sebastian, Aug. and Sept., 1813, battles of the Nivelle, Nive and Orthes, and the affairs of Vera; subsequently in the action in front of New Orleans and capture of Paris. He received the war medal with four clasps for Vittoria, Pyrenees, Nivelle, Orthes.

43rd Light Infantry.

HARRIS, John	16 Sept. 1763	..	From the Staff 43rd, 27th March, 1835; died at St. John's, New Brunswick, 24th Dec, 1836.
HAMILTON, William	29 May, 1835	..	
HENDERSON, Walter	25 June, 1744	..	
HENRY, John James	28 Aug. 1857	..	From the Staff, 18th Jan., 1856; exchanged back to Staff, 29th Nov., 1864.
HODKINSON, R.	23 Jan. 1793	..	Died 30th May, 1793.
HUME, Thos. David, M.D.	28 Nov. 1834	..	Assistant-Surgeon 84th Regt., 11th Oct., 1827; appointed to Staff, 2nd July, 1841; Surgeon, 2nd July, 1841; exchanged to 82nd Regt., 14th June, 1842; Surgeon-Major, 26th Nov., 1852; Deputy-Inspector-General, 29th June, 1855; Inspector-General, 31st Dec., 1862. Served at the siege of Sebastopol, and was principal medical officer of the 3rd Division during the winter of 1855, and afterwards of the 4th Division, until the end of the war (medal and clasp, 5th class of the Medjidie, and Turkish medal).
JACOB, Adolphus	10 Oct. 1795	..	Appointed to 75th Regt., 3rd April, 1849.
JOHNSTON, John Lawrence	31 Dec. 1847	..	
JONES, John	8 Dec. 1795	..	Resigned 24th Aug, 1797.
JONES, William, M.D.	12 May, 1803	9 Mar. 1809	Expedition to Copenhagen; appointed to 1st Dragoon Guards, 25th Feb, 1817; retired on h.-p. of the Regt., 17th April, 1838.
LAWSON, Robert, M.D.	..	16 Dec. 1845	Assistant Surgeon, 15th May, 1835; appointed to Staff 47th Regt, 27th Oct., 1846; Surgeon-Major, 27th Oct., 1846; Deputy Inspector-General, 8th Dec., 1854. Was present at the storm and destruction of the fortified native Mandingo town of Sabajee on the Gambia, 1st June, 1853. Served in the Crimea from 8th Nov., 1854, to 15th Jan., 1855 (medal and clasp for Sebastopol, 4th class of the Medjidie, and Turkish medal).
LIND, Robert Robinson	..	8 Oct. 1803	Assistant Surgeon 4th Foot, 27th Dec, 1796; expedition to Copenhagen; died of fatigue in the retreat to Corunna.
LEITH,	..	..	Resigned 25th Dec, 1784.
MACARTNEY, John	..	28 Aug. 1743	
MADDEN, Charles Dodgson, M.D.	31 Aug. 1855	..	From Assistant Surgeon 39th, 14th Dec, 1854; appointed to the Staff, 26th Oct., 1860.
MADDEN, John, M.B.	3 April, 1849	..	Assistant Surgeon 1st West India Regt., 2nd Oct., 1846; promoted to Surgeon 8th Regt., 2nd Oct, 1857. Served with the 43rd Light Infantry the Kaffir war of 1851-3 (medal).
McKINTIRE, Donald	15 Jan. 1803	13 Mar. 1772	To General Hospital, 1st Mar., 1782.
McMAHON, John	..	..	From the 83rd.
MILLER, John	..	Nov. 1829	From Staff, 8th Feb, 1821; crossed the Portage of the Madawaska with the Regt.; appointed a Staff Surgeon, 1st class, 16th Dec, 1845; appointed to North British recruiting district, April, 1850; died at Glasgow, 3rd May, 1850. The officers of the Regt. erected a monument with the following inscription:—"In affectionate remembrance, the officers who served with him in the 43rd Light Infantry, of which Regt. he was surgeon for 18 years, have erected this monument. His remains rest in Lighthill Cemetery at Glasgow."
MORRIS	..	..	Promoted 13th June, 1768.
O'CONNEL, Richard	7 July, 1808	..	7th Garrison Batalion, 15th Jan., 1807; present at Vimiero and Corunna; appointed Surgeon 45th, 16th Mar, 1813.

Names.	Assistant Surgeon.	Surgeon.	Remarks.
Parrot, Thos. Montgommery	25 Mar. 1813	..	88th Regt, 26th April, 1810; Assistant Surgeon 14th Light Dragoons, 6th Feb., 1812; h.-p., 25th Mar., 1817; appointed to 3rd Veteran Battalion, 1st Nov., 1819; to 41st Regt., 28th Feb., 1822; exchanged to h.-p. of Staff, 12th April, 1831; retired 1839. Medal for Salamanca and St. Sebastian.
Peryn, Fred.	26 Dec. 1785	..	
Philips, Thomas	..	3 Jan. 1749	On formation of the Regt.
Robson, James	22 Feb. 1810	..	Appointed to 95th Rifles, 21st Nov., 1811; exchanged to h.-p. of 1st Dragoons 11th Feb., 1819. Medal for Waterloo; died 1821.
Salmon, Robert	..	11 June, 1794	Vice Hodkinson.
Simms,	13 June, 1768	..	
Stott, Samuel	..	25 Mar. 1768	Resigned 20th Sept.
Sullivan, Cornelius	7 April, 1800	..	Promoted in 28th, 29th July, 1803; appointed to 63rd, 28th April, 1808.
Taylor, John Butt	7 Nov. 1805	..	Surgeon 25th Regt., 23rd June, 1808; appointed to 25th Regt, 25th Aug., 1809; died 1813.
Thompson, Chris, M.D.	24 Sept. 1841	..	Appointed to Staff, 20th Aug., 1841; resigned 19th April, 1844.
Thompson, William	21 July, 1808	..	Retired 12th Nov., 1812.
Turner, Aug. Frederick	..	8 July, 1862	From Staff; Assistant Surgeon, 26th July, 1853.
Waugh, Robert	..	1 Mar. 1781	Retired 27th May, 1791.
Webb, William	24 Feb. 1745⅗	..	
Younge, William	..	20 Aug. 1751	To Hospital, 18th Dec., 1762.

QUARTERMASTERS.

Names.	Date of Appointment.	Remarks.
Armstrong, John	3 Jan. 1787	From 73rd Regt.; resigned 31st July, 1792.
Barr, Edward	17 Feb. 1803	5th Foot, 23rd Aug, 1799.
Bruce, Robert	11 July, 1794	Died 1794.
Burnet, Robert	31 July, 1793	Died, 30th April, 1794, of fever, in West Indies.
Campbell, James	10 Mar. 1747/8	Vice Ingram, made Ensign.
Cooper, Joseph	3 Jan. 1865	Served in the suppression of the Indian mutiny, including the action at Sahao (medal); also in the New Zealand war, 1864-5.
Denton, James	27 May, 1856	Died 29th Oct., 1858.
Denton, Joseph	15 Aug. 1848	To Paymaster, 27th May, 1856.
Elliott, James	23 Nov. 1804	Placed h.-p. of the Regt., 25th April, 1817; appointed to 65th Regt., 12th April, 1831; retired on h.-p. of the Regt., 26th April, 1839. Served with the expedition to Copenhagen in 1807. Medal for Vimiero and Corunna.
Fraser, David	22 Aug. 1805	Expedition to Copenhagen. Appointed Paymaster of the Regt., 11th Oct., 1810. *Vice* Richards to 1st Battalion, *vice* Havelock resigned.
Hall, Edward	27 Aug. 1762	Out, 14th Mar., 1765.
Hawkins, John	11 Nov. 1761	
Hessey, James	17 Nov. 1773	
Ingram, William	26 Nov. 1741	*Vice* Threlkeld, made Lieutenant.
Kennedy, John	8 July, 1780	To 73rd Reg, 2nd Jan, 1787; from Quartermaster-Sergeant.
Knight, Jas. Henry	16 June, 1760	Resigned 11th Nov, 1761.
Loftus, Thomas	19 April, 1798	Exchanged to 5th Foot, 17th Feb, 1803; placed on h.-p. of the Regt., 17th Feb, 1803.
Mackenzie, Robert	14 Mar. 1765	
Mallis, John	25 Oct. 1794	To Invalids, 18th April, 1798.

Names.	Date of Appointment.	Remarks.
Potts, George M.	31 July, 1792	To Ind. Co., 30th July, 1793.
Rand, Samuel	8 Oct. 1830	Retired h.-p. of the Regt, 15th Aug., 1848; appointed Military Knight of Windsor, 1849. Served in the Peninsula, and was present at the battles of Vimiero and Corunna; expedition to Walcheren in 1809; also in the Peninsula from 1811 to the end of the war, including the siege and storming of Badajoz (severely wounded), battles of Salamanca and Vittoria, attack on the heights of Vera, battles of Nivelle, Nive, and Toulouse; battle in front of New Orleans, 8th Jan., 1815. War medal and nine clasps for Vimiero, Corunna, Badajoz, Salamanca, Vittoria, Pyrenees, Nivelle, Nive, Toulouse; died 1850.
Threlkeld, Thomas	3 Jan. 1740/1	At formation; appointed Lieutenant in the Regt., 26th Nov, 1741.
Williams, Arthur	29 Oct. 1858	From Colour-Sergeant.
Williams, David	29 Nov. 1810	Retired 8th Oct., 1830; served in the West Indies, and in most of the actions in the Peninsula, and was distinguished for his activity and courage, and greatly respected by all of his comrades of the 43rd; was also at New Orleans, and with the expedition to Portugal, 1826-7; appointed Military Knight of Windsor, 1830; died there, 1832.
Wilson, David	9 Mar. 1757	

www.ingramcontent.com/pod-product-compliance
Lightning Source LLC
Chambersburg PA
CBHW080633230426
43663CB00016B/2852